Best Places
to Stay in
the Southwest

THE BEST PLACES TO STAY SERIES

Best Places to Stay in America's Cities
Second Edition/Kenneth Hale-Wehmann, Editor

Best Places to Stay in Asia
Jerome E. Klein

Best Places to Stay in California
Third Edition/Marilyn McFarlane

Best Places to Stay in the Caribbean
Third Edition/Bill Jamison and Cheryl Alters Jamison

Best Places to Stay in Florida
Third Edition/Christine Davidson

Best Places to Stay in Hawaii
Fourth Edition/Bill Jamison and Cheryl Alters Jamison

Best Places to Stay in Mexico
Third Edition/Bill Jamison and Cheryl Alters Jamison

Best Places to Stay in the Mid-Atlantic States
Second Edition/ Dana Nadel Foley

Best Places to Stay in the Midwest
Second Edition/John Monaghan

Best Places to Stay in New England
Fifth Edition/Christina Tree and Kimberly Grant

Best Places to Stay in the Pacific Northwest
Fourth Edition/Marilyn McFarlane

Best Places to Stay in the Rockies
Second Edition/Roger Cox

Best Places to Stay in the South
Second Edition/Carol Timblin

Best Places to Stay in the Southwest
Fourth Edition/Anne E. Wright

Best Places to Stay in the Southwest

FOURTH EDITION

Anne E. Wright

Bruce Shaw, Editorial Director

HOUGHTON MIFFLIN COMPANY
BOSTON • NEW YORK

For information about permission to reproduce selections from
this book, write to Permissions, Houghton Mifflin Company,
215 Park Avenue South, New York, New York 10003.

Fourth Edition

ISSN: 1048-549X
ISBN: 0-395-70009-4

Printed in the United States of America

Illustrations prepared by Eric Walker
Maps by Charles Bahne
Design by Robert Overholtzer

This book was prepared in conjunction
with Harvard Common Press.

VB 10 9 8 7 6 5 4 3 2 1

Contents

Introduction

This isn't another "inn book," nor is it an attempt to judge all of the lodgings in Arizona, New Mexico, and Texas by one rigid criterion. Instead, we have looked at the full range of places to stay in the Southwest and noted first and foremost their astonishing variety, from grand new resorts to national park lodges, and we have picked only the outstanding examples. *Best Places to Stay in the Southwest* describes historic hostelries, family favorites, and health spas. It includes places to ride horseback and inns catering especially to golfers, tennis players, hikers, and birding enthusiasts. It includes elegant urban hotels and working ranches covering tens of thousands of acres, as well as lake resorts and ski resorts. Throughout, there are lodgings with the historical mix of Southwest Indian, Hispanic, and Anglo-American cultures for which the Southwest is justly famous.

Obviously, we judge guest ranches and city hotels by different criteria. Our primary standards are cleanliness, the palpable presence of a host or, at the larger hotels, a personal style of service, and a conviction that we would like to stay in the place for more than one night. As with all the books in this series, no fees have been collected for inclusion — these are not paid advertisements.

Anne Wright has over eight years of traveling experience in the Southwest. She covered a total of 25,000 miles preparing for this book, and she understands the distinct traditions of lodging and hospitality that make the Southwest different from, say, New England.

Innkeepers tell us that these days travelers want more and are willing to pay for it. Certainly there are many small places with high prices, but there are also many bargains. The key to planning a trip for yourself, we believe, is value — what you get for your money. For example, families can stay comfortably and economically in many of the new condominium resorts, where the rate is per unit rather than per person. On the other hand, a number of fine old resorts, large and small, maintain the same standards and traditions that have attracted generations of devotees, and many hotels with illustrious histories have been brilliantly refurbished to stand as superior alternatives to the standard (that is, dull) motel.

We have done our best to provide you with accurate and up-to-date information. For each accommodation in the book, we've given basic facts that you'll probably want to know before booking a room. In general, lodgings will accept personal checks (with proper identification) except where noted, and those that take major credit cards will accept one of the top three: Visa, MasterCard, and American Express. We suggest that you list the four or five points that most concern you and, when making reservations, ask the clerk or host about them. If money is important, be sure you know what your room rate will be. If noise bothers you, be sure that you ask for a quiet room. We have found over and over that we get what we ask for.

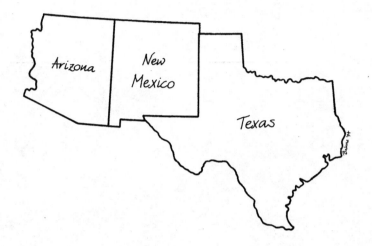

Arizona

Grand Canyon

Flagstaff

Northern Arizona

Prescott

Central Arizona

Wickenburg

Phoenix

Apache Junction

Southern Arizona

Oracle

Tucson

Bisbee

Behne '94

Arizona: the land of cactus, sunny skies, and the Grand Canyon. A Spanish Franciscan friar, Marcos de Niza, was the first European to explore the Arizona territory back in 1539. He came in search of gold. Over the years, many more were to come prospecting, and towns such as Prescott, Bisbee, Jerome, and Tombstone all came about because of the riches of the earth beneath them. Now, thousands of retirees and vacationers come to Arizona in search of treasure of a different kind — a warm climate, a beautiful landscape, or perhaps a lush green golf course — and almost all find what they are looking for.

While Arizona may be a peaceful escape today, it was not always so. Gunfights were common in the 1800s, and some, such as Wyatt Earp's shootout at the O.K. Corral, reached legendary status. The white man and Indians, led by powerful chiefs such as Geronimo and Cochise, fought for territory as the settlers pushed west. Although Geronimo ultimately surrendered in 1886, all was not totally lost, for Arizona still has the largest Native American population in the United States; and today Native American culture plays an important role in Arizona's appeal.

Arizona also has an air of mystery about it. No one really knows why the apparently thriving Sinagua Indians suddenly disappeared from northern Arizona in the 13th century. Then there's Sedona — many believe that the land surrounding the town has mystical qualities. And just about every abandoned ghost town feels like it's hiding long-buried secrets.

Almost nowhere else in the United States have the landscape and climate so strongly affected the fates and fortunes of the inhabitants as in Arizona. Happily, in the 1990s, those fortunes seem to be mostly positive. The state's population is growing quickly as more Americans discover its bounty. Luckily, there's lots of room in which to expand, and the state's economy seems to be improving right along with the development. Even if you don't decide to move to Arizona after visiting, you're likely to fall prey to the same magnetic charms that drew the first residents to the 48th state — a comfortably arid climate, spectacular scenery, open space, multicultural communities, a storied history, fine arts, good restaurants, great shopping, and superb recreational facilities.

Central Arizona

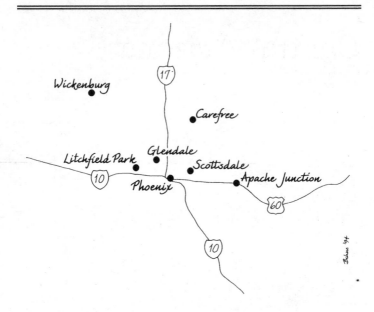

Best Bed-and-Breakfasts

Phoenix
Maricopa Manor
Scottsdale
Bed and Breakfast Inn Arizona
Inn at the Citadel

Best City Stops

Phoenix
The Ritz-Carlton, Phoenix

Best Family Favorites

Scottsdale
Red Lion's La Posada
Wickenburg
Wickenburg Inn

Best Guest Ranches

Wickenburg
Flying E Ranch
Kay El Bar Ranch
Rancho de los Caballeros

Best Historic Hostelries

Phoenix
San Carlos Hotel

Best Resorts

Apache Junction
Gold Canyon Ranch
Carefree
The Boulders

Litchfield Park
  The Wigwam
Phoenix
  Arizona Biltmore
  The Pointe at Tapatio Cliffs
Scottsdale
  Hyatt Regency Scottsdale at Gainey Ranch
  John Gardiner's Tennis Ranch on Camelback
  Marriott's Camelback Inn
  The Phoenician Resort
  Scottsdale Princess
  Stouffer Cottonwoods Resort
  Wyndham Paradise Valley Resort

Best Spas

Phoenix
  Maine Chance

Central Arizona is a desert playground. The Phoenix area is fittingly called the "Valley of the Sun," and the sun really does shine here almost every day of the year. Winters are pleasant; spring and autumn are just about perfect. Although summers are hot, the low humidity often makes the extreme desert heat more bearable than in other parts of the country where high humidity is the norm. Nights are almost always refreshingly cool.

Because of the climate, it's no wonder that the Southwest's largest concentration of fine resorts is centered around **Phoenix** and **Scottsdale,** and in outlying towns such as **Litchfield Park** and **Carefree.** Resorts here offer everything from excellent golf against scenic desert backdrops to tennis and deluxe accommodations to camp programs for kids. The weather is bound to cooperate, and low rates in the warmer months can make even a summer visit appealing.

Yet Phoenix is more than just a fun place to play. It's Arizona's capital, and a city that is rapidly gaining in stature on a national level. The Heard Museum has a highly respected Native American collection, and students of architecture continue to perfect their trade at Frank Lloyd Wright's renowned Taliesin West. The visions of futuristic urban planner Paolo Soleri are on exhibit at the Cosanti Foundation. For an informative introduction to the unique plants of the desert, a trip to the Desert Botanical Garden is a must, and devotees of Impressionist painting will want to seek out the works of American artists at the Fleischer Museum. Phoenix also has a zoo, an art museum, and a museum just for kids. For spectator sports, the city is the home of the Phoenix Suns basketball team and the Arizona Cardinals football team, and several major league baseball teams play in the area during spring training.

Scottsdale is a glamorous extension of Phoenix. You can shop here for days in chic boutiques and tony malls. Galleries line the quaint streets of Scottsdale's old town, and you may be able to locate a good piece of Indian art or jewelry here as well. The Borgata shopping center in North Scottsdale, built to resemble an Italian hill town, is especially attractive.

Near Chandler, south of Phoenix, there's an area of citrus groves that are more reminiscent of Florida or California than the Arizona desert. Further south, the Indian ruins at Casa Grande make for an interesting side trip. **Wickenburg,** northwest of Phoenix, is guest ranch country, offering travelers a more western-style and horse-oriented vacation than can be found at the golf and tennis resorts in the metropolitan area.

APACHE JUNCTION

Gold Canyon Ranch

6100 S. Kings Road
Apache Junction, AZ 85219
602-982-9090
800-624-6445
Fax: 602-830-5211

A golf resort in the Superstition Mountains

General Manager: Bruce Eaglesham.
Accommodations: 57 rooms. **Rates:** $96–$220 double. **Added:** 6.55% tax. **Payment:** Major credit cards. **Children:** Under 16 free in room with parents. **Pets:** Not permitted. **Smoking:** Permitted. **Open:** Year-round.

In the foothills of the Superstition Mountains, about 45 minutes from downtown Phoenix, Gold Canyon Ranch offers some of Arizona's best golf. Enthusiasts of the sport will particularly enjoy playing Gold Canyon's renowned 11th, 12th, and 13th holes, or signing up for one of the ranch's packages that includes rounds of golf at other popular resort courses in the area. A pro shop and the Nineteenth Hole Bar and Grill also cater to golfers.

Golf is not the only activity to be found at Gold Canyon Ranch. There's also a swimming pool and two lighted tennis courts, and horseback riding can be arranged through a neighboring stable.

Dinner at Kokopelli's, the resort's fine restaurant, is a good way to cap off a day on the fairways. The menus, imprinted on stone to resemble petroglyphs, are Southwestern and inventive in both appearance and content. Sea bass is served with red chili aioli, sautéed lamb medallions come with roasted pumpkin seed and habanero goat cheese pesto, and desserts are artfully prepared.

While the lodging is not as posh as it is at neighboring Phoenix and Scottsdale resorts, rooms are spacious and have interesting configurations. A kitchenette or wet bar is standard in each room, as is a fireplace and a patio designed to take in the mountain views. Some rooms even come with a private hot tub — both indoor and outdoor spas are available.

CAREFREE

The Boulders

34631 North Tom Darlington
P.O. Box 2090
Carefree, AZ 85377
602-488-9009
800-553-1717
Fax: 602-488-4118

> *A fine resort in
> an almost surreal
> landscape*

General Manager & Vice President: Kenneth B. Humes. **Accommodations:** 160 casitas. **Rates:** $215–$415 single, $450–$475 double. **Included:** Use of resort facilities. **Added:** 10.25% tax. **Payment:** Major credit cards. **Children:** Under 12 free in room with parents. **Pets:** Permitted; additional $50 charge. **Smoking:** Permitted. **Open:** Early September to early July.

The Boulders is an exclusive resort hidden away in the foothills of Scottsdale on a desert plateau dotted with palo verde, mesquite, and sweet acacia trees, as well as saguaro cacti. Jackrabbits and chipmunks scurry across your path here, but it's the tremendous boulders that dominate the landscape — like the toys of a wayward giant haphazardly discarded as he ambled through the countryside. At first glance, you have to look twice to distinguish the casitas from the surrounding rock formations. A wonderful free-form pool set amid the rocks looks almost natural.

There's plenty to do at the Boulders, but not so much that you have to schedule frantic days to get it all in. A residential community as well as a resort, it has 36 holes of golf and six Plexi-cushioned tennis courts, all set against spectacular desert scenery. The concierge will arrange such things as horseback riding, Jeep tours, hot-air ballooning, and flights to the Grand Canyon.

The main lodge is a stone extravaganza, and entering it is like stepping into a science fiction movie. A circular struc- ture, it has boulderlike doors and polished stone floors, and space is used in an unusual way. The architecture reflects the physical setting, and the interior reflects the area's Indian heritage.

The Boulders is about 30 minutes north of Scottsdale. Next door is El Pedregal, a collection of boutiques and restaurants.

The casitas are luxuri- ous and quite large, with beamed ceilings, adobe walls, and sitting areas in front of fire- places (winter temperatures drop into the forties at night). Thoughtful touches include down comforters, terry robes, wall safes, irons and ironing boards, wet bars, large walk-in closets, coffeemakers, Mexican glassware, alarm clock-radios, and even umbrellas (although you probably won't have much need for one). The baths have vanities with lighted make-up mirrors, hair dryers, and step-in showers as well as large oval tubs.

There's a choice of five dining areas. Latilla is the formal dining room (jackets are required). It has a pleasing circular shape representative of a Hopi kiva, and the menu consists of American and Continental classics including pan-seared loin of buffalo served with a juniper berry sauce ($26.50). Presenta- tion and the use of indigenous spices are at the heart of Palo Verde's Southwestern fare, and its exhibition kitchen is the focal point of the restaurant. The Club Restaurant, overlook- ing the golf course, serves grilled meat and seafood. The Can- tina, at the adjoining El Pedregal shopping complex, is more casual and specializes in Sonoran/Mexican cuisine. There's also a bakery in El Pedregal, and snacks are available poolside as well.

Transportation can be arranged between the resort and Sky Harbor Airport in Phoenix, and rental cars are available on the property.

LITCHFIELD PARK

The Wigwam

300 E. Indian School Road
Litchfield Park, AZ 85340
602-935-3811
800-327-0396
Fax: 602-856-1081

A venerable and popular resort

General Manager: Cecil Ravenswood. **Accommodations:** 331 rooms. **Rates:** Rooms $250 single, $270 double; suites start at $380; rates lower in summer. **Added:** 9.05% tax. **Payment:** Major credit cards. **Children:** Under 18 free in room with parents. **Pets:** Small pets permitted. **Smoking:** Nonsmoking rooms available. **Open:** Year-round.

The Wigwam sprawls over 75 acres in Litchfield Park, a small, quiet, palm-lined community 17 miles west of Phoenix. With three championship golf courses and excellent service, it has long been a top choice for golfers. The Gold and the Blue courses were designed by Robert Trent Jones, Sr., the West Course by Robert Lawrence. The Gold Course has been named one of the hundred best in the country.

Dating from 1929, the Wigwam has an interesting history. In 1915, the vice president of Goodyear, Paul Litchfield, developed a revolutionary tire that used fabric woven from staple cotton. This cotton was grown in only two places: the Sea Islands off the Georgia coast and the Nile Valley in Egypt. Both sources were threatened, one by boll weevils and the other by World War I. When Litchfield found an area in southern Arizona that approximated the Nile's climate, he bought thousands of acres and began producing cotton. Goodyear then developed a community to support the operation. A lodging house built for business visitors was later opened to the public. Over the years, the Wigwam helped establish the Phoenix area as a winter vacationland.

In late 1986, the resort was sold to SunCor Development, which undertook an extensive renovation project. The results are stunning: green lawns and thriving gardens bring glorious color to the desert. The common areas in the main building are tastefully accented with original art and sculpture. There are intimate lounges and sitting areas throughout.

The rooms are in low casas, some looking out onto the golf course, or in the newer two-story buildings spread over the grounds. The extra-large interiors are attractively decorated in muted tones and southwestern themes. Rooms have wet bars, refrigerators, safes, Mexican glassware (a nice change from the standard hotel glasses), televisions, VCRs, phones, large closets, and private patios or terraces. The baths have scales and makeup mirrors. Most units can sleep up to four people. Some rooms have Murphy beds. Premier rooms have fireplaces and sitting areas.

> In the summer, the resort operates the Pow Wow program, a day camp for children aged four through teens. Pow Wow activities include horseback riding, bicycling, roller-skating, swimming, and movies.

At mealtime, there are many options. The Arizona Kitchen, with its busy open kitchen, is the most inventive. Dishes such as rattlesnake fritters and chocolate tacos are artfully presented. Even the bread here is special — Indian fry bread with jalapenos, and blue corn and onion rolls. Dinner entrées average about $20.

The Grill on the Greens, with indoor/outdoor dining overlooking the golf course, serves a breakfast buffet, a soup, salad, and deli buffet at midday, and specializes in steaks and seafood for dinner. The Terrace Dining Room is the resort's main restaurant, serving American bistro cuisine and a popular Sunday brunch in a pleasant atmosphere. Tables on the terrace overlook the pool, and dinner entrées such as venison, mixed grill, and pot roast average about $15. The Kachina Lounge just down the hall has a copper-topped bar, and the Arizona Bar has live entertainment in season.

The main swimming pool is free-form, with a water slide and fountain. There's a volleyball net on one side, and a poolside cabana serves drinks, snacks, and a full lunch every day. Nearby is a children's playground, shuffleboard, and an outdoor fireplace surrounded by a circular sofa designed to take the chill out of an evening swim.

The estatelike resort is also known for its tennis on eight Plexi-Pave courts and its western program. There's a stable on the grounds, and special events include stagecoach and hay wagon rides and desert steak broils. An activities director makes sure that everyone has a good time, including children.

PHOENIX

Arizona Biltmore

24th Street and Missouri
Phoenix, AZ 85016
602-955-6600
800-950-0086
Fax: 602-381-7600

*The grande dame
of Phoenix resorts*

General Manager: Bill Lucas. **Accommodations:** 500 rooms.
Rates: $280, suites from $650. **Added:** 10.35% tax. **Payment:**
Major credit cards. **Children:** Under 18 free in room with parents. **Pets:** Small pets permitted with deposit. **Smoking:** Nonsmoking rooms available. **Open:** Year-round.

Built in 1929, the Arizona Biltmore offers much more than a
long and distinguished history. Spread over 200 acres, it's
filled with activities — a pair of 18-hole championship golf
courses, 17 tennis courts (16 lighted), three outdoor swimming pools, a putting green, lawn chess, shuffleboard, a
health club, croquet lawns, bicycle paths, and jogging trails.
Two of its restaurants, the Orangerie and the Gold Room,
have won awards for cuisine and decor. Best of all, the hotel's
staff works hard to please guests, providing a full range of services with a smile and a high degree of professionalism.
  Few hotels can claim such a totally distinctive look, both
inside and out. Frank Lloyd Wright was the consulting architect on the project, and his inspiration is clear throughout the
hotel. Precast concrete blocks, molded on the site using Ari-

zona sand, are the primary building material. This technique was developed by Wright, and the Biltmore was the first large structure to be constructed in such a manner. Newer buildings have been added on over the years, each designed to resemble the original structure both outside and in, with wooden checkerboard-paneled hallways.

The rooms are in one of five buildings or in cottages spread over the lush, exquisitely planted grounds. They range from good-size spaces with a mini-bar to extra-large units with a bedroom and sitting room, a mini-bar and refrigerator, a large bath with a tub and separate shower, and a private balcony or patio. Newly refurbished, the rooms are attractively decorated in cream, tan, and beige with patterned carpeting once again mirroring the buildings' exterior walls. They have monogrammed woven cotton bedspreads, extra pillows, and TVs hidden in armoires. Old photos of the hotel hang on the walls, and marble-tiled baths are outfitted with hair dryers and scales. Rooms have views of the golf courses, mountains, or the beautiful gardens.

> **The entire hotel seems transported from a slower, more gracious time, and ongoing renovation is further enhancing it. At press time, plans were underway to extend the lobby lounge's windows to two stories in order to expand its view of Squaw Peak.**

Recent renovations to the resort include the addition of an attractive new pool complex complete with fountains, flowers, whirlpools, a water slide, and private cabanas. For tradition's sake, the Biltmore's original pool has been saved nearby, but it pales in comparison to its younger neighbor.

Dining is important at the Biltmore. The Gold Room, named for its gold-leaf ceiling, has always been the main dining room. The Orangerie is the fine restaurant, where you can expect meals such as grilled Colorado lamb chops with braised artichokes, glazed root vegetables, and Zinfandel pan jus ($28), and braised moulard duck with couscous and coriander, and apricot compote ($22.50). For lighter fare, the Café Sonora features American and Mexican dishes. There's also a snack bar by the pool, two cocktail lounges, and the Aztec Theatre, where plays are performed in a cabaret setting.

Self-parking at the resort is free. There are a few fine gift shops just beyond the hotel lobby, but if you desire a more extensive shopping excursion, an exclusive shopping center, the Biltmore Fashion Park (the hotel came first), is just down the road.

Maine Chance

5830 East Jean Avenue
Phoenix, Arizona
602-947-6365
800-326-2772
Fax: 602-481-9654

A first-class women's spa

General Manager: Susan Hooper. **Accommodations:** Maximum 60 guests. **Rates:** $3,750–$4,500 single, $3,250–$3,500 per person double for one-week spa package; rates lower in off-season; partial week packages available. **Included:** All meals, spa program, tax and gratuities. **Payment:** Major credit cards. **Children:** Not permitted. **Pets:** Not permitted. **Smoking:** Outside only. **Open:** Late September through mid-June.

Run by the Elizabeth Arden Company, Maine Chance prides itself on the privacy and personal attention it affords its all-female clientele. So security-conscious is the spa, and so closely is privacy guarded, that notable guests have included several first ladies. With fitness programs designed to suit each individual's needs and a limit of 60 participants at a time, it is no wonder that women leave feeling truly pampered. Many of Maine Chance's guests return year after year.

Spa programs are generally six days long, with Sunday as the arrival and departure day. Physical and mental fitness and beauty are all stressed, so a daily schedule could include a mountain hike, step aerobics, water exercise, and body sculpting, as well as hair and nail care, a massage, facial, or mud bath. Self-defense and stress management classes are also offered. To help maintain physical fitness, caloric intake is limited to 1,100 calories per day. Spa meals are nutritionally based and are low in fat and salt. Dishes sometimes include fresh herbs and fruit grown on the property, or honey from the spa's own bees.

In keeping with Maine Chance's emphasis on beauty, it is not surprising that its surroundings are visually appealing.

With Camelback Mountain as a backdrop, hot pink bougainvillea is brilliant against the white stucco walls of the red tile–roofed buildings sprinkled throughout the spa's 110 acres. Yellow and orange African daisies are ablaze with color behind the Main House, feathery tamarisk trees offer dappled shade, and a garden-bordered waterfall spills into a fish pond by the West Garden House.

> **Activities include shopping trips to nearby Scottsdale boutiques on Thursday evenings, bingo on Friday nights, and farewell dinners on Saturday.**

Guest rooms, amply adorned with feminine floral and chintz fabrics, feel like gardens themselves. Individually decorated and comfortably sized, sitting areas and fainting couches add to the indulgent milieu. The Hilltop House, which can accommodate up to six guests, provides the most luxurious living quarters with its own swimming pool, Jacuzzi, and formal dining room.

The Main House is decorated with Elizabeth Arden's own ornate antiques, and her portrait still hangs over the fireplace in the living room. As a rule, guests gather for dinner in the Main House, where dress is "dressy casual," although guests can have meals served in their own rooms if they wish. Alcoholic beverages are not permitted at the spa.

Maricopa Manor

P.O. Box 7186
15 West Pasadena Avenue
Phoenix, AZ 85011
602-274-6302
Fax: 602-266-3904

> *A B&B where
> decor ranges from
> Victorian to modern*

Innkeepers: Mary Ellen and Paul Kelley. **Accommodations:** 6 suites. **Rates:** $79–$159. **Included:** Breakfast. **Added:** 10.35% tax. **Payment:** Major credit cards. **Children:** Over 6, $15 additional. **Pets:** Not permitted. **Smoking:** In designated areas only. **Open:** Year-round.

On a quiet residential street, one block from bustling Camelback Road and not far from downtown Phoenix, Maricopa Manor offers comfortable accommodations for a variety of tastes. The manor is a member of the American Association of Historic Inns — a fact that owner Paul Kelley says foreigners and travelers from the East get a real chuckle over, since the inn was only built in 1928. In modern Phoenix, almost anything dating to the 1920s is considered historic.

The red-roofed Spanish-style house is surrounded by towering palms, giving it a Floridian feel. The old-fashioned pull doorbell with musical chimes adds a nostalgic air. Inside, the formal parlor is decorated with antique furniture and inlaid end tables. The dining room next door has an Oriental rug and a crystal chandelier.

The two-story back living room, called the "gathering place," is very casual. It has a double-sided fireplace, a sunken TV viewing area, and a basketball hoop.

Although its bathroom is across the hall, the Victorian

suite is one of the prettiest rooms at the inn. The bed is covered with an embroidered satin spread, and the bedside tables are marble-topped. A charming sitting room is set off in an alcove. The Library suite is popular with honeymooners and business travelers. A white comforter with lace trim and pillow shams make the four-poster bed inviting. The bedroom opens onto a backyard deck. The separate library has a business-size desk, some well-stocked bookshelves, a sofa bed, and a TV.

> **Twelve children have lived in the house, three of the Kellys' own and the rest foster children or exchange students; the basketball hoop in the common room is not just for show.**

The remaining guest suites are in an adjacent building that was once a separate residence. Palo Verde is a two-bedroom suite with an adjoining sunroom. The larger bedroom is decorated in pinks and mint greens. It has a wicker settee with matching chairs, a Franklin stove, and a king-size canopy bed. The small bedroom is delightfully cozy with a three-quarters size spool bed draped by a lacy canopy, a country print quilt, and matching curtains and pillow shams. Mirrors line one wall of the living room in the masculine Reflections Past suite. There's a gas fireplace in the living room, a king-size bed in the bedroom, a spacious bath, and a large closet. Reflections Future is ultramodern, with black and brass furniture and a mirrored coffee table, a full kitchen, and a breakfast nook. All suites have ironing boards, irons, TVs, and phones.

A breakfast of juice, fruit, homemade breads, jams, and quiches arrives at your door in a basket each morning. The china is from an interesting and eclectic collection. In the backyard, bordered by oleander, there's a gazebo with a hot tub.

The Pointe at Tapatio Cliffs

11111 North Seventh Street
Phoenix, AZ 85020
602-997-6000
800-876-4683
Fax: 602-866-6353

A sprawling Mediterranean-style resort village

General Manager: Bob Brooks.
Accommodations: 591 suites. **Rates:** $79–$260. **Added:** 10.35% tax. **Payment:** Major credit cards. **Children:** Under 18 free in room with parents. **Pets:** Not permitted. **Smoking:** Nonsmoking suites available. **Open:** Year-round.

The mood is festive at the Pointe. With pool parties and a host of special activities, it's like a giant cruise ship moored at an inland shore. The lobby, three stories high, has a central fountain, and large windows overlook the resort's main pool, which always seems to be surrounded by happy guests. Cocktails are served poolside in the evenings. Beside the glass elevators is a plaque listing famous Pointe guests, such as Robert Redford, Julius Irving, Liza Minelli, Walter Mondale, and many others, from rock stars to professional athletes.

Spread over 400 cliffside acres, the Pointe is a complete vacationland with seven pools, 16 lighted tennis courts, four racquetball courts, horseback riding, hiking, mountain biking, three major restaurants, and an 18-hole golf course. The tennis is excellent; the court quality is good and extensive landscaping between the courts adds to their appeal. There is an extra fee for tennis. There's a pro shop for golf and tennis, and there are four golf pros on staff. Horseback rides are available by the hour or half-day; special rides include breakfast, lunch, and pony rides for children under seven.

- The guest suites are in the main building or in smaller buildings with arches, courtyards, and fountains. Standard are separate sitting rooms with wet bars and refrigerators, bedrooms with armoires, baths divided into sections, and balconies. Other features include room safes, two TVs, coffeemakers, tile baths, and rich marble vanities. Twenty-eight "presidential suites" on the hill have good views and are especially roomy, with large living rooms, bedrooms, and baths. Each has 1½ baths, a kiva fireplace (firewood is supplied), and stained glass windows above the baths. They can connect with a standard suite.

The Pointe In Tyme restaurant has Mexican marble at its entrance, crystal chandeliers, and Honduran mahogany–paneled ceilings and walls decorated with old photos of famous restaurants taken in their heyday. There's a huge oval bar in the center, a large fireplace on one side, and comfortable booths all around. The restaurant serves all three meals; the breakfast buffet is especially popular.

> **The Pointe publishes a monthly newsletter called *Pointes of Interest* to inform guests of current happenings at the resort, and there's a children's day camp called Coyote Camp. A 2,700-acre preserve adjoins the resort.**

The crème de la crème for dining is Étienne's Different Pointe of View, on top of the mountain. Étienne's has innovative architecture, a sleek and modern decor, and an unequaled setting. In the highest building in Phoenix, it has windows all around and impressive views. Guests may enjoy cocktails overlooking the city on the multileveled terrace and then dine on roast chicken with périgourdine sauce or baked salmon fillet with green peppercorn butter. Entrées range from $22 to $27. The restaurant boasts a long list of awards and has one of the most impressive wine lists in the country: more than 20 pages of unusual bottles, including an extensive selection of California Cabernets. Be sure to stop down and see the glass-encased wine cellar. For after dinner, the adjacent lounge is a popular spot, with two shows a night featuring Al Raitano, Phoenix's "entertainer of the year."

More casual dining is available at La Cabana, a snack bar between the resort's two main pools, and the Watering Hole Chuckwagon and Saloon. A shuttle service runs throughout the resort, which in this hillside setting can be a real plus — especially if you're dining at Étienne's.

The Ritz-Carlton, Phoenix

2401 East Camelback Road
Phoenix, AZ 85016
602-468-0700
800-241-3333
Fax: 602-468-0793

A centrally located, first-class hotel

General Manager: John Rolfs.
Accommodations: 281 rooms. **Rates:** $95–$350, suites $270–$800. **Added:** 10.25% tax. **Payment:** Major credit cards. **Children:** Under 18 free in room with parents; rollaways $20 extra per day. **Pets:** Permitted with some restrictions. **Smoking:** Nonsmoking rooms available. **Open:** Year-round.

The modern pink exterior of the Ritz-Carlton is deceptive. When you walk into the lobby expecting contemporary decor, you're greeted by gleaming Italian marble, Oriental rugs, and priceless antiques. The feeling of Old World elegance is remarkable for a new hotel.

Off to the side is the Lobby Lounge, where high tea is served every day from 2:00 to 4:30 P.M. The scones with Devonshire cream are a real treat. During the Christmas season, Teddy Bear Tea is served for children: the lounge is filled with teddy bears, hot chocolate is served, and stories are read. At night, couples dance here to live entertainment.

Next door, the Grill has a men's-club atmosphere. Original paintings of sporting and equestrian scenes, all predating the 1890s, hang on the paneled walls. The fireplace came from a castle in Germany. The Grill's specialties are prime aged meats, fresh fish, and pheasant, but if you don't see what you want, just ask; the chef will whip up something special for you. The Restaurant is formal and features beautifully presented Continental cuisine. The menu changes weekly to take the best advantage of seasonal ingredients.

> **The front desk keeps a record of guests' special requests for their next visit.**

The guest rooms are plush and attractive in gray and salmon. Two telephones, marble baths, hair dryers, robes, honor bars, safes, twice-daily maid service, and nightly turndown with chocolates are just a few of the many extras the Ritz offers. Guests on the keyed-access club level can take advantage of complimentary meals throughout the day, including Continental breakfast, midmorning snacks, evening hors d'oeuvres and cocktails, and late cordials and sweets.

Recreation has not been overlooked at this city hotel. In addition to the requisite pool, there's a fitness center, sun deck, and two tennis courts. Massages are available for $25 a half hour, $40 per hour. Tee times on the nearby Biltmore golf course can be arranged; transportation is free.

More than anything, attention to detail stands out at the Ritz. Even the public restrooms are marble, with fresh flowers and a supply of washcloths. The paneled elevators have marble floors covered with Persian rugs. The devoted staff is unequaled. The hotel offers concierge, valet, and 24-hour room service. Shoeshines are complimentary; valet parking is $9.50 per day.

The Ritz has a convenient central location about 15 minutes from the airport and near downtown Phoenix and Scottsdale's many golf courses. It is directly across the street from the Biltmore Fashion Park.

San Carlos Hotel

202 North Central Avenue
Phoenix, AZ 85004
602-253-4121
800-528-5446
Fax: 602-253-4121 ext. 209

> *A historic hotel in the heart of downtown Phoenix*

Owners: The Melikian family.
Accommodations: 111 rooms and suites. **Rates:** $89–$129,

suites $129–$159. **Added:** 10.25% tax. **Payment:** Major credit cards. **Children:** Welcome, additional $10 charge. **Pets:** Not permitted. **Smoking:** 2 nonsmoking floors. **Open:** Year-round.

When the San Carlos Hotel opened in 1928, it was considered one of the most modern hotels in the Southwest, for it had air conditioning and circulating ice water. It was the first high-rise hotel in Phoenix; now its seven stories seem modest in comparison with the taller skyscrapers surrounding it. The San Carlos has seen its fortunes come and go, as has downtown Phoenix, but with the recent revival of the city center, the hotel has once again risen to prominence.

> In the past, celebrities such as Clark Gable, Carole Lombard, and Spencer Tracy stayed at the San Carlos. Today, a healthy portion of the guests are business travelers, and the hotel operates a concierge communication center on the second floor.

Just one look inside the elegant bistro will assure you of the San Carlos' renewed glory. The maitre d' snaps to attention and leads you to your table in the pleasant dining room. The lobby is an intimate, pretty space, with crystal chandeliers and potted palms.

The guest rooms are also attractive; some are decorated in mauves and greens with rich wood furnishings while others are decked out in chintz. At the request of Historic Hotels of America, of which the San Carlos is a member, some of the baths still have original fixtures. Older washbasins have an extra faucet that draws up the coldest water from the well in the hotel's basement. All rooms have the expected amenities, but executive king suites have two baths, two large closets, a TV in the living room and in the bedroom, ceiling fans, and a refrigerator.

For workouts, there is a rooftop swimming pool and a small fitness room. The Herberger Theatre, the Museum of Science and Technology, the convention center, and Symphony Hall are all within walking distance. The staff at the San Carlos is friendly and eager to please.

SCOTTSDALE

Bed and Breakfast Inn Arizona

P.O. Box 11253
Glendale, AZ 85318
602-561-0335
Fax: 602-561-2300

*A reservation
service with
lots of choice*

Manager: B. Kennedy. **Accommodations:** More than 200 listings statewide, including Bisbee, Flagstaff, Grand Canyon, Phoenix, Prescott, Scottsdale, Sedona, Tombstone, and Tucson. **Rates:** $45–$200. **Included:** Breakfast. **Added:** 6.5–10.5%; varies from city to city. **Payment:** Major credit cards. **Children:** Discouraged in many homes. **Pets:** Not permitted. **Smoking:** Not permitted in most inns. **Open:** Year-round.

Bed and Breakfast Inn Arizona, with hundreds of bed-and-breakfast listings throughout the state, is true to its name. If you're having trouble finding a B&B on your own, or if you'll be traveling throughout Arizona and want to book all your reservations with just one phone call, then this service may be the answer. Every property listed has been inspected, and the service has made a special effort to find innkeepers native to Arizona whenever possible.

Among the service's many and diverse listings are properties with special amenities, such as swimming pools, hot tubs, and fireplaces.

Bed and Breakfast Inn Arizona offers traditional B&B homes with resident owners as well as guest houses and ranches. Some of the B&Bs are in cities, offering intimacy in a bustling metropolis; others are more remote, with superb mountain or desert views. Some are furnished with fine antiques, others are more modest but offer a friendly and welcoming environment.

Hyatt Regency Scottsdale at Gainey Ranch

7500 East Doubletree Ranch Road
Scottsdale, AZ 85258
602-991-3388
800-233-1234
Fax: 602-483-5550

A refreshing desert playground

Manager: Bill Eider Orley. **Accommodations:** 493 rooms.
Rates: $125–$375, suites $250–$2,200. **Added:** 10.25% tax.
Payment: Major credit cards. **Children:** Welcome. **Pets:** Not
permitted. **Smoking:** Permitted. **Open:** Year-round.

The Hyatt Regency Scottsdale is a true oasis in the midst of
the desert, with a water playground and a beautiful setting
that surpass just about anything else in the Southwest. It also
has 27 holes of golf, a health and fitness center, eight tennis
courts, lawn croquet, and jogging and cycling trails.
The hotel opened in late 1986 as part of the Gainey Ranch complex, which includes residential and re-
tail development. With
hundreds of palm trees
and other lush foliage, it's
an elegant resort. So special is the landscaping
outside and the artwork
inside that weekly tours
are given of the art and
the flora and fauna.

The Regency Spa surpasses the typical hotel fitness center. In addition to sunny workout rooms, excellent exercise equipment, saunas, massage rooms, and herbal wraps, it has the Mollen Clinic, a physical fitness and medical facility offering personal health evaluations and programs.

The water playground
is truly dazzling. Built on
several levels, it has 28 fountains, 10 pools, and a three-story
water slide — but statistics don't tell the story. It's a water
fantasy, a quasi-Roman-Grecian creation with a pure American sandy beach. Adding to the family appeal are the Fort
Kachina playground and Camp Hyatt Kachina for kids.

The lobby, decorated with international art, leads down to
three dining rooms. The Squash Blossom, offering southwestern cuisine, has all-day service with both indoor and outdoor

dining. It is tastefully decorated, particularly for an informal restaurant, with nice touches such as hand-blown Mexican glassware. The more formal Golden Swan overlooks the Koi Pond. Sandolo offers the most intimate dining experience, with waiters who sing as you enjoy Italian specialties, and the meal is followed by a romantic gondola ride on the resort's waterway. Sandolo's dinner entrées range from $10 to $16. Reservations are necessary.

The guest rooms are decorated in plum, mauve, and gray and have private balconies and stocked mini-bars. Cactus print robes are a refreshing change from the standard terrycloth. Regency Club rooms on the third floor have complimentary breakfast, afternoon hors d'oeuvres, and upgraded amenities. Several deluxe casitas, with a living room, two to four bedrooms, and stereo system, are on the lake.

Inn at the Citadel

8700 East Pinnacle Peak Road
Scottsdale, AZ 85255
602-585-6133
800-927-8367

An inn offering luxury and fine dining

Owners: The Keyes family. **Accommodations:** 11 rooms. **Rates:** $145–$195 September through December, $225–$265 January through May; lower in summer. **Included:** Deluxe Continental breakfast. **Added:** 10.2% tax. **Payment:** Major credit cards. **Children:** Additional $20 per day if more than two people per room. **Pets:** With prior approval only. **Smoking:** Not permitted. **Open:** Year-round.

The Citadel is a complex of fine shops and restaurants on the road to Pinnacle Peak on the northern edge of Scottsdale. The center was developed by the Keyes family, who put a lot of care into creating a compound that was both visually appealing and personally meaningful. The businesses surround a central courtyard filled with trees, lagoons, and boulders. The three entrance archways represent the Keyes daughters, and the two chimneys, their parents.

The inn, which opened in 1991, is upstairs. Rooms are luxurious and spacious, with interesting configurations. Beautifully decorated by Anita Keyes, they have TVs and mini-bars hidden in armoires, safes, hair dryers, and terrycloth robes. Some rooms have balconies, four have fireplaces, and all have gray marble tile in the baths.

Room 11, with a Mexican feel, is dominated by a large, colorful oil painting over the bed. The bed itself is covered in a silver

> **Guest room doors are painted turquoise to keep evil spirits away, a tradition the Keyes encountered in their sometime home of Santa Fe.**

satin comforter, and two chairs sit invitingly in front of the fireplace. Room 3 has an Oriental theme, with a lacquered screen inlaid with mother of pearl and an ornately carved blanket chest used as a coffee table. The bed's headboard is made from a bamboo screen. In Room 6, a wooden door has been cleverly turned into a headboard. If rooms look somewhat different during your visit, it's because many of the art objects in the guest rooms are for sale.

The Keyes also operate the three restaurants at the Citadel center, and a Continental breakfast is served for inn guests at the Market, the most casual of the restaurants. The Market serves all three meals, with southwestern breakfasts and dinners, salads and sandwiches at lunch, and fun exotic drinks in the evenings. The Marque Bar and Grill has splendid sunset views and specializes in sophisticated western cuisine.

The award-winning 8700 is the place to go for fine dining. Candlelight, classical music, and artwork from the Keyes' own collection add to the elegant ambience, but it's the food people come for. Appetizers such as southwestern cured salmon served with avocado blini, caviar, and habanero sour cream ($8), and cabrito, mushroom and chenel goat cheese strudel served with cilantro-mint pesto, apple compote, and pecan-raisin sauce ($8.25) are inventive to say the least. The creativity continues with the main course with entrées like grilled achiote-rubbed sea bass accompanied by a black bean potato cake, fried plantains, lobster, hominy, and smoked bacon sauce ($23), or roasted loin of lamb served with Sonoran ratatouille, cilantro corn mashed potatoes, goat cheese fritters, and chipotle sauce ($28.50).

John Gardiner's Tennis Ranch on Camelback

5700 East McDonald Drive
Scottsdale, AZ 85253
602-948-2100
800-245-2051
Fax: 602-483-7314

> *The place to go for tennis in the Scottsdale area*

General Manager: Adrian Bizri. **Accommodations:** 100 units, including casitas and 4- and 5-bedroom casas, some with private tennis court. **Rates:** Rooms $160–$190, 2-bedroom casitas $480–$540 for up to 4 people, weekend packages from $680 per person double, 1-week packages from $1,620 per person double. **Included:** Court time in daily rates; meals, court time, and tennis clinic in multiple-day packages. **Added:** 9.05% tax and 15% service charge. **Payment:** Major credit cards. **Children:** During junior clinics only. **Pets:** Not permitted. **Smoking:** Permitted (few guests smoke). **Open:** September through June.

If you like tennis combined with luxury, John Gardiner's Tennis Ranch is the place for you. The resort's 50-plus acres are beautifully landscaped: citrus trees, bougainvillea, and oleander seem to be in bloom everywhere you turn. Scottsdale's glitzy resorts are a stone's throw away, but here on Camelback Mountain, the rest of the world seems distant.

Tennis is king at this private club resort, which holds such tournaments as the annual invitational U.S. Senators' Cup. Take your choice of 24 championship courts. In keeping with tradition, players almost always wear white on the court. (The ranch's dress code specifies "predominantly white.") Weekly clinics offer 21 hours of instruction, six hours of optional tournaments, complimentary court time, and two half-hour massages, which you may need after all that tennis. Weekend "tiebreaker" packages are also available. More than 30 pros provide instruction at a ratio of one pro to every four guests. Workouts include computerized ball machines and videotape replay. In between sessions on the court, guests can relax in three swimming pools, saunas, and whirlpools or have a massage.

Lodgings are in casas or casitas off of palm-shaded paths with names like Forty Love Lane and High Lob Avenue. Casitas have a living room in the middle and a bedroom on either side; you rent any part or the entire unit. Some have sunrooms and private balconies with views of Camelback or the valley below. Since all of the units are privately owned, each is individually decorated, but southwestern themes predominate. All are luxuriously comfortable, with spacious living rooms, fireplaces, and kitchenettes fully equipped with tableware, coffeemakers, cutlery, ice makers, full-size refrigerators, toasters, and blenders. Each casita section has a phone and TV, and some units have VCRs and washer-dryers.

> **Although the casitas feel like private homes, touches such as daily housekeeping service, fresh fruit upon arrival, and fresh-squeezed orange juice and a newspaper on your doorstep each morning let you know that you're at a fine resort.**

For the ultimate in tennis luxury, opt for a casa. Casa Rosewall, the home of Ken Rosewall, has a rooftop court and a private pool. The spacious Gardiner house also has its own pool and tennis court. Additional bedrooms with separate entrances that open onto the pool can be rented by small groups or families requiring more than the casa's one main bedroom.

Meals are served buffet-style in the clubhouse, which by day wears a sporty look and at night is more formal. Guests are asked to wear evening attire. You can eat indoors or outdoors, overlooking the valley.

Marriott's Camelback Inn

5402 East Lincoln Drive
Scottsdale, AZ 85253
602-948-1700
800-242-2635
Fax: 602-951-2152

> *Guests have been returning to this resort for years*

General Manager: Wynn Tyner.
Accommodations: 423 units. **Rates:** $305, suites for up to 5 people $375–$1,500. **Added:** 10.25% tax. **Payment:** Major credit cards. **Children:** Under 18 free in room with parents. **Pets:** Permitted. **Smoking:** Nonsmoking units available. **Open:** Year-round.

The Camelback Inn dates from 1936, when it was built by Jack and Louise Stewart. With hospitality and dedication, they wrote a romantic chapter in the story of American resorts. Their inn attracted noted guests from around the world, many of whom returned year after year to the popular desert resort. "In all the world, only one," was the Stewarts' guiding principle as they molded a lodging of rare charm, emphasizing attention to detail and personal service.

In 1967 the Stewarts sold the resort to the Marriotts, a family that had been visiting Camelback for 14 years. Today's resort is much larger than the one the Marriotts bought. But you don't have to look far to sense the tradition, a rarity in an area now crowded with posh new playgrounds.

Spread over 125 acres of desert terrain, numerous recreational facilities help "real world" cares slip away quickly. Camelback has two highly acclaimed 18-hole championship golf courses where greens fees, including golf cart rental, range from $25 to $85 depending on the season, a driving range, putting green, 10 tennis courts ($10 per hour), three pools, and four restaurants and lounges. The front lawn is an 825-yard executive golf course. Stables are nearby. Hiking trails lead up Mummy Mountain, at the resort's back door. There's a playground for kids, bikes to rent, shuffleboard, and lots of space to roam. Social programs during holiday seasons reflect the spirit of the Stewarts' resort.

> **The words "Where time stands still" are emblazoned on the inn's clock tower and at the entrance to the lobby. The message to guests is clear: forget about the outside world — just relax and enjoy.**

Guests stay in rooms scattered over the rolling grounds, which are studded with citrus, olive, and mesquite trees and more than 40 varieties of cactus. Lodgings include single rooms, rooms with adjoining sun decks, and a variety of suites. There is a four-bedroom manor house with a full kitchen, washer-dryer, and private pool. All the rooms have refrigerators and small cooktops. Even standard rooms are spacious, with such extras as two phones, built-in hair dryers, coffeemakers, ironing boards, safes, stocked mini-bars, and remote control TV. The decor is southwestern in style.

The main lodge, small for a resort of this size, looks like a real lodge. Decorated with an Indian theme, it has wonderful painted beams, Navajo rugs, and light fixtures made from arrows. The lobby is listed on the National Register of Historic Places.

Dining offers lots of choices, both in cuisine and price, and everyone, even finicky children, should be able to find something to suit their taste and mood. MAP, FAP, and CAP (Camelback American Plan, with breakfast and lunch) rates are available. Popular with both guests and residents, Chaparral specializes in classic Continental cuisine. Entrées such as beef Wellington, steak Diane, rack of lamb, scampi flambé, and Dover sole range from $18 to $26.

The Camelback has its own spa, with state-of-the-art exercise equipment, a wellness center, revitalizing skin and body treatments, and a highly trained staff. Guests can use the facility for $22 per day or $10 after 5:00 P.M. The outdoor massage rooms are especially pleasant, as is the spa's own outdoor 25-meter lap pool, surrounded by terraced cacti with a glorious view of both the city and the mountains. Sprouts, the spa's attractive café, has a tempting menu even if you're not keeping track of calories, fat, and cholesterol.

Above the spa, there's a mock Old West town where popular steak fries and cookouts are held. The inn also has its own hiking trail up Mummy Mountain.

The Phoenician Resort

6000 East Camelback Road
Scottsdale, AZ 85251
602-941-8200
800-888-8234
Fax: 602-947-4311

*A posh
desert resort*

General Manager: Alan Fuerstman. **Accommodations:** 442 rooms, 107 casitas, 31 luxury suites. **Rates:** Rooms and casitas $310–$445 single or double, each additional person $50 per night; 1-bedroom suites $950–$1,200; 2-bedroom suites $1,350–$1,550. **Added:** 10.355% tax. **Payment:** Major credit cards. **Children:** Under 12 free in room with parents. **Pets:** Not permitted. **Smoking:** Nonsmoking rooms available. **Open:** Year-round.

The Phoenician plays up its desert location in the Valley of the Sun with a sun motif in the marble floor of the lobby and with the name of its lobby bar, the Thirsty Camel. The resort really does feel like an luxurious oasis. The Phoenician opened in late 1988 as the newest and perhaps the most opulent resort in the area. Spread over 130 acres, the lushly landscaped property is dotted with lagoons and streams, with Camelback Mountain as a backdrop. The hotel is semicircular; casitas, a spa, a clubhouse, and an 18-hole golf course complete the lower half of the circle, with multilevel pools (one with mother-of-pearl tile) and fountains in between.

The guest rooms are light, airy, and spacious. Furnished with painted rattan furniture and soft pastel fabrics, they are among the largest around. The luxurious baths have commodious oval tubs, separate showers, and marble floors and washbasins. Robes are provided: terrycloth in winter, cotton in summer. All the rooms have closet safes, hair dryers, ironing boards, scales, and telephones in the baths. The televisions are bigger than average, and VCRs are available upon request. Most rooms have balconies. Governor's suites have two terraces, a sitting room with a day bed, and two baths, one with a huge walk-in shower. The casitas have a more residential feeling; some have fireplaces. For those who require even more space, the two elaborate Presidential suites offer 3,200 square feet of pure luxury.

The Phoenician has a number of restaurants. The Terrace Dining Room serves Italian cuisine with entrées ranging from $15 to $25, and an elaborate Sunday brunch. For southwestern cuisine, try Windows on the Green, which overlooks the golf course. The Lobby Tea Court serves a fancy afternoon tea, and the Oasis serves meals by the pool. Mary Elaine's, with wonderful views of the valley below, specializes in contemporary cuisine highlighting the influences of the Mediterranean and Asia.

> **Once a year the street outside Windows on the Green is turned into a Bavarian village to celebrate Oktoberfest. Food booths and a lively band add to the festivities.**

In addition to swimming and golf, there are 11 lighted tennis courts, including one with an automated practice court, in the attractive tennis garden. Greenery has been planted between the courts to keep them cool and private.

The Phoenician's Centre for Well Being is a full-service health and fitness center. It has an aerobics studio with a suspended wooden floor, saunas, steam rooms, exercise machines that overlook the resort grounds and Camelback Mountain, and a skylighted meditation atrium with plants and a fountain providing a soothing background. Guests can use the center for $16 daily, with treatments such as massage and aromatherapy available at an hourly rate. Bicycles can be rented for $10 per hour or $20 for half the day. For younger guests, there is a children's clubhouse with supervised programs. There's also a playground beyond the tennis garden, and kids are sure to enjoy the twisting and turning water slide next to the main pool.

Next to the lobby is a hallway lined with shops and an ice cream parlor that also serves light meals. Up against the mountain is a tranquil cactus garden, where the plants have names like desert spoon, Mormon tea, Morocco mound, and warty aloe. Strangely enough for an active desert resort, there are no drinking fountains in the public areas, although the bartender will happily provide an ice cold glass of water in the Thirsty Camel Lounge.

Red Lion's La Posada

4949 East Lincoln Drive
Scottsdale, AZ 85253
602-952-0420
800-547-8010
Fax: 602-852-0151

A fun-filled, family-oriented resort

General Manager: Derick MacDonald. **Accommodations:** 264 rooms. **Rates:** Rooms $95–$215; suites $450–$1,500. **Added:** 10.25% tax. **Payment:** Major credit cards. **Children:** Under 18 free in room with parents. **Pets:** Permitted. **Smoking:** Nonsmoking rooms available. **Open:** Year-round.

Red Lion's La Posada brings water to the desert and adds an extra dollop of glitz to Scottsdale's hotel row. Standing in the lobby — more like Las Vegas than the Southwest, with a profusion of fuchsia, gold, and sparkle — you can tell this is no ordinary resort.

La Posada is a lively place, where the tone is definitely upbeat and the staff greets you with a smile.

Out back there's a half-acre swimming pool, actually more of a lagoon, with a manmade boulder mountain, splashing waterfalls, and a partly hidden grotto bar. Directly behind the hotel is the area's most distinctive landmark, Camelback Mountain. The Garden Terrace Restaurant is a great place to eat while overlooking the pool and the mountain. Like the lobby below, it has a refreshingly energetic decor. The Sunday champagne brunch, at $17.95, is a popular event. The adjoining Terrace Lounge has live entertainment.

The guest rooms are in long stucco buildings with red tile roofs arranged over the resort's 32 acres. Inside, brocades, formal furniture, and mirrors prevail. The smallest room is 450 square feet, large by hotel standards. The cabanas are 759 square feet, the casitas, 950 square feet. All the rooms have small refrigerators, honor bars, TVs in armoires, and patios or balconies.

La Posada has six tennis courts, two racquetball courts, a volleyball court, fitness center, massage services, a putting green, table tennis, horseshoes, basketball, a sauna, and hot tubs. There's also a camp for children, concierge service, car rental, and airport transportation. A shopping plaza on the grounds has an Italian restaurant.

Scottsdale Princess

7575 East Princess Drive
Scottsdale, AZ 85255
602-585-4848
800-223-1818
Fax: 602-585-0086

A truly first-rate resort on the edge of Scottsdale

General Manager: Stephen J. Ast.
Accommodations: 600 rooms. **Rates:** Rooms $125–$385, suites $480–$2,400 double; each additional person $20 in summer, $30 in winter. **Added:** 10.25% tax. **Payment:** Major credit cards. **Children:** Under 12 free in room with parents. **Pets:** Not permitted. **Smoking:** Nonsmoking rooms available. **Open:** Year-round.

Opened in 1987, the first Princess hotel in the U.S. is an estatelike resort covering 450 acres several miles north of the other Scottsdale resorts. Hand your car keys to a parking attendant when you arrive; with all that this resort has to offer, and a capable staff to attend to your every need, there's really no reason to leave.

Built in a Mexican colonial style, the main building is truly grand. There are majestic palms, fountain courts, and intimate nooks and crannies with wicker sofas. Two thirds of the guest rooms are in the sprawling main building; the casitas are clustered near the tennis courts, and the villas are next to the golf course.

Recreational choices cover the grounds. There are two 18-hole TPC (Tournament Players Club) golf courses designed by Jay Morrish and Tom Weiskopf (the Phoenix Open is held here); nine tennis courts, including a 10,000-seat stadium court that hosts the Arizona Men's Tennis Championships in late February; three swimming pools, one especially large and with an interesting shape; and a health club and spa with racquetball and squash courts, state-of-the-art exercise equipment, saunas, whirlpools, and health and beauty treatments. Club usage is $12 per day, which includes squash and racquetball court time.

The guest rooms are large and with more interesting configurations than standard hotel rooms. They are attractively furnished in southwestern peach, cream, and earth tones, and they have big terraces and wet bars. The extra-large baths are luxurious, with deep oval soaking tubs, separate showers, a telephone, loofah sponges, robes, and other top-of-the-line amenities.

> Next to the hotel, the city of Scottsdale has built a 400-acre horse park with nine equestrian arenas, two stadium arenas, a polo field, a grand prix jumping course, and stables for 500 horses.

The casitas afford lots of privacy. They come in two styles, bed–sitting and casita suites. The casita suites have large, separate sitting rooms with sleeper sofas, a wet bar, and TVs in both the living and bedrooms. All have balconies and fireplaces and share a swimming pool. The villas are similar to the casitas but do not have fireplaces.

The beautifully decorated Marquesa is the resort's fine restaurant, specializing in Catalan cuisine. (Notice the unusual centerpieces made by the chef from beans, herbs, pastas and other natural ingredients.) On Sundays, a nearby courtyard is turned into a Spanish market serving a bountiful brunch. La Hacienda's Mexican food is some of the highest rated in the country, and spit-roasted suckling pig is a specialty. The casual Las Ventanas serves all three meals, and the Cabana Café serves food and frosty drinks by the pool. The Grill at the TPC clubhouse, which serves sandwiches and salads at lunchtime, and grilled meats and seafood in the evening, is popular with hotel guests and golfers alike. At the end of the day, you can head to Club Caballo Bayo for a night of dancing.

Stouffer Cottonwoods Resort

6160 North Scottsdale Road
Scottsdale, AZ 85253
602-991-1414
Fax: 602-951-2434

> *A quiet resort for romantic getaways*

General Manager: Richard Bibee.
Accommodations: 171 rooms. **Rates:** Rooms $109–$215 single, $119–$225 double; suites $139–$305. **Included:** Continental breakfast. **Added:** 10.25% tax. **Payment:** Major credit cards. **Children:** Permitted. **Pets:** Under 25 pounds permitted with a $50 deposit. **Smoking:** Nonsmoking rooms available. **Open:** Year-round.

Scottsdale Road is lined with glamour, a mix of golden resorts, boutiques, and restaurants. In the midst of it all, the Stouffer Cottonwoods provides a tranquil hideaway, close to the glitter yet removed, offering the best of both worlds. Scottsdale's cosmopolitan atmosphere is literally a few steps away. The Borgata Shopping Village, designed after an Italian hill town, with boutiques, galleries, and restaurants, is across the parking lot; but there's a residential, clublike feeling about the resort.

> **The Moriah Restaurant is comfortably elegant and serves outstanding southwestern dishes. Tumbleweeds, the poolside bar and grill, is open daily. Other dining choices can be found in the Borgata Shopping Village next door.**

One-story villa suites are scattered over the 25 acres of grounds, with flower-lined paths draped with cottonwoods. The pace is unhurried. Tucked among the villas and courtyards is a large swimming pool that invites you to lounge. The sunken tennis courts, along grassy banks, have an intimate feeling. A jogging track with par exercise stations circles the grounds, leading past natural desert landscapes. There's a putting green and croquet course on the property, and you can play golf at any of five nearby courses. Bicycles can be rented at the gift shop.

The villas have been designed for privacy, and each has a secluded patio. Decorated in a southwestern scheme, they have beamed ceilings and touches of regional art. The Flagstaff rooms are the smallest, though somewhat larger than the average hotel room. They are furnished with a king-size or two double beds, a refrigerator, and a safe. The Tucson suites have a living room with a wet bar, large bedroom, and a private spa on the patio. The Phoenix suites are top-of-the-line, with a large living room and fireplace, a kitchen, a huge bath, a bedroom with a king-size bed, and an enclosed court-yard with a hot tub — truly a romantic setting. In the morning, croissants, newspaper, coffee, and orange juice are delivered to your room with your wake-up call.

Wyndham Paradise Valley Resort

5401 North Scottsdale Road
Scottsdale, AZ 85253
602-947-5400
800-822-4200
Fax: 602-946-1524

*A friendly
family resort in the
center of things*

General Manager: Randy Kwas-nieski. **Accommodations:** 387 rooms and suites. **Rates:** From $79 in the off-season and $180 in high season; suites from $425. **Added:** 10.25% tax. **Payment:** Major credit cards. **Children:** Under 18 free in room with parents. **Pets:** Not permitted. **Smoking:** Nonsmoking rooms available. **Open:** Year-round.

The Wyndham Paradise Valley Resort has an unusual facade: it is built of angular cement blocks that seem to mirror the bark patterns of the surrounding palm trees. At the entrance is a striking brass fountain of horses rising from the water.

The resort has two swimming pools, one with a waterfall, the other with an adjacent hot tub and bar.

The guest rooms surround attractively landscaped courtyards, and colorful desert flora seem to be in bloom everywhere. The rooms are pleasantly furnished with light woods and modern furniture with a southwestern air. Most have small sitting areas, terraces, and a vanity apart from the bath. All the rooms have mini-bars, coffeemakers, remote control

TVs, and phones in the bath. The Presidential Suite is especially handsome, with large glass doors that open onto a terrace overlooking one of the main pool courtyards. Guests staying there will have no need to use that pool, however, since the suite has its own outdoor pool and Jacuzzi.

Tennis is available on four outdoor clay courts and two indoor courts. The health club has two racquetball courts, steam rooms, saunas, and whirlpools. Golf can be arranged nearby.

Lunch and light meals are served in the Palm Pavilion. For dinner, Spazzizi's offers Italian and regional cuisine. Of course, a menu is also available for those who just want to lounge by the pool all day.

WICKENBURG

Flying E Ranch

Box EEE
2801 W. Wickenburg Way
Wickenburg, AZ 85358
602-684-2690

A relaxed, friendly guest ranch

Owner/Manager: Vi Wellik. **Accommodations:** 16 units. **Rates:** $110–$140 single, $190–$250 double; family house $225. **Included:** All meals and ranch activities except riding. **Minimum stay:** 2 nights; 4 nights over holidays. **Added:** 6% tax. **Payment:** No credit cards. **Children:** Up to 2 years $30, 3–6 $40, 7–12 $50, 13 and over $70; children in separate rooms at adult rates. **Pets:** Not permitted; kennels are available nearby. **Smoking:** Discouraged. **Open:** November to May.

By the flip of a coin, Vi Wellik and her husband, George, discovered the Flying E Ranch in 1949, thereby changing their lives. The couple, both flyers, first noticed the ranch on a flight to Texas in their private plane. "It looked like a motel in the middle of the desert," says Vi. Their curiosity was sparked. That night they tossed a coin to decide whether to go back. Not only did they return, but they ended up buying the ranch and have operated it as a guest ranch since 1960.

Guests, many of whom visit Flying E year after year, find friendly folks and a relaxing atmosphere at this small ranch. The clock by the pool sets the tone: instead of hands, it says, "Who cares?" This is the kind of place where you can do what you want when you want.

Ranch owner Vi Wellick is a history buff who also restores old properties. She enjoys entertaining guests with local lore.

Horseback riding is a good option. There's an extra fee: $15 per day for one ride, $24 for two, or $125 weekly. With more than 20,000 acres of riding terrain, there's lots of room to roam, starting from the ranch's site on a 2,500-foot mesa. The rides, all led by wranglers, are separated into groups according to riders' abilities. When you aren't riding, you can soak in the pool and hot tub, play tennis (one court), basketball, volleyball, shuffleboard, or life-size chess, exercise in the small workout room, or socialize with other guests. Meals are served family-style on red and white checked tablecloths and feature good ol' home cooking. Breakfast cookouts and chuck wagon dinners are highlights. Nonriders are escorted to the serving site via haywagon. Cocktail hour (BYOB) is from 6 P.M. to 7 P.M. in the ranch's cozy "saloon."

The guest rooms are in motel units spread out from the main living–dining room. With wood paneling, traditional furnishings (twin or king-size beds), Navajo rugs, and baths with bird and cactus tiles, they're comfortable and well maintained. All have wet bars and refrigerators; they are electrically heated and cooled and stocked with electric blankets for extra-nippy nights. TVs with VCRs are available for rent.

Kay El Bar Ranch

Box 2480
Wickenburg, AZ 85358
602-684-7593

This guest ranch is a National Historic Site

Hosts: The Martins and Nashes.
Accommodations: 10 rooms, all with private bath. **Rates:** Rooms $125 single, $235 double; suites $250. **Included:** All meals

and horseback riding. **Minimum stay:** 2 nights mid-October through February 15; 4 nights February 15 through May 1 and all holidays. **Added:** 6% tax and 15% gratuities. **Payment:** Major credit cards. **Children:** Welcome; additional charge over age 2. **Pets:** Not permitted. **Smoking:** Nonsmoking rooms available. **Open:** Mid-October through May 1.

With only 20 guests at a time, Kay El Bar is low-key, laid-back, and downright friendly. The breakfast bell, nestled in the trees, rings at about 8:00 A.M. Guests gather in the dining room, where photographs of Hollywood cowboys line the walls and guests have contests to see who can name the most stars. The morning ride goes out at around ten. Depending on the crowd, it may come back in mid-afternoon or stay out all day, ending with a cookout. Those who choose not to ride can lounge by the heated pool all day and arrive at the cookout site just in time for barbecued chicken or fajitas.

> **The Kay El Bar's first guests checked in back in 1926, making it one of the oldest guest ranches in Arizona. The ranch's buildings include several hacienda-style adobes, shaded by magnificent salt-cedar and eucalyptus trees.**

At night, guests gather in the main lodge, a cozy sort of room with a mock bearskin rug in front of a crackling fire in the big stone fireplace, shelves upon shelves of books, and an array of games. Sometimes the hosts show an old western on the VCR. When the mood is right, somebody may play a tune on the piano. Over to the side there's a stocked bar.

Eight guest rooms are in the main lodge. Their ranch-style furniture dates from the 1920s dude ranch. These rooms have a nostalgic air, with Remington prints, cowboy lampshades, and Indian rugs.

A separate two-bedroom, two-bath cottage with a living room and fireplace can be rented as a whole or as a two-room suite.

Rancho de los Caballeros

P.O. Box 1148
Wickenburg, AZ 85358
602-684-5484
Fax: 602-684-2267

> *No luxury*
> *is spared at this*
> *top-notch ranch*

General Manager: Dallas Gant, Jr.
Accommodations: 74 rooms. **Rates:**
Rooms $160–$205 single, $265–$365 double; suites $465;
group rates available. **Included:** All meals. **Added:** 6% tax.
Payment: Personal checks; no credit cards. **Children:** Welcome. **Pets:** Not permitted. **Smoking:** Permitted in some areas. **Open:** Early October to mid-May.

In the Wickenburg area, renowned for its guest ranches, Rancho de los Caballeros reigns supreme, adding a touch of class to the Southwest. Its name, meaning Ranch of the Gentlemen on Horseback, pays tribute to the Spanish explorers who introduced horses to the Indian culture. Both a working and a guest ranch, with 20,000 acres of hills and desert terrain, Los Caballeros has been welcoming guests since 1948. Although the overall style is casual, men are required to wear sports jackets or western shirts with vests or bolo ties in the evening, and women sports suits or dresses.

The main lodge sets the tone. Its spacious living room has a vaulted ceiling, fanciful trim and molding, lots of sofas and chairs for lounging, and a large copper-shielded fireplace. Off to one side is the library, overlooking a putting green. Card tables are set in window nooks for amicable contests, and in an adjoining room there's a pool table. Outside, lush green lawns and flower borders alternate with natural desert landscaping, including native grasses and saguaros and other cacti.

Naturally, horseback riding is a star event at the ranch. With 75 or more horses, two rides are offered each day at an extra fee: $28 for morning rides, $19 for afternoon rides. A wrangler will come to your table in the dining room to sign you up.

Los Caballeros Golf Club is on the ranch grounds; its 18-hole championship course is one of the finest in Arizona. There's an extra charge of $37 for 18 holes and $13 for cart rental. The resort also has trapshooting, four tennis courts, a swimming pool, and miles of wide-open spaces. During appropriate seasons, a children's program for ages 5–12 is offered at no extra charge. Activities include riding, hiking, swimming, and games.

> **Twice a week the ranch throws a western cookout at South Yucca Flats or Vulture Peak, featuring barbecued ribs and hot apple crisp, followed by campfire entertainment.**

Before dinner, guests congregate in Los Caballeros Saloon, which is colorful, fun, and friendly. Large windows offer views of the Bradshaw Mountains. Meals are served in the adjacent dining room, with ornate Spanish decor. Lunch is served buffet-style; breakfast and dinner entrées are ordered from the menu.

The accommodations, in wide variety, are spread over the grounds. Sun Terrace rooms, in one wing of the main building and in bungalows, have hand-painted beds, simple curtains and carpeting, and small modern baths with Mexican tile accents. Sunset rooms, which face the mountains and the open desert, are the most secluded. From their patios, quail and roadrunners are often seen scampering across the desert terrain. Available in one-, two-, or three-room units, they have fireplaces and Mexican furnishings. Bradshaw Mountain rooms are the most modern. They have one or two large bedrooms, ample closet space, a parlor with lots of comfortable seating, a fireplace, and a kitchenette. You can rent just a bedroom portion of a Bradshaw Mountain unit, or you can combine a bedroom with the living room–kitchenette segment.

Wickenburg Inn

P.O. Box P
Highway 89
North Wickenburg, AZ 85358
602-684-7811
800-942-5362
Fax: 602-684-2981

*A fine,
family-oriented
getaway*

General Manager: Roger E. Wilcox. **Accommodations:** 47 rooms. **Rates:** $95–$240 single, $165–$310 double; additional persons aged 7 and up, $50 extra per day. **Included:** All meals, ranch activities, horseback riding, and tennis. **Added:** 5.5% state tax; 15% service charge. **Payment:** Major credit cards. **Children:** Welcome. **Pets:** Not permitted. **Smoking:** Permitted. **Open:** Year-round.

Wickenburg Inn offers an innovative mix of attractions in an informal atmosphere that's especially suited to families. Tennis, horseback riding, nature observation, and arts and crafts are popular events. Spread over gently rolling desert landscape studded with saguaro cactus, the inn consists of a ranch-style lodge, luxurious adobe casitas, and a host of recreational facilities. The 11 acrylic tennis courts are among the best in the state. Its instruction center has automatic ball machines, strategy boards, fixed targets, and practice walls. Clinics and individual lessons are easy to arrange.

The stables house about 100 horses during the winter months, 40 or so in the summer. Rides go out daily, with special cookout, breakfast, and moonlight rides according to the season. Private lessons and horsemanship clinics are also offered.

One of the inn's most imaginative offerings is its nature program. A resident naturalist introduces guests to the Sonoran Desert through interpretive walks, slide presentations, and stargazing seminars, as well as exhibits and a natural history library in the nature center. Surrounding the resort is a 47,000-acre wildlife preserve, the home of more than 200 species of animals and 300 kinds of plants. Special desert ecology programs and desert study weekends are scheduled during the year. Day-long guided excursions to the Grand Canyon, Oak Creek, Sedona, and Prescott are also offered. Check with the inn before you arrive.

Of course, the resort has a pool, as well as a hilltop outdoor spa, archery, a children's playground, and a jogging trail. The main lodge's dining room serves all three meals — buffet-style when the inn is full, but there is usually a choice of entrées such as prime rib, crab cakes, or chicken Alfredo. The menu changes daily. Saturday nights are special, with western cookouts and maybe a hay ride. For parents, there's a bar in the main lodge with a stone fireplace and big-screen television.

Most accommodations are in the casita complexes scattered around the grounds; a few rooms are in the main lodge. There's nothing rustic about these lodgings, though Wickenburg Inn is often referred to as a ranch. Well decorated and spacious, the casitas have modern southwestern furnishings and such amenities as fireplaces, TVs, and wet bars with a two-burner cooktop and refrigerator. The deluxe suites are definitely deluxe, with their own rooftop decks.

> **The arts and crafts center, unusual at a resort, has excellent programs for all ages, including leatherwork, stained glass, pottery, and weaving. Local artisans may be on hand to demonstrate their crafts.**

Best of all for a family is the attention the staff gives to its younger guests. Not only are there plenty of activities for children, but the staff members really enjoy "working" with them and go out of their way to make their stay special. One guest said a staff member helped her son catch a gecko. Another reported that prized stuffed animals accidently left at the inn were promptly returned by mail. On one visit, the front desk clerk cheerfully tried to locate the room number of a young guest's newfound friend with only the first name to go on. There must have been over 50 children staying at the resort at the time, but she was able to track down the little girl's playmate and the two girls went off happily to dinner together.

Northern Arizona

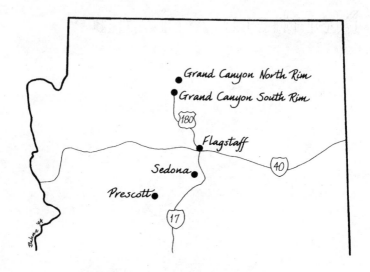

Flagstaff
Birch Tree Inn Bed & Breakfast, 58
The Inn at Four Ten, 60
Grand Canyon, North Rim
Grand Canyon Lodge North Rim, 64
Grand Canyon, South Rim
Bright Angel Lodge and Cabins, 61
El Tovar Hotel, 63
Prescott
Hassayampa Inn, 65
Hotel Vendome, 67
Lynx Creek Farm, 68
The Marks House, 69
Sedona
Canyon Villa, 71
Casa Sedona, 72
Enchantment Resort, 74
Garland's Oak Creek Lodge, 75
The Graham Bed & Breakfast Inn, 77
Junipine Resort Condo Hotel, 79
L'Auberge de Sedona, 80
Los Abrigados, 81
Territorial House, 83

Best Bed-and-Breakfasts

Flagstaff
Birch Tree Inn Bed & Breakfast
The Inn at Four Ten
Prescott
Lynx Creek Farm
The Marks House
Sedona
Canyon Villa
Casa Sedona
Garland's Oak Creek Lodge
The Graham Bed & Breakfast Inn
Territorial House

Best City Stops

Sedona
L'Auberge de Sedona
Los Abrigados

Best Family Favorites

Sedona
Junipine Resort Condo Hotel

Best National Park Lodging

Grand Canyon
Bright Angel Lodge and Cabins
El Tovar Hotel
Grand Canyon Lodge North Rim

Best Historic Hostelries

Prescott
Hassayampa Inn
Hotel Vendome

Best Resorts

Sedona
  Enchantment Resort

Since it is deservedly one of the seven natural wonders of the world, there is no question that the **Grand Canyon** is the highlight of any visit to northern Arizona, but it is only one of the many natural phenomena that grace this part of the state. From the magical topography of Sedona's red rock country to the quiet serenity of Canyon de Chelly, northern Arizona seems to have gotten more than its fair share of natural splendor.

In addition to the Grand Canyon's awesome beauty, there are the surreal rock formations of Monument Valley at the state's northern border, the pastel colors of the Petrified Forest and Painted Desert, the lava-strewn landscape of Sunset Crater National Monument, the snow-capped drama of 12,663-foot Humphreys Peak outside Flagstaff, and the deep pit of the Meteor Crater, created by the impact of an otherworldly mass.

History has also played an important role in the development of northern Arizona's character. The Sinagua Indians were among the first known inhabitants of the area. They lived in various locales along the Verde Valley between A.D. 1100 and 1400, and ruins of their former villages can be seen today at Montezuma Castle National Monument, Tuzigoot National Monument, and Walnut Canyon National Monument. (What is not known is why they seem to have mysteriously disappeared during the 1400s.) The unprotected ruins at Wupatki National Monument have been attributed to at least three Indian groups: the Sinagua, Anasazi, and Cohonina.

More modern history was made in the 1860s when gold was discovered in the **Prescott** area. Thousands flocked to Prescott in search of fortune, and before long the city became Arizona's territorial capital. It was a wild town in those days, and a main street in downtown Prescott is still referred to as Whiskey Row because of the revelry that took place there a century ago. A visit to the nine exhibit buildings of the Sharlot Hall Museum provide an in-depth look at Prescott's territorial days.

From Prescott, a scenic drive through the Mingus Mountains brings you to Jerome. Active copper mines made Jerome a booming metropolis at the turn of the century, but when the mines closed in 1953, the town just about died. Today the mountaintop town is being revitalized by artists. Although some buildings still look as though they could slide off the mountainside at any moment, many have been converted to shops, restaurants, and galleries, giving the town a somewhat bohemian atmosphere. The exhibits at Jerome Historic State Park offer the visitor views of the town in its heyday.

While the Grand Canyon still draws the most visitors in northern Arizona, **Sedona** is rapidly gaining a tourist following. Lured by striking scenery and a comfortable climate, many travelers find themselves returning to Sedona again and again. Exploring on foot, by car, by Jeep, or hot-air balloon are all popular pastimes here; as are dining and shopping in the town's many galleries, or visiting Tlaquepaque, a recreation of a traditional Mexican village.

Although many travelers simply pass through **Flagstaff** on their way to the Grand Canyon, the town does have a few sights worth stopping for. The delightfully eclectic Riordan Mansion merits seeking out. The Museum of Northern Arizona highlights the geography, history, and heritage of the region; and stargazers will be pleased to learn that the Lowell Observatory, where Pluto was first sighted, is here.

Finally, the pièce de résistance — the Grand Canyon — a chasm 277 miles long, 18 miles wide at its widest point, and one mile deep, carved out over millions of years by the Colorado River. There's quite simply no other place on earth like it. Every first-time visitor to northern Arizona must see it, and if you get the chance, try to experience it at sunset, when the walls of the canyon spring to colorful life with the rays of the setting sun. The South Rim, which is only 80 miles from Flagstaff, is heavily touristed. The North Rim, which is 200 miles further, offers a more tranquil view of this incredible wonder.

FLAGSTAFF

Birch Tree Inn Bed & Breakfast

824 W. Birch
Flagstaff, AZ 86001
602-774-1042

> *A B&B with*
> *an atmosphere*
> *of camaraderie*

Innkeepers: Donna and Rodger Pettinger, Sandy and Ed Znetko. **Accommodations:** 5 rooms. **Rates:** $55–$75 single, $60–$80 double. **Included:** Full breakfast and afternoon refreshments. **Added:** 8.61% tax. **Payment:** Major credit cards. **Children:** Age 10 and over permitted; additional $5 per day. **Pets:** Not permitted. **Smoking:** Not permitted. **Open:** Year-round.

On the local register of historic sites, the Birch Tree Inn was built in 1917 by a builder from Chicago to resemble a midwestern farmhouse. In keeping with its midwestern roots, the home has an open, welcoming feel fostered by the inn's warm and friendly hosts, Donna and Rodger Pettinger and Sandy and Ed Znetko (all childhood friends), and resident dog Daisy.

Downstairs there's a large comfortable living room, a game room outfitted with a pool table and piano, and a breakfast room that has a cheerful country look. Upstairs, the five guest rooms are individually furnished, and many reflect the owners' heritage.

The Pella room, named after a Dutch festival in Pella, Iowa, called Tulip Time, has Dutch lace curtains, a painted spool bed, a patchwork quilt with a tulip motif, and a mirrored armoire. It shares a hall bath. Carol's room is decorated in hunter greens and Shaker pine furniture and has its own bath. The Wicker room, furnished of course with wicker, has mountain views.

The Wagner-Znetko room, or "Grandma's attic," as the owners call it, contains a number of heirloom pieces from Ed's family, including an old-fashioned wooden washstand (the plumbing still works) and his grandmother's old 1913 sewing machine. The Southwest suite, decorated in cool greens and peaches, is the most modern of the rooms. Its giant bathroom is hard to miss, with aqua and black fixtures.

> **Stargazers take note: the historic Lowell Observatory, where Pluto was first sighted, is just up the street from the inn.**

Breakfasts are not taken lightly at the Birch Tree. Skillet breakfasts of potatoes, eggs, sausage, and vegetables are popular, and Sandy's sinfully delicious raisin bread French toast stuffed with cream cheese and pineapple and topped with a homemade pecan praline sauce keeps guests coming back for more. No matter what the dish, you won't leave hungry.

If you're looking for a way to burn off breakfast calories, there's a park across the street with four tennis courts, and tennis rackets and bicycles can be borrowed from the inn. Fifteen miles from the inn is the Snowbowl ski area, a Nordic track for cross-country skiing is ten miles away, and the Grand Canyon with its many hiking trails is an hour and a half away. The Museum of Northern Arizona is nearby.

The Inn at Four Ten

410 N. Leroux Street
Flagstaff, AZ 86001
602-774-0088

A welcoming B&B in the heart of Flagstaff

Innkeepers: Howard and Sally Krueger. **Accommodations:** 9 rooms. **Rates:** $100–$135 single or double, additional persons $25. **Included:** Full breakfast. **Added:** 9.06% tax. **Payment:** Major credit cards. **Children:** Welcome. **Pets:** Not permitted. **Smoking:** Not permitted. **Open:** Year-round.

About four blocks from the center of downtown Flagstaff, the Inn at Four Ten offers guests fine accommodations in a pleasant environment. The swing and wicker furniture on the front porch are inviting, and once inside the 1907 home you'll see plenty of evidence of the superior craftsmanship of the day. The staircase and moldings, made from golden oak, and the polished hardwood floors exemplify a quality rarely seen in houses built today. In keeping with that attention to detail, the inn is decorated with charm and style.

What was once an entrance hall has been converted to a living and breakfast room. On one side of the room are comfortable sofas and an Oriental rug; on the other, wicker-backed chairs are pulled up to tables covered in red and white checked cloths. Lace curtains drape the many windows; old bird cages hang overhead. In the morning, a full home-cooked breakfast is served here.

Separated from the breakfast room by lace-covered French doors is a ground floor guest suite. Once the dining room, it has a beautiful built-in mahogany buffet. The high-ceilinged room is feminine, its white iron bed topped with a pretty yellow spread. There's a white sofa at the end of the bed, a walnut armoire, and a rocking chair. The suite has a kitchenette and a breakfast nook.

The Southwest suite has an exposed brick wall, lodgepole pine furniture, a fireplace, tile bath, kiva ladder, turquoise armoire, and a kitchenette. Upstairs, two rooms share a bath. The smaller of the two has slanted ceilings. Decorated in yellow and blue, the room is cheerful and cozy. The room next door is similar in design and decor but is larger and has a washbasin.

> **Home-baked breads, sometimes low in fat and calories, are the high point of breakfasts at the inn.**
>
> **A typical breakfast consists of frothy orange nog, a "honey of a fruit cup," Paul's oat pancakes, pumpkin chocolate chip muffins, and raisin scones.**

The Garden suite, in a separate building, has a handicapped-accessible bath — rare for a bed-and-breakfast. The room is attractively furnished in plum, ivory, and green, and opens onto the inn's backyard, complete with covered gazebo. The two-bedroom Dakota suite has an Old West decor with rustic bent willow furniture.

GRAND CANYON

Bright Angel Lodge and Cabins

P.O. Box 699
Grand Canyon, AZ 86023
602-638-2631
Reservations: 602-638-2401
Fax: 602-638-9247

> *Enjoy the view from your stone cabin*

General Manager: Bill Bohannon.
Accommodations: 71 rooms. **Rates:** $59–$124, suites $244.
Added: 6.05% tax. **Payment:** Major credit cards. **Children:** Under 12 free in room with parents. **Pets:** In kennels; not allowed in lodgings. **Smoking:** Permitted. **Open:** Year-round.

Bright Angel Lodge dates from 1896, when it began as cabins and tents on the very edge of the Grand Canyon's South Rim. The name comes from Bright Angel Creek, which was christened by John Wesley Powell, the first white man to explore the inner gorge of the Grand Canyon.

Today the lodge is a conglomeration of facilities. At the low end of the scale are simple rooms with shared baths or half baths. The most expensive unit is the Bucky Suite, an 1890s cabin built by Bucky O'Neil. Right at the canyon's rim, it is a delightful old structure with two rooms, a king-size bed, a double sofa bed, a fireplace, full bath, a phone, and two TVs.

> **Bright Angel Lodge is always heavily booked. It's best to make reservations four to six months in advance, although it is sometimes possible to get a room at the last minute. Reservations are accepted as far as "two years minus two days" in advance.**

The stone and log rim cabins, from 1935, are the best choice. Views don't get any better than this, and the price is right. The cabins are roomy, and their simple furnishings are more than adequate. With the incredible view outside your window, it's hard to ask for more. Some of the cabins have stone fireplaces. All have a bathroom with shower and tub, phone, and TV. The cabins labeled "historic" have little to recommend them except their location within a few hundred feet of the Grand Canyon.

The standard rooms are in rambling, one-story buildings connected to the main lodge by breezeways. A typical room has two double beds, a dresser, and two chairs, with pine walls and shag carpeting. The bathroom has a claw-foot tub.

In the main lodge, a casual restaurant serves sandwiches and burgers as well as steak and seafood entrées ($6–$11). The lobby is the headquarters for booking bus tours and mule rides.

El Tovar Hotel

P.O. Box 699
Grand Canyon, AZ 86023
602-638-2631
Reservations: 602-638-2401
Fax: 602-638-9247

> *A venerable
> hotel on the edge
> of the canyon*

General Manager: Bill Bohannon.
Accommodations: 65 rooms. **Rates:** $122–$185, suites $190–$300. **Added:** 6.05% tax. **Payment:** Major credit cards. **Children:** Under 12 free in room with parents. **Pets:** In kennels; not in lodgings. **Smoking:** Permitted. **Open:** Year-round.

The grandest place to stay at the grandest of all canyons is El Tovar. Built on the South Rim in 1905 by the Santa Fe Railroad, the hotel sits just 50 feet from the edge of the dramatic chasm carved by the Colorado River.

This lodge was named for Don Pedro de Tovar, who in 1540 became the first European to visit the Hopi Indians. It was built using native limestone and logs shipped from Oregon. Although it was renovated a few years ago, El Tovar Hotel retains its historic character. The rooms are stylishly furnished and most are spacious, with a pair of double or queen-size beds

> **For the best views of one of the world's grandest natural sites, head for the cocktail lounge or dining room of El Tovar.**

or one king-size. The baths are larger than average and have showers and tubs. Some rooms look out over the canyon; four suites are designated as "guaranteed view" accommodations.

The front porch, lined with rockers, is welcoming. The lobby, handsome and dark with its log columns and hunting lodge design, bustles with activity. A cocktail lounge is off to one side. So is the dining room, like a lodge in architecture yet with a more formal air. Stone fireplaces stand tall at each end. The menu features fowl, beef, and seafood ($10–$23).

One of the most pleasant areas in the hotel is the mezzanine lounge, overlooking the lobby. Reserved for guests, it serves Continental breakfast and light meals in a relaxed atmosphere above the activity of the lobby.

Adventurous travelers may want to stay at the Phantom Ranch, which is also run by Grand Canyon National Park Lodges. At the bottom of the inner gorge, it can be reached only by foot, mule, or river raft. Reservations can be made through the same phone number as El Tovar.

Grand Canyon Lodge North Rim

602-638-2611
Reservations: TW Recreational
  Services
P.O. Box 400
Cedar City, UT 84721
801-586-7686
Fax: 801-586-3157

Cabins and a motel on the canyon's quiet side

Accommodations: 200 units. **Rates:** $49–$80 double. **Added:** 9% tax. **Payment:** Major credit cards. **Children:** Welcome. **Pets:** Not permitted. **Smoking:** Permitted. **Open:** Mid-May to late-October.

In the spruce and fir forests on the Grand Canyon's North Rim, far from the crowds of the South Rim, this lodge's accommodations are in three types of log cabins and a wood-frame motel. Frontier cabins are the smallest, with one double bed, one single bed, and a bathroom with a shower. Pioneer cabins have two rooms, each with two twin beds, and a small bath. Motel rooms have two double beds and a bath with a shower. Western cabins are the top of the line, with two double beds, a private porch, full bathrooms, and a telephone. All the units are carpeted and heated.

The Grand Canyon Lodge, built of native stone and logs, has one of the best porches in the world, directly overlooking the magnificent canyon. There are no guest rooms here, but the dining room serves all three meals. Dinner entrées range from $8 to $14; be sure to make reservations. You can also arrange for a picnic lunch.

The pace is slower here at the north rim. There's time to experience the serenity and to drink in the grandeur of the surroundings. You can hike, ride mules, or drive to see more of the canyon's splendor. Mule trips take

> **By air, the North Rim is 15 miles from the more commonly visited South Rim; on the road, it's about 200 miles.**

from one to eight hours. Hiking trails are from half a mile to ten miles long. The North Kaibab Trail is the only one that leads into the canyon. The hike to Roaring Springs, 3,041 feet below the rim, and back takes from six to eight hours.

PRESCOTT

Hassayampa Inn

122 E. Gurley Street
Prescott, AZ 86302
602-778-9434
800-322-1927
Fax: 602-778-9434

> *An elegant hotel in Arizona's territorial capital*

Owners: William and Georgia Teich. **Accommodations:** 67 rooms. **Rates:** $95–$115, suites $130–$170. **Included:** Breakfast and evening cocktail. **Added:**

8.5% tax. **Payment:** Major credit cards. **Children:** Over 6, additional $10 per day. **Pets:** Not permitted. **Smoking:** Non-smoking rooms available. **Open:** Year-round.

Hassayampa Inn was truly a grand hotel when it opened in 1927. A product of its age, it was flamboyantly elegant. As a social leader, it was one of the first hotels in Arizona to cater to automobile travelers. The El Paso architect Henry Charles Trost, also responsible for the historic Gadsden Hotel in Douglas, Arizona, designed the red brick Hassayampa, combining Mission and Italian Renaissance styles.

> A suite with a porch overlooking Prescott's main street is rumored to be haunted by a young woman who was abandoned here on her honeymoon. Apparently she's a friendly ghost; members of the housekeeping staff claim that she has helped them clean the room.

In 1985 the restored grande dame resumed her rightful place in society. Now listed on the National Register of Historic Places, the Hassayampa offers a sense of history coupled with style. The lobby has tile floors, Oriental rugs, oversize easy chairs, a leather sofa, an antique piano, and potted palms, but the focal point is the beamed ceiling, decorated with Spanish and Indian motifs. During the renovation the ceiling was meticulously restored from photographs of the original.

Ride up the attended birdcage elevator, part of the original building, to the second- and third-floor rooms. More than half of the rooms feature Castilian walnut furniture inset with Spanish tiles — the same pieces that decorated the rooms in 1927. Televisions, air conditioning, and heating are modern additions. With color schemes of deep blue and mauve or peach and green, the spacious rooms have high ceilings and are fresh and inviting. Original watercolors of local Prescott scenes adorn the walls. Beds are dressed in comforters, dust ruffles, and pillow shams, with coordinating draperies and lace curtains. Several suites are available, including one with a large whirlpool tub.

The Peacock Room is the hotel's pleasant dining spot, with tapestry print booths and etched glass accents. All three meals are served here. For lunch, there is a wide variety of salads and sandwiches as well as a list of hot entrées that includes beef liver, an item you don't see on many menus these days. Dinner entrées range from pork schnitzel to Scapparelli (chicken fillets and sausage sautéed with broccoli topped with white wine sauce and served on fettuccine) and start at $9. For light lunches or evening cocktails, try the Hassayampa Bar and Grill. It's decorated with beveled glass, a copper ceiling, and fringed cocktail tables.

Hotel Vendome

230 S. Cortez Street
Prescott, AZ 86303
602-776-0900

A small, historic hotel with an appealing simplicity

General Manager: Catherine Lemons. **Accommodations:** 21 rooms, all with private bath. **Rates:** $70–$85, suites $100–$115. **Added:** 8.5% tax. **Payment:** Major credit cards. **Children:** Free in room with parents. **Pets:** Permitted with prior approval. **Smoking:** Nonsmoking rooms available. **Open:** Year-round.

This wood and brick hotel, built in 1917 and restored in 1983, sits near the center of downtown. It's a pleasant lodging that doesn't pretend to be elegant. The tiny lobby doubles as an informal bar. Guests can sit at the cherry counter and enjoy wine or coffee and doughnuts.

The guest rooms stretch along wood-paneled central hallways accented with brass light fixtures on the first and second floors. All have a tailored, uncluttered look and either a queen-size or two twin beds. Two-room suites, with a sofa bed in the parlor, are a good choice for families. The bathrooms, which have also been nicely renovated, have either a claw-foot tub with a shower or an oversize sunken tub. The lighting is good, with open bulb fixtures reminiscent of theatrical dressing rooms. Cable TVs, phones, and ceiling fans in lieu of air conditioning are in every room.

Behind the front desk is a charming reminder of the hotel's vintage — a two-way signaling system that enables guests to buzz the front desk or vice versa. The system still works; ask for a demonstration.

Lynx Creek Farm

P.O. Box 4301
Prescott, AZ 86302
602-778-9573

*A delightful B&B
in a
delightful setting*

Innkeepers: Greg and Wendy Temple. **Accommodations:** 6 rooms. **Rates:** $95–$120, suites $140. **Included:** Full breakfast and afternoon refreshments. **Added:** 5.5% tax. **Payment:** Major credit cards. **Children:** Age 2–16, $15 extra. **Pets:** Permitted with prior approval. **Smoking:** Not permitted in guest rooms. **Open:** Year-round.

Seven miles east of Prescott, a sign points to Lynx Creek Farm, Orchards, and Bed and Breakfast, and you drive down a farm road through the orchards to the home of Greg and Wendy Temple. In the mid-1980s, this energetic young couple from Phoenix bought the 20-acre hillside orchards on Lynx Creek, intending to run a B&B. It opened in 1987, offering a country getaway in beautiful surroundings.

> **Guests are served home-baked cookies at check-in, and evening hors d'oeuvres are served out on the deck of the main house in nice weather. Every month the inn hosts cooking classes with names like Fall in Tuscany and A Taste of the Sun in Provence.**

Two guest rooms are in a wood building about 50 feet from the family's home. A wonderful cedar deck with a large hot tub and chaises looks down on the creek below. The rooms are like a fairy tale come true. Victorian antiques, country crafts, and imaginative decorating create romantic, enchanting interiors. Everywhere you look there's something special — an old-fashioned school desk, antique quilts, old Farmer's Almanacs, and framed pages from old Prescott newspapers. More like small apartments than bedrooms, the units are spacious and comfortable. The Sharlot Hall Suite, named for Prescott's first historian, has two king-size beds, one in a cozy loft. The White Wicker Suite has a queen-size bed with a canopy and a down comforter as well as a day bed.

The log cabin rooms, the Country Garden and the Chaparral, have large picture windows and private decks with hot tubs that offer fine views of the creek and mountains. Decorated in florals, the Country Garden is feminine, while the Chaparral has a western flavor. The lower cabin rooms are the inn's newest. The Sunflower is accented with sunflower fabrics, prints, and crafts, while the Liberty is fittingly decorated in red, white, and blue. Fresh flowers, sherry decanters, and fluffy robes add a welcoming touch to all of the rooms.

Breakfast is geared to suit the taste of any guest, whether it's fresh fruit and homemade granola or heartier fare such as huevos rancheros and homemade tortillas. Muffins, coffee cakes, and cobblers made from the farm's own apples are specialties.

After breakfast you can hike by the creek, pick fruit in the orchard, and enjoy the seclusion. The Temples can arrange for horseback rides or restaurant reservations. Nearby Prescott is a historic town with museums, antiques shops, and many festivals. Catering to families, this B&B has a playground and sandbox, part of an attitude that truly means "Children welcome." Babysitters are arranged upon request.

The Marks House

203 E. Union Street
Prescott, AZ 86303
602-778-4632

A Victorian B&B in the heart of Prescott

Innkeepers: Dottie and Harold Viehweg. **Accommodations:** 4 rooms. **Rates:** $75–$90 single, $75–$120 double; suite $105 for 2, $135 for 3–4. **Included:** Full breakfast and afternoon refreshments. **Added:** 8.5% tax. **Payment:** Major credit cards. **Children:** Older children preferred. **Pets:** Not permitted. **Smoking:** Not permitted. **Open:** Year-round.

The Marks House perches on a hill in downtown Prescott, a maize-colored Queen Anne house with turrets, gables, and an inviting front porch. Built in 1894, the Marks House is on the National Register of Historic Places, and rightly so. During the Depression the house was divided into five apartments, and it's been converted into a charming bed-and-breakfast.

Guests are welcomed in a parlor furnished with Victorian pieces, including a display case that came from an old Prescott drug store and a fainting couch. The patterned trim around the ceilings is hand-painted, and portraits of the Viehwegs' grandparents adorn the walls. A full breakfast and afternoon hors d'oeuvres are served in the adjoining dining room.

> **The Marks House is just a block from Prescott's main square, the site of many arts and crafts and antiques shows as well as other civic events throughout the year.**

The two-bedroom Ivy suite, the largest suite, is on the main floor. The larger bedroom has a real feather mattress covered with an ivy print spread. The smaller bedroom is sweet, with lace curtains that give it a comforting feel. Upstairs, the Princess Victoria suite has a copper bathtub that dates to 1892; its wooden exterior is painted with roses. A family christening gown hangs on the wall, and the walk-in closet has ample room to accommodate extended visits. The Tea Rose suite, in rose and cream, is the only room with a hall bath, which is not shared.

The Queen Anne suite was originally the home's master bedroom. Now a favorite with honeymooning couples, the room is decorated in cool green with white wicker furniture and lace pillows. Bow windows create a sunny sitting area and offer a view of Prescott's natural rock formation called Thumb Butte.

In the upstairs hallway there's an antique vanity said to have come from FDR's White House. Throughout, attractive floral wallpaper and dried flower arrangements add a country touch to this urban home.

SEDONA

Canyon Villa

125 Canyon Circle Drive
P.O. Box 204
Sedona, AZ 86336
602-284-1226
800-453-1166

> *A professionally run*
> *inn with*
> *lots of extras*

Innkeepers: Chuck and Marion Yadon. **Accommodations:** 11 rooms. **Rates:** $85–$145 single, $95–$155 double; additional persons $25 per day. **Included:** Full breakfast and afternoon refreshments. **Added:** 10.5% tax. **Minimum stay:** 2 nights on weekends and holidays. **Payment:** Major credit cards. **Children:** Over age 10 welcome; additional $25 per day. **Pets:** Not permitted. **Smoking:** Not permitted. **Open:** Year-round.

Since Canyon Villa, which opened in the summer of 1992, was built as an inn, many distinctive features were incorporated into its design that add to the overall appeal of the inn. Prior to opening Canyon Villa, innkeeper Chuck Yadon had worked in commercial real estate for over 20 years, so when it came time to create the inn he knew just what he was doing. His expertise is in evidence as soon as you walk into the inn's dramatic, high-ceilinged living room and are immediately captivated by Sedona's spectacular scenery exquisitely framed by the room's lofty arched windows.

Each guest room has its own patio, strategically angled to

view the landscape but not neighboring patios. All baths have relaxing whirlpool tubs accented by stained glass windows that coordinate with the room decor, and instant hot water.

> **Although Courthouse Butte and Bell Rock feel as though they're literally at Canyon Villa's back door, there is enough room in the yard for a good-size swimming pool and an outdoor fireplace.**

And then there are things that you don't see (or hear) that were included in the inn's construction, such as extra thick walls for soundproofing and individual climate controls.

The rooms, which are named for desert plants, are all individually and beautifully decorated. On the first floor, the Gold Poppy has an Oriental theme, the Evening Primrose is decorated in green and rose, the Claret Cup has a carved four-poster king-size bed, and the Mariposa's iron bed is topped with a white eyelet lace spread and pillows. Upstairs, the Strawberry Cactus has white wicker furniture; the Ocotillo, in mauves and desert colors, has a southwestern flavor; the Desert Daisy is pure Americana; and the Spanish Bayonet has an oversize whirlpool tub right in the bedroom. Several rooms have fireplaces.

Breakfast is served in the elegant dining room. The night before, the morning menu is posted in case any guest needs to alert the chef to dietary restrictions. The full breakfasts are prepared by innkeeper Marion Yadon and rotated in an 18-day cycle so that long-term guests aren't constantly being served the same meal time and again. Every afternoon there are fresh hors d'oeuvres, and guests are always welcome to help themselves to beverages from the dining room fridge.

Casa Sedona

55 Hozoni Drive
Sedona, AZ 86336
602-282-2938
800-525-3756

> *Gracious living
> at a relaxed pace*

Innkeepers: Misty and Lori Zitko and Dick Curtis. **Accommodations:** 11 rooms. **Rates:** double

$95–$150; additional persons $25 per day. **Included:** Full breakfast and afternoon refreshments. **Added:** 10.5% tax. **Payment:** Major credit cards. **Children:** Over age 10 welcome. **Pets:** Not permitted. **Smoking:** Not permitted. **Open:** Year-round.

Casa Sedona was designed by Mani Subra, a protégé of Frank Lloyd Wright, and from the moment you see the inn's exterior, stuccoed to match the surrounding red rock terrain, you'll know setting plays a key role at this inn, both inside and out.

The wooden front door is beautifully carved and has feather and turquoise accents; even the doorbell has a turquoise push button. Inside, the Sierra Vista room, which serves as the living room, and the Library are both comfortably welcoming.

> Casa Sedona's lush backyard lures many a guest into an afternoon of lazing about in the hammock or swing, perhaps with a book from the inn's library. Others may prefer to gaze at the view of the Mongollon Rim or Cathedral Rock from an upstairs terrace. For hikers, trails into the forest start at the edge of the property.

You'll soon notice the photographs on the wall from "The Jonathan Winters Show" and other television programs. One face crops up time and again in all of the pictures: that of Casa Sedona's host, Dick Curtis. Dick worked in show business for many years, but in the fall of 1992 he opened Casa Sedona with Misty Zitko and her daughter Lori. He calls innkeeping his proudest role, and judging by his warmth and hospitality, it's a role he was born to play, as were Misty and Lori.

In the mornings, Dick performs for guests (he varies the revue each day so long-term visitors don't see the same show over again) while Lori cooks a delicious breakfast, maybe a chile relleno souffle one day and special whole wheat pancakes topped with fruit the next. In good weather, which is fairly often thanks to Sedona's marvelous climate, breakfast is served outdoors on one of the inn's patios.

No two guest rooms are alike, and each is tastefully furnished. The Hozoni is pretty in rose and sea foam green chintz fabrics, and light wood furnishings. The Cowboy is masculine, with a four-poster pole bed, cowhide rocking chair, and prints of cowboys on the walls. The Sunset room opens onto a large terrace and has a Jacuzzi tub and fireplace. The Anasazi has Native American decor including a painted Indian drum, and the Hopi has an incredible bath. Serena Vista, pretty and romantic in peach French country fabrics, is a favorite. All rooms have private baths and patios, fireplaces, refrigerators, and telephones.

In the afternoon, hors d'oeuvres such as quiche and Mexican sushi (flour tortillas wrapped around black beans, salsa, and cilantro) are served with lemonade.

Enchantment Resort

525 Boynton Canyon Road
Sedona, AZ 86336
602-282-2900
800-826-4180
Fax: 602-282-9249

A luxurious escape in a breathtaking setting

Resident Manager: Mark Grenoble. **Accommodations:** 56 casitas. **Rates:** $145–$230 single, $210–$275 double; suites $425–$475. **Added:** 7.5% tax. **Payment:** Major credit cards. **Children:** Over $12, additional $20 per day. **Pets:** Not permitted. **Smoking:** Permitted. **Open:** Year-round.

Enchantment Resort is surrounded by the Coconino National Forest and the glowing rock formations of Boynton Canyon. About 10 minutes from the center of town, Enchantment is right in the heart of Sedona's magical red rock country.

When you're not out exploring the area's glorious terrain, there is plenty to keep you busy at the resort. Twelve tennis courts and four swimming pools are spread throughout the grounds, giving the resort an uncrowded feel and making each casita more convenient. Court time is free for guests, but for those who want more intensive tennis programs, instructional packages are available. There's a full-service spa and fitness center with steam rooms, saunas, and whirlpools. Also on the property is a croquet course; and if the pitch-and-putt won't satisfy your golf craving, a round of 18 holes can be arranged at a nearby course.

The casitas are so roomy they feel like private homes. Built of adobe to blend in with the landscape, they are decorated tastefully in a southwestern style. Black Indian pottery and Taos drums add personality. Two-bedroom casitas have a large central living room with a kiva fireplace, a deck with a built-in barbecue, and a kitchenette. Two casitas have private pools, one with a poolside Jacuzzi, and a number have garages.

> **A trail leading to the ruins of Indian canyon dwellings starts right at the edge of the resort. In the evening, deer snack on the lush green grass of the pitch-and-putt golf course.**

Guests who don't feel like whipping something up in their kitchenette can eat in the fine dining room at the resort's clubhouse, which has outstanding views, or order from room service. The restaurant cuisine is primarily southwestern, and spa meals are available for the health-conscious. On Friday and Saturday nights there is musical entertainment; on Sundays a champagne brunch is offered.

A security gate at the entrance to the resort ensures that it remains a secluded hideaway for guests only. A concierge is on duty in the clubhouse from 8:00 A.M. to 6:00 P.M., and there are laundry facilities on the property.

Garland's Oak Creek Lodge

8067 North Highway 89A
P.O. Box 152
Sedona, AZ 86336
602-282-3343

> *A cozy hideaway in Oak Creek Canyon*

Innkeepers: Mary and Gary Garland. **Accommodations:** 16 units. **Rates:** $120–$140 single,

$155–$175 double. **Included:** Breakfast and dinner. **Minimum stay:** 2 nights. **Added:** 5% tax. **Payment:** Major credit cards. **Children:** Additional $35 per day. **Pets:** Not permitted. **Smoking:** Permitted. **Open:** April 1 through mid-November (closed on Sundays).

To get to Garland's, turn off Highway 89A at the Banjo Bill Campground, about eight miles north of Sedona. Then drive through the campground, over the creek, and onto the property. All of a sudden you're in a private world — peaceful, serene, and far removed from the tourists in Sedona. Garland's Lodge is right on Oak Creek, the same creek that created the surrounding canyon renowned for its beautiful views. In the family's orchards around the lodge are about 200 fruit trees, including apples, pears, peaches, and cherries.

> **Run by the Garlands since 1972, the lodge is so popular that guests often make reservations a year in advance. Note that Garland's is unusual in two ways: there's a two-day minimum stay, and the lodge is closed on Sundays.**

The main lodge is a rambling log building that serves as office, dining room, and social center. With rustic furniture, a piano, and a stone fireplace, it has a casual, inviting atmosphere.

Sixteen log cabins are scattered over the grounds, each with a porch overlooking the creek, the orchards, or the gardens abloom with luminous sunflowers or purple cosmos. Some cabins have views of the red cliffs that enclose the canyon. Large cabins have a combination bedroom–sitting room and a fireplace with either one king or two double beds. Small cabins have one queen-size bed. This is a true retreat; the cabins have no TVs, radios, or phones.

Breakfast features homemade breads, hot entrées such as griddle cakes, or a smoked trout and leek frittata made with eggs from the farm's chickens, and fruit from the orchard. Dinner is a fancy affair; you don't have to dress, but you dine rather than simply eat. Even though the lodge itself is rustic, tables are set with crisp linens. The menu changes daily, but there is always an emphasis on fresh ingredients from the Lodge's own gardens. A typical meal starts with French onion soup, followed by Caesar salad, shrimp with a red garlic sauce, linguine with creamy basil sauce, fresh carrots and cauliflower, and Kahlua cheesecake. Another night you may dine on sesame oat bread, minestrone soup, warm cabbage salad with walnuts and gorgonzola cheese, breast of chicken al Limone, carrots and broccoli, and orange and black currant sorbet. The wine list, featuring California wines, has about 30 choices by the bottle, as well as a number of selections by the glass. In the afternoons, an informal or "low" tea is served.

When guests aren't enjoying the seclusion amid the forest, they can fish in Oak Creek, hike, browse in Sedona's shops and galleries, and take day trips to numerous sights, especially the Grand Canyon, 100 miles to the north.

The Graham Bed & Breakfast Inn

150 Canyon Circle Drive
Sedona, AZ 86351
602-284-1425
800-228-1425
Fax: 602-284-0767

> *Thorough and thoughtful innkeepers set this B&B apart*

Innkeepers: Carol and Roger Redenbaugh. **Accommodations:** 5 rooms, 1 suite, all with private bath. **Rates:** $80–$140 single, $95–$160 double; suite $195. **Included:** Full breakfast and afternoon refreshments. **Added:** 5.5% tax. **Payment:** Major credit cards. **Children:** Additional $20 per child. **Pets:** Not permitted. **Smoking:** Outside only. **Open:** Year-round.

This two-story western contemporary house sits at the base of Bell Rock in the Village of Oak Creek, about six miles south of Sedona. The inn is a pleasant lodging, professionally run by resident owners who enjoy getting to know their guests.

> The innkeepers' attention to detail is truly extraordinary. Color schemes in the baths, down to the tiles and terry robes, completely match the guest rooms. Even the ironing boards are covered in matching fabrics.

Built as a B&B in 1985, the house is designed to take full advantage of its setting in red rock country, with lots of glass in the living areas and a balcony off each guest room. The decor brings the outdoors in. For example, the terra cotta–colored rug downstairs reflects the red of the mountains visible through the windows.

Since the house itself is new, the Redenbaughs have imbued one of the guest rooms with their personal history. The Country room is a reflection of Carol's childhood in Kansas. Her parents' wedding picture sits atop a dresser in the living room, her cousin in Dodge City made the log cabin patchwork quilt on the bed, a picture of her grandmother adorns one wall, dried flowers hang from a stair rail that came from the family farmhouse, and her mother's porcelain angel collection is on display. Other rooms include the art deco–style San Francisco room, the lively Garden Room in red and green, with white wicker furniture, and the Southwest room, with a pole bed and an attractive metal and glass coffee table.

With a large separate living room and bedroom, a private patio, and a fireplace, the Sedona suite is the most deluxe. Like the Southwest room, it is furnished with a regional air. The suite comes with a television/laser disc player and library of movies on laser disc. In the bath, there's a roomy whirlpool tub and separate double shower. Every room has a private bath, balcony, air conditioning, hair dryer, curling iron, set of bathrobes, iron, ironing board, fudge at bedside, and a flashlight — there are no streetlights in Sedona.

Guests eat together in the dining room, and a window open to the kitchen lets them converse with the innkeepers as they prepare the morning meal, something that's easy to do, as the Redenbaughs are truly a genial couple. The breakfast menu changes daily, but German pancakes served with lemon juice and powdered sugar or fruit, artichoke frittatas, puffed apple pancakes, cheese strata, and walnut sticky rolls are examples of the tasty treats guests can expect.

In the backyard there's a nice pool and spa. Other activities are shopping at the nearby boutiques and art galleries, playing golf at one of two excellent courses half a mile away, Jeep rides through the countryside, and day trips to the Grand Canyon, two and a half hours away.

Junipine Resort Condo Hotel

8351 North Highway 89A
Sedona, AZ 86336
602-282-3375
800-742-7463
Fax: 602-282-7402

> *Condominium
> accommodations
> among the pines*

General Manager: Jolynn Green-field. **Accommodations:** 23 units. **Rates:** $110–$250. **Added:** 6.05% tax. **Payment:** Major credit cards. **Children:** Under 12 free in condo with parents. **Pets:** Not permitted. **Smoking:** Nonsmoking condos available. **Open:** Year-round.

Oak Creek Canyon, north of Sedona, is one of the area's top scenic attractions, a combination of evergreen forests and rugged mountain vistas. Junipine Resort, nestled among huge ponderosa pines on the banks of Oak Creek, provides spaciousness and comfort in a beautiful wooded setting.

All privately owned, the condos — called "creekhouses" by management — were built in 1985. Attractive natural wood structures, they blend well with the surrounding forests. The modern interiors are comfortable, with southwestern decor, but the outdoors is the prime focus, so every unit has a large deck, accessible from both the living and sleeping areas through sliding glass doors. Families will appreciate the out-door activities, such as hiking, volleyball, horseshoes, and swimming in Oak Creek, which runs behind the property.

> **Those seeking seclusion will find it here, since the creekhouses are designed for privacy.**

Each creekhouse has a small but quite functional kitchen, complete with all you need. All units have fireplaces, and baths have separate vanities. Some units have lofts.

L'Auberge de Sedona

301 L'Auberge Lane
Sedona, AZ 86339
602-282-7131
800-282-6777
Fax: 602-204-5757

> *A taste of
> French country
> in Sedona*

General Manager: Dirk Oldenburg.
Accommodations: 96 units. **Rates:** Cottages $200–$385, lodge rooms $130–$180, Orchards rooms $100–$165. **Added:** 11.1% tax. **Payment:** Major credit cards. **Children:** $20 per day. **Pets:** Not permitted. **Smoking:** Not permitted. **Open:** Year-round.

L'Auberge de Sedona is four establishments rolled into one. The hostelry operates a gourmet French restaurant, a lodge, a motel, and charming cottages, all with a French country theme. The restaurant is situated beside babbling Oak Creek, and tables on the restaurant's porch have a view of a small waterfall. Inside, pink table linens and fresh flowers complement Pierre Deux print wallpaper and upholstery. But of course it's the food that takes center stage. You can expect dishes such as sautéed rib-eye of veal served with a saffron rice timbale and Spanish hollandaise, or grilled salmon in an onion butter sauce with California citrus. Prix fixe meals run about $45 per person. Perhaps because the menu changes daily, the quality of the dishes has been known to be somewhat inconsistent in recent years.

The most luxurious accommodations at L'Auberge are in the creekside cottages. With distinctive combinations of

French country fabrics, canopied beds, cushiony sofas, stone fireplaces, and dried flower wreaths, the rooms are a visual delight, and highly romantic. Outside you can hear the soothing sounds of Oak Creek, and the surrounding grounds are beautifully landscaped. It is easy to imagine that you have been somehow transported to Provence.

Lodge rooms are similar in decor to the cottages, but with less space and privacy. Rooms at the Orchards, the motel atop the hill, have traditional

> **The Armoire Boutique is L'Auberge's charming French country gift shop. If you like the inn, you'll enjoy the shop.**

motel decor, but they also have red rock views and retain a few country touches that are distinctly L'Auberge. There's a restaurant at the Orchards, and an outdoor pool. A "hilavator" connects the Orchards with the lower portion of the inn so that guests can travel between the two with ease.

Since L'Auberge is in the center of Sedona, it's an ideal jumping-off point for area sightseeing. The inn's staff is happy to arrange Jeep tours, golf, and horseback riding excursions.

Los Abrigados

160 Portal Lane
Sedona, AZ 86336
602-282-1777
800-521-3131 in U.S.
Fax: 602-282-2614

> *An ideal base for exploring Sedona and its environs*

General Manager: Ed Zielinski. **Accommodations:** 175 rooms. **Rates:** Suites $215–$375, Old Stone House $1,000. **Included:** Spa facilities. **Added:** 11.01% tax. **Payment:** Major credit cards. **Children:** Under 16 free in room with parents. **Pets:** Not permitted. **Smoking:** Permitted. **Open:** Year-round.

Los Abrigados is in the center of town, yet it is easy to miss because it's tucked behind Tlaquepaque, Sedona's popular shopping village. Tlaquepaque is modeled after an arts and crafts village in Mexico, and Los Abrigados has a Mexican look as well. A massive terra cotta and tile fountain stands at the entrance to the hotel; lodgings are spread among red tile–roofed buildings that are peppered with small fountain courtyards.

Guest rooms are decorated in rich plum complemented by soothing green and pink. Furnishings are contemporary but not distinctive. Suites all have TVs in both the bedroom and living room, refrigerators, coffee makers, microwaves, and sleeper sofas; some also have fireplaces, and others have private patio spas.

> **For a really special occasion you can rent the entire Old Stone House, built over 60 years ago.**

Los Abrigados has an excellent spa with a weight room, an aerobics room, and fully equipped locker rooms that have hot tubs and steam rooms. For an extra fee, pampering services such as massage, body wraps, and tanning beds are available. The inn also has a pleasant outdoor swimming pool and a poolside bar, as well as several tennis courts.

At mealtime, the hotel's Canyon Rose restaurant presents interesting fare that can best be described as nouvelle southwestern. For dinner, entrées such as seared ahi tuna dusted with southwestern seasonings and veal chops topped with a mango salsa sauce and served with potato Napoleon range from $17 to $24. For lunch, dishes such as beer-battered halibut in a tarragon tartar sauce add zest to more traditional noontime offerings. The restaurant's Sunday brunch is a festive affair.

Territorial House

65 Piki Drive
Sedona, AZ 86336
602-204-2737
Fax: 602-208-2230

*A homey
"Old West" B&B*

Innkeepers: John and Linda Steele.
Accommodations: 4 rooms. **Rates:** $75–$115 single, $90–$130 double; suites $160. **Included:** Full breakfast. **Added:** 10.5% tax. **Payment:** Major credit cards. **Children:** Additional charge if over age 6. **Pets:** Not permitted. **Smoking:** Outside only. **Open:** Year-round.

Staying at Territorial House is like visiting old friends. Guests enter through the kitchen door, and new arrivals are greeted by a welcome note on a chalkboard there. On the table there's fresh gingerbread or some other afternoon treat. Beyond the kitchen is a comfortable living room centered around a large stone fireplace. Guests are welcome to relax or watch television here when they're not out exploring Sedona's glorious terrain.

The B&B is run by friendly hosts, John and Linda Steele, two Midwesterners who fell in love with Sedona on a golfing vacation. Many of the furnishings throughout the house were either handbuilt by the Steeles or are attached to their childhood memories. Each guest room is different. Fans of westerns should request Grasshopper Flats, which comes with a TV/VCR and a collection of old western movies, some of them filmed in the Sedona area. The two-bedroom, one-bath Schnebly Station is a good choice for families. One of the bedrooms has a king bed and gas fireplace. The other, smaller room has a queen bed and a built-in twin. There's a cute closet with a half moon cut out of its door, and John and Linda's initials are branded into one of the beams overhead. Indian Garden is cozy and rustic, with a bed tucked at an angle under the dormered ceiling. There's a lively red-striped Indian print spread on the bed and a dreamcatcher on the wall. It has its own staircase and, best of all, a private balcony with a telescope for celestial viewing.

Although Territorial House is only 20 years old, pieces of western history have been built in. The brickwork in the kitchen came from a bordello in Jerome, the beam above the living room fireplace came from a Zane Grey cabin, and the copper window in Indian Garden was once part of a building in Jerome.

Red Rock Crossing is the deluxe suite. With a king-size pine four-poster canopy bed bursting with pillows topped by a flower garland, pine night tables, and hunter green, wine, and ivory fabrics, the room has a clean, country look. This room is a favorite with honeymooners because of its deep whirlpool tub and glass-enclosed shower. All the rooms have guardian angels incorporated into their decor (Linda collects them), a supply of magazines, and a small basket of chocolates at bedside.

Breakfast is served family-style at the long farmhouse table in the kitchen. There are always fresh baked goods, maybe followed by Linda's delicious fruit taco and hot egg dish such as huevos rancheros, artichoke frittata, or chile egg puff. Meats are served on the side. Bandana print napkins and cowboy hat napkin rings add a playful western touch to the meal. Afterwards, John gives new guests a map of the area and helpful suggestions for hiking and sightseeing.

Southern Arizona

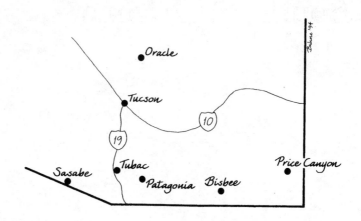

Best Bed-and-Breakfasts

Bisbee
  The Bisbee Inn
Oracle
  Triangle L Ranch
  Villa Cardinale Bed & Breakfast Inn
Tucson
  Casa Alegre
  Casa Tierra
  El Presidio Bed & Breakfast Inn
  La Posada del Valle
  The Peppertrees
  The SunCatcher

Best Guest Ranches

Douglas
  Price Canyon Ranch
Patagonia
  Circle Z Ranch
Sasabe
  Rancho de la Osa
Tucson
  White Stallion Ranch

Best Historic Hostelries

Bisbee
  Bisbee Grand Hotel
  Copper Queen Hotel

Best Resorts

Tubac
  Tubac Golf Resort
Tucson
  Arizona Inn
  Loews Ventana Canyon Resort
  Sheraton Tucson El Conquistador Golf and Tennis Resort

Tucson
 Tucson National Golf and Conference Resort
 Westin La Paloma
 Westward Look Resort

Best Spas

Tucson
 Canyon Ranch Spa

Southern Arizona may be less popular with tourists than the central and northern parts of the state, but it is no less appealing. Winters are just as pleasant, and the landscape is just as beautiful. Those who want an active vacation will find a good selection of dude ranches, as well as golf and tennis resorts to choose from; and travelers in search of traditional sightseeing activities will not be disappointed.

 Tucson, Arizona's second largest city, is at the heart of this southern region, both literally and figuratively. It may surprise some to learn that Tucson is the oldest continuously inhabited settlement in the United States. Jesuit missionary Father Eusebio Francisco Kino founded a mission here in 1687, and in the 1770s the Spanish established Fort Tucson. Today Tucson is a growing, multicultural city influenced by a variety of ethnic groups.

 Many of Tucson's most popular attractions are out of doors. The wonderful Arizona-Sonora Desert Museum is the best place to become acquainted with the flora and fauna of the Sonoran desert. Afterwards, be sure to visit the adjacent Saguaro National Monument, where majestic saguaro cacti, unique to the Sonoran Desert, dot the landscape by the thousands. Nearby is the International Wildlife Museum.

 Closer to downtown, Tohono Chul Park, with its nature trails, demonstration gardens, and excellent tea room, is worth discovering. The Reid Park Zoo and Tucson Botanical Gardens are also within the city. On the outskirts of town, a tram trip into Sabino Canyon makes for an enjoyable outing, and the ski area at Mount Lemmon is the southernmost in the United States. For those willing to travel a bit, the controversial but fascinating Biosphere II is located in **Oracle,** to the north of Tucson, Kitt Peak Observatory is about an hour southwest of the city, and Colossal Cave, an enormous dry cave, is 22 miles southeast of Tucson.

History buffs should walk through Tucson's downtown Presidio district. Not far from the Presidio district, downtown Tucson springs to life on special Saturday nights. Boutiques and galleries stay open late on these scheduled nights, and the streets fill with people and street musicians. Another free entertainment is a visit to the Flandrau Science Center and Planetarium at the University of Arizona. There is a charge for tickets to planetarium shows, but the exhibit halls and celestial viewing through the center's telescope are free.

And there is still more to occupy the visitor. The Amerind Foundation is a museum of Native American art and culture. There's the Tucson Museum of Art, the Arizona Historical Society, the Pima Air Museum, the Titan Missile Museum south of the city, the exquisite Mission San Xavier Del Bac also south of town, and Old Tucson, where movies such as *Tombstone* have been filmed, is just a short drive west of downtown. Speaking of Tombstone, the actual town where the infamous battle at the O.K. Corral took place is an easy side trip from Tucson. Now strictly a tourist town, the boardwalked streets of Tombstone, lined with saloons and gift shops, are still worth a visit if you want a taste of the Wild West.

A pleasant day trip in southern Arizona takes in **Tubac** and Nogales. The town of Tubac was once a Spanish military post; now it's the home of a variety of gift shops and art galleries. Arts and crafts shows regularly draw art lovers to the small town, and the mission ruins at Tumacacori National Monument just south of town are also well-frequented. From Tubac, it's half an hour further south to Nogales, Mexico, the largest town along the Arizona/Mexico border. Many enjoy walking into Mexico to shop in Nogales's lively markets.

A visit to the fascinating copper mining town of **Bisbee** is another worthwhile excursion in southern Arizona. Many turn-of-the-century buildings that were constructed during the mine's heyday have been well preserved, and you can tour the Queen Mine or the Mining and Historical Museum. As with Jerome in northern Arizona, artists have flocked to this mining town, fostering an interesting assortment of shops and galleries. The colorful and cavernous mine pit on the edge of town is dramatic in its sheer depth and size.

BISBEE

The Bisbee Grand Hotel

P.O. Box 825
61 Main Street
Bisbee, AZ 85603
602-432-5900
800-421-1909

A turn-of-the-century B&B and saloon

Owner: Bill Thomas. **Accommodations:** 8 rooms and 3 suites. **Rates:** $50 without private bath, $65 with private bath, $75 for rooms with queen beds, suites $110. **Included:** Continental breakfast. **Added:** 10.55% tax. **Payment:** Major credit cards. **Children:** Permitted in one suite only. **Pets:** Not permitted. **Smoking:** In restricted areas only. **Open:** Year-round.

In a town that has remarkably preserved its origin as a bustling turn-of-the-century mining town, the Bisbee Grand Hotel recaptures the lively, almost bawdy spirit of the day. The hotel, originally built in 1906, burned to the ground in the great fire of 1908. Immediately rebuilt, it stands today as a reminder of an earlier era. In the late 1980s, Bill Thomas purchased the hotel and turned it into a stylish bed-and-breakfast with a sense of fun.

Guests check in at the saloon on street level. The saloon itself dates back to 1883 and has fixtures once owned by Wyatt Earp, red velvet–cushioned bar stools, and a pressed tin ceiling. Adjacent to it is an elegant ladies' parlor with a large fireplace, sofa, baby grand piano, and a number of easy chairs that invite guests to socialize in a more refined environment.

Guest rooms are reached by climbing a staircase carpeted in vibrant maroon. A shimmery stuffed peacock stands at one end of the stairwell, and velvet-upholstered chairs add to the central hallway's plush Victorian feel. Each room is decorated with antiques and has its own theme. The Hunter Room is small but appealing. There are bird prints on the walls, and a riding crop rests across the bed. The Gray Room, furnished in gray and burgundy, has a brass bed. The Coral Room is feminine in decor.

The Oriental and Victorian suites are the most luxurious. The Oriental has an ornate brass bed topped with satin pillows embroidered with Asian motifs, and there's an elaborate gold fan above the bed. In the living room, an attractive chest with intricate scenes sits in one corner, an Oriental screen shields the fireplace, and Oriental prints adorn the walls. Fabric wallpaper printed with Oriental themes and bamboo print curtains throughout the suite add to the mood.

> **Next to the ladies' parlor is a theater where the inn's murder mystery weekends are staged.**

The Victorian suite is opulent, furnished with period pieces — most notably the bed, lavishly canopied in fringed red velvet drapes. Both suites have private bathrooms. The rooms share appealing baths with lace shower curtains.

Breakfast is served in the guest rooms or on the second-floor balcony overlooking the street below. If you can't live without television, there's a big-screen TV in the saloon. In Bisbee, you can take the City Mine Tour or visit the Mining and Historical Museum. Bisbee has many interesting shops, and the town of Tombstone, not far away, is worth a visit.

The Bisbee Inn

45 OK Street
P.O. Box 1855
Bisbee, AZ 85603
602-432-5131

*Affordable rooms
next to
Brewery Gulch*

Owners: John Thorup and Joy Timbers. **Accommodations:** 18 rooms with shared baths. **Rates:** $29 single, $39–$45 double; $6 each additional person. **Included:** Full breakfast. **Added:** 10.55% tax. **Payment:** Major credit cards. **Children:** Over 1, $6 additional per day. **Pets:** Permitted. **Smoking:** Outside only. **Open:** Year-round.

On one of the steepest streets in a town known for steep streets is the Bisbee Inn, with very affordable prices. When it opened as the LaMore Hotel in 1917, the saloon-lined strip across the street was known as Brewery Gulch.

In the morning, guests gather around oak tables for a generous breakfast of fresh fruit, French toast, cereal, hash browns, pancakes, bacon and eggs. Then it's time to explore the town of Bisbee.

With a certified historic restoration, the inn reflects its past yet also has a fresh appeal. Many of the furnishings have a history of their own. The iron beds, recently sandblasted and repainted, are from the original hotel. The oak tables and chairs came from the old Brooks Apartments next door.

Each guest room is different, both in decor and configuration. All have period wallpaper, perhaps deep blue with flowers or another dainty design. Quilted spreads and antique dressers complete the look.

Bed arrangements include one double, two doubles, or one double and one twin. Central air conditioning and heating have been added. There are no TVs in the guest rooms, but there is a TV room on the main floor. Each room has a washbasin, but bathrooms are down the hall. Also available are a coin-operated washer and dryer.

Nearby, tours of Bisbee's old Queen Mine, narrated by former miners, include turn-of-the-century mining demonstrations. Also nearby are Chiricahua National Monument, Fort Huachuca, and the western town of Tombstone.

Copper Queen Hotel

P.O. Box Drawer CQ
Bisbee, AZ 85603
602-432-2216
800-247-5829
Fax: 602-432-4298

*A historic hotel
in the heart
of Bisbee*

General Manager: Karen Schonwit.
Accommodations: 43 rooms. **Rates:** $65–$90. **Added:** 10.55% tax. **Payment:** Major credit cards. **Children:** $5 additional if more than 2 people in a room. **Pets:** Seeing-eye dogs only. **Smoking:** Nonsmoking rooms available. **Open:** Year-round.

Sit on the upstairs porch of the Copper Queen Hotel and look down on the bustling town below. Straight ahead is a mountain, so near you can almost touch it. Below you is the historic town of Bisbee, stair-stepping up the side of Mule Pass Gulch. It doesn't take much imagination to pretend that you're in a turn-of-the-century mining town.

In 1902, when the Copper Queen was built, Bisbee was the largest copper-mining town in the world. Right around the corner was Brewery Gulch, the site of about 40 bars where the miners caroused. Today's

The saloon looks like a western movie come to life.

residents like to point out that Bisbee was not just a hastily constructed boom town but was built to last. At one time it had two opera houses, in addition to a host of brick buildings, many of which remain.

The Copper Queen has lots of character. On one wall of the

saloon hangs a painting of a reclining nude with a winged cherub. There's an old-fashioned safe behind the check-in desk. Red patterned wallpaper and old trunks give the hallways an old-fashioned feel.

The guest rooms are upstairs, and each is individual in size and decor. In one of the nicest rooms, burgundy curtains are tied back with lace. The wallpaper is also burgundy, and the bed is covered with a colonial white spread. The Teddy Roosevelt is a three-bedroom suite with a sofa in the large bedroom and slanted ceilings in the two smaller rooms. Another room in rich green, pink, and cream has two brass beds, an armoire, and a large bath. Baths and modern conveniences such as air conditioning, telephones, and televisions have been added to all the rooms. In an unexpected touch for a historic hotel, the Copper Queen has a swimming pool.

The Copper Queen has a picturesque dining room and a sidewalk café that's great for people-watching. Waitresses wearing long blue skirts serve such dishes as veal Sonoita, chicken dream (chicken stuffed with cheese and asparagus tips and topped with hollandaise), and scampi Carrera. Dinner entrées are priced from $8.50 to $17.

ORACLE

The Triangle L Ranch

P.O. Box 900
Oracle, AZ 85623
602-896-2804
Fax: 602-896-9070

The pace of an earlier era at a desert hideaway

Innkeepers: Tom and Margot Beeston. **Accommodations:** 4 cottages.
Rates: $60–$75 single, $80–$95 double; $15 per day each additional person. **Included:** Full breakfast. **Added:** 6.6% tax. **Payment:** Major credit cards. **Children:** $10 additional per day per child. **Pets:** Not permitted. **Smoking:** Outside only. **Open:** Year-round.

Although the entrance to Triangle L Ranch is only a couple of hundred yards from Route 77 in Oracle, the ranch is set down in a valley all its own. You feel yourself being drawn into an earlier era as the gate closes behind you. A lazy dog sleeps on the dusty dirt road as you approach the main house. Off to one side, a windmill stands high above the low-lying buildings, which are spread out over the 80-acre property. In spring, the front garden is alive with color.

The ranch was established in the 1890s by William Ladd, a sheep and cattle rancher. In the 1920s, Triangle L became the first guest ranch in southern Arizona, and cattle remained on the property until the 1960s. In 1978 the Beestons bought the ranch and began restoring the buildings, most of which were built during the late 1800s and early 1900s. The Beestons began welcoming guests in four cottages in 1988.

The cottages are simple and cheerful. Rooms decorated with family pieces and original furnishings

A visit to the ultra-modern environmental experiment Biosphere II, just four miles down the road, offers a fascinating contrast to the ranch's old-time flavor. Tucson and its many sights are just a 45-minute drive, and nearby hiking opportunities abound.

from the ranch — old-fashioned refrigerators, stoves that predate the 1940s, hooked rugs, brass and metal beds, and clawfoot tubs — have a nostalgic air. The Hill House is the largest cottage, with three bedrooms, a full kitchen, and nice views from the front porch. The Foreman's House is the most secluded. It has a screened porch, kitchen cabinets made from packing crates, and a patio with a ramada. Yellow tombstone roses drape over the front entrance to the Trowbridge House. Inside there's a large stone fireplace and a Victorian bed that belonged to the owner's great-grandmother. The Guest House has a darling sleeping porch with two twin beds. All of the cottages offer a great sense of privacy.

Full breakfasts, cooked on an old-fashioned wrought-iron stove, are served in a cheerful sun room overlooking the iris garden, on a long screened porch with views of wild birds as they come to dine at feeders, or in the traditional adobe dining room of the main house. Eggs come from the ranch's chickens, and visiting children are welcome to help collect the fresh eggs right from the source. For guests wanting a stronger than average cup of coffee, cappuccino or espresso are offered; and the breads, pancakes, and waffles are always homemade.

It's not uncommon to see quail and various desert animals crossing the ranch grounds. Margot, an avid birder and animal lover (she is a licensed wildlife rehabilitator), can help identify unfamiliar species for guests. Tom restores stringed instruments and is happy to give tours of his workshop.

Villa Cardinale Bed & Breakfast Inn

1315 Oracle Ranch Road
P.O. Box 649
Oracle, AZ 85623
602-896-2516
Fax: 602-896-2516

> *This B&B is ideal for birders*

Owners: Donna and Glenn Velardi. **Accommodations:** 4 rooms. **Rates:** $55–$65. **Included:** Breakfast and tax. **Payment:** Major credit cards. **Children:** Welcome with prior approval; $10 additional per child per night. **Pets:** By prior arrangement. **Smoking:** Outside only. **Open:** Year-round.

Just off Highway 77 in Oracle, Villa Cardinale is far enough from Tucson to have a country feel, yet close enough to make the city and its sights easily accessible. The house was built in 1987, and opened as a bed-and-breakfast in 1988.

> **The area is known for excellent birding, and the rooms are named for birds.**

The rooms surround an outdoor courtyard highlighted by a central copper fountain. The Hummingbird room has two twin half-canopy beds from the '20s; the Cactus Wren has a double bed and antique dresser. The Quail room features antique peacock chairs, lace curtains, Wedgwood plates, and a queen-size bed. Roadrunner, the only room for smokers, has pigskin tables and chairs, a queen bed, and an antique oak dresser. All rooms have little Mexican fireplaces, tile floors, and private baths. Some have TVs, others have stereos. Since business travelers are regular guests, there are telephone outlets and a fax machine available.

Breakfast, which changes daily, is served in the dining room in the main house. A typical meal might include apricot frittata, fresh fruit, bran muffins, and kielbasa.

PATAGONIA

Circle Z Ranch

P.O. Box 194-BP
Patagonia, AZ 85624
602-287-2091

> *Arizona's oldest guest ranch*

Owner: Lucia Nash. **Accommodations:** 24 rooms; maximum 45 guests. **Rates:** $725–$900 single or double; cabin $3,000–$3,900 per week for 4; special rates for long weekends in November, December, and January. **Included:** Horseback riding, all meals. **Minimum Stay:** 3 nights. **Added:** 5.5% tax, 15% gratuity recommended. **Payment:** Personal checks; no credit cards. **Children:** $525–$675 per week for children aged 5–13. **Pets:** Not permitted. **Smoking:** Limited. **Open:** November 1 through May 15.

Forget what you've heard about guest ranches looking rugged and dusty; these adjectives simply don't apply to the Circle Z. There's a sense of gentility about the place that one does not normally associate with a ranch.

But a guest ranch the Circle Z certainly is, and, established in 1925, it's the oldest continuously operating one in Arizona. With 70 horses for a maximum of 45 guests, there are plenty to go around, and riding on more than 6,000 acres is what most people come here for. Instruction is available for beginners, and each is given plenty of attention, thanks to the limited number of guests. Trail rides go out twice daily for about two hours, and there are picnic rides on Saturdays and day-long rides once a week.

After a day on the trail, guests unwind in the cantina with hors d'oeuvres and BYOB cocktails and then sit down to a hearty meal of mesquite-cooked steak, lasagna, or barbecue. All breads and desserts are homemade. The pleasant dining room, with hand-painted chairs and wooden tables, has a nice view and is perfect for birding.

> **Children eat a half hour earlier than adults in a separate dining room. They also have their own cantina, complete with juke box and pool table.**

Lodgings are in small adobe casitas that surround the central lawn. Simply furnished, the casitas have cheerful hand-painted furniture, ceramic Mexican plates, and tile baths. There are no phones or televisions in the rooms; guests are encouraged to socialize in the main lodge's living room, where one can play cards or sink into a comfortable sofa and enjoy a fire on chilly evenings. The ranch is at an elevation of 4,000 feet, and it gets much colder at night here than in other parts of southern Arizona.

Riding is the only planned activity, but the ranch does have a pool and tennis court. Nogales, Mexico, is not far away, and makes for a fun trip across the border.

PRICE CANYON

Price Canyon Ranch

P.O. Box 1065
Douglas, AZ 85608
602-558-2383

> *An authentic working ranch*

Owners: Scotty and Alice Anderson. **Accommodations:** 5 units. **Rates:** $100 single, $200 double. **Included:** All meals, riding, and tax. **Minimum Stay:** 2 nights. **Payment:** Personal checks. **Children:** 1–5 years, $10; 6–9, $25; 10–12, $35; 13–15, $45; 16 and older at adult rate. **Pets:** With some restrictions, permitted if well-behaved. **Smoking:** Permitted. **Open:** Year-round.

Price Canyon Ranch, between Douglas and Apache on the slopes of the Chiricahua Mountains (elevation 5,600 feet), feels like it's far from anywhere. The bumpy dirt road that leads to the ranch is long, but at the end the hospitable Andersons are ready to introduce you to their way of life. A working ranch — and working is the operative word — Price Canyon invites visitors to experience real ranch life by pitching in with the chores, from branding and rounding up cattle to repairing fences. And Scotty Anderson leads half-day, day-long, and overnight rides across the desert and up into the mountains. There are some 400 miles of trails to explore.

> **Groups can rent a spacious "people barn," with kitchen and bath facilities as well as living, sleeping, and recreation space. Ten camper and trailer sites are also on the premises.**

Although riding is the only scheduled activity, guests can also go hiking, birding, or cave exploring. For those interested in archaeological study, the ranch sits on a pre-Columbian Indian site. Hunters can arrange guided hunts for deer, bear, and javelina. Adventure seekers can arrange one- to 12-day guided pack trips (for 4 to 20 people). The ranch also has a youth riding program in the summer.

The ranch can house three or four families or 30 individuals. Accommodations are in the Andersons' 1870s ranch house, with loft rooms that are good for families; a nearby bunkhouse; and a modern apartment with its own full kitchen, living room, and large bedroom. All are pleasant and comfortable. Explain your needs to the Andersons and they'll match you with the best unit.

Home-cooked meals are served family-style. For breakfast you can expect bacon and eggs, pancakes, or waffles. At lunch there are cold cuts and salads. Dinners feature meals made with fresh vegetables, beef raised on the ranch, and hot apple pie.

You don't have to know how to ride to enjoy a stay at Price Canyon. Scotty has been in the ranching business for almost 30 years, and his hands are experienced riding instructors. And there are 400 miles of trail to practice on. There's also a small bass and catfish pond and a spring-fed swimming pool on the property.

SASABE

Rancho de la Osa

P.O. Box 1
Sasabe, AZ 85633
602-823-4257
Fax: 602-823-4238

*A family
guest ranch with
historic origins*

Hosts: The Davis family. **Accommodations:** 18 rooms. **Rates:** $95–$110 per person per night; nonriding packages available. **Included:** All meals and horseback riding. **Added:** 6.5% sales tax, 15% service charge. **Payment:** Major credit cards. **Children:** Newborn to 2 years, $10; 3–4, $30; 5–13, $75; 14 and older at adult rate. **Pets:** Not permitted. **Smoking:** Nonsmoking rooms available. **Open:** Year-round.

About 65 miles southwest of Tucson, near the Mexican border and far from the city resorts, there's a ranch that dates from the 1730s. Here you can retreat into an earlier time while enjoying riding, nature study (especially birds), and excursions to nearby sites in Arizona as well as Mexico.

Of special interest is the Buenos Aires National Wildlife Refuge, where birders can hope to see more than 200 species, just a few miles from the ranch. Other nearby attractions include Kitt Peak Observatory, Tubac, Tucson, and Nogales, Mexico.

The Davis family has been operating the ranch since 1982. Their program is flexible, and their facilities work well for groups. The adobe cantina was built as a mission in about 1737 by Franciscan monks. While it retains a historic feeling, it's quite modern inside, with pool tables, a big-screen TV with a VCR, and a bar.

The rambling adobe hacienda, or main house, was built in 1860. Today vacationers gather here for hearty ranch meals. The dining room is open to the public for lunch every day and for Sunday afternoon dinner. Special arrangements for groups include cookouts under the trees.

The guest rooms are in low adobe block buildings with walls up to three feet thick. Although far from plush, they have lots of southwestern character: hand-painted furniture, Mexican pigskin chairs, and Indian throw rugs. Every room has a fireplace, and fires are lit twice a day. There are electric blankets in the winter and ceiling fans overhead for the warmer months (no air conditioning). The bathrooms, remodeled in the mid-1980s, have showers and tubs.

Rides led by wranglers go out twice a day. The ranch raises its own quarter horses, and there are always plenty to go around. Rides are leisurely, with riders are grouped according to ability. The swimming pool and spa, shaded with palm trees, are good for relaxing.

TUBAC

Tubac Golf Resort

1 Otero Road
P.O. Box 1297
Tubac, AZ 85646
602-398-2211
800-848-7893
Fax: 602-398-9261

A small golf resort with splendid mountain views

Owner: Al Kaufman. **Accommodations:** 16 casitas and 16 posadas. **Rates:** $78–$110 for posada rooms, $98–$142 for casitas without kitchenettes, $111–$155 for casitas with kitchenettes; extended stay and golf packages available. **Added:** 6.05% tax. **Payment:** Major credit cards. **Children:** Over 12, $15 per day. **Pets:** Permitted. **Smoking:** Permitted. **Open:** Year-round.

Built on the 400-acre site of the Otero Ranch, established in 1789, the Tubac Golf Resort is about a mile outside of the artsy town of Tubac. While not as posh as some of Tucson's large resorts, the Tubac Golf Resort offers comfortable lodging and 18 holes of golf in a tranquil setting. People come here to relax, not to be seen.

Beautiful views of the Santa Rita Mountains enhance any round of golf at the resort, and the course, dotted with cottonwoods and mesquites, is well maintained. There's a convenient pro shop, and after a day on the greens, the lobby lounge overlooking the course is a genial spot for drinks and complimentary chips and salsa. Montura's restaurant, in a building next door that was once the ranch's stables, serves three meals a day. Dark wooden booths, stone floors, copper light fixtures, Indian rugs, and a stone fireplace add atmosphere. Steak, seafood, and Mexican dinner entrées range from $9.50 to $18.

> Tubac Presidio State Historic Park and Tumacacori National Monument are nearby, and Nogales is about a half hour's drive from the resort.

Lodging is in red tile–roofed buildings sprinkled around lawns and a central swimming pool. Casitas are the largest units, with a separate living room and bedroom, a fireplace (firewood is supplied), and a kitchenette; one unit has a full kitchen. The posadas are smaller and have more traditional hotel room configurations. Decor in both is Mexican and southwestern, and all rooms have Mexican tile baths with separate vanities.

In addition to golf and swimming, there is a tennis court on the resort, as well as facilities for volleyball and horseshoes. Tubac has many shops and galleries worth investigating, and arts and crafts festivals are held in town on a regular basis.

TUCSON

Arizona Inn

2200 East Elm Street
Tucson, AZ 85719
602-325-1541
800-933-1093
Fax: 602-881-5830

> *This beautiful inn is a classic*

General Manager: Patty Doar. **Accommodations:** 80 rooms. **Rates:** $65–$162 single, $75–$172 double; suites start at $130. **Added:** 10% tax. **Payment:** Major credit cards. **Children:** Ad-

ditional $10 for children over 10; $15 charge for rollaways.
Pets: Not permitted. **Smoking:** Permitted. **Open:** Year-round.

A mourning dove watches as two tennis players approach the court along a walk lined with hedges. Near a fountain surrounded by flowers, a young couple sips coffee. Palms and oleander, cypress and citrus trees grace the grounds of this estate. The Arizona Inn acted as grand hostess of the Southwest for six decades. It is now on the National Register of Historic Places. Many of the staff are students from the nearby University of Arizona, and their youth and enthusiasm add spirit to the inn.

> **Guests often become attached to particular rooms. It is said that one guest was so disappointed when his "regular room" was already booked that he asked that all its furniture be moved to the room he was staying in.**

From the beginning, the Arizona Inn was designed to have a residential feeling and a sense of privacy. It opened in 1930 as the creation of Isabella Greenway, a sophisticated, dynamic community leader. She was Arizona's only congresswoman, serving from 1933 to 1936, and she established a furniture company to employ disabled World War I servicemen. One of the original purposes of the inn was to serve as a market for their furniture, and their craftsmanship can be seen throughout the inn today.

Mrs. Greenway had a hand in every aspect of the inn. During construction, to be sure that her guests would wake up to the sights of flowers, birds, and trees, she went around the site with a makeshift bed to check that each windowsill was at just the right height; if it wasn't, she'd have the workmen change it. The inn is still owned by the same family (Patty Doar is Mrs. Greenway's granddaughter), and Mrs. Greenway's commitment to quality and service remains at the heart of its operation.

The pink adobe inn is surrounded by vine-covered walls that screen it from the rest of the world. Inside, it is so peaceful that you forget you're just a hop, skip, and a jump from downtown Tucson. Low buildings sprawl over 14 acres of beautifully landscaped grounds connected by winding paths.

The public rooms are grand and gracious. The library, with a vaulted ceiling and polished wood floors, comfortable seating and shelves of books, feels like a lodge. It's the type of place where guests, many of whom return year after year, borrow a book and return it on their next visit. Notice the large photograph taken of the inn in 1935. You'll see how little it has changed — though the vegetation has gotten taller.

The Audubon Bar, with a white piano and a skylight encircled by a vine, is decorated with 19th-century Audubon prints. One of the dining rooms has hand-colored George Catlin lithographs from Mrs. Greenway's collection.

The guest rooms are charming; each is well-furnished, and has its own character, size, and configuration. The pieces were individually selected, and many were made by the servicemen. Window frames handpainted with delicate patterns, writing desks, overstuffed chairs, and sofas are just a few of the special touches. Some newly redecorated rooms have a classy English air with four-poster beds topped with cream-colored colonial spreads, tapestry print easy chairs, and botanical and bird prints on the walls.

The rooms are designated standard, mid-range, and deluxe. Some have fireplaces, many have private patios with comfortable patio furniture, and all have TVs, radios, and air conditioning. The closets are bigger than average; in the 1930s, guests often brought their trunks and settled in for a season.

The inn's swimming pool is a private world, adjoined by glassed-in gardens and a bar beneath vine-covered arbors. The porches alongside the pool can be heated on cool days; ceiling fans circulate the air in warmer weather. If you're enjoying a day in the sun, you needn't leave the pool area for lunch, as burgers, sandwiches, and salads are served here in good weather. The pool itself always seems to be just the right temperature, and the nearby Har-Tru clay tennis courts are also popular. Guests need only sign up on a chalkboard to reserve court time.

Dining at the inn is a pleasure, especially in the romantic courtyard. Entrées such as steamed fresh fish with ginger and leeks ($14), grilled vegetables with rice, legumes, pasta, and red chile pesto ($11.50), and linguini with sun-dried tomatoes, goat cheese, roasted pine nuts, black olives, and basil ($12.50) are delicious, healthful, and attractively presented.

Because of the inn's popularity, reservations should be made well in advance. On fall weekends, the inn fills up quickly for the University of Arizona's home football games.

Canyon Ranch Spa

8600 East Rockcliff
Tucson, AZ 85715
602-749-9000
800-742-9000
Fax: 602-749-7755

*A coed spa
run by professionals*

Owner: Mel Zuckerman. **Accommodations:** 153 rooms. **Rates:** From $1,660 single and $1,340 per person double for a 4-night, 5-day spa getaway; 7-night, 10-night, and other special packages also available. **Included:** Meals, airport transportation, medical screening, local calls, and spa programs. **Added:** 18% service; 6.5% tax. **Payment:** Major credit cards. **Children:** Over 14 welcome. **Pets:** Not permitted. **Smoking:** Nonsmoking rooms available. **Open:** Year-round.

Canyon Ranch is a place where people go not only to relax but to change their lives — for recreation in the literal meaning of the word. Geared to the health of the body and mind, it's a professionally run, coed fitness resort and spa with an amazing array of facilities, classes, and services. Since spa guests select the activities they want to participate in rather than the staff, the programs offer a higher degree of flexibility than can be found at some other spas. However, Canyon Ranch's highly trained staff does work closely with participants to insure that individuals are selecting the activities best suited to their ability level and goals. With over 700 employees, there is no shortage of help.

People go to Canyon Ranch with different goals: to lose weight, to reduce stress, to become more fit, or to stop smoking. Through a combined program of exercise and nutrition, many find what they want. Unlike some spas, this one attracts as many men as women, all seeking rejuvenation through a healthier lifestyle.

On 70 acres in the Sonoran Desert on the edge of Tucson, the spa offers exercise options that take advantage of the area's beauty, such as hikes to nearby waterfalls and bike rides through Sabino Canyon. The entire complex is webbed with paths flanked by desert landscaping.

The spa building itself pulsates with energy. The locker rooms overflow with amenities and are decorated in energizing yellow, red, and orange. More than 30 classes are taught here, from water aerobics to yoga. Personal services are all-encompassing, including massage, herbal wraps, life change counseling, nutrition counseling, astrology, and biofeedback. Facilities include a weight room, racquetball courts, and nine gymnasiums. Four swimming pools (three exercise pools and one quiet pool) and eight tennis courts, all lighted, are also on the grounds.

> **To help guests continue healthy eating habits when they leave, the spa has a demonstration kitchen to teach food preparation the Canyon Ranch way.**

At mealtime, guests dine in soothingly beautiful surroundings on such delicacies as grilled tenderloin, chicken teriyaki, sautéed shrimp in red chile sauce, pasta with spicy lobster sauce, and hearty vegetarian chile. Menus come with a calorie count, and guests choose what they eat. Whole grains, fresh fruits and vegetables, and the absence of refined flour and sugar, along with small portions, are at the heart of the cuisine. Meals are low in salt and have no additives or preservatives, and no caffeine or alcoholic beverages are served.

Accommodations are in small buildings scattered over the resort's 70 acres. The standard rooms are fairly small, while executive kings have a sitting area, and casitas have a living room and kitchen in addition to the bedroom. The furnishings are modern and plush.

In addition to traditional spa activities, Canyon Ranch can arrange horseback riding, golf, shopping trips to Nogales, Mexico, gallery tours of Tucson's arts district, and sightseeing trips to Biosphere II or the Arizona-Sonora Desert Museum. There are in-room movies, with a different feature each night, or guests can borrow a video from the spa's video library. Guests are also free to socialize in the clubhouse's living room, borrow books from the spa's library, or join in line dancing or bingo in the pavilion. Classes at Canyon Ranch's creative arts center range from pottery to watercolor.

Casa Alegre

316 E. Speedway
Tucson, AZ 85705
602-628-1800
Fax: 602-792-1880

> *A warm hostess
> presides over this
> downtown B&B*

Innkeeper: Phyllis Florek. **Accommodations:** 4 rooms. **Rates:** $70–$85 single, $75–$95 double. **Included:** Full breakfast and afternoon refreshments. **Added:** 9.5% tax and $1.00 per day. **Payment:** Major credit cards. **Children:** Over age 12 preferred. **Pets:** Not permitted. **Smoking:** Permitted only outside. **Open:** Year-round.

Casa Alegre means "happy house," a name well suited to this pleasant B&B. The white stucco exterior with bright blue trim is cheerful, and a Mexican fountain bubbles in the front yard. From the moment you are greeted by innkeeper Phyllis Florek, you feel right at home.

The Craftsman-style bungalow was built for a pharmacist in 1915 when Speedway was just a dirt road, not the main thoroughfare in the heart of Tucson it is today. The home was later owned by a doctor and his family for 50 years, and the doctor practiced here as well.

Casa Alegre's living room has a big front window, bringing lots of light into the house. A piano invites the musically inclined to sit down and

> **Full breakfasts are served each morning in the sun room, where colorful papier-mâché birds hang from the ceiling and pretty stained glass panels adorn the windows.**

play a tune, while sofas and a stone fireplace entice others to relax. The room is accented with mahogany trim and ivy stenciling. The adjoining dining room has a built-in mahogany cupboard and more stenciling. An unusual chandelier highlighted by porcelain insets is painted with old-fashioned romantic scenes.

Each of the four guest rooms has a theme reflecting a different aspect of Tucson's history. The Rose Quartz room is dedicated to mining: there's a small rock collection, and a miner's hard hat and lantern on the molding above the window. The morning glory wallpaper in the Amethyst Room is original, and the Victorian theme is complete with a four-poster bed, floral print pillows, a needlepoint footstool, mirrored vanity, potpourri, quilt stand, and a christening gown that belonged to the innkeeper's father. The bath next door has a claw-foot tub and lavender wallpaper reminiscent of a Monet painting.

The high-ceilinged Spanish Room, once the doctor's examining room, has a massive carved bed that was made in Mexico for a priest. The appliqued quilt is hand-painted and has matching pillows. Chairs are covered in bright Mexican weavings, and a 1920s armoire, hand-carved in Mexico, serves as a closet. On the wall, a tin mirror with a peacock motif is especially appealing, and is complemented nicely by the surrounding pheasant print wallpaper.

The Saguaro Room is furnished in southwestern pink, cream, and aqua. The decor includes willow and pigskin chairs, an armoire with saguaro rib doors, a queen-size bed topped with a cozy down comforter, a Mexican dresser, a stone slab table with a petroglyph, a working fireplace, and live cactus plants. The innkeeper has employed a few inventive touches of her own, using saguaro ribs for curtain rods and a small kiva ladder to hold towels and washcloths in the bath. All of the rooms have ceiling fans, private baths, and terrycloth robes.

In the back of the house is a sunny sitting room with a large dollhouse and a television and VCR. Guests may help themselves to cold sodas from a Coca-Cola cart that came from a movie set, lounge on the garden patio, soak in the outdoor Jacuzzi, or take a dip in the swimming pool — rare amenities for a downtown B&B. There's a carport for parking, and the University of Arizona and downtown Tucson are only minutes from the inn.

Casa Tierra

11155 West Calle Pima
Tucson, AZ 85743
602-578-3058

*The perfect B&B
for nature lovers*

Innkeepers: Karen and Lyle Hymer-Thompson. **Accommodations:** 3 rooms. **Rates:** $75–$85. **Included:** Full breakfast. **Added:** 6.5% tax. **Minimum Stay:** 2 nights on weekends. **Payment:** Cash or travelers checks. **Children:** Well-behaved children welcome. **Pets:** Not permitted. **Smoking:** On patios only. **Open:** September through May.

Nature is the operative word to use when describing Casa Tierra bed-and-breakfast. The solar home, built of adobe bricks made in Sasabe, Mexico, has an earthy feel and was designed and built in the late 1980s by the owners. Lyle builds solar adobes for a living. Off a dirt road on the northwestern outskirts of Tucson, miles from the city center, the inn is convenient to the Arizona-Sonora Desert Museum and only two miles from trailheads in Saguaro National Monument West.

> The view of majestic saguaros, desert birds, and distant powder blue mountains from the Casa Tierra's dining room picture window is exquisite. The saguaros almost seem to be in the same room with you.

In fact, the inn is an ideal base for those wishing to explore the desert terrain on foot. You won't feel uncomfortable lounging about in your hiking gear, for the mood here is casual and unpretentious. If you do return from the trail dusty and a little worse for wear, you can head straight for the shower, because each of the three guest rooms has a private entrance. There's also an outdoor hot tub where you can soothe overworked muscles and watch the moon rise over the desert.

Guest rooms all have saguaro cactus rib cabinetry, adobe walls, latilla ceilings, microwaves, refrigerators, wet bars, photographs taken by Karen (she's a photographer by trade), watercolors painted by Lyle in Mexico, and private patios. There's talavera tiling in each of the baths, and in keeping with the innkeepers' commitment to the environment, they are stocked with natural products in refillable containers rather than individually packaged toiletries.

Rooms open onto a central, open-air courtyard. Alive with colorful bougainvillea and grapefruit and mesquite trees, it is a pleasant gathering spot where guests can help themselves to coffee, curl up with a book on one of the Mexican sofas, or share their desert experiences with other guests, one of the two resident cats, or Emiliano Zapata (E.Z. for short), a desert tortoise, adopted from the Arizona-Sonora Desert Museum on Cinco De Mayo, who makes his home in the courtyard.

Breakfast is served in your room, in the courtyard, or, in cooler weather, in the dining room of the Hymer-Thompsons' own residence. The morning meal always includes fresh fruit, fresh baked goods such as banana buckwheat walnut cake, baked apple calzone, or blue corn pancakes, and a hot entrée such as broccoli and mushroom quiche, Mexican green chile and cheese egg bake, or a low-cholesterol spinach and rice torte with chile con queso. There is ample nourishment to get any hiker or sightseer off to a good start.

El Presidio Bed & Breakfast Inn

297 North Main Avenue
Tucson, AZ 85701
602-623-6151

Lush gardens and tasteful Victorian furnishings

Innkeepers: Patti and Jerry Toci. **Accommodations:** 3 suites. **Rates:** $70–$90 single, $85–$110 double. **Included:** Full breakfast. **Added:** 9.5% tax and $1 per day. **Payment:** Major credit cards. **Children:** Over 13 preferred. **Pets:** Not permitted. **Smoking:** Permitted only outside. **Open:** Year-round.

El Presidio is a charming Victorian adobe with wraparound porches and gingerbread trim in Tucson's historic district. Built in 1886, it is listed on the National Register of Historic Places. The owners, Patti and Jerry Toci, have won awards for their beautiful restoration work. But as lovely as the house is, it's the gardens one notices first. Pink oleanders and orange nasturtium spill onto the front sidewalk. The fountain courtyard in the back is ablaze with color, and there's always something blooming: yellow cat's claw, bright red bottlebrush, roses from the Victorian garden, blossoms on the citrus trees. The air is perfumed by the fragrant blooms.

The guest rooms are equally enjoyable. The Victorian Suite in the main house is like an indoor garden, with white wicker furniture, floral cushions, plants in the fireplace, and a sideboard painted with flowers in the living room. The bedroom is decorated in pink and light green, with country quilts and botanical prints. Glass doors lead from the living room out to the front porch overlooking the South and Victorian gardens.

The Gate House Suite has its own entrance, tan wicker furniture, French country fabrics, shuttered windows, a hand-painted blanket chest, and a small galley kitchen.

The Carriage House Suite is in a separate building. The owners' love of gardens is clearly evident here: there's a floral screen in the living room, flower patterns on the china plates and the bedspread, and a dried flower wreath hanging on the wall above the bed. The suite has its own kitchen. All of the suites have

> **The highlights of Tucson's historic district are an easy walk from the inn.**

pleasant private baths and top-quality mattresses and linens. They have ample living space, but guests are also welcome to use the formal living room in the main house. This elegant room is appointed with antique furnishings including a grandfather clock, Oriental rug, a corner cupboard filled with flow blue china, another cabinet displaying Indian artifacts, and more plants and dried floral arrangements. The small sitting room next door has a television and VCR.

Patti caters luncheons for resort guests who come into town for historic tours, gives classes on the use of Victorian herbs, and is writing a cookbook. Her breakfasts, served in the Veranda Room overlooking the garden courtyard, are a treat. She describes her breakfasts as southwestern (as opposed to Mexican) using ingredients from her own gardens whenever possible. You may sit down to eggs Benedict southwestern style, chile rellenos, vegetable frittatas, or stuffed French toast. Her specialty is muffins, such as strudel-topped lemon-pecan with lemons from her own trees, spiced orange-pineapple bran, and corn topped with homemade marmalade.

For guests on business, El Presidio has a fax machine and can provide other business services when needed. Guests may use the facilities at a nearby YMCA free of charge.

La Posada del Valle

1640 North Campbell Avenue
Tucson, AZ 85719
602-795-3840

> *Southwestern
> and art deco style
> from the 1920s*

Innkeepers: Tom and Karin Dennen. **Accommodations:** 5 rooms.
Rates: $90–$115. **Included:** Full
breakfast on weekends, Continental on weekdays. **Added:**
9.5% tax plus $1.00 city room tax. **Payment:** Major credit
cards. **Children:** Over age 12 preferred. **Pets:** Not permitted.
Smoking: Not permitted. **Open:** Year-round.

In a fine residential section of Tucson, behind a gray stucco
wall, stands this pristine gray adobe with a red tile roof. A
fountain adds grace to its courtyard, and orange trees, palms,
and colorful container plants are scattered about the mani-
cured grounds. Designed in 1929 by a renowned Tucson architect, Josias T. Joesler, the home exemplifies the early
Santa Fe style of architecture.

Inside, La Posada del Valle sparkles with art deco furnishings, and it's the extra touches that make it special, from
stained glass art to peach potpourris. The living room is large
and inviting, with a Japanese screen, satin couches, an old-
fashioned radio, and a good selection of books and magazines.

Each room honors an illustrious woman of the 1920s. Zelda's room is a tribute to Zelda Fitzgerald — her biography is
on the dresser, along with several of F. Scott Fitzgerald's
works, and a photo of husband and wife rests on the vanity.
The dresser, vanity, bed, and bedside table are a lovely matching inlaid set. If the literary surroundings spark a creative
urge, the armoire in the corner has a pullout writing desk, or
you can step out onto the adjoining patio and dream of a more
glamorous era.

Isadora's room is decorated in pale green with geometric
designs. Claudette's is mauve, featuring a maple king-size
bed. Sophie's room, done in peach, has a Victorian bedroom
set that once belonged to a fan dancer at the notorious Crystal
Palace in Tombstone, a fainting couch, and an 1818 king-size
bed. In keeping with the mood, a feather boa is draped over
the dresser mirror, and a fancy lace hat rests on the vanity.
Every room has a private bath and a private entrance. Zelda's
bath is especially attractive, with an embroidered shower cur-

tain and floral tiles. There are no TVs in the rooms, but they can be supplied upon advance request. Guests are welcome to use the set on the sun porch while lounging in cushioned wicker sofas and chairs.

Breakfast, served in the dining room or out on the patio, features fresh fruit, fresh bread, bagels, and cereals during the week. Weekends, guests feast on entrées such as vegetable

> **On the sunny porch, the Dennens sell baskets and other African artifacts from their native South Africa.**

strudel with Parmesan, gingerbread pancakes with lemon curd, or cream cheese blintzes topped with fresh raspberry sauce. In the afternoon, apricot and raspberry teas are served with homemade scones, shortbread, and cheesecakes. Turn-down service, complete with a mint on the pillow, is provided in the evening.

The University of Arizona and University Medical Center are an easy walk from La Posada.

Loews Ventana Canyon Resort

7000 North Resort Drive
Tucson, AZ 85715
602-299-2020
800-234-5117
Fax: 602-299-6832

> *A modern resort complements its natural setting*

Managing Director: Johnny So. **Accommodations:** 398 units. **Rates:** $95–$305 single, $105–$325 double; suites $135–$1,400; golf, tennis, spa, and holiday packages available. **Added:** 6.5% tax. **Payment:** Major credit cards. **Children:** Under 18 free in room with parents. **Pets:** Not permitted. **Smoking:** Nonsmoking floor available. **Open:** Year-round.

The setting of Loews Ventana Canyon Resort could hardly be more dramatic. Ventana Canyon, with an 80-foot waterfall in the center, is the tranquil backdrop for this new resort, made of deep taupe cement to blend with the mountains behind. The natural landscape has been kept very much intact.

Loews, with 94 acres of facilities, is part of a 1,000-plus-acre planned community. Guests have privileges at the Lakeside Spa and Tennis Club next to the hotel, which has ten championship tennis courts, a lap pool, fitness trail, exercise center, and a spa. Loews guests also have access to two 18-hole PGA golf courses.

> A path leads to a waterfall — an invitation to explore the mystical desert landscape. Desert lizards scurry in front of you, stately saguaros dot the hillside above, and within minutes you've forgotten there's a world somewhere with traffic jams and deadlines.

Behind the hotel is a large, pretty pool where lunch buffets are served, a croquet lawn, and a shallow lake at the base of the mountain.

Art is integral to the hotel's decor, from the Arizona landscapes in the foyer to the lithographs in the guest rooms. The rooms, with views of either the mountains or the city, have private balconies or terraces, mini-bars, and armoires with concealed TVs. The bathrooms, accented in marble, feature double whirlpool tubs.

The Ventana restaurant, serving dinner only, specializes in new American cuisine. Entrées such as range-fed hen with a pecan crust in a honey-mustard sauce and grilled quail with roasted garlic sauce and foie gras range from $17 to $26. Canyon Café serves all day. The Flying V Bar and Grill serves lunch and dinner overlooking the golf course. After 9:00 P.M. it's transformed into a video disco.

The Peppertrees

724 East University
Tucson, AZ 85719
602-622-7167

> *English hospitality at a downtown inn*

Innkeeper: Marjorie Martin. **Accommodations:** 3 rooms, 2 2-bedroom guesthouses. **Rates:** $50–$80 single, $60–$90 double; guesthouse $140–$160. **Included:** Breakfast and afternoon tea. **Minimum Stay:** 2 nights. **Added:** 9.5% tax and $1 per day. **Payment:** Major credit cards. **Children:** Permitted in guest houses only. **Pets:** Not permitted. **Smoking:** Permitted outside only. **Open:** Year-round.

This pleasant brick territorial house, built in 1905, is named for the two large California peppertrees that dominate the front yard. Innkeeper Marjorie Martin can show you an old photograph of the house taken when it looked like a lone homestead in the desert; today it is just a couple of blocks from the University of Arizona and convenient to the downtown sights.

> **Because both of the guesthouses and the Annex have kitchens, the Peppertrees is becoming increasingly popular with long-term visitors to Tucson.**

Inside, guests are welcomed by refreshments, sunny rooms, Oriental rugs on hardwood floors, lace curtains, and Victorian family furnishings from Marjorie's native England. The guest room in the main house is romantic, with lots of windows, French doors that open to the outside, and an inviting white wrought-iron bed covered by a flowered spread and extra pillows. Across the hall, its bathroom is finished in green Italian marble, brass fixtures, and wooden cupboards.

Behind the main house, there's a plant-filled courtyard with a central fountain, and two guesthouses. Each house has two bedrooms, a living room, a full kitchen with washer and dryer, a bathroom, and a private patio. The Annex, next door to the main house, has two bedrooms, one with a queen bed, the other with two twins that can be made up as a king, a large living room with a television, and a full kitchen.

Marjorie is an excellent cook whose recipes have appeared in a number of cookbooks, including the inn's own. Her breakfasts, often served on the porch near the fountain in nice weather, are memorable. Her shortbread, served at afternoon tea, is the house specialty.

Marjorie once owned a travel agency, and she is more than happy to give you sightseeing tips. The Peppertrees is right on the main trolley route, which travels to such places as the Arizona State Museum, Flandrau Planetarium, and the Children's Museum.

Sheraton Tucson El Conquistador Golf and Tennis Resort

10000 North Oracle Road
Tucson, AZ 85737
602-544-5000
800-325-7832
Fax: 602-544-1222

> *Recreational opportunities abound*

Hotel Manager: Tom Kreitler. **Accommodations:** 432 rooms. **Rates:** single or double, $260; suites $300; $15 each extra person; tennis and golf packages are also available. **Added:** 8.5% tax. **Payment:** Major credit cards. **Children:** Under 17 free in room with parents. **Pets:** Permitted. **Smoking:** Nonsmoking rooms available. **Open:** Year-round.

Spread over 150 acres of high rolling desert about ten miles north of Tucson, the Sheraton El Conquistador looks up at the 2,000-foot Pusch Ridge cliffs directly beyond. A resort with a colonial Mexican theme, it's a composite of one- to three-story buildings. The lobby itself is expansive, with many sitting areas and a desert scene above the front desk that is said to be the largest copper mural in the country.

The guest rooms have traditional furniture and southwestern decor in attractive cool colors. All the rooms have irons and ironing boards, hair dryers, and private patios or balconies. Junior suites are spacious, with writing desks, cushioned bancos and sofas for extra seating, tie racks and wooden valets in the closet, makeup mirrors, coffeemakers, and telephones in the bath. The most luxurious accommodations are the Casita suites, with their own fireplaces.

A variety of recreational facilities are available, highlighted by El Conquistador's 45 holes of championship golf. Its 31 lighted tennis courts are excellent. There's a stadium court, two pro shops, and ten tennis instructors. About 40 horses are stabled on the grounds for trail rides into Coronado National Forest. Cookout and sunset champagne rides can be scheduled upon request. For groups, hayrides, barbecues, and square dances can also be arranged. Of course, there's a large central swimming pool and a smaller one in the midst of the casitas, along with such extras as seven indoor racquetball courts, jogging paths, and fitness centers.

Summer is an excellent time to get top value, with the lowest prices for both rooms and recreation. There is Camp Conquistador for kids during the summer, with supervised activities such as tennis, arts and crafts, swimming, and movies.

El Conquistador's five restaurants and the poolside snack bar, the Desert Spring, give both dimension and variety to the resort's dining choices. The Sundance Café serves casual breakfast and lunch; it has a children's menu, and kids under six eat free. The Last Territory is a rustic steakhouse with entertainment and dancing. Dos Locos, fashioned after a Baja beachside cantina, serves Mexican food to the music of live mariachis, and turns into a lively disco after 9:00 P.M.

> **Resort services such as a concierge, 24-hour room service, a morning newspaper at your door, free self-parking, a daily activities program featuring sunrise and sunset nature walks, a weekly newsletter of events at the resort and in Tucson, and a friendly staff contribute to El Conquistador's appeal.**

The White Dove is El Conquistador's newest restaurant. Gourmet pizzas, grilled meats, and seafood are prepared with southwestern flair and spice. La Vista, atop the clubhouse at El Conquistador's country club, offers panoramic views.

The SunCatcher

105 North Avenida Javalina
Tucson, AZ 85748
602-885-0883
800-835-8012
Fax: 602-885-0883

> *A sophisticated B&B in glorious desert terrain*

Innkeeper: Dave Williams. **Accommodations:** 4 rooms. **Rates:** $160–$190 single or double; each additional person $25. **Included:** Full breakfast and afternoon hors d'oeuvres. **Added:** 6.5% tax. **Payment:** Major credit cards. **Children:** Welcome; additional $25 per day. **Pets:** Not permitted. **Smoking:** Permitted outside only. **Open:** Year-round.

When you pull into the driveway at the SunCatcher, on the outskirts of Tucson, you will instantly understand why innkeeper Dave Williams, a veteran world traveler, chose to settle in this spot. Magnificent mountains and desert flora surround you. You half expect a lizard or coyote to run across your path at any moment, and you can hear the call of coyotes in the distance when darkness falls.

Active guests will enjoy the heated swimming pool, hot tub, and tennis court. The trailhead at Saguaro National Monument is only a quarter mile from the inn. For some, lounging by the pool and soaking up the sun and relaxed ambience are vacation enough.

The rather modest exterior of the 1960s house does not prepare you for the beauty and elegance inside. Clerestory windows shed lots of light on a large living room, dining room, kitchen, and bar area. Exquisite Oriental rugs, bought on an excursion to the Far East, adorn the floor. At one end of the room is a sunken sitting area encircling a fireplace; nearby is a mesquite bar. Large picture windows frame the majestic mountains and desert landscape, and the best spot to enjoy the view is the graceful dining table that extends the length of one wall.

With the exception of the Oriental room, the guest rooms lack such extraordnary views, but in these impeccable rooms, the view is within their own four walls. Each is modeled after a world-class hotel: the Oriental after the Oriental in Bangkok, the Four Seasons after the Four Seasons Hotel in Chicago, the Connaught after the Connaught Hotel in London, and the Regent after the Regent Hotel in Hong Kong. Dave has visited these hotels in his travels, and all are known for their style and service. The Connaught room is decidedly British in tone, with classic mahogany and Chippendale-style pieces. The Four Seasons, decorated in green and beige, has a canopy bed, a mahogany drop-lid writing desk, and a stained glass window in the bath.

The Regent's decor blends the best of modern and Asian styles for a sophisticated look. A stunning hand-painted fan from China is on display, as is a Tibetan prayer rug; and a cloisonné plate rests on a desk with an inlaid leather top, accompanied by a yew-backed writing chair. The Oriental-looking television table was actually purchased by the owner in Nogales, Mexico. The bath has a large sit-in shower, and the room itself opens onto the swimming pool and patio.

The Oriental is the most luxurious guest room, with matching inlaid Oriental furnishings including a graceful writing desk. Most sumptuous of all is the Oriental's bath. With marble floors, brass fixtures, a bidet, a large oval Jacuzzi, and a separate shower, you could spend hours pampering yourself here. Amenities such as a hair dryer, makeup mirror, scales, extra towels, and large bath sheets for the pool are standard in all of the rooms. Also standard are a TV, VCR (there's a video library for guests to borrow from), telephone, extra pillows and blankets, reading chairs, and nightly turndown complete with a chilled bottle of mineral water. As further evidence of the care taken with each room, wastebaskets are lined with rice paper and sprinkled with potpourri made from the SunCatcher's own rose garden. Fresh flowers from the garden along with a welcoming note from the inn's gracious host await each guest in their room upon check-in. This is an inn where comfort and service are truly first rate.

Breakfasts, which alternate between sweet and savory, are served in the dining room. Perhaps it's an egg strata one day, stuffed French toast the next, and southwestern eggs the following day. Dave always tries to prepare meals according to his guests' tastes; if you prefer a cold breakfast, there will be bagels, muffins, cereal, and fruit. In any case, you won't go away hungry. There is a different flavor of coffee each morning, and in the afternoon, hors d'oeuvres are served on the bar or by the pool.

Tucson National Golf and Conference Resort

2727 West Club Drive
Tucson, AZ 85741
602-297-2271
800-528-4856
Fax: 602-297-7544

> *Golf gets top billing at this resort*

General Manager: Brian Rickert. **Accommodations:** 167 units.
Rates: $85–$350; spa and golf packages available. **Added:**
6.5% tax. **Payment:** Major credit cards. **Children:** Under 18
free in room with parents. **Pets:** Not permitted. **Smoking:**
Nonsmoking rooms available. **Open:** Year-round.

About 15 miles north of downtown Tucson, the Tucson National resort is surrounded by 650 acres of saguaro-studded
desert. It is a resort that wears many faces. Designed as a private golf club, its 27-hole USGA championship golf course
has hosted such tournaments as the Tucson and Northern
Telecom opens. The 18th hole is known for being one of the
most challenging finishing holes on the PGA tour. As a family resort, it has a large attractive pool, tennis courts, two
restaurants, several lounges, and beautifully designed rooms
and suites. As a spa, it has few equals, offering a variety of services, professional attention, and flexibility in its programs.

The club opened to the public in 1986. The spa, downstairs
in the main building, is one of the highlights of the resort.
It offers herbal wraps and massages, loofah rubs and body
facials, hydrotherapy pools and tanning beds. Special services on the women's side include Swiss showers (water ranging in temperature from 60 to 105 degrees comes from 14
shower heads and sprays from all directions) and steam cabi-

nets. There's also a panthermal, said to break down cellulite, along with a Finnish sauna. The locker room is equipped with robes, spa shoes, high-quality toiletries, and hair dryers; and there's a full-service beauty salon.

The men's spa features a Scottish water massage (16 needle-spray shower heads and two high-pressure hoses controlled by an attendant, with varying pressure and temperature) and a Russian bath, a kind of steam room.

Both men and women have inhalation rooms, where aromatic eucalyptus and other herbs help open sinuses. Lounges are plush, quiet, and relaxing. Exercise classes include aerobics, water exercise, stress management, and creative movement. The exercise machines are designed primarily for lower body workouts. Spa programs are extremely flexible: you can enjoy just one of its services or buy a two- to seven-day package that includes room, meals, and an abundance of spa services.

> **The Fiesta Room, the resort's main restaurant, serves all three meals. Dinners include steak and seafood choices, and those with smaller appetites will find a number of light entrées and sandwiches on the menu as well. In pleasant weather there is outdoor dining, and Sunday brunch is always a popular event.**

The rooms are designated as villas (hotel size), poolside, casitas (ranging from hotel size to near-suites), and executive suites. All have a patio or balcony with views of the golf course, swimming pool, or the Catalina mountains. Some have fireplaces. The rooms are spacious, with sitting areas, refrigerators, and a separate tub and shower in the bath. While the rooms differ in decor, each has special touches such as beamed ceilings, copper light fixtures, and southwestern fabrics.

Westin La Paloma

3800 East Sunrise Drive
Tucson, AZ 85718
602-742-6000
800-876-DOVE
Fax: 602-577-5878

*A pink palace
in the desert*

General Manager: Tom Cortabitarte. **Accommodations:** 487
rooms. **Rates:** $95–$335; suites from $200. **Added:** 6.5% tax.
Payment: Major credit cards. **Children:** Under 18 free in room
with parents. **Pets:** Not permitted. **Smoking:** Nonsmoking
rooms available. **Open:** Year-round.

The Westin La Paloma is a grand new resort with first-class
facilities, among the best in the Southwest. The arched entry-
way is dramatic, as are the massive arched windows in the
lobby that frame the dis-
tant mountain view. Just
beyond the lobby, a small
waterfall cascades over
rocks into a lily pond.

> **La Paloma's developers
> were sensitive to the desert
> landscape. With careful
> planning, they were able
> to save more than 7,000
> of the 8,000 saguaro cacti
> on the site of the resort.**

The resort's 27-hole
championship Jack Nick-
laus golf course is chal-
lenging; its unusual lay-
out takes advantage of its
Sonoran Desert setting
while making a minimal
impact on it. The tennis courts (eight hard surface courts and
four clay) are top quality, in a scenic setting, and next to a
good pro shop. La Paloma's free-form pool has bridges, adjacent waterfalls, and lagoons, like pools at Caribbean resorts.
Hot tubs are tucked away invitingly among the shrubs.
There's also a health club with racquetball, Nautilus equipment, and aerobics, a spa with massage, facials, waxing, and
body wraps, and a game area with croquet, volleyball, and
bike rentals.

At mealtime, choose from the gracious and elegant La
Paloma Dining Room, part of the private La Paloma Country
Club; La Villa, in a charming hacienda; and Desert Garden, in
the main building. The menu changes regularly at La Paloma,
but you can expect imaginative presentations of fine popular
dishes.

Throughout the resort, the look is refined Southwest with a modern flair. Accommodations are in two- and three-story buildings arranged in a semicircle facing the mountains. All are painted La Paloma rose, a color that suggests the sunset. The interior colors reflect the desert: sage green, cobalt blue, mauve, and gray.

While the rooms tend to be small, they are cleverly decorated and arranged, with beds placed at angles and unusual layouts. Each has a patio or balcony, a refrigerator, and a remote TV in an armoire. The baths are also on the small side but have a separate tub and shower, phone, and robes.

Day care is available for children from 6 months to 12 years old.

Westward Look Resort

245 East Ina Road
Tucson, AZ 85704
602-297-1151
800-722-2500
Fax: 602-297-9023

A popular place where guests return year after year

General Manager: Jim McCullough. **Accommodations:** 244 rooms. **Rates:** $85–$140; suites $170–$280. **Added:** 6.5% tax. **Payment:** Major credit cards. **Children:** Welcome. **Pets:** Small ones permitted with a $50 deposit. **Smoking:** Nonsmoking rooms available. **Open:** Year-round.

Westward Look, about eight miles north of Tucson, glistens on the high desert landscape. It has a wide assortment of sports, a highly rated restaurant, and well-designed lodging, plus a friendly atmosphere conducive to family vacations.

Spread over 84 acres, the resort has three swimming pools and hot tubs, eight Laykold tennis courts, basketball and volleyball courts, a fitness center, and a fitness trail with desert plants identified, plus such extras as horseshoes and shuffleboard. Tennis gets lots of attention at Westward Look. There's a pro shop, a clubhouse, and a viewing deck. An hourly fee is charged for court time, but tennis packages are offered. The resort has no golf course, but the staff can arrange for you to play at one of seven courses in the area.

The Gold Room restaurant has an inventive and inviting

menu, plus beautiful views of Tucson and the mountains to the west — hence the resort's name. Loin of lamb served with spinach and chicken mousse and rosemary Bordelaise, grilled tenderloin of pork with black figs and Bermuda onions, and sautéed shrimp topped with a julienne of celery and leek in a Chardonnay beurre blanc sauce are a few of the dinner entrées; papaya and prosciutto, and duck confit in wonton served over avocado beurre blanc are among the tempting appetizers. Entrées range between $5.25 and $9.50 for lunch, $16.50 and $22 for dinner. Sunday brunch is always popular.

> **For light meals, there's the Lookout Bar and Grille. The Lounge frequently has live entertainment, and guests can enjoy Sunday afternoon tea dances to the music of a swing band.**

The lodgings are sprinkled over the beautifully landscaped grounds, with nearby parking for each unit. Units themselves have different configurations, but all are comfortable and well designed for privacy. The decor is pure Southwest, with light wood furnishings, terra cotta lamps, beamed ceilings, and desert art. Each unit has a private balcony or patio, small refrigerator, stocked servi-bar, coffeemaker, cable TV, and a choice of one king or two double beds. The baths are large and accented with painted tiles. Extra towels, hair dryers, and night lights are thoughtful touches.

White Stallion Ranch

9251 West Twin Peaks Road
Tucson, AZ 85743
602-297-0252
800-782-5546
Fax: 602-744-2786

> *Down-home hospitality at a friendly ranch*

Owners: The True family. **Accommodations:** 29 rooms. **Rates:** $130–$145 single, $215–$260 double; suite $250–$315. **Included:** All meals and horseback riding. **Added:** 6.5% tax and 15% service charge. **Payment:** Personal checks; no credit cards. **Children:** Welcome. **Pets:** Not permitted. **Smoking:** Permitted. **Open:** October through April.

White Stallion Ranch spreads over 3,000 acres of beautiful desert and mountain terrain 17 miles northwest of Tucson. Both a working and a guest ranch, it's been owned and run by the True family since 1965. It's the nicest guest ranch in the Tucson area, everything you expect a ranch to be.

Year-round, the Trues raise Texas longhorn cattle, but in the winter season they go all out to show guests a slice of the West. Over the years, visitors have arrived from 50 or so countries (look for the collection of flags representing the guest list). Many return year after year for what White Stallion offers: four rides a day, informal rodeos, nature walks led weekly by a wildlife biologist, home cooking, and a warm family atmosphere.

> **The ranch's wildlife zoo has fallow deer, mouflon bighorn sheep, llamas, pygmy goats, miniature horses, and pheasants. The zoo attracts lots of attention from adults as well as children. A favorite is Dewey, the Vietnamese potbellied pig that answers to his name when you call him.**

The Trues own about 60 horses, and one of their specialties is matching riders with the right horses. Some rides are designed to be slow and scenic, others, fast and exhilarating. Trails lead from flat desert up into the mountains. Children 5 and older can ride on their own; younger children ride with their parents.

Some guests never ride, preferring to soak up the western atmosphere. There's a Saturday afternoon rodeo, which features roping, bulldogging, and barrel racing. Other favorite events include breakfast rides, hayrides, cookouts, and a weekly barbecue, with the whole meal — roast beef, carrots, onions, and potatoes — cooked in an outdoor Indian brick oven.

Areas for relaxing include the comfortable and spacious main lodge open around the clock, with a TV room, pool room, library, and self-serve bar, an outdoor pool surrounded by palms, and an enclosed redwood hot tub that's one of the most popular spots on the ranch. There is also tennis on two courts, horseshoes, volleyball, basketball, and shuffleboard; and sometimes guests form their own impromptu softball games. Kids have their own air-conditioned rec room with pool table, television, and piano.

Accommodations are comfortable and fairly simple. Three units are in the main lodge; the others are scattered over the grounds. Most have a double and a twin bed and can be rented either as a bedroom or suite. Baths are modern. The newest units, called deluxe suites, have fireplaces and whirlpool tubs. Several small units at a lower price have been designed for single people. All rooms are air-conditioned. There are no phones or TVs in the rooms, but for those who need to keep in touch with the outside world, there is a TV in the main lodge, a pay phone, and *USA Today* and the *Wall Street Journal.*

Meals, often buffet-style, are served in the main lodge. Chicken, pasta dishes, and quiches are alternated with traditional meat and potatoes to give guests a variety. White Stallion can arrange transportation to and from the airport.

New Mexico

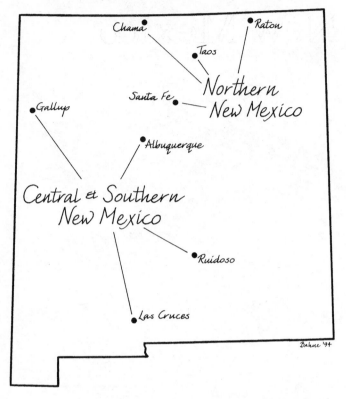

Chama •   • Raton

• Taos

Northern
New Mexico

Santa Fe •

• Gallup

• Albuquerque

Central & Southern
New Mexico

• Ruidoso

• Las Cruces

Bahne '94

New Mexico lives up to its "Land of Enchantment" sobriquet quite well, with expansive mesas, seemingly endless high desert plateaus, and dramatic mountain peaks, some of them soaring over 13,000 feet. Pueblo Indians, who have long considered the land sacred, have made their home in New Mexico for centuries. Spaniards such as Coronado explored the area as early as 1540, and today the rest of America seems to be discovering the magic of this beautiful state.

Perhaps nowhere else in the United States do Hispanic, Native American, and Anglo cultures mingle and intermesh as closely and as frequently as they do in New Mexico. Spanish is spoken as often as English, modern buildings incorporate Indian kiva fireplaces, grocery stores stock masa meal for making tamales alongside hot dogs, and events such as Santa Fe's annual Fiesta draw on traditions from all three cultures.

The fiesta starts off with mariachi music, then there's the pagan ritual of burning Zozobra (Old Man Gloom) and then it's on to the plaza for enchiladas, burritos, Navajo tacos, and Indian fry bread.

Tourist activities are equally diverse. In spring you can ski in the morning, play golf in the afternoon, and maybe take in a concert in the evening in places such as Albuquerque, Santa Fe, Ruidoso, and Angel Fire. Or maybe it's an art exhibit in the morning and horse-racing in the afternoon. With the exception of deep-sea fishing, whatever your passion, you're bound to be able to indulge it somewhere in New Mexico.

If your adventures take you out of doors, the weather is likely to comply. New Mexico is almost always blessed with clear, sunny skies and reasonable temperatures. In summer, brief late afternoon showers temper the heat of the day, making evenings refreshingly cool. Winter snow is common in northern New Mexico; it generally melts quickly at lower altitudes and sticks to the ski slopes at higher altitudes, which is as it should be.

Among the greatest joys of a visit to New Mexico is sampling its hearty and spicy cuisine. Much of it is made with green chile grown in the southern part of the state. Once you've tried a few dishes made with this tasty morsel, you may find yourself lugging tubs of the vitamin C–rich pepper home. It's a good idea to bring along extra baggage in any case because with all of the locally crafted art, pottery, and jewelry available, you're certain to return home with a lot more than you came with.

Central and Southern New Mexico

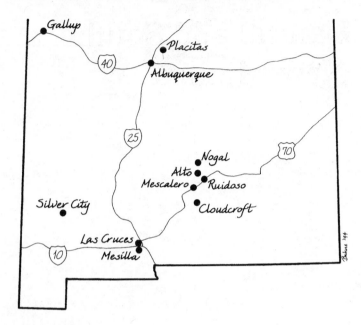

Best Bed-and-Breakfasts

Albuquerque
Adobe and Roses
Casas de Sueños
Casita Chamisa
Sarabande Bed and Breakfast
William E. Mauger Estate
Las Cruces
Lundeen's Inn of the Arts Bed and Breakfast
Mesilla
Meson de Mesilla
Nogal
Monjeau Shadows
Placitas
Hacienda de Placitas
Silver City
Bear Mountain Guest Ranch

Best City Stops

Albuquerque
Barcelona Court All Suite Hotel
Holiday Inn Pyramid
Hyatt Regency Albuquerque
La Posada de Albuquerque
Ramada Hotel Classic

Best Family Favorites

Ruidoso
Story Book Cabins

Best Guest Ranches

Alto
La Junta Guest Ranch

Best Historic Hostelries

Cloudcroft
The Lodge
Gallup
El Rancho Hotel

Best Resorts

Mescalero
Inn of the Mountain Gods

Best Ski Lodges

Ruidoso
Best Western Swiss Chalet

At the heart of central New Mexico is **Albuquerque,** New Mexico's largest city. Blessed with a fairly moderate climate and an expanding job market, Albuquerque is also one of the country's fastest growing metropolitan areas. Some of the same factors that contribute to the city's livability, such as climate and a healthy cultural scene, also add to its appeal for visitors.

Albuquerque's historic Old Town and plaza, with the many surrounding shops and galleries, is a good place to begin a visit to the city. Nearby is the Albuquerque Museum with changing exhibits, the fun and accessible Museum of Natural History, and the excellent Rio Grande Zoo. The University of New Mexico has several specialty museums including the Maxwell Museum of Anthropology, the Geology Museum, and the Meteorite Museum. The Indian Pueblo Cultural Center, representing the state's 19 Indian pueblos, offers a fine introduction to the Native American way of life. To get a scenic overview of the city, travel to the top of Sandia Peak via the world's longest tram.

For entertainment, a number of theaters throughout Albuquerque mount theatrical productions and concerts. Sports fans may be able to see a baseball player on his way up to the major league at an Albuquerque Dukes game, or a horse on its way to the Kentucky Derby at Albuquerque Downs. Each

September the New Mexico State Fair is held in Albuquerque, but it's the annual International Balloon Fiesta held every October that really draws the crowds. With more than 500 hot air balloons from all over the world, the fiesta is an exciting visual feast for the eyes.

About an hour west of Albuquerque is Acoma Pueblo, a striking community called "sky city" because it's built atop a mesa. Farther west, almost to the Arizona border, **Gallup** is heavily influenced by Native American culture as it lies between the Zuni and Navajo reservations.

In the southwestern part of the state, the mining town of **Silver City** sits on the edge of the Gila wilderness, and Deming holds the famous Deming Duck Race each year.

Las Cruces, close to both the Texas and Mexico borders, is New Mexico's third largest city. Home of New Mexico State University, many of the city's activities are centered around the school; but Las Cruces is also gaining stature as a comfortable retirement area. Nearby, the tiny town of **Mesilla** was once the largest and most important settlement in the region. For a time it was the Confederate capital of a huge territory, and the Gadsden Treaty was signed in the town's plaza.

The Capitan Mountains, and 12,003-foot Sierra Blanca peak on the Mescalero Apache Reservation in particular, offer some of the most dramatically beautiful scenery in the southern part of the state. For this reason, **Ruidoso** has become a year-round tourist destination. There's hiking in the fall, skiing in the winter and spring, and horse-racing at Ruidoso Downs in the summer. With skiing, the Sacramento Peak Observatory, and golf on one of the highest courses in the world, the mountain town of **Cloudcroft** on the southern side of the reservation is also a popular getaway. White Sands National Monument lies between Cloudcroft and Las Cruces.

The Carlsbad Caverns, perhaps better known than any other tourist destination in southern New Mexico, are miles from anything and aren't even visible above ground. The extensive network of caves, filled with an incredible array of stalactites, stalagmites, and other intriguing formations, fascinate young and old alike. A visit to the caverns is certainly worth a drive out of the way.

ALBUQUERQUE

Adobe and Roses

1011 Ortega NW
Albuquerque, NM 87114
505-898-0654

*A rural B&B
on the outskirts
of Albuquerque*

Innkeeper: Dorothy Morse. **Accommodations:** 3 rooms. **Rates:** $55 single, $65–$75 double, $115 for guesthouse up to 4; $10 surcharge for single night stays. **Included:** Full breakfast. **Added:** 5.5% tax. **Payment:** Personal checks; no credit cards. **Children:** $10 additional per day if more than two people in room. **Pets:** Allowed. **Smoking:** Permitted outside only. **Open:** Year-round.

Adobe and Roses is the type of bed-and-breakfast that lets you truly be yourself. There are no rigid check-in or breakfast hours here. If you want a full hot breakfast, one will be cooked for you. If you prefer a Continental breakfast, you will awake to fresh fruit and muffins instead. If you like privacy, you may come and go as you please, as each unit has its own entrance. If you enjoy socializing, innkeeper Dorothy Morse is an affable host, and it is easy to get lost in conversation with her. No matter what your taste, you're likely to feel right at home here.

Two of the rooms are in a new adobe guest house at the back of the property. The larger of the two accommodations has a kitchenette, separate living room and bedroom, skylights, a nice Mexican tile bath, and a TV, stereo system, and clock radio in the bedroom. The smaller unit includes a beautifully carved wooden bench in the shape of a swan and has a microwave and toaster oven rather than a kitchenette. The two rooms share a porch overlooking a lovely Japanese lily pond, and they may be rented as one unit.

The remaining suite is connected to the main house. With an entrance hallway, separate living room, large kitchenette, bedroom, and a spacious bath, the suite feels like a private home. Horses graze on the lawn just outside the living room's big windows, and musically inclined guests will enjoy the suite's piano. All the guest rooms have kiva fireplaces, Oriental rugs, brick floors, ceiling fans, plenty of books, and reading lamps above each bed. In appropriate seasons, vases of fresh flowers from Dorothy's handsome gardens are placed in the guest rooms.

> **About 20 minutes from downtown Albuquerque, Adobe and Roses feels secluded, yet with most of the area's attractions only a short drive away, the inn is conveniently located for sightseeing.**

Sometimes the Adobe and Roses sponsors musical evenings. Dorothy is associated with the local symphony and occasionally puts up visiting musicians. On such occasions, she puts together an impromptu evening of music, company, and food, and any guest staying at the inn is welcome to join in the festivities.

Barcelona Court All Suite Hotel

900 Louisiana Boulevard NE
Albuquerque, NM 87110
505-255-5566
800-222-1122
Fax: 505-255-5566, ext. 6116

> *A conveniently located all-suite hotel*

General Manager: Steve McKiernan. **Accommodations:** 164 suites. **Rates:** $125 single, $145 double. **Included:** Full breakfast, afternoon cocktails. **Added:** 10.813% tax. **Payment:** Major credit cards. **Children:** Additional $5 per day. **Pets:** Not permitted. **Smoking:** Nonsmoking rooms available. **Open:** Year-round.

This hotel is different in both layout and atmosphere from all the other all-suite hotels you've seen. From the outside, it's not particularly impressive, but the front doors open to a gracious lobby with Mexican tile floors, Oriental rugs, and curved staircases trimmed in wrought iron.

> **Because of their size, the suites at Barcelona Court are perfect for families. Couples will enjoy the "special occasion" suites with fireplaces and whirlpools.**

The hotel was once a cluster of apartments. In 1984, the open areas were enclosed and the complex converted into a hotel, hence its sprawling nature and unusual spaces. The suites, which are larger than those in most all-suite hotels, are on the first two floors. With a southwestern decor, they're inviting and comfortable. The living rooms have a sofa bed, an easy chair with an ottoman, and a game table. The bedrooms have two queen- or one king-size bed and a marble vanity alcove. The well-equipped kitchenette includes a microwave oven and is geared to light meals. Three telephones and two TVs add to the convenience.

At the center of activity is Fountain Court, a huge, enclosed atrium. A complimentary breakfast, cooked to order, is served here, as are the free afternoon cocktails; you may invite guests to join you, and no tipping is allowed. Although there is no restaurant on the premises, room service is offered through a nearby restaurant. There is also a supermarket across the street where you can shop for your own meals.

There's an indoor pool with a whirlpool and sauna, a small outdoor pool, and laundry facilities. Also available are free underground parking, free transportation to the airport and to malls and restaurants Monday through Thursday, and valet service.

On the edge of a residential area in uptown Albuquerque, the Barcelona Court is convenient to the Coronado and Winrock shopping malls and next to the New Mexico State Fairgrounds, which has thoroughbred racing from January through May, arts and crafts shows all year, and a state fair in September. The University of New Mexico is about ten minutes away.

Casas de Sueños

310 Rio Grande SW
Albuquerque, NM 87104
505-247-4560
800-CHAT W/US
Fax: 505-842-8493

> *Variety*
> *on the edge of*
> *Old Town*

Owner: Robert C. Hanna. **Accommodations:** 15 casitas. **Rates:** $85–$200. **Included:** Full breakfast and afternoon tea. **Added:** 10.8125% tax. **Payment:** Major credit cards. **Children:** Over 12 welcome; $15 additional. **Pets:** Not permitted. **Smoking:** Not permitted. **Open:** Year-round.

Casas de Sueños, which means "houses of dreams," is named for the various casitas that were built here as artists' residences and studios in the 1930s by J.R. Willis, an artist himself. Over the years, noted artists have lived and worked on the property. Robert Hanna has tried to retain the communal feel of the compound while affording guests plenty of privacy for relaxation and contemplation. The inn's staff goes out of its way to ensure every comfort is extended to guests.

The most obvious reminder of the inn's early roots as an artists' colony stands at the entrance: a unique, futuristic, cylindrical structure made from brick, glass, and wood. Created by architect Bart Prince, who designed the Los Angeles County Museum, the structure is functional as well as intriguing. Inside, lounges and terraces on several levels offer views of the mountains, city, and golf course; there are also comfortable spaces for relaxing, reading, socializing, or watching television (the televison set is hidden behind sliding wooden doors when not in use). Sofas are built into the semicircular walls, and the unusual mix of glass, brick, and carpeting gives the interior a distinctive Japanese, if thoroughly modern, look.

The dining room, where breakfast is served, was once a writer's and artist's studio. Vibrant stained glass now graces the sunny room, and changing exhibits from local artists adorn the walls. Breakfasts such as asparagus soufflé with green chiles served with English scones, homemade tomato jam, fresh pumpkin or sweet potato empañadas, bizcochos, coffee cakes, and granola are works of art in their own right. The inn has its own blend of coffee, and meals are served outside on the patio in the summer.

Rooms vary greatly in size and decor. Some are tucked away in quiet corners, others overlook courtyard gardens. The Taos and Zuni casitas are furnished with southwestern and Indian pieces, while the Rose room has a more romantic air. The Elliot Porter suite is a tribute to the famed photographer, and some of his fine pictures hang on the walls. La Miradora suite, meaning "the vision," is located in J.R. Willis's original residence and is the most elegant of the suites. A beautifully intricate Oriental table is the centerpiece of the large living room, and the two bedrooms, one with a four-poster pine bed, are both tastefully appointed.

> **Casas de Sueños is next to the Albuquerque Country Club Golf Course, which hosts an enchanting hot air balloon glow every Christmas Eve.**

The Albuquerque Museum, the New Mexico Museum of Natural History, and the historic Old Town with its many shops, restaurants, and galleries are all within walking distance of the inn. The Rio Grande Zoo is also nearby.

Casita Chamisa

850 Chamisal Road NW
Albuquerque, NM 87107
505-897-4644

> *A comfortable B&B on an archaeological site*

Owners/Hosts: Kit and Arnold Sargeant. **Accommodations:** 2 units. **Rates:** $70 single, $85 double; $10 each additional person. **Included:** Breakfast. **Payment:** Major credit cards. **Children:** Additional $10 per night. **Pets:** Permitted with prior approval. **Smoking:** Outside only. **Open:** Year-round.

Casita Chamisa made local headlines in the late 1980s when an archaeological excavation on the property uncovered some 150,000 pottery shards and 15,000 animal bones left by six different American Indian pueblos that occupied the site for 350 years, from around A.D. 1300. The Sargeants knew their house was on an archaeological site when they purchased it in the 1970s, but they had no idea what the excavation would yield when they decided to add a bedroom and a pool. Kit is an archaeologist, and he supervised much of the excavation; he is now working on a book about the project.

Although most of the excavated area has been covered for preservation purposes, a small exposed portion remains in the basement, and Kit will be happy to interpret the site for interested guests. It is just one aspect of this truly special B&B.

Casita Chamisa, with wide floorboards and low ceilings, has all the charm of an adobe farmhouse built in the 1850s. Deco-

> **Casita Chamisa, in one of the loveliest and lushest parts of Albuquerque, is a beautiful five-mile drive from historic Old Town. The Sargeants gladly provide guests with information on attractions in the area and can even arrange a massage for you at the end of a long day.**

rated with artifacts from the Sargeants' travels in Central and South America, the living and dining rooms are intriguing. In warmer months, breakfast is served in the adjoining sun room, whose skylight is shaded by an intricate network of bamboo branches, grown in the yard, that make unusual patterns on the adobe walls below.

Outside, horses neigh from their corral, roosters and chickens roam the property, as do several friendly dogs and cats, and honeybees buzz in their hives (at a safe distance from the house, of course). There are porch swings for lounging, two redwood decks for sunning, fragrant flower gardens, and a small orchard to enjoy. Casita Chamisa has a good-size heated indoor swimming pool with a diving board (a rare amenity for a B&B) and a hot tub. Another unusual treat: robes and sandals are provided.

The accommodations are designed for privacy. The large guest room attached to the main house, directly above the excavation, has its own entrance, patio, and bath. The hall that leads from the guest room to the swimming pool has a small sitting area under a mollusk shell–shaped bay window sculpted by Arnold. A separate guest house has a Mexican tile bath, a small kitchenette, a sitting room with a cute kiva fireplace, and two bedrooms, one with a queen-size bed, the other with two twins that can be made up to form a king.

There's a greenhouse off the back bedroom and a lively mural painted on one side of the cottage. Conveniences such as TVs, clock radios, and telephones have not been forgotten.

Even breakfast at Casita Chamisa has its own story. There is always homemade jam and either fresh or baked fruit from the orchard, honey from the bees, and fresh orange juice. But the real highlight is Arnold's sourdough: blueberry sourdough Belgian waffles, sourdough pancake roll-ups, and sourdough bread made with freshly ground wheat.

Arnold got the sourdough starter in Pocatello, Idaho, 20 years ago. At that time it was 90 years old, and its origins could be traced to a Basque sheepherder. When the Sargeants took it with them to Central America, they had to find an ice-house every two days in order to keep the dough alive in such a hot climate. Now Arnold celebrates the dough's birthday on July 1 with a traditional birthday cake and ceremony. Special guests are allowed to take a small portion of the sourdough with them, but they must promise to send a birthday card every July. This may seem like a lot of fuss over a sourdough, but when you taste its truly delicious products, you'll realize how extraordinary it is.

The Holiday Inn Pyramid

I-25 North at Paseo del Norte
5151 San Francisco Road NE
Albuquerque, NM 87109-4641
505-821-3333
800-461-4329
Fax: 505-828-0230

*A modern hotel
on the north side
of town*

General Manager: Mark Gundlach. **Accommodations:** 311 rooms. **Rates:** $100–$112 single, $110–$132 double; suites $125–$275. **Added:** 10.75% tax. **Payment:** Major credit cards. **Children:** Under 18 free in room with parents. **Pets:** Permitted. **Smoking:** Nonsmoking floors available. **Open:** Year-round.

Opened in 1987, the Pyramid is in the Journal Center business complex, about seven miles north of downtown. True to its name, it is a modern version of Mexico's pyramids, reflecting Albuquerque's heritage. Inside, the hotel is built around a ten-story atrium and a tiered 50-foot waterfall. The lobby is decorated with plenty of plants (not live ones, unfortunately) and in green and rose colors, creating an outdoor feeling.

> **The Pyramid is one of the closest hotels to the spectacular Albuquerque International Balloon Fiesta, which takes place every October. It is also a good jumping-off point for Santa Fe and points north.**

Glass elevators lead to rooms traditionally furnished in upbeat tones such as peach and blue. The rooms range from standard to queen suites. King rooms have a king-size bed, living area, and desk; king executive rooms have larger living areas than kings; king suites have a large living–dining room, wet bar, and separate bedroom. Deluxe suites are upgraded kings. The Presidential Suite has a large living room, a dining room, and a whirlpool. One floor has been designated as a concierge floor.

The Gallery serves American and regional cuisine ($11–$16), while the Terrace Café in the atrium offers casual dining, with sandwiches and southwestern fare for $4.75–$7.50. The Pyramid Club is a contemporary dance lounge.

In addition to the small indoor-outdoor pool, there are two indoor hot tubs, a sauna, and an exercise room. Jogging trails wind through the 313-acre Journal Center. Attractive shops are off the lobby, a concierge is on duty, and parking is free. Best of all, the staff is cordial and eager to please. The hotel is owned and operated by the local John Q. Hammons Hotels.

Hyatt Regency Albuquerque

330 Tijeras NW
Albuquerque, NM 87102
505-842-1234
800-233-1234
Fax: 505-766-6710

*Albuquerque's
downtown
luxury hotel*

General Manager: Dave Phillips.
Accommodations: 395 rooms. **Rates:** $110–$140 single, $130–$160 double; suites $325–$725. **Added:** 10.8125% tax. **Payment:** Major credit cards. **Children:** Under 18 free in room with parents. **Pets:** Not permitted. **Smoking:** Nonsmoking rooms available. **Open:** Year-round.

The 20-story Hyatt Regency opened in 1990 in conjunction with the expansion of the Albuquerque Convention Center. This modern high rise was designed as the premier luxury hotel in the downtown area. The exterior is Texas red granite, while the interior has a neoclassical flavor with geometric stained glass decorations, black Andes marble, and fanciful light fixtures. Close to half a million dollars' worth of contemporary art is displayed throughout the hotel.

The guest rooms are plush. Modern dark wood furniture and marble-topped tables make an appealing contrast to the overall lavender and silver color scheme. Clock radios, full-length mirrors, video check-out, irons and ironing boards are standard features.

There are two bars in the lobby, but McGrath's is the hotel's only restaurant. Although named for Lizzie McGrath, a well-known turn-of-the century madam whose "parlor house" stood nearby, Mc-Grath's is strictly above-board. The dinner menu is dominated by steak and seafood; prices range from $11 to $19. Breakfast and lunch dishes are up to $9.

> **The shops off the lobby include a Native American art gallery and a boutique dedicated to New Mexico's favorite food, the chile pepper.**

The Hyatt has more extensive exercise facilities than other hotels in the area; the large workout room has state-of-the-art equipment. The locker rooms have hair dryers and toiletries. There is a dry sauna, an outdoor heated pool, and massages are available for $40 to $53.

A concierge is on duty until 10:30 P.M., room service operates from 6 A.M. to midnight, and the airport shuttle is free.

La Posada de Albuquerque

125 Second Street NW at Copper
Albuquerque, NM 87102
505-242-9090
800-777-5732
Fax: 505-242-8664

> *A bit of the old
> Southwest
> in downtown
> Albuquerque*

General Manager: Tilden L. Drinkard. **Accommodations:** 114 rooms. **Rates:** Rooms $102 single, $112 double; suites $225. **Added:** 10.8125% tax. **Payment:** Major credit cards. **Children:** Under 19 free in room with parents. **Pets:** Not permitted. **Smoking:** Nonsmoking rooms available. **Open:** Year-round.

In 1939, Conrad Hilton built his first hotel in his native New Mexico. Now restored, renamed, and no longer a Hilton, La Posada de Albuquerque is the only downtown hotel that really captures the spirit of the old Southwest. It is listed on the National Register of Historic Places. The lobby recalls colonial Mexico, with its muted lighting, arched doorways, Mexican tile floors, tin chandeliers, and tile fountain. The lobby bar is popular with residents and guests alike.

Upstairs, the guest rooms reflect their southwestern heritage with furnishings that are beautiful in their simplicity. Wooden shutters cover the windows, regional art accents the walls, carved Mexican furniture and hammered tin light switch covers add interest. Standard, mini-suite, and deluxe units differ primarily in size. Because of the hotel's age, the standard rooms tend to be a little smaller than more modern ones, but all the rooms have small refrigerators.

> **Across the street from Albuquerque's convention center, La Posada is about five minutes from Old Town and ten minutes from the University of New Mexico.**

Conrad's Downtown is La Posada's restaurant. Southwestern dishes dominate the breakfast menu, while at lunch and dinner the cuisine takes on more of a Spanish bent. Dinner entrées range from $12–$21, and paella is a specialty. On weekend nights a classical guitarist entertains.

For a small daily fee, guests can visit the Downtown Athletic Club across the street: it has an indoor pool, racquetball courts, and exercise equipment. Room service, free airport transportation, and free parking are nice extras.

Ramada Hotel Classic

6815 Menaul NE
Albuquerque, NM 87110
505-881-0000
800-2-RAMADA
Fax: 505-881-3736

> *A hotel across from the city's biggest mall*

General Manager: Bill Caskey. **Accommodations:** 272 rooms and 24 suites. **Rates:** $86 single, $96 double; suites $120–$260. **Added:** 10.75% tax. **Payment:** Major credit cards. **Children:** Under 18 free in room with parents; $10 additional if more than three people in room. **Pets:** Permitted with approval. **Smoking:** Nonsmoking rooms available. **Open:** Year-round.

From the public areas to the guest rooms, the Ramada Hotel Classic is visually pleasing. The lobby and adjoining areas, done in peach, mauve, and green, have skylights and lots of plants, creating a cool, soothing environment in Albuquerque's uptown business district. Built in the mid-1980s, this hostelry was the dream of George Maloof, an Albuquerque businessman who died soon after it opened. His portrait hangs in the entranceway.

Outside, the hotel is surrounded by activity. The city's largest mall, Coronado, is across the street. Winrock Shopping Center is half a mile away, and many corporate addresses are within a few miles. Guests have easy access to the city yet can relax in calming surroundings.

> **Take time to see the ornate white pipe organ with five keyboards and 27 sets of pipes. A true showpiece, it originally entertained audiences at the Roxy Theater in New York. Now it is played during Sunday brunch.**

The guest rooms have a sophisticated air. Their colors are soft and warm and their design emphasizes comfort. Extras include small refrigerators, double vanities, and shower massages in the baths. The suites have deluxe whirlpools, and some king rooms have large wet bars complete with bar stools.

The Café Fennel serves all three meals. The menu runs the gamut from southwestern dishes to burgers and pasta ($3.50–$10.50 lunch or dinner), but the desserts get the most attention. The delicious pastries, pies, and cakes are so popular that the restaurant sells them to go. Try to sit in the "train" section: the cozy booths are lined up as if they were in a train, and photographs of an older America pass by slowly like the landscape from a moving train.

Chardonnay's is the hotel's fine restaurant, serving Continental cuisine in an elegant setting. Entrées include lamb chops Madagascar and saffron scallops ($6–$11 for lunch, $12–$20 for dinner). The hotel's nightclub, Quest Lounge, serves early evening drink specials and hors d'oeuvres and has a dance floor and live entertainment. The Lobby Bar serves complimentary hors d'oeuvres during the week.

The Ramada has a small indoor heated swimming pool with an adjacent hot tub. There are dry saunas in the men's and women's locker rooms and a coed fitness room.

The Albuquerque Visitors Bureau has an office on the second floor of the hotel. Parking in the hotel lot is free, as is airport transportation.

Sarabande Bed and Breakfast

5637 Rio Grande Blvd. NW
Albuquerque, NM 87107
505-345-4923

*A small,
romantic B&B in
the North Valley*

Innkeepers: Margaret Magnussen and Betty Vickers. **Accommodations:** 2 rooms. **Rates:** $75–$110. **Included:** Full breakfast and afternoon refreshments. **Added:** 5.75% tax. **Payment:** Major credit cards. **Children:** Not permitted. **Pets:** Not permitted. **Smoking:** Outside only. **Open:** Year-round.

Sarabande is a charming bed-and-breakfast in Albuquerque's affluent North Valley. Run by two nurses who wanted to try their hand at a new occupation in their retirement, the inn is firm evidence that they made the right choice.

Two guest rooms share the main portion of the house (Betty and Margaret live in a separate wing), affording guests lots of living space and privacy. The large living/dining room has a shepherd's fireplace and an elegant dining table accented with a fine silver tea service and candlesticks.

The Rose room has a four-poster bed topped with a rose coverlet. There is a ceiling fan, TV, viga ceilings, and an interesting frosted glass door with a dragonfly pattern. The best part is a raised platform with a deep tub that you step down into. There's also a vanity, a wash basin with brass fixtures, and a separate shower across the room. A door at the far end of the room opens onto a fountain patio with a climbing rose bush.

> **The inn has all-terrain bicycles to lend for a trip to the nearby nature center.**

The Iris room across the hall is smaller but equally inviting. Decorated in mauve and gray, it has twin beds that may be made into a king. A striking stained glass window with an iris motif gives the room its name. The room opens onto the front fountain and garden courtyard with a built-in barbecue for guests to enjoy. Thoughtful touches in both the guest rooms include fresh flowers, electric towel warmers, and plush terry robes.

On one side of the house there's a wonderful garden complete with shady ramadas and a lily pond. On the north side, there's a Japanese garden inviting meditation to the sound of falling water. Out back there's a garden room where greenery hangs from skylights. Double doors lead from the garden room to a 50-foot lap pool and adjoining hot tub — a real treat, especially when you consider that with only two guest rooms you're likely to have them all to yourself.

Full breakfasts are served in the dining room each morning. German pancakes with apples, eggs, coffee, and fresh orange juice is a typical meal, but the hosts always try to accommodate special dietary needs. In the afternoon, guests can unwind with a cool refreshment of their choice.

William E. Mauger Estate

701 Roma Avenue NW
Albuquerque, NM 87102
505-242-8755

Owners: Chuck Silver and Brian Miller. **Accommodations:** 8 rooms, all with private bath.

A turn-of-the-century home on the edge of downtown

Rates: $65–$85 single, $75–$95 double; suite $105–$115. **Included:** Breakfast. **Added:** 10.8125% tax. **Payment:** Major credit cards. **Children:** Permitted with prior approval; additional $1 per year of age. **Pets:** Permitted with prior approval. **Smoking:** Permitted only outside. **Open:** Year-round.

Just where downtown Albuquerque gives way to a residential section stands a charming brick three-story inn. Built in 1897 for $1,600, it's a stately Queen Anne that puts you in touch with history yet is filled with modern comforts.

The William E. Mauger opened to guests in late 1987 after being beautifully restored. Great effort was expended during the renovation process to preserve as much of the original home as possible. In the entrance sitting room, the light fixture still has its original Edison bulbs. The current owners have a fully documented history of all the home's past owners (the only turn-of-the-century building in Albuquerque to have such a record), and old photos of previous occupants are on display on the second-floor foyer.

> **The Mauger Estate is close to the Sunshine Opera House and the Kimo and El Rey theaters. All in all, the inn is an excellent alternative to the city's traditional lodgings.**

Decorated with period furnishings, the guest rooms have an air of elegance. The pleasant Tuers room is the smallest. The Boston Sleeper suite can accommodate five. Hardwood floors are covered with Oriental rugs, stuffed animals sit on the brass beds, and lace-covered satin hangers are found in the closet. The suite has a split bath, and the sofa on the sun porch opens into a twin bed. The Britannia room is spacious, with a brass king bed, a small sitting area with a table and easy chairs, and a large closet. The Wool room was Mr. Mauger's office. It has a private balcony. Greystone B, on the third floor, has a slanted roof and two queen beds draped with lace. Greystone A, decorated in black and fuchsia, is the most modern.

Rooms on the ground floor include the Williams room, which has a queen bed, and the Garden room, originally a conservatory and sun porch, with twins. All rooms have a surprising number of amenities, including small refrigerators, coffeemakers, hair dryers, ironing boards and irons, clock radios, curling irons, air conditioning, ceiling fans, and individual heat controls.

The parlor, with its pretty floral wallpaper, player organ, and old-fashioned phonograph, looks at first glance as if it belongs to another age, yet it too is filled with modern conveniences. There's a laser disc player and VCR with a vast disc and videocassette library. The refrigerator is always stocked with refreshments. At five o'clock, hors d'oeuvres are served, and freshly baked goods are available all day long. On one table, the hosts have compiled a directory of local restaurants and travel brochures, and they've even put together their own guidebook of photographs of local tourist sights.

Southwestern breakfasts, served outdoors on the deck in

nice weather, vary daily. A typical breakfast might be burritos served with refries and a yogurt and granola fruit cup. Or you might rise to a green chile and bacon soufflé accompanied by pan-fried potatoes and zucchini bread.

Chuck and Brian's commitment to hospitality makes a visit to this inn unusually pleasant; they really enjoy their guests and go out of their way to make everyone's stay as comfortable as possible. They keep a scrapbook of visitors' photos and letters, and many guests return again and again.

ALTO

La Junta Guest Ranch

Alto, NM 88312
505-336-4361
800-443-8423

A group-oriented hideaway near the Apache ski area

Owners: The Finley family. **Accommodations:** 27 rooms. **Rates:** $65 single, $75 double, large cabins $200. **Added:** 7.125% tax. **Payment:** No credit cards. **Children:** Additional $5 per child per day. **Pets:** Additional $5 per day. **Smoking:** Discouraged; nonsmoking rooms available. **Open:** Year-round.

La Junta means "meeting place," which is exactly what this lodging offers: an informal gathering spot for groups of up to 75, whether they want to ski at nearby Ski Apache Resort or enjoy the wooded surroundings at any time of year. The managers are eager to help groups meet their specific needs.

Spread over seven acres of beautiful countryside six miles north of Ruidoso, with the smell of pine in the air and occasional mountain vistas, La Junta has a central recreation room and guest rooms in five buildings. Picnic tables and grills are scattered among the trees.

The owners are transplanted Louisianians, and happily, they have brought a touch of their native state with them to New Mexico. Each room is named for a Louisiana parish, and the decor reflects the Finleys' penchant for Cajun country. For example, tucked into the basket of goodies awaiting guests — items such as coffee, tea, and ketchup — is a bottle of Trappey's pepper sauce.

> **The atmosphere at La Junta is camplike and low key, allowing groups to create their own mood.**

Each of the buildings is different, offering a variety of accommodations, and each one has a well-equipped kitchen and fireplace. Vermilion and St. Charles, on top of the recreation building, can be rented as separate or adjoining units; together they can accommodate 12. The two units have a wide upstairs porch and two living room–kitchen combinations in addition to bedrooms. Guest rooms have a rustic flavor.

CLOUDCROFT

The Lodge

P.O. Box 497
1 Corona Place
Cloudcroft, NM 88317
505-682-2566
800-395-6343
Fax: 505-682-2715

*A historic
mountain getaway*

General Manager: Lisa Thomassie. **Accommodations:** 47 rooms. **Rates:** $69–$89, suites $99–$189. **Added:** 9.25% tax. **Payment:** Major credit cards. **Children:** Free in room with parents. **Pets:** Not permitted. **Smoking:** Nonsmoking rooms available. **Open:** Year-round.

Even in July, the air is cool high in the Sacramento Mountains. In the lobby of the Lodge, guests enjoy a crackling fire, while at the mountains' base, 15 miles away, folks swelter in the desert heat.

The Lodge, intimate and secluded, is a romantic escape. Here you can play golf or hike during the summer, ski or snuggle by the fire in the winter. The original lodge, built in 1899 by the Alamogordo and Sacramento Mountain Railway, was destroyed by fire in 1909; this lodge was constructed two years later. Over the years it has undergone numerous renovations, though its Bavarian-style exterior has remained essentially the same.

You should know that the hotel has a friendly and flirtatious ghost named Rebecca. According to the legend, beautiful Rebecca was a chambermaid at the Lodge in the early

1930s. She mysteriously disappeared after her lumberjack lover found her in the arms of another man. People swear that they see her ghost from time to time wandering the halls of the old inn. The legend is so popular that the Lodge's restaurant is named for her, and her portrait hangs at the entrance. Some say that Rebecca's image in this portrait is missing from their photographs when they're developed.

> **A family-oriented hostelry, the Lodge will arrange for babysitters upon request. Nearby family activities include skiing at Cloudcroft, with 25 runs, outdoor fun in Lincoln National Forest, and seasonal festivals.**

The restaurant is renowned for its Continental cuisine, which includes dishes such as piñon trout, mahogany chicken with a honey-pecan sauce, and peppercorn tournedos. Tableside presentations are a house specialty — the dessert flambés are particularly popular. The breakfast and lunch menus are equally extensive, and the menu itself is printed like a newspaper informing guests of the inn's history as well as seasonal events. Entrées range from $13 to $24 at dinner, from $3 to $8 at breakfast and lunch. Down in the basement is the Red Dog Saloon, with a history of its own; ask about the dollar bills encased in glass. Upstairs is a Victorian bar from Al Capone's home.

One of the Lodge's most distinctive features is its five-story copper tower. Judy Garland wrote her name on the wall here. So did Clark Gable. For a romantic tête-à-tête, reserve the tiny parlor at the base of the tower; more than one couple has gotten engaged here. Climb the stairs to the summit and look out over miles of alpine scenery. White Sands National Monument glistens, 40 miles away, and on a clear day you can see much farther — 150 miles, it's claimed.

The lobby of the hotel looks like a lodge, with leather couches, bearskins, even a stuffed bear. The guest rooms are much more romantic, decorated in a French country style with antique furniture, matched bed and drapery fabrics, and brass accents. Every room in this personable inn is different in size and shape, and has its own decorating scheme. Common to all are high ceilings, clicking steam radiators, down comforters, and French eyelet linens, TVs, and phones. Family rooms, sleeping up to four, are especially spacious. King rooms tend to be dormer style, with four-poster beds, dormer seating, and shutters with fabric insets.

The Honeymoon Suite features a gold-crowned, mirror-topped bed — you have to see it to believe it — and a Jacuzzi built for two. The Governor's Suite, a real bargain at $169, is the most elegant room at the Lodge. It has a four-poster bed, lace curtains, a plush living room with antique furniture and velvet upholstery, a phone, an old wooden radio that still works, its own entrance hallway, a writing desk in a sunny window alcove, and Oriental rugs. They say that this is Rebecca's favorite room.

The Lodge's 9-hole golf course, at 9,200 feet, is among the highest in the world. Golfers can pause to enjoy the spectacular scenery punctuated with blue spruce and ponderosa pine. The outdoor pool, kept at 80 degrees year-round, and outdoor hot tub are attractive modern features of a hotel that's a throwback to a more graceful era of travel.

GALLUP

El Rancho Hotel

1000 East 66 Avenue
Gallup, NM 87301
505-863-9311
800-543-6351
Fax: 505-722-5917

> *Movie stars once frequented this historic hotel*

Owner: Armand Ortega. **Accommodations:** 98 rooms. **Rates:** $39 single, $52 double; suites $75. **Added:** 11.1875% tax. **Payment:** Major credit cards. **Children:** Under 6 free in room with parents. **Pets:** On leash and with owner supervision only. **Smoking:** Nonsmoking rooms available. **Open:** Year-round.

The stone and timber exterior of El Rancho looks out of place among the fast-food restaurants, gas stations, and modest motels that surround it, but the hotel existed long before fast food was invented. El Rancho was built in 1937 and is on the National Register of Historic Places. It served as the headquarters for numerous movie stars and production teams while filming in the area during Hollywood's heyday: Ronald Reagan, Gregory Peck, William Holden, and Kirk Douglas are just of few of the luminaries who made pictures here. After a period of decline, the hotel was restored and reopened in 1988 with new vigor.

The balcony walls upstairs from the lobby look like a veritable who's who of movie-making — one could spend hours looking at the photos of Hollywood idols. Many have been autographed with endearing messages for the hotel.

With a timbered ceiling, a stone and log double staircase, casual sofas, Navajo rugs, stuffed elk and deer heads, and a stone fireplace, the lobby has the feel of a hunting lodge. On one wall a mural depicts the early history of New Mexico, and a striking amethyst crystal encased in wood stands near the registration desk.

Guest rooms, western in tone, are decorated in pleasant shades of rose and cream. The rooms have wagon wheel headboards, attractive wood furniture, ceiling fans, clock radios, TVs, phones, sand paintings, and southwestern prints. Suites include a bridal suite and a presidential suite. El Rancho also rents out rooms in an adjacent motel.

El Rancho's restaurant has a Mexican feel, though the theme here is Hollywood as well, and dishes are named after stars. The "Errol Flynn" is a French dip sandwich; the "Mae West" is a stacked ham or beef sandwich; the "Rita Moreno" is an enchilada plate. The 49'er bar is down the hall. A gift shop beside the lobby sells Indian jewelry, and there is a laundry room on the premises.

LAS CRUCES

Lundeen's Inn of the Arts
Bed and Breakfast

618 South Alameda
Las Cruces, NM 88005
505-526-3327
Fax: 505-526-3355

> *An artistic feast for the eyes*

Innkeepers: Linda and Gerald Lundeen. **Accommodations:** 20 rooms. **Rates:** $55 single, $62 double; suites $88; long-term rates available. **Included:** Continental breakfast, afternoon hors d'oeuvres and cider. **Added:** 11% tax. **Payment:** Major credit cards. **Children:** With approval only; additional $10 per day. **Pets:** With approval only; additional $15 charge. **Smoking:** On balconies and in courtyard only. **Open:** Year-round.

Lundeen's is run by a creative and energetic couple, Linda and Gerry Lundeen. Linda runs an art gallery in the same adobe building that holds the B&B and the Lundeens' home. Gerry is an architect, and his handiwork can be seen throughout the inn.

The main building is actually a combination of three separate adobe homes, one built in 1896, one in 1901, and one in 1921, that the Lundeens have connected with a lofty merienda or "afternoon gathering" room. With its high ceilings, arched windows, expansive oil paintings, and plant-filled alcove, the merienda room is the appealing focal point of the inn and serves as both the main living and dining room for guests. In the afternoon, guests, who are often as interesting as the inn itself, gather here for hors d'oeuvres and apple cider. At breakfast, the Lundeens serve perhaps huevos rancheros, blueberry muffins, or cinnamon swirls accompanied by fruit, herb tea, and coffee.

If you want to be surrounded by art you needn't confine yourself to Linda's gallery or the merienda room; artwork is sprinkled throughout the B&B, creating a lively look. Also in evidence is the Lundeen's imaginative design sense. The antique organ used as a serving bar, the balustrade above the merienda room that includes pieces taken from a synagogue in El Paso, and a pressed tin segment from a Baptist church are a few examples of the Lundeens' creative flair.

In keeping with the B&B's artistic theme, each guest room is named for an artist, with furnishings that reflect that artist's style. The Georgia O'Keeffe Room, decorated in black, gray, and white, has an antique bed and a private balcony. The Olag Wieghorst Room, with its blue quilts and red accents, has a pair of double beds and a red claw-foot tub draped with netting. Pottery is on display in the sunny Maria Martinez room. About half the guest rooms have their own televisions and phones, and some have bidets in the baths.

> You don't have to be an art expert to stay at Lundeen's, but if you are, you won't be disappointed. Either way, you will enjoy being surrounded by the work of contemporary artists.

As Las Cruces's warm winter climate has become more widely known, the Lundeens have gotten an increasing number of repeat guests who want to stay several weeks, a month, or even longer. To accommodate them, the Lundeens have built several casitas on the property. Like large one-room studios, the casitas have living/dining areas, fireplaces, and fully equipped kitchens.

Catering to groups as well as individuals, the hosts can coordinate such special functions as theater nights, art and elder hostels, watercolor and silversmithing workshops, mystery weekends, archaeological digs, and even trips to the nearby Deming Duck Races.

MESCALERO

Inn of the Mountain Gods

P.O. Box 269
Carrizo Canyon Road
Mescalero, NM 88340
505-257-5141
800-545-9011
Fax: 505-257-6173

*A beautiful setting
and plentiful
recreation*

General Manager: Fredda Draper. **Accommodations:** 250 rooms. **Rates:** $115–$125; suites $125–$135. **Added:** 9.5% tax. **Payment:** Major credit cards. **Children:** Under 12 free in room with parents if no crib or rollaway required; over 12, additional $12 per day. **Pets:** Not permitted. **Smoking:** Nonsmoking rooms available. **Open:** Year-round.

High in the Sacramento Mountains, the Inn of the Mountain Gods sprawls along the shore of Lake Mescalero below the spectacular snow-capped Sierra Blanca peak. Although the tourist center of Ruidoso is only 3½ miles north, this resort is a world of its own, beautiful in its seclusion. Owned and run by the Mescalero Apache Indian Reservation, it sits at the heart of its forested land. The inn, built in 1975, is made up of a series of rambling buildings connected by long enclosed walkways. Be sure to drive as close as possible to your room with your luggage after check-in, because unless your room is in one of the hallways closest to the lobby, you'll have to carry your bags quite some distance. There's no pretension about the place, just informality and relaxed fun.

Every room has a balcony or patio and overlooks the lake or the mountains. The decor is modern, with some Indian art accents. These accommodations rank high in spaciousness and convenience; in the bathrooms, the vanities and mirrors are separate from the rest of the bath. Suites have a Murphy bed–sitting area and wet bar.

The inn has three restaurants, five lounges, and a hot dog stand by the pool that specializes in international versions of the snack food. The Apache Tee serves breakfast and lunch. The finest restaurant, Dan Li Ka Room (Mescalero Apache for "good food"), has excellent fare and an attractive environment. Entrées such as mountain trout, and a southwestern sauté made with venison, chicken breast, and beef medallions in a Marsala cilantro sauce range from $14 to $18. The Top of the Inn coffee shop is open in summer only.

Golfing, boating, tennis, fishing, riding, archery, and trap and skeet shooting are enough to keep most vacationers happy. The inn's 18-hole championship golf course is one of the finest in the Southwest. Scenic, challenging, and well maintained, it's a prime drawing card for the resort. The greens fee for guests is $35; full cart rental is $20, half cart rental $10.

For hunters, the inn operates a hunting program from mid-September through December. Trophy-size elk, whitetail deer, pronghorn herds, turkey, mountain lions, and black and brown bear are among the possible game.

Tennis is also important here, with six outdoor courts, a pro shop, and viewing deck. Court time is $10–$20 per hour. Boaters can rent canoes, rowboats, and pedal boats; motor boats are not permitted. For anglers, the lake is stocked with rainbow and cutthroat trout, and there's a bait and tackle shop by the pier. The stables, about a mile and a half from the inn, offer hour-long to all-day rides.

The inn runs a bus service to Ski Apache, also owned by the tribe, during ski season and to Ruidoso Downs Race Track on race days. For guests with a yen for gambling, Casino Apache is open from 10:00 A.M. to 1:00 A.M. daily.

MESILLA

Meson de Mesilla

1803 Avenida de Mesilla
P.O. Box 1212
Mesilla, NM 88046
505-525-9212
800-732-6025

Fine dining is the main attraction

Innkeeper: Chuck Walker. **Accommodations:** 13 rooms, all with private bath. **Rates:** $45 single, $60 double; suite $72–$82. **Included:** Full breakfast. **Added:** 6.3175% tax. **Payment:** Major credit cards. **Children:** Additional $10 for rollaway. **Pets:** Not permitted. **Smoking:** Nonsmoking rooms available. **Open:** Year-round.

Mesilla was once the largest town in the southern New Mexico territory. During the Civil War, it was declared the Confederate capital of a territory that extended to California. Billy the Kid stood trial in Mesilla, and the Gadsden Treaty, transferring 45,000 square miles of land that is now southern Arizona and New Mexico, was signed on Mesilla's plaza. About six blocks from the plaza is the Meson de Mesilla, an adobe inn vintage 1985.

Meson de Mesilla was designed as an inn, hence the large, airy rooms and the spacious restaurant. The guest rooms, all on the second floor, open onto a porch that leads down to the pool and covered patio. Honeysuckle twines up the wrought-iron stairway. Beyond the pool, past the yard, stretch miles of cotton fields. Every room at Meson de Mesilla is different, and some have views of the distant mountains. With names like Yucca and Roadrunner, their decor reflects the surrounding locale. Brass beds and ceiling fans provide comfort, while handsome vertical window blinds provide seclusion. The three suites have kiva fireplaces. There are no phones in the rooms, but all have TVs and clock radios.

Breakfast is beautifully served in the restaurant downstairs. Through the windows you look out on a landscaped cactus garden. Inside you enjoy such dishes as eggs Creole and orange yogurt pancakes, all presented with panache.

> **Old Mesilla, now a village of about 2,000, is known for its galleries, shops, and restaurants, while nearby Las Cruces, population 45,000, is the economic leader of the region.**

While breakfast is quite good, dinner is a meal to savor. The menu always includes seven or eight choices, such as sea scallops with curried apples, veal roulade Florentine, quail sauté à la messine, and king salmon piccata. You might begin with escargots followed by soup, salad, and then the main course, served with wild rice pilaf. The price of the entire meal, including dessert, ranges from $14 to $25. A wine connoisseur, Chuck Walker offers a wide selection of California, Spanish, Italian, German, and New Mexican wines.

Although the cuisine is Continental, the restaurant's decor has a Mexican feel, with tiled fountains and carved wooden columns. It is open for dinner Tuesday through Saturday and for lunch Wednesday through Friday. Sunday brunch is a highlight. Reservations are recommended.

NOGAL

Monjeau Shadows

Bonito Route
Highway 37
Nogal, NM 88341
505-336-4191

> *A hillside*
> *guest home*

Owners: J.R. and Kay Newton. **Accommodations:** 5 rooms. **Rates:** $50 single, $75 double; suite $100. **Added:** 7.125% tax. **Included:** Breakfast. **Payment:** Major credit cards. **Children:** Additional charge for children over 12; younger children not encouraged. **Pets:** Not permitted. **Smoking:** Outside only. **Open:** Year-round.

The highway leading to Ruidoso is only a few hundred feet below. But Monjeau Shadows feels removed from the crowds. From any of the three porches, you look out over miles of wooded terrain. To the northeast is Capitan Mountain, where a frightened bear cub was found after a devastating forest fire in 1950, inspiring a campaign for national awareness of forest conservation led by Smokey the Bear.

Monjeau Shadows, built as a home on ten acres in 1980 and transformed into a B&B four years later, is an excellent hub for a New Mexico mountain vacation any time of the year. Ski Apache, with eight lifts including a four-passenger gondola, is 18 miles away. Hiking and fishing enthusiasts can find plenty to do. One of the most popular attractions in the area is Ruidoso Downs, where races are held from May to September.

Birding is a special activity here. Hummingbirds are constant visitors to the feeders on the second-floor balcony. The owners claim that when the feeders are empty, the birds let them know by flying around the kitchen windows.

Breakfast is included in the room rate, and generally J. R. will fix whatever you'd like. If you want a high-energy breakfast to fuel a day of skiing, he'll oblige; if you prefer something light, he'll do that too. Breakfast hour is flexible, according to the needs of the guests. The meal can be served in your room, in the dining room, or outside. For an extra charge, and with advance notice, other meals can be arranged.

> **The inn can accommodate groups of up to 16. Special arrangements can be made for groups upon request, including meals and entertainment.**

The guest rooms are on four levels, from the basement to the loft. Bryan's room is red, white, and blue, and has a nautical theme. The adjoining bath has several surprises — wallpaper that you can read (advertisements from a Victorian-era catalog) and a red, white, and blue claw-foot tub. Elaina's room is the nicest, with lace curtains, a chenille bedspread, a straw heart wreath over the bed, and a marble-topped bedside table. It can be rented alone or with Lisa's room to form a suite. Every room has a TV, a digital clock, and well-matched furnishings.

A look of orderliness and comfort prevails throughout. In the living room, distinctive with its apricot carpet and yellow walls, a stained glass skylight is the focal point.

There's lots of space available for guests. Especially popular in winter is the basement game room, with a tournament-size pool table, a dart board, and a sitting area beside the fireplace. For games like badminton, croquet, and horseshoes, you don't have to go any farther than the front lawn.

PLACITAS

Hacienda de Placitas

491 Highway 165
Placitas, NM 87043
505-867-3775

A pleasant place to indulge your senses

Innkeepers: Carol and François Orfeo. **Accommodations:** 2 guesthouses. **Rates:** $115–$150 double; additional persons $15 per day. **Included:** Full breakfast. **Added:** Tax. **Payment:** Major credit cards. **Children:** Welcome. **Pets:** Welcome. **Smoking:** Outdoors only. **Open:** Year-round.

In the attractive community of Placitas just north of Albuquerque, Hacienda de Placitas offers comfortable accommodations in a historic, artistic, and natural setting. As you head east on Highway 165 toward the Sandia Mountains, you'll easily be able to spot the inn on the left side of the road because of its windmill; locals call it the windmill house. Pull in the drive and you'll see a tepee that came from a movie set and the remnants of an old covered wagon.

The interior of the main hacienda is a definite surprise — not at all rugged, as the covered wagon, tepee, and windmill might lead you to believe. In fact, the reception room has a museumlike quality. Although the viga ceiling is traditional for an adobe home, the lattice-patterned brick floor is unique, and the furnishings are far from ordinary. There's a grand piano, two sofas in front of an ornate French 17th-century fireplace, a gothic sideboard that came from a church, and a bishop's chair. At one end of the room there's an expansive dining room table set with tall brass candlesticks just waiting for a medieval feast. Renaissance-style paintings on the wall by innkeeper François Orfeo only add to the European flavor.

Adjacent to the main reception room is a sunroom outfitted with a hot tub, Nordic track, and exercise bicycle. In the oldest section of the hacienda, which is more than 100 years old, the Orfeos have an art gallery, where works for sale include paintings by François and jewelry by his wife and fellow innkeeper, Carol Orfeo.

Guest lodging is in two separate and very private guesthouses. The Piñon is a two-story adobe house with turquoise trim. Downstairs is a kitchen, small dining table, bath, and living room with a sleeper sofa. Upstairs is a loft bedroom with a queen bed. The Piñon also has a large, private slate patio and grill.

> **Behind the hacienda is a terrace with built-in banco seating and an outdoor grill. The terrace offers terrific sunset views of Cabezon Volcano and Mt. Taylor.**

The Pecos cabin is an authentic log cabin that was moved to the property from the Pecos wilderness. Once inside you'll truly believe you've been transported to a remote cottage in the woods. Furnishings are rustic and fun. There's an old wooden sled on one wall, a four-poster pole bed, an animal skin rug, and antlers adorning the stone fireplace. Modern conveniences such as a kitchen, bath, and television haven't been overlooked, but they have been incorporated in a manner befitting a wilderness retreat. The bath has a pull-chain toilet, and the kitchen cookware is of the blue enamel variety that brings to mind campfires and chuckwagons. The cabin's front porch affords excellent views.

Breakfast is served in the reception room in the main hacienda, on a large terrace by the kidney-shaped swimming pool, or in the guesthouses. Since both Carol and François have been in the restaurant and catering business, breakfasts are delicious. House specialties include egg and shrimp Orfeo, an omelet served on a croissant with shrimp, melted Swiss cheese, and hollandaise served with potatoes provence; blue corn waffles topped with apple-rum-raisin sauce, honey-yogurt, and piñon nuts; and plum au flan, a walnut pastry filled with plum halves and cinnamon sour cream custard.

Despite the secluded air of Hacienda de Placitas, the inn is actually only 20 minutes from downtown Albuquerque and 40 minutes from Santa Fe. It is a short drive from Albuquerque's Balloon Fiesta Park, site of the world's largest hot air balloon festival each October.

RUIDOSO

Best Western Swiss Chalet

1451 Mechem Drive
P.O. Box 759
Ruidoso, NM 88345
505-258-3333
800-477-9477
Fax: 505-258-5325

A European-style lodge with glorious mountain views

General Manager: Giddings Brown. **Accommodations:** 82 rooms. **Rates:** $54–$81 single, $62–$89 double; suites $135. **Added:** 10.68125% tax. **Payment:** Major credit cards. **Children:** Over 12, additional $8 per day. **Pets:** Small ones permitted with $10 additional charge. **Smoking:** Nonsmoking rooms available. **Open:** Year-round.

Although the Swiss Chalet is set on a hill just off Highway 48 in Ruidoso, it has the remarkable feel of an inn in the Swiss Alps. The inn's alpine look is in its white exterior accented with bright blue trim and its light pine–paneled lobby. Ahna-Michelle's, the hotel's German-style restaurant with checked tablecloths and cuckoo clocks, seems to stretch right out into the trees. It

The Swiss Chalet is one of the closest inns to Ski Apache; Ruidoso Downs is only eight miles away.

has floor-to-ceiling views of Sierra Blanca peak. A German buffet is offered on Friday nights, and entrées such as Weiner schnitzel, a German sausage platter, and Die Drei Ecken, an omelette with German sausage, swiss cheese, potato pancakes, and applesauce, add to the Bavarian ambience.

Rooms on the back side of the building have views of Sierra Blanca, a striking peak that remains snow-capped for about two-thirds of the year. Rooms are spacious and tastefully decorated in soft rose and blue. The rich wood furnishings are good reproductions of fine antiques. Guest rooms at the front of the hotel are off a glassed-in hallway, and although they don't have views, they are cheerful, with painted headboards and dressers. Family and king suites have sleeper sofas.

The Honeymoon Suite is the best in the house. It has a

canopied four-poster king bed, extra pillows and dust ruffles, pretty prints, a comfortable sitting area, and a Jacuzzi bath.

For leisure, there is a small swimming pool in a glassed-in atrium designed to capture mountain vistas. A hot tub and sauna are nearby.

Story Book Cabins

P.O. Box.472
410 Main Road
Ruidoso, NM 88345
505-257-2115
Fax: 505-257-7512

Comfortable family lodging in cabins

Owners: Kaye and Bruce Kernodle.
Accommodations: 10 cabins. **Rates:** $79–$139; rates lower in some seasons. **Added:** 10.8% tax. **Payment:** Major credit cards. **Children:** Welcome. **Pets:** Not permitted. **Smoking:** Permitted. **Open:** Year-round.

Story Book Cabins are certainly not hidden in the woods. Indeed, they are among the many groups of cabins that line Upper Canyon Road just off Highway 70, which runs through the center of Ruidoso. But if you want a pleasant place to stay in the area, Story Book is a good choice.

> **Only a few steps from Story Book Cabins is the Rio Ruidoso, popular for trout fishing.**

The cabins have from one to three bedrooms. Interiors are cozy, with large stone fireplaces and comfortable country furnishings. The kitchens have gas ranges and full-size refrigerators. The bathrooms, while not large, are nicely decorated. Each cabin has cable TV in the sitting room, a swing or rocker on the porch, and an outdoor grill.

Nearby Ruidoso Downs is a major attraction, with thoroughbred and quarter-horse racing from May through early September. During the winter, Ski Apache, 16 miles to the northwest, draws skiers of all abilities.

SILVER CITY

Bear Mountain Guest Ranch

P.O. Box 1163
Silver City, NM 88062
505-538-2538
800-880-2538

*A mountain inn
popular with
nature lovers*

Owner: Myra McCormick. **Accommodations:** 15 units. **Rates:** $54–$79 single, $95–$130 double; suites $105–$130. **Included:** All meals. **Added:** 10.55625% tax. **Payment:** Credit cards not accepted. **Children:** Welcome. **Pets:** Permitted with a refundable deposit. **Smoking:** In guest rooms or outdoors only, not in public areas. **Open:** Year-round.

Nature is the star attraction at Bear Mountain Guest Ranch, which has been run by Myra McCormick since 1959. An expert nature guide, she cordially invites guests to get to know her part of the world. More than 200 species of birds have been spotted in the Bear Mountain area. Mountain chickadees, Mexican jays, canyon towhees, and Gambel's quail are among the frequent visitors.

Myra's specialties are birding, wild plants, archaeology, and ghost towns. Throughout the year, special events are held at the ranch, such as archaeological digs and birding expeditions. She also helps guests plan excursions — spelunking, whitewater rafting, exploring canyons, rock hunting, fishing, and sightseeing.

Guided tours to archaeological sites of the Mimbres Indians, a culture that flourished between A.D. 1000 and 1150, can be arranged. The Mimbres produced sophisticated pottery;

Myra explains that their work was decorated with black on white geometric designs and human and animal figures.

Bear Mountain Guest Ranch is about four miles outside Silver City. Ringed by distant mountains, it sits on grassy meadowland speckled with junipers. The location is peaceful and secluded. Even the stars shine more brightly at the ranch.

The main hacienda was built in the 1920s as a home and school for emotionally handicapped children. The main room has native stone fireplaces, cupboards filled with rocks and minerals, casual sitting areas, and a vast array of magazines. To one side is the sun porch, or as Myra calls it, the bird-watching room.

> **Guests are asked to introduce themselves at the table just before each meal. This usually stimulates lively conversation, for the ranch's guests tend to be as interesting as the place itself.**

You can choose among seven rooms in the main house (three downstairs, four upstairs) or in nearby cottages. Furnishings are casual and simple, reminiscent of the 1920s and 1930s, with electric blankets to warm the chilly mountain nights. The windows are large and seem to be everywhere, letting in the fresh air and the sun. A cottage called the Bear's Den has five bedrooms, each with a private bath, and a large central sitting area. The other two cottages have one bedroom each. Since the cottages have kitchens, guests there may cook for themselves or eat in the ranch's dining room.

Meals are served family-style in the main house. Everything is cooked from scratch using natural ingredients. Dinner usually consists of homemade bread, meat and potatoes, vegetables, salad, and homemade dessert. At breakfast there's a hot entrée, generally eggs of some sort, as well as cereal and fresh muffins, often made from Mrs. McCormick's secret low-calorie recipes. Guests are sent off with bag lunches to fortify them on their birding or sightseeing excursions.

The ranch holds special six-day programs on subjects such as the geology of New Mexico, Indians of the Southwest, and stress management Southwest style. The programs are popular and reasonably priced, so be sure to arrange your stay as far ahead as possible.

Northern
New Mexico

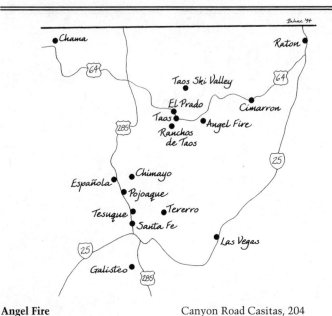

Best Bed-and-Breakfasts

Chimayo
  Hacienda Rancho de Chimayo
  La Posada de Chimayo
El Prado
  Salsa del Salto
Española
  Inn at the Delta
  Rancho de San Juan
Galisteo
  Galisteo Inn
Ranchos de Taos
  Adobe and Pines Inn
Santa Fe
  Adobe Abode
  Alexander's Inn
  Canyon Road Casitas
  Dancing Ground of the Sun
  Dos Casas Viejas
  Four Kachinas Inn
  Grant Corner Inn
  Guadalupe Inn
  Spencer House Bed and Breakfast
  Water Street Inn
Taos
  Casa Benavides
  Casa de las Chimeneas
  El Rincón Bed and Breakfast
  Hacienda del Sol
  Taos Bed & Breakfast Association

Best City Stops

Santa Fe
  Hotel Plaza Real
  Inn of the Anasazi
  Inn on the Alameda

Best Family Favorites

Pojoaque
  Rancho Jacona

Best Historic Hostelries

Cimarron
St. James Hotel
Las Vegas
Plaza Hotel
Santa Fe
Hotel St. Francis
La Fonda
Taos
The Taos Inn

Best Hunting and Fishing Lodges

Chama
The Lodge at Chama Land and Cattle Company
Unser's Oso Ranch and Lodge
Raton
Vermejo Park Ranch
Tererro
Los Pinos Guest Ranch

Best Resorts

Taos
Quail Ridge Inn Resort
Tesuque
The Bishop's Lodge
Rancho Encantado

Best Ski Lodges

Angel Fire
The Legends Hotel
Taos Ski Valley
Austing Haus Hotel
St. Bernard Condominiums

The landscape of northern New Mexico ranges from dry, high desert terrain to the heavily forested ridges of the Rocky Mountain range, and all of it is beautiful. There's the dramatic gorge carved by the Rio Grande near Taos, the apple orchards of Dixon and Velarde, the colorful outcroppings of rock at Abiquiu, the haunted mesas in the Española river valley, the remote woods of the Pecos wilderness, the golden fields of Tierra Amarilla (which means "yellow land"), and captivating mountain peaks — often capped with a blanket of snow — running from Santa Fe all the way north to the Colorado border.

Of northern New Mexico towns, **Santa Fe** is the undisputed trend-setter, a role it has long been accustomed to playing. Coronado's search for the Seven Cities of Gold led him to Santa Fe in 1540, and by 1598 a permanent Spanish settlement had been established in the area. Later the city was to see a boom in traffic and trade as it became a major stop on both the Camino Real and Santa Fe Trail. In 1912, Santa Fe was named the state capital when New Mexico became a state, but the city never lost its ties to the Spanish traditions of its early European settlers, or to the Native American heritage of the Pueblo Indians, who had inhabited the land long before Coronado's visit. Today, visitors to Santa Fe can experience the legacy of the three cultures that have most influenced the city's history: Native American, Hispanic, and Anglo.

For a relatively small city (the population is less than 60,000), Santa Fe has a remarkable arts scene. Art galleries are everywhere, surrounding the central plaza and lining nearby Canyon Road. The Museum of Fine Arts, which adjoins the plaza, counts a number of Georgia O'Keeffe's works among its collection, and the Girard Wing at the Museum of International Folk Art is not to be missed. The Museum of Indian Arts and Culture, the Institute of American Indian Arts Museum, and the Wheelwright Museum of the American Indian are all devoted to the art of American Indians. Musical organizations include the Orchestra of Santa Fe, the Santa Fe Desert Chorale, the Santa Fe Chamber Music Festival, the Santa Fe Symphony, and the Santa Fe Women's Ensemble. In addition, there are a number of local groups that regularly mount local theatrical productions, but it is the world-famous Santa Fe Opera that garners the artistic accolades during the summer.

The Santa Fe dining scene is equally rich. The number of restaurants is staggering for such a small population, but the standards maintained by most dining establishments are generally quite high. Santa Fe has everything from nationally known eateries, to small, family-run spots serving home-cooked native dishes, to a surprising variety of ethnic restaurants.

Shoppers need not go home empty-handed either; there seems to be at least one boutique in town for every gallery or restaurant. Many visitors enjoy purchasing jewelry and crafts directly from the Native Americans who sell their creations under the portal of the Palace of the Governors on the plaza.

The Palace of the Governors itself has long been the focal point of Santa Fe's central plaza. It was built in 1609 to house the Spanish governor and is the oldest government building in the United States. Other city landmarks include the beautiful St. Francis Cathedral one block from the plaza, the Loretto Chapel with its miraculous stairway, the San Miguel Mission, and what is supposedly the "Oldest House in the U.S.A." a block from the capitol building. The Santa Fe Ski Basin is just 18 miles from downtown.

Taos, about 80 miles north of Santa Fe, has an appeal that rivals the capital city's but on a smaller scale. The extraordinary "high road to Taos," which passes through the weaving village of **Chimayo** with its sacred Santuario and the alpine village of Truchas, is the most scenic but not the fastest route between Taos and Santa Fe.

The arts are also important in Taos, and the skiing at **Taos Ski Valley** is among the best in the country. The Millicent Rogers Museum collections include Hispanic art and colorful weavings, the historic Kit Carson home is one block from the Taos plaza, and charming Bent Street is lined with fine shops and galleries.

Pueblo de Taos, on the outskirts of town, is one of the most visited sights in the area. The unique multilevel adobe structures of the pueblo are reputed to be the oldest continuously inhabited residences in the United States. Other interesting pueblos in Northern New Mexico include San Ildefonso, Santa Clara, San Juan, and Nambe.

The **Chama** area near the Colorado border is popular for hunting, fishing, and cross-country skiing, and the Cumbres-Toltec steam train ride from Chama into Colorado is a scenic journey. At Los Alamos, high in the Jemez Mountains, one is acutely aware of the contrast between the modern birth of the atomic bomb at Los Alamos National Laboratory, and the ancient cliff dwellings at nearby Bandelier National Monument. Other ancient Indian ruins in northern New Mexico include the Puye Cliff Dwellings, Pecos National Monument, and Chaco Culture National Historic Park.

ANGEL FIRE

The Legends Hotel

P.O. Drawer B
Angel Fire, NM 87710
505-377-6401
800-633-7463
Fax: 505-377-4200

> *A ski lodge
> in the heart of
> Angel Fire*

General Manager: Gary Plante. **Accommodations:** 139 rooms. **Rates:** $90–$225 during ski season, $70–$125 other times. **Added:** 11.63% tax. **Payment:** Major credit cards. **Children:** Free in room with parents. **Pets:** Not permitted. **Smoking:** Nonsmoking rooms available. **Open:** Year-round.

In the Moreno Valley of the Rocky Mountains, 26 miles east of Taos, Angel Fire is a sprawling year-round resort village. Skiing gets top billing, with a 2,180-foot vertical drop and 55 downhill ski trails. A sophisticated snow-making system covers 60 percent of the terrain, making this resort a good bet whatever the yearly snowfall.

When the ski slopes close in early April, Angel Fire transforms. Its championship 18-hole golf course has rolling greens backed by mountains. Tennis, horseback riding, and boating are all popular. Fishing is in a private, stocked lake (no license is needed). Big- and small-game hunting can be arranged through Resort Sports in the resort village. Chamber music concerts and community theater productions highlight the summer season.

Spread over 12,000 acres, Angel Fire has both condos and single-family residences. The Legends Hotel, the only hotel at the resort, opened in late 1987. Originally the Plaza, the new hotel is a complete renovation, although its site, an Indian burial ground, has caused some to speculate that the building is haunted. At the base of the ski slopes, the Legends has a contemporary design. A five-story atrium encloses a small pool and hot tub.

> **The Mill serves breakfast and lunch; Springer's is the elegant dining room. Annie O's, named for Annie Oakley, is the place to relax over drinks.**

The guest rooms lack personality, but they are unusually spacious, an advantage for skiers with lots of gear. All have two queen-size beds. The studios, which accommodate two people, have cooking facilities (four-burner stove, oven, refrigerator) and a Murphy bed. Suites, which are a combination of a studio and hotel room, can sleep six. Presidential rooms are extra large and have private patios with mountain views.

CHAMA

The Lodge at Chama Land and Cattle Company

P.O. Box 127
Chama, NM 87520
505-756-2133
Fax: 505-756-2133

> *A luxurious and comfortable hunting lodge*

General Manager: Frank Simms. **Accommodations:** 11 rooms. **Rates:** $200 per person per day, suites $100 additional per day. **Included:** Meals, guide, transportation, horseback riding, and fishing; lodging-only rates available for nonhunting/fishing companions. **Added:** 5.375% tax. **Payment:** Personal checks; no credit cards. **Children:** Under 12 not permitted; over 12, $200 per night. **Pets:** Not permitted. **Smoking:** Permitted. **Open:** Year-round; hunting September–January.

Chama Land and Cattle Company, in the San Juan Mountains of northern New Mexico, is a working ranch of more than 32,000 acres. The ranch spreads over beautiful terrain ranging from oak foothills and meadows of aspen and spruce to alpine country up to 10,000 feet. Here, hidden from public view, is an exclusive, luxurious lodge catering to hunters and anglers as well as business groups. Repeat visitors account for three-fourths of its clientele.

> **In winter, the lodge is a great place for a mountain vacation, especially if you like cross-country skiing, sleigh rides, and observing wildlife.**

Elk hunting is at the heart of the lodge's operation. The ranch has one of the largest elk herds on private land in the country. Ninety percent of its hunters take 6x6 bull elk or better; the rest take 5x5s. Each hunter has a private guide, and travel is by four-wheel-drive vehicle, horseback, or on foot. Hunts last about three or four days. Other game hunted include mule deer and black bear.

Guests fish in mountain lakes stocked with rainbow, German brown, brook, and native cutthroat trout. Comments in the guest register tell the story. "Better fishing than in Alaska," wrote one guest.

The stone lodge is a sprawling ranch house on a hill overlooking the Chama Valley. (There's a security gate at the entrance, so be sure you're expected.) The main room, called the Great Room, is truly handsome, with a 22-foot stone fireplace in the center and original western art. Stuffed elk, deer, and bear, all native to the area, as well as wildlife from other parts of the world, set the tone.

The guest rooms line the adjoining hall. Large and well appointed, each has its own theme, with wildlife as the focal point. Leather and wood, Indian pottery and woven work make the rooms distinctive. The huge junior suites have kiva fireplaces and rugs made by the famous Ortega weavers in Chimayo.

Guests take meals in the Great Room. All of the food is made from scratch and served with a flair. An open bar is included in the rate. For relaxation, there's a hot tub and sauna.

Unser's Oso Ranch and Lodge

P.O. Box 808
Chama, NM 87520
505-756-2954
800-882-5190, ext. 25

A friendly lodge owned by the racing Unsers

Managers: John and Pamela Adamson. **Accommodations:** 6 rooms.
Rates: $90–$140 single, $115–$165 double. **Included:** Breakfast and facilities. **Added:** 6% tax. **Payment:** Major credit cards. **Children:** Charged as adults. **Pets:** Not permitted.
Smoking: Not permitted. **Open:** Year-round.

On the banks of the Chama River, about two miles south of Chama, is a lodge geared to year-round outdoor enthusiasts. Guests fish in the river or lake in spring, summer, and fall, and there's ice fishing in winter. In summer there's riding, hiking, and birding; in the winter, snowmobiling and cross-country skiing. Hunting gets the emphasis in the fall. Friendly managers and Oso Ranch's intimate size make it an inviting place to visit during any season.

Horseback riding, pack trips, hayrides, and cookouts can be arranged by Oso Ranch. The Cumbres and Toltec Scenic Railroad, with departures from Chama, is a popular day trip. The train runs daily from June to mid-October.

Built as a private lodge, Oso Ranch is now owned by well-known race car drivers Al Unser, Sr. and Jr., who live nearby. The ranch covers 1,400 acres of rolling country dotted with juniper, pine, and spruce. The guest rooms are in a log building that doubles as a dining room and social center.

The main lodge room is log cabin rustic, decorated with hunting and fishing trophies, Indian and western art, and a large stone fireplace. Guests can relax by the antique woodstove and enjoy the wide-screen satellite TV, pool table, and a library of western history. Meals are served family-style. The fare is good country food — soups, stews, biscuits, and grilled meats. Breakfasts are hearty.

One hall leads to the guest rooms, with a choice of twin or

king-size beds. The door of each room is a work of art, a suede and leather creation depicting an animal indigenous to the area. The rooms are not only comfortable but thoughtfully decorated, and the work of local artists hangs on the walls. Each room takes its theme from the animal on the door; for instance, the one with a rainbow trout on the door has such accents as a rod, creel, and tackle box mounted on the wall and a display of fishing flies. Some rooms have ceiling fans; all have TVs and private baths.

Without a doubt, fishing is the most popular activity at Oso Ranch. Anglers have a choice of the Chama, Little Navajo, and Brazos rivers and private streams for rainbow, brook, or brown trout and Kokanee salmon. The ranch also has two stocked ponds that can be fished without a license.

Oso Ranch becomes a hunting lodge in the appropriate seasons. Elk, mule deer, mountain lion, and black bear (*oso* is Spanish for bear) are the predominant game. Hunt packages include private-land hunting permits; New Mexico license and hunting fees are not included. The ranch will also assist in arrangements for taxidermy, meat storage, and freezing.

CHIMAYO

Hacienda Rancho de Chimayo

P.O. Box 11
State Road 520
Chimayo, NM 87522
505-351-2222

Guests flock to the restaurant here

Owners: The Jaramillo family. **Accommodations:** 7 rooms, all with private bath. **Rates:** $49–$85 single, $59–$95 double. **Included:** Continental breakfast. **Added:** 8.75% tax. **Payment:** Major credit cards. **Children:** Over age 9 welcome; additional $10 per night. **Pets:** Not permitted. **Smoking:** Not permitted. **Open:** Year-round.

Heading north from Santa Fe, the road to Chimayo turns east at Pojoaque. Once you leave U.S. 285, between Santa Fe and Taos, you're definitely on "the road less taken." Highways 503 and 520 are beautiful stretches of road, rising and falling over the wide-open countryside, with expansive views of the Sangre de Cristo Mountains in the distance.

Chimayo, with a population of about 3,500, is an old Spanish settlement dating from 1598. Known today for its weavers, it is one of New Mexico's most famous craft villages, continuing a tradition begun by the Ortega family eight generations ago. Shops in the area include Ortega's Weavers and Art Gallery, Trujillo's Weavers, and El Chimayo Weavers. Visitors come from all parts of the country to buy their creations, especially blankets, rugs, curtains, and place mats.

> So popular is Rancho de Chimayo's cuisine that a cookbook has been published featuring the restaurant's most loved recipes.

The Jaramillos, another old Chimayo family, trace their roots to the area's first Spanish settlers, and they have created their own tradition in recent years. Today they have two operations, a large restaurant serving native cuisine and an inn across the street. In the 1880s, two Jaramillo brothers helped each other build family homes, now separated by the little road leading into town. In 1965, their descendants restored one of the homes and converted it into a hacienda-style restaurant.

Highly popular despite its remote location, Restaurante Rancho de Chimayo is a festive spot. The dining areas are authentic Southwest, with hand-stripped vigas and white-washed walls. Terraced patios spill down the hillside. Everybody has a great time, developing a sense of camaraderie in this place well off the beaten track.

Comidas nativas (native dishes) are all tempting: chicken breasts topped with red chili and melted cheese; sopapillas stuffed with beef, beans, Spanish rice, carne adovada (pork marinated and cooked in a red chili sauce); and more than a dozen other choices. For less adventurous palates, such dishes as hamburgers and trout amandine are on the menu as well.

The restaurant is usually open from noon until 9:00 P.M. but closes on Mondays during part of the year. Whatever the season, be sure to make reservations (505-351-4444).

Since the restaurant was so successful, the Jaramillos restored the second home across the road and opened it as an inn in 1984. Now travelers can dine at the restaurant and spend the night at Hacienda Rancho de Chimayo.

The hundred-year-old brown adobe home, trimmed in white, has a wreath of dried peppers on the front door. The atmosphere is casual, with a country flavor. All the guest rooms open onto a sunny courtyard with a central fountain, and all have fireplaces. Stepping into any of them is a beautiful surprise: the decor is not Santa Fe or Taos but country Victorian. Antique mahogany beds, Queen Anne chairs, and touches of lace combine for a look of casual elegance.

Uno, which can adjoin Dos, is the largest room, with high ceilings, twin pine-cone beds that can be pushed together to form a king, a sofa, an easy chair with ottoman in front of the fireplace, and double doors that open onto a private balcony. The antique dresser, mirrored wardrobe, and desk make a nice matching set. Even the bath is appealing, with a wooden vanity and a water closet. Siete is exquisite, with a king-size four-poster bed, a Queen Anne chair, and antique mirror.

Most rooms can be joined with at least one other for families or couples traveling together. Cuatro can adjoin Tres to form a two-bedroom–living room suite. Guests have a choice of twin, double, queen-, and king-size beds.

Continental breakfast, served in your room, the lobby, or the courtyard, is likely to be croissants and fresh fruit. You can spend the morning visiting the weavers' shops and El Santuario, a church where miraculous cures are said to have taken place since it was built in the early 1800s. Every Easter, thousands of faithful New Mexicans make a pilgrimage on foot to visit the sacred Santuario.

La Posada de Chimayo

P.O. Box 463
Chimayo, NM 87522
505-351-4605
Fax: 505-351-4605

A B&B with southwestern charm

Innkeeper: Sue Farrington. **Accommodations:** 2 suites and 2 rooms, all with private bath. **Rates:** $75–$80 single, $90–$100 double; $25 additional for third person in room; reduced weekly rates in winter. **Included:** Breakfast. **Added:** 5.375% tax. **Payment:** Personal checks; credit cards for reservation deposits only. **Children:** Over 12 welcome. **Pets:** With approval. **Smoking:** Permitted only outside. **Open:** Year-round.

The tiny village of Chimayo, renowned for its masterful weavers, is not exactly on the beaten path. From Santa Fe, 25 miles to the south, you wind through wide-open countryside after leaving the highway. Taos, via the High Road, which passes through the craft villages of Cordova and Truchas, is 45 miles north.

> **Breakfast is not for the faint-hearted, the innkeeper warns. Bring a big appetite, because breakfast portions are generous, and there is always plenty to go around.**

Even more remote is La Posada de Chimayo. You turn off Highway 76 onto a narrow dirt road that ambles by the landmarks noted in the directions Sue Farrington has sent you: "Moose," "a building with a fan-shaped roof," and "a house with blue trim." Just when you think you must have missed it — or that you're on the wrong road altogether — there it is, with a sign in front to prove it.

The rooms are in separate buildings, two in a guesthouse next to Sue Farrington's own home and two in a restored farmhouse down the road. Built in 1981, the guesthouse blends beautifully into the surroundings, quite a trick considering that the ancient settlement of Chimayo dates from 1598. Sue calls it a "new old adobe."

A traditional adobe structure, the guesthouse has viga ceilings, brick floors, and corner fireplaces. The furniture is comfortable, and the decorations are pure Southwest, with Mexican rugs and handwoven bedspreads as accents. The house has two separate apartments. Each has a sitting room with a "Taos bed" (sleeps one), a small bedroom with a double bed, and a bath. There's a porch swing on the shared front porch.

The farmhouse is just around the bend. It was built in stages beginning in 1891, and Sue completely renovated it in 1992. The two spacious guest rooms have Mexican furnishings and their own fireplaces. Guests staying in these rooms are free to use the adjoining common living area, where breakfast is served family-style for all guests.

Sue's breakfast specialties include Spanish tortillas made with green chiles, cornmeal pancakes topped with honey-lemon syrup, bread pudding, and French toast stuffed with cream cheese, chopped nuts, and vanilla, topped with apricot-orange sauce.

In addition to visiting the local sights, notably the weavers' shops and a historic church where miraculous cures are said to have taken place, you can take day trips to several Indian pueblos, Bandelier National Monument, Santa Fe, and Taos. Skiers who want to avoid the crowds can head to Sipapu Ski Area. There are also hiking trails in the nearby desert country and alpine forests.

CIMARRON

St. James Hotel

Route 1, Box 2
Cimarron, NM 87714
505-376-2664
Fax: 505-376-2623

The site of many real-life Wild West dramas

Owners: The Champions. **Accommodations:** 13 rooms in hotel, most with private bath, 12 rooms in annex. **Rates:** $50 single, $70 double; suites $100. **Added:** 9% tax. **Payment:** Major credit cards. **Children:** Welcome. **Pets:** With prior approval only. **Smoking:** Permitted. **Open:** Year-round.

In the dusty little town of Cimarron, about an hour's drive southwest of Raton, is a historic hotel with delightfully different rooms and a restaurant guaranteed to please. It all started back in 1870, when the man who had been Abraham Lincoln's personal chef headed west to seek his fortune. Henri Lambert, a French immigrant, never found gold, but he bought some land at a stop along the Santa Fe Trail and built a saloon. In 1880, he added a hotel of thick adobe.

Back then, Cimarron was a tough kind of place, a hangout

for desperadoes, horse thieves, mountain men, and traders. The hotel, as the center of the town's social life, was the last stop for some of its patrons: 26 men were killed within its walls. Bullet holes in the tin ceiling of the former bar, now the restaurant, bear testament to violence that became legendary. Outlaws like Blackjack Ketchum, Jesse James, and the notorious gunman Clay Allison all stayed at the St. James. So did plenty of respectable folks. Annie Oakley met with Buffalo Bill Cody here and joined his Wild West show. Zane Grey wrote a novel here. Frederic Remington stayed here while he sketched nearby scenery. Wyatt Earp and Doc Holiday also stayed at the St. James.

> With such a past, it's no wonder that the St. James is rumored to have ghosts. But the Champions are excellent hosts, and the food is fantastic, so have another glass of wine and enjoy.

The St. James has been charmingly restored. Furnished throughout with period pieces, the hotel is a showcase of western history. The lobby is furnished with Victorian velvet sofas, and an elk, moose, or buffalo head hangs on each wall. There's an old safe in one hallway, a roulette table in another, and old photos line the main hallway to the guest rooms.

The Jesse James room has red brocade wallpaper, red velvet chairs, a brass bed with a red quilt, and a cranberry lamp. Bat Masterson's room has green velvet wallpaper, a marble-topped dresser, a mountain lion rug, lace curtains, and a separate sitting room with a daybed. Buffalo Bill's room is the largest. Next door is a tiny poker-playing room — past and present. Mary Lambert's room, named for the original hotel owner's wife, is especially attractive, with a fabric-draped ceiling and white fireplace. Some claim Mary's presence can still be felt in the room.

Most of the rooms have fireplaces (no longer used), marble washstands, and private baths, and some of the tubs have hand-held showers. There are no TVs or phones in the rooms, but both are available in the lobby and lounge. Motel-style rooms are available in the annex, but these are not recommended; the point of coming to the St. James is for its history.

It's only fitting that a classic hotel have a fine restaurant. Crystal chandeliers and cloth napkins lend a touch of elegance, and the food is the best for miles around. Feast on stuffed flounder Florentine, filled with crabmeat and fresh vegetables and topped with velouté sauce. Or pollo Gismonda: breaded chicken breast in a spiced spinach ring, covered with sautéed mushrooms. Broiled swordfish steak, shrimp Diablo, veal Marsala, tournedos of beef, pasta carbonara, plus a dozen or more other entrées give you plenty of choice. Dinner entrées range from $11 to $19.

The St. James also has an informal dining room and a bar, with patio dining in the summer. Across the street is the history-filled Old Mill Museum, open from late spring to early fall. A National Historic District, Cimarron has other sites worth a visit. Two miles down the road is the Philmont Scout Ranch, the national campground for the Boy Scouts of America. Fishing, hunting, and skiing are popular area attractions.

EL PRADO

Salsa del Salto

P.O. Box 1468
Taos Ski Valley Road
El Prado, NM 87529
505-776-2422
800-530-3097
Fax: 505-776-2422

> *An inn*
> *on the road to*
> *Taos Ski Valley*

Innkeepers: Mary Hockett and Dadou Mayer. **Accommodations:** 8 rooms. **Rates:** $85–$160; $10 each additional person. **Included:** Breakfast. **Added:** 9.32% tax. **Payment:** Major credit cards. **Children:** Over age 6 welcome. **Pets:** Not permitted. **Smoking:** Not permitted. **Open:** Year-round.

Soon after passing the funky town of Arroyo Seco, you will see the sign for Salsa del Salto. At the end of a private road in the Taos valley, the inn has expansive views in all directions. But the inn's location, about halfway between Taos and the Taos Ski Valley, and the incredible vistas are only two of the reasons to visit Salsa del Salto. The pool, hot tub, and tennis court allow guests to enjoy resort amenities without having to share them with the crowds of a typical resort.

The inn itself is a newer two-story adobe designed by noted architect Antoine Predock. Among the unique features he included are special corner windows that make the most of the surrounding views. The house itself wraps around a quiet courtyard.

> **Gourmet breakfasts are served next to a huge stone fireplace and an old-fashioned cast iron stove. Fresh croissants and homemade jams and jellies are specialties. Chips and salsa are served here in the afternoon.**

Guest rooms are crisply and very comfortably furnished with whitewashed wooden furnishings and southwestern prints covering down comforters. The Master's room is a favorite of honeymooners, with its panoramic views, high pitched ceilings, a huge bath, and a fireplace. The Truchas has views of the Truchas peaks, and La Familia has two connecting rooms. All have private baths and king-size beds. The are no TVs in the rooms, but there is one for guests at the top of the stairs.

For skiers, who make up a large part of the inn's winter clientele, there's a ski rack in the entrance hall. Throughout the inn, the recognition of one's need for rest and recreation sets it apart from more average bed-and-breakfasts.

ESPAÑOLA

Inn at the Delta

304 Paseo de Onate
Española, NM 87532
505-753-9466
Fax: 505-753-9466

> *This luxurious inn exudes south-western charm*

Owners: The Garcia family. **Accommodations:** 10 rooms. **Rates:** $85–$150 double; additional persons $10 per day. **Included:** Breakfast. **Added:** Tax. **Payment:** Major credit cards. **Children:** Under 12 free in room with parents. **Pets:** Call first. **Smoking:** Most rooms are nonsmoking. **Open:** Year-round.

Anthony Garcia is a man of many talents. He's a dentist, he operates a flower shop, and he runs the best restaurant in Española. In 1994, he opened a southwestern-style inn beside the restaurant. To be fair, he had some help getting started. His parents and grandfather opened the Delta Bar on the property in 1949. Because it paralleled the highway they ended up building it in a triangular shape. Rooms have been added to the structure so that its original deltoid shape can barely be detected, but the name has stayed with the place.

> **Española is centrally located in northern New Mexico, making it equally convenient to Santa Fe, Taos, and Bandelier National Monument, as well as other area sights.**

Anthony turned the adjoining family home into a restaurant and decorated it with art, antiques, and artifacts from his own private collection. Specializing in steaks and seafood ($11–$24), Anthony's at the Delta quickly became one of the most popular eateries around, even drawing diners from out of town. Since first-rate accommodations in Española were sparse, Anthony decided to open Inn at the Delta. Frequent diners at the restaurant quickly discovered that Anthony had created yet another appealing and successful enterprise.

Set well back from the highway, the inn comprises several one- and two-story adobe buildings that house a total of ten guest rooms. Each room has its own private entrance and front portal accented with hand-carved columns. Inside there are more hand-carved columns and moldings, split cedar viga ceilings providing a fresh cedar scent, and over 600 square feet of space.

Each room has plenty of amenities, such as a fireplace, telephone, large TV, sitting area, and one or two queen beds; but the handcrafted furnishings by local artisans set these rooms apart. Headboards are beautifully carved, as are armoires, used here as closets, or roperas. Some pieces are whitewashed, others have a sheer turquoise stain, while some are left in their natural state, but all are lovely and have a Spanish flavor. Large decorative mirrors of tin and copper and colorful retablos are also locally crafted and add visual appeal, as do rich southwestern print fabrics, tile floors, and Native American art. Every bath has cheerful Mexican tile with coordinating ceramic wash basins and a Jacuzzi tub.

Brick walkways lined with flowers lead from the guest rooms to Anthony's own home, where breakfast is served. Not surprisingly, the Garcia home is filled with art. Large high-ceilinged rooms showcase charcoal portraits of Native Americans, kachina dolls, Indian pottery, Navajo rugs, and straw basketry. Even breakfasts are artfully presented. Chile cheese cornbread is baked in a heart-shaped pan, omelettes are served inside loaves of bread, and fresh fruit parfaits arrive in Mexican glasses. Fruit flan, quiche, yogurt, coffee, tea, and fresh juice round out the morning meal. For your evening repast, of course, you don't have to go far; Anthony's at the Delta is just at the end of the driveway.

Rancho de San Juan

P.O. Box 4140
Fairview Station
Española, NM 87533
505-753-6818
Fax: 505-753-6818

> *A high desert
> oasis at the base
> of Black Mesa*

Innkeepers: David Heath and John Johnson. **Accommodations:** 5 rooms. **Rates:** $85–$135 double; $10 less per room in low season; $20 additional per night over some holidays; discounts for stays of a week or more. **Included:** Full breakfast. **Added:** 5.375%. **Payment:** Major credit cards. **Children:** Over 6 welcome. **Pets:** Not permitted. **Smoking:** Outside only. **Open:** Year-round.

Although it seems a little remote, Rancho de San Juan is actually fairly well situated for exploring northern New Mexico; and if you're looking for a true hideaway you could hardly find a more tranquil spot. David Heath and John Johnson built the inn on 225 acres of piñon-studded high desert terrain at the base of Black Mesa, about seven miles north of San Juan pueblo. To the west are beautiful views of the Ojo Caliente river valley below, outlined by majestic cottonwoods, and the Jemez Mountains in the distance. To the east there are striking sandstone rock formations for guests to explore.

Guests check in at a pueblo-style hacienda that houses the common living room, dining room, two guest rooms, and the innkeepers' own home. A gracious space, the high-ceilinged hacienda is southwestern in style and attractively decorated in desert tones with art and antiques from the innkeepers' private collection. Guests can enjoy sunset views from the living room before dining on fine fare in Rancho de San Juan's intimate dining room.

Seating only 18 at a time (there are two sittings per night), the restaurant serves dinner Wednesday through Saturday, and brunch on Sunday. Since space is limited, reservations are required, but overnight guests get first priority. Although the menu changes daily, the cuisine has a northern Italian and French country slant, and there's usually a choice of two entrées and two desserts each day. A typical meal could include vichyssoise, a salad with toasted sunflower seeds, swordfish provençale in a tomato, wine, herb and garlic sauce, twice-baked potatoes, fresh asparagus, and a strawberry and kiwi fruit tart for dessert.

> **Attention to detail makes Rancho de San Juan a standout. When the innkeepers were planning the half-mile-long driveway, they walked it over and over, hand-staking every foot, so as to give their guests the best views on the drive in.**

The Acoma and San Juan, named for area pueblos, are guest rooms attached to the main hacienda, although they do have private entrances. The Acoma is handicapped-accessible, with twin beds topped by patchwork quilts. The queen bed in the San Juan is covered in a lacy crocheted spread, and the framed dried flower and butterfly arrangement above was made by David. Both rooms have fireplaces and small porches ideal for taking in evening sunsets.

Zia, Santa Clara, and Black Mesa Garden are in a separate building across the inn's central courtyard. Zia is the smallest but most colorful, with lively Mexican woven drapes, an antiqued red chest, and pressed tin mirror. Santa Clara is romantic, with a rose print duvet, a rocking chair in front of the fireplace, and a private patio. Black Mesa Garden, decorated in French country prints, is the most deluxe, with a private garden patio and fireplace. Decanters of cream sherry, terry robes, starched linens, and Mexican tile baths add luxury to every room. The inn can arrange for in-room salon services such as leg waxing, herbal wraps, facials, and massages.

Since Rancho de San Juan is set in some of the prettiest

countryside around, you may not feel the need to venture far, but if the sightseeing bug does bite, the inn is 35 miles from Santa Fe's plaza, 49 miles from Taos, 35 from Bandelier National Monument, 25 from the Puye Cliff Dwellings, and only 13 miles from the hot springs at Ojo Caliente.

GALISTEO

Galisteo Inn

HC 75, Box 4
Galisteo, NM 87540
505-982-1506

A country inn designed for relaxation

Owners: Joanna Kaufman and Wayne Aarniokoski. **Accommodations:** 12 rooms, 8 with private bath. **Rates:** $60–$70 single, $95–$175 double. **Included:** Breakfast. **Added:** 8.75% tax. **Payment:** Major credit cards. **Children:** Over 12 welcome; additional $15 per day if more than 2 people in room. **Pets:** Not permitted, though horses can be boarded. **Smoking:** Outside only. **Open:** Year-round except for last 3 weeks in January and early February.

A sleepy cat curls up on a Mexican bench. Visitors sit on willow furniture on the front porch and talk about their day while they watch a croquet match on the lush green lawn. Out back, the athletes are swimming in the pool or riding horses. Others are stealing a quiet moment with a book in the library.

About 250 years ago, what is now the Galisteo Inn was built as a Spanish homestead. Today, ancient trees shade its grounds, and a picturesque stone wall surrounds the property. The road out front is dirt. Santa Fe is a comfortable 23 miles away.

Here is a historic hacienda-style inn offering tranquility yet decorated with a modern eye. The living room has a big fireplace, a piano, and an extensive library. The guest rooms, all named for trees (the inn even smells like new wood), are airy and fairly spacious, decorated with Mexican furniture. Several have kiva fireplaces. Eight rooms have private baths; the others share two baths that are especially attractive, with viga ceilings and lots of Mexican tile.

Breakfast features homemade pastries such as blue corn muffins and scones, fresh fruit, juice, granola, and coffee. Special southwestern dinners are served Wednesday through Sunday evenings (about $25). The menu changes weekly, but you can expect inventive entrées such as antelope medallions with three-cheese tamales and roasted vegetable salsa or

> The inn has its own horses, and guided rides can be arranged. Mountain bikes for touring the desert are available, and guests can rest their tired bones in the hot tub or sauna.

grilled chicken cannelloni with ancho cream and Indian bean relish.

LAS VEGAS

Plaza Hotel

230 Old Town Plaza
Las Vegas, NM 87701
505-425-3591
800-328-1882
Fax: 505-425-9659

> *A historic hotel on Las Vegas's plaza*

General Manager: William Slick. **Accommodations:** 38 rooms. **Rates:** $55–$75 single, $60–$85 double; suites $95–

$120. **Added:** 9.88% tax. **Payment:** Major credit cards. **Children:** Welcome. **Pets:** Permitted with $25 deposit. **Smoking:** Nonsmoking rooms available. **Open:** Year-round.

In 1879, the railroad came to Las Vegas, making it the first large town in the territory to be reached by rail. Of course, a railroad town needed a hotel, so in 1881 the local businessmen, headed by Don Benigno Romero, formed the Plaza Hotel Company. Their three-story hotel, hailed as "the Belle of the Southwest," opened in 1882.

> **Now on the National Register of Historic Places, the Plaza Hotel is a lodging with charm. Touches such as fringed lampshades, botanical prints, frosted glass fixtures, and lace curtains add nostalgia.**

In its earliest days, notorious outlaws such as Billy the Kid were among the Plaza's patrons. Then in 1913, the hotel brushed shoulders with Hollywood: the popular silent film star Romaine Fielding selected the Plaza as his studio headquarters, renaming it the Hotel Romaine (the lettering can still be seen on one facade of the building). Later, cowboy actor and director Tom Mix came to town. Scenes for several of his movies were filmed in Las Vegas and included shots of the renamed Plaza Hotel.

An agricultural depression hit the area in the mid-1920s, and the hotel suffered along with the rest of the town. The decline of the one-time "Belle" continued until 1982, when William and Katherine Slick joined with its owners, Lonnie and Dana Lucero, to restore it.

The guest rooms were doubled in size and are now spacious and airy, with high ceilings. The antique furnishings include a superior collection of armoires, some with inlaid patterns, not only convenient for the traveler but also good for camouflaging TVs. The baths are simple, with separate dressing areas. Happily, modern comfort has not been overlooked. The rooms are air-conditioned, and there are telephones.

Just off the lobby, furnished with antiques but not opulent in style, are Byron T's western saloon and a pleasant dining room. Breakfast in the dining room is very reasonably priced. The lunch menu is basic, consisting mainly of sandwiches, burgers, and salads, while dinner selections range from New

Mexican specialties to filet mignon ($7–$14). Byron T's often features entertainment in the evenings.

Las Vegas has other historic sites, beginning with a walking tour of the Plaza area. There's also the Rough Riders Memorial and City Museum, with Rough Rider memorabilia, Indian artifacts, and city history. Outdoor activities include horseback riding, fishing, hay rides, and pack trips into the Pecos Wilderness. The Indian ruins at Pecos National Monument, about halfway between Las Vegas and Santa Fe, are worthwhile, as is the drive between the two cities.

POJOAQUE

Rancho Jacona

Route 5 (Pojoaque)
P.O. Box 250
Santa Fe, NM 87501
505-455-7948

> *Spacious casitas
> ideal for families*

Innkeeper: Sheri Tepper. **Accommodations:** 6 casitas. **Rates:** $80–$165. **Added:** 8.75% tax. **Payment:** Major credit cards. **Children:** Welcome. **Pets:** With prior approval. **Smoking:** Permitted outside only. **Open:** Year-round.

Rancho Jacona is a world unto itself, about halfway between Santa Fe and Los Alamos. Casitas dot the expansive grounds; the Sangre de Cristo mountains can be seen in the distance. Rare breeds of farm animals such as the San Clemente goat and Shetland sheep, of which there are only six herds in the entire United States, are raised here. The Pojoaque riverbed backs the property, and from there it's a quick escape to the high desert mesas.

Accommodations are comfortable and unusually spacious. Rabbit House is the largest casita, with a huge living room, kiva fireplace, cable television, two bedrooms (one with its own fireplace), and a full kitchen complete with a washer, dryer, and ironing board. Piglet House and Parrot House are the only casitas to share a common wall. Billed as two-room studios, they are still roomier than an average hotel room.

Each has a sitting area, kitchen, and fireplace. Views of the Rio Grande valley and Jemez Mountains are framed by the bedroom window in Piglet House. Lifelike parrots hang from the ceiling in Parrot House. Raccoon House also has a studio arrangement with an eat-in kitchen, large fireplace, queen-size Murphy bed, and twin bunk beds.

> **Parents should know that there is plenty here to capture the attention of little ones. Koi swim in a pond out front, a swimming pool is open in summer, and each casita has an outdoor grill. One of the goats is just for petting, and pigs are also raised on the ranch.**

Coyote House is a personal favorite, and the most private because it is farthest from the main house and other casitas. The views from Coyote's front porch and living room window are among the best on the property: you can almost see the ski runs at the Santa Fe Ski Basin; with binoculars you probably would. Lace curtains, colorful rag rugs and wood furniture add a homey touch. Rooster House, a long adobe with a low ceiling, is the oldest casita. Built about 200 years ago to house farmhands, it is cheerfully furnished in yellow and blue. Both Coyote House and Rooster House have two bedrooms, and all of the casitas have fireplaces and kitchens. Because they have cooking facilities, and because the rates are based on the size of the casita rather than the number of guests staying in each unit, the casitas are economical for families or couples traveling together. A full-size crib is available.

Although Rancho Jacona feels remote, it is a convenient jumping-off point for sightseeing in northern New Mexico. Santa Fe and Los Alamos are both 20 minutes away; Bandelier National Monument is just 15 minutes from Los Alamos; the beginning of the "high road to Taos" is a five-minute drive from the ranch; and the Puye Cliff Dwellings are nearby, as are a number of Indian pueblos.

RANCHOS DE TAOS

Adobe and Pines Inn

P.O. Box 837
Ranchos de Taos, NM 87557
505-751-9047
800-723-8267
Fax: 505-758-8423

*A pleasant inn
in a 150-year-old
adobe home*

Innkeepers: Chuck and Charil Fulkerson. **Accommodations:** 5 rooms. **Rates:** $85–$145. **Included:** Full breakfast. **Added:** 10.25% tax. **Minimum stay:** 2 nights when Saturday included. **Payment:** Major credit cards. **Children:** Over 12 welcome. **Pets:** Not permitted. **Smoking:** Outdoors only. **Open:** Year-round.

The green pasture out front immediately begins to soothe when you turn into the Adobe and Pines driveway off Highway 68 on the outskirts of Taos. The relaxation process deepens when you leave your car and cross the old stone bridge on foot; and by the time you reach the inn's 80-foot-long portal you're ready to sink into one of the cushioned willow chairs that line the porch. At the far end of the portal is a 50-year-old mural painted by a Taos Pueblo Indian, and exterior doors and window trim are painted in a lively royal blue. Inside, you're greeted by two of the warmest innkeepers around, Chuck and Charil Fulkerson, and then shown to one of five individually decorated guest rooms.

Visiting from California, the Fulkersons fell in love with the 150-year-old adobe structure, bought it, and went home to pack their bags. Leaving their hectic California life-style behind, they say it only took about 15 minutes to adjust to the slower pace of northern New Mexico. At the Adobe and Pines, it might not even take you that long. The Fulkersons spent about six months renovating the hacienda-style building, and the result is an inn that is both peaceful and friendly.

Full breakfasts of Chuck's "killer muffins" (cranberry, blueberry, and lemon poppyseed, to name a few) and hot entrées such as stuffed French toast or southwestern soufflés are served in the sun room, added to the original building by the innkeepers in 1991. Even confirmed night owls will feel cheerful while dining on their morning meal in this festive room. Bright yellow walls and lots of windows with royal blue trim coordinate with the sunny yellow placemats and blue Mexican glassware. The whimsical china is made by local potter Steven Killborn, the willow furniture by a Dixon artisan. The room itself overlooks the garden, with its terraced cobblestone walls and colorful flower beds.

> This warm and tranquil hideaway is set back in a hollow on the edge of Taos. From the inn it is only a short walk to the historic Saint Francis de Assisi church.

All the guest rooms have private entrances, either through the garden or the front portal. All have queen-size beds, down comforters and pillows, and at least one fireplace. The cozy Puerta Azul is the smallest room. It has an iron bed, a built-in cupboard with carved doors, and a dutch door over a century old that can be opened to a view of the mountain peaks in the distance. The innkeepers liked the dutch door so much they had another one made for the entrance to the Puerta Verde room next door. In Puerta Verde there's a retablo built into the wall above the kiva fireplace and an iron four-poster bed.

The guest cottage has 460 square feet of space that includes a full kitchen and two fireplaces, one in the bathroom and one in the bedroom. The four-poster pole bed is topped with a pastel comforter that complements the unusual pastel mosaic floor. Charil's hand-painted windows in the kitchen add to the cottage's playful tone, and the tile bath is very inviting.

If the guest cottage's bath is pleasant, Puerta Rosa's is incredible. Several steps down from the bedroom, Puerta Rosa's bath is the size of a guest room all on its own. A large two-person tiled tub is sunk into the center of the hardwood floor. Off to one side is a shower. On the other side of the room is a fireplace with nearby bancos and a refrigerator perfect for storing a bottle of champagne. But it gets better; the bath even has a two-person sauna, perfect for restoring an aching body after a day on the ski slopes.

The inventive wrought-iron headboard and other pieces throughout Puerta Rosa's bedroom were made especially for it, and an old wooden door from Chuck's parents' homestead placed horizontally on a ledge near the ceiling adds a surprisingly decorative and rustic touch. Pink adobe walls and rich teal accents throughout give the room an earthy feel.

If you want views, Puerta Violeta is the room for you. The only upstairs guest room, Puerta Violeta has a private deck with views of Taos Mountain, and large picture windows in the bedroom and bath draw the mountain scenery right into the room, along with lots of New Mexico sunshine. Decorated in pastels, it's Charil's favorite.

When you're not spending time in your room, the Fulkersons are happy to help you with sightseeing and restaurant ideas. They'll also give you a map they made using back roads to get to the Taos Ski Basin that will help you avoid much of the traffic. Guests are also welcome to unwind on the garden terrace or gather for conversation in the guest living room.

RATON

Vermejo Park Ranch

P.O. Drawer E
Raton, NM 87740
505-445-3097
505-445-3474

> *A hunting ranch
> on over half a
> million acres*

General Manager: John Conner.
Accommodations: 45 rooms. **Rates:**
$275 per person per day; 5-day hunt packages from $1,500 per person. **Included:** Meals and fishing privileges with daily rate; meals, guides, and transportation with hunt packages. **Added:**

5.5% tax. **Payment:** Personal checks; no credit cards. **Children:** Ages 5–14 $140 additional per day. **Pets:** Not permitted. **Smoking:** Nonsmoking rooms available. **Open:** April through December.

Vermejo Park Ranch is one of the largest blocks of privately owned land in the country. Its 588,000 acres in the Sangre de Cristo Mountains date from an 1840s land grant encompassing 2 million acres. The ranch, owned since 1973 by the Penzoil Company, is now an outdoor recreation resort and a working cattle ranch. As a hunting and fishing destination, it offers extensive private grounds far removed from the masses.

> **Casa Grande, the former owner's mansion, is truly grand, with hand-carved ceilings, interior marble columns, Oriental rugs, and a 1904 Steinway. Its remote location makes you feel as if you've stumbled upon a forgotten castle. Be sure to ask for a tour.**

The nucleus of the resort is about forty miles from Raton, reached partially over a private road. In the early 1900s, a businessman from Chicago owned the ranch, and he built a mansion for himself and several houses for guests. Today's guests stay in seven of the houses or in wonderfully rustic Costillo Lodge, 28 miles from the headquarters. Accommodating up to 12 guests, it is usually reserved for groups. The mansion, exquisitely furnished with antiques, is used only on special occasions.

In 1911, elk were reestablished at Vermejo Park after having been killed off in the entire area in the early 1890s. Today, Vermejo claims to have New Mexico's largest elk herd. Its hunters generally have an overall 85 percent success rate, and more than 70 percent of all bulls taken score 6 x 6 or larger. Heavily populated with wildlife, the ranch also offers hunts for mule deer, antelope, bear, mountain lion, buffalo, and Merrium turkey. All the hunt packages include a private guide, a four-wheel-drive vehicle, hunting license, and game skinning and quartering.

Anglers can fish in ten lakes and 25 miles of creeks. Cutthroat, brook, rainbow, and brown trout, along with Coho salmon, are the featured catches. Fly-fishing schools are scheduled several times during the season. There's a limit of

12 fish per day. Other activities include horseback riding, hiking, and skeet shooting.

The lodging here is truly different from anywhere else in the Southwest. The setting is magnificent; you're surrounded by miles and miles of open wilderness. The guesthouses are indeed houses, with a variety of floor plans, and are set apart from each other like a little village. The furnishings are modern but not particularly luxurious or atmospheric. The bedrooms have either double or twin beds.

Meals are served in a log cabin lodge with a rustic, southwestern interior. The cuisine leans toward meat and potatoes, and guests choose from the menu that is printed daily. While lunch is served in the dining room, most guests ask for box lunches. Costillo Lodge has its own dining room.

SANTA FE

Adobe Abode

202 Chapelle
Santa Fe, NM 87501
505-983-3133
Fax: 505-983-3133

A B&B with a sense of fun

Innkeeper: Pat Harbour. **Accommodations:** 5 rooms. **Rates:** $95–$140 single, $100–$145 double; additional $25 for third person in room. **Included:** Full breakfast. **Added:** 10.25% tax. **Payment:** Major credit cards. **Children:** 10 and older preferred. **Pets:** Not permitted. **Smoking:** Permitted outside only. **Open:** Year-round.

Adobe Abode, on a residential street several blocks from Santa Fe's plaza, was built in 1907 by the Army to house officers from nearby Fort Marcy. The only exterior feature that makes Adobe Abode stand out from its neighbors is a purplish blue door. It's a hint of the creativity and whimsy that await inside.

The sunny living room, a gathering spot, is an eclectic mix of styles. A needlepoint chair from the Philippines, a comfortable easy chair with matching ottoman, Indian pottery, folk art animals, and a bright painting by the owner that hangs over the fireplace add color and visual interest to the room. Here guests are welcome to help themselves to cookies and sherry, or build a fire.

> The cowboy is celebrated in the Bronco casita. There are cowboy hats on the wall, and a saddle hangs on one corner of the large canopy bed spread with a cowboy print comforter. Atop the armoire is a colorful collection of kid's cowboy boots. Even the shower curtain is made of cowboy print fabric.

Two of the guest rooms have British themes, and three are uniquely southwestern. The art nouveau bed in the English Garden room is topped with a pretty floral spread and an antique quilt. Attractive artwork adorns the walls, and there's a marble-topped writing table for jotting down inspired thoughts. The Bloomsbury room has a four-poster bed draped in fabric patterned after that made popular by the famous artistic and literary Bloomsbury group of London. The tiles in the bath were painted in nearby Madrid especially for the inn to match the Bloomsbury print fabric. The cheerful bedside table is a piece that innkeeper Pat Harbour picked up at a flea market and brought back to life with her paint brush.

The remaining three rooms are located in casitas behind the house. Each has a private entrance from a pleasant patio. In the Casita de Corazon, the twin aspen-pole beds made by the innkeeper double as sofas during the day. Cowhide print pillows and spreads add fun. There's a table lamp made from a pre-Columbian ceramic figure thought to be the rendering of a Mayan god. Weathered old Mexican doors covered in lace stand between the bedroom and the bath, and the bath is equipped with a telephone and towel warmer.

Cactus casita has color-washed viga ceilings, quality bedding woven in Oaxaca, Mexico, a bench made from a baby's crib, another paper art–backed bench made by Pat's daughter, African and Ecuadoran masks, and a pottery cactus light fixture. The handicapped-accessible bath has a huge walk-in shower accented by green tiles handmade in Dixon. All of the baths are tiled and have soft terry robes. All the rooms have clock radios, coffee makers, color cable TVs, private phones, and an information book put together by the innkeeper to help guide her guests to local sights and restaurants.

Full breakfasts are served in the kitchen on different china each day. Fresh juice, fruit, and homemade muffins or scones are staples, but entrées vary. Crustless quiches are a specialty, and some of Pat's recipes are going to be published in an upcoming cookbook.

Alexander's Inn

529 East Palace Avenue
Santa Fe, NM 87501
505-986-1431

A homey cottage on the edge of downtown

Innkeeper: Carolyn Lee. **Accommodations:** 7 rooms, some with private bath. **Rates:** $70–$150. **Included:** Continental breakfast and afternoon refreshments. **Added:** 10.25% tax. **Payment:** Major credit cards. **Children:** Over 6 welcome; additional $15 if more than 2 people in room. **Pets:** Permitted. **Smoking:** Not permitted. **Open:** Year-round.

Alexander's Inn is a cozy 1903 cottage facing a field of wildflowers. With a traditional brick face and shingled roof, it's a departure from the adobe construction of Santa Fe. Stenciled patterns, hardwood floors, and beautiful furnishings, many of them antiques, add to the country flavor.

The array of old family photographs that greets you in the

entrance hall suggests a warm family welcome. The guest rooms are similarly warm and inviting. Wide dormer windows attractively draped with floral print curtains fill the upstairs rooms with sunshine. Room 4 has a four-poster brass bed and a private deck. Room 1, which shares a large, sunny bathroom with Room 2, has sloping ceilings with gingerbread trim and is decorated in pink, making it the most feminine of the rooms. Room 5, on the ground floor, has a king-size four-poster bed, a stained glass window, and a fireplace.

> **Two casitas behind the main cottage have a living room downstairs and a bedroom upstairs. Alexander's casita, named for the innkeeper's son, has a full kitchen.**

Continental breakfasts of fresh breads, muffins, granola, cereal, fruit, juice, tea, and coffee are served on the backyard deck in summer or inside by the fire in winter. In the afternoon there are salsa and chips or homemade cookies and other goodies and a wide selection of teas. Guests are welcome to help themselves to cold drinks in the fridge.

Canyon Road Casitas

652 Canyon Road
Santa Fe, NM 87501
505-988-5888
800-279-0755
800-445-9923

> *A secluded hide-away steps from gallery row*

Innkeeper: Trisha Ambrose. **Accommodations:** 2 units. **Rates:** Casita $85, suite $165. **Included:** Continental breakfast, tax. **Payment:** Major credit cards. **Children:** Free under 12. **Pets:** Not permitted. **Smoking:** Permitted outside only. **Open:** Year-round.

Lined with galleries, boutiques, restaurants, and fine homes, Canyon Road is Santa Fe's most exclusive street. Hidden down a quiet driveway, Canyon Road Casitas offer a secluded environment for travelers craving both privacy and downtown convenience. Guests check in at the quilt shop on Canyon Road, run by the same owner, and are given a key to a walled courtyard shared by parties in the casita and the suite. Wisteria, lilacs, and roses surround the pleasant patio, and there's an outdoor dining table and grill ready for a barbecue.

The suite is the larger of the two units. It has a glass-roofed dining room, kitchenette, a kiva fireplace, bedroom, bath, and sitting room. The decor is southwestern, with Indi-

> **A bottle of wine and a cheese tray await guests upon check-in.**

an rugs, tin light fixtures, dried flower arrangements made with chiles, and Mexican tile in the kitchen and bath. The carved queen-size bed is covered with a patchwork quilt, and the futon in the sitting room opens to a double bed. The casita is similarly furnished, but is much smaller, and has a wood-burning stove rather than a fireplace.

Breakfast foods are stored in the kitchenettes, so guests can help themselves whenever they choose to rise.

Dancing Ground of the Sun

711 Paseo de Peralta
Santa Fe, NM 87501
505-986-9797
800-645-5673
Fax: 505-986-8082

> *A charming downtown inn*

Innkeeper: Connie Wristen. **Accommodations:** 5 suites. **Rates:** $115–$180; $20 each additional person. **Included:** Continental breakfast. **Added:** 10.25% tax. **Payment:** Major credit cards. **Children:** Over 12 welcome. **Pets:** Not permitted. **Smoking:** Not permitted. **Open:** Year-round.

If you are looking for private and spacious accommodations in a convenient downtown location, Dancing Ground of the Sun more than fits the bill. Only a few blocks from Santa Fe's plaza, the inn has five casitas, each with a private entrance, full kitchen, fireplace, living room, cable TV, and telephone. Two casitas, Buffalo Dancer and Rainbow Dancer, have washers and dryers.

> **Each casita has its own breakfast nook. Fresh orange juice, muesli, fruit, and pastries are provided for the morning meal.**

Connie Wristen is an interior designer, and she has taken great care with the decorating throughout the inn. Only the finest furnishings have been used. Each casita has a hand-painted mural reflecting its name — corn dancers in the Corn Dancer casita, buffaloes in the Buffalo Dancer casita — and terra cotta light fixtures outside the entrance. Wherever possible, the works of local artisans were used. Taos artist Katherine Henry painted the murals, Santa Fe artist Rebecca Parson created the light fixtures, and the living room sofas were made by Harley Designs.

Buffalo Dancer, furnished in earth tones, has lots of willow furniture and Taos drums. Rainbow Dancer, in maroon and blue, has a unique aspen headboard with matching dresser. Corn Dancer, the smallest casita, is a cheerful space in teal, sage, and burgundy, and has an especially nice bath. In the living room there's a nicho painted with a lovely mural of a Santa Fe mountain landscape in addition to the corn dancers on the walls. Clown Dancer is whimsical, with a watermelon motif painted on the kitchen chairs, rainbow fabrics, and an especially fun clown dancer bench in the living room. Be sure to look behind it — it's just as fun from the back.

The Kokopelli casita, named for a figure in Anasazi legend, is the most elegant, with a remarkable sinewy driftwood table at its entrance, an aspen and willow chair with ottoman in the living room, and a king-size willow bed (all other rooms have queens) with a matching willow fainting couch in the bedroom. Kokopelli also has a small balcony.

Although the casitas do afford lots of privacy, innkeeper Connie Wristen is a gracious host, always willing to help her guests in any way she can. Dancing Ground of the Sun offers the best of both worlds: solitude when you want it and attention when you need it.

Dos Casas Viejas

610 Agua Fria Street
Santa Fe, NM 87501
505-983-1636

This inn surrounds you with Santa Fe style

Innkeepers: Jois and Irving Belfield. **Accommodations:** 5 rooms and suites, all with private bath. **Rates:** $135–$185. **Included:** Continental breakfast. **Added:** 10.25% tax. **Payment:** Major credit cards. **Children:** Discouraged. **Pets:** Not permitted. **Smoking:** Not permitted. **Open:** Year-round.

Dos Casas Viejas, which means "two old houses" in Spanish, is so named for the pair of historic adobes dating back to the 1860s that make up the inn. In a walled adobe compound just off a busy Santa Fe street, Dos Casas Viejas is a secluded, peaceful escape from the world beyond.

For breakfast there are home-baked muffins and yeast breads, fruit, and fresh orange juice.

With rust-colored sofas comfortably arranged in front of a fireplace, Navajo rugs, handsome book-lined walls, and classical music playing in the background, the main reception area in one of the old homes sets the tone for the rest of the inn. At one end is the small breakfast room with cowhide-covered chairs. Just outside, a courtyard with a fountain spilling into a swimming pool, surrounded by amply cushioned willow chairs and plush oversize towels, provides an air of true luxury.

Handsomely decorated guest rooms, with woven rugs, Mexican antiques, saltillo tile floors, tiled baths, viga ceilings, kiva fireplaces, and desert colors, really have an old Santa Fe flavor. The pole bed in Room 3 is built into the wall and ceiling, and there is cozy banco seating in front of its fireplace. In Room 5 there's a Mexican wrought-iron bed, a sofa overflowing with pillows, and built-in bookshelves stocked with reading material. All rooms have private patios, baths, and entrances, televisions, coffeemakers, clock radios, telephones, ceiling fans, down bedding, and fresh flowers. Four rooms have refrigerators.

Four Kachinas Inn

512 Webber Street
Santa Fe, NM 87501
505-982-2550
800-397-2564

A quiet inn offers lots of privacy

Innkeepers: John C. Daw and Andrew Beckerman. **Accommodations:** 4 rooms, all with private bath. **Rates:** $88–$113. **Included:** Continental breakfast. **Added:** 10.25% tax. **Minimum stay:** 2 nights on weekends. **Payment:** Major credit cards. **Children:** Over 10 welcome. **Pets:** Not permitted. **Smoking:** Not permitted. **Open:** Year-round.

Four Kachinas Inn is close to everything, yet it feels hidden away. Although it is on the edge of downtown Santa Fe, it's on a one-way street that sees little non-resident traffic, so peace and quiet reign. The Acequia Madre flows past at one end of the property, and the innkeeper's 1912 cottage stands at the opposite end. In between is a new adobe that houses the four guest rooms, and a separate older adobe that serves as the lounge, stocked with snacks and guidebooks.

Since breakfast is served in your room, and all rooms have separate entrances, Four Kachinas affords more privacy than can be found at some other B&Bs. Only a block from the State Capitol and a five-minute walk from the Plaza, Four Kachinas is centrally located.

Each room is named for a kachina. On the ground floor are Poko, Hon, and Koyemsi, each with high ceilings and private patio. Upstairs is Tawa, with a banco seating area at the top of the stairs and lightly stained wood paneling. All rooms have a crisp clean look and are furnished with Navajo weavings, Indian drums, baskets, small dining tables, surprisingly attractive headboards made from lumber taken from an old barn, and of course kachina dolls. The rooms also have private baths, telephones, TVs, clock radios, and ceiling fans.

Breakfast arrives at your door at the time you requested the night before, when you made your choices from the menu provided. Although the breakfast is Continental rather than full, guests still rave about the delicious home-baked pastries.

For those who want to socialize, the lounge is open to all guests, and many do enjoy swapping stories over a cup of tea or hot chocolate there. The innkeepers next door are always happy to help guests with sightseeing plans.

Grant Corner Inn

122 Grant Avenue
Santa Fe, NM 87501
505-983-6678

> *This delightful inn is a Santa Fe favorite*

Innkeepers: Louise Stewart and Pat Walter. **Accommodations:** 12 rooms, 10 with private bath. **Rates:** $70–$85 single, $80–$140 double. **Included:** Full breakfast. **Added:** 4% room tax. **Payment:** Major credit cards. **Children:** Over 8 welcome. **Pets:** Not permitted. **Smoking:** Not permitted. **Open:** Year-round.

This Colonial manor home was built in 1905 by a wealthy ranching family, and was opened as an inn in 1982 by Louise Stewart, daughter of Jack Stewart, the founder of the Camelback Inn in Scottsdale, and her husband, Pat Walter. Past the white picket fence and softly swaying weeping willows, through the etched glass front door, you walk into a living room furnished in antiques. From the Wedgwood blue ceiling and walls to the gleaming wood floors and the Oriental carpets, the house exudes warmth. The adjoining dining room gets lots of use, for the inn serves breakfast to the public as well as to its guests. It takes only a moment to start noticing the rabbits — calico rabbits, wooden rabbits, furry rabbits, porcelain rabbits, even rabbit napkin holders on the dining room table.

Throughout the house are other touches that give the inn its special charm. Arriving guests find a small fruit basket, a carafe of wine, fresh flowers in a demivase, chocolates on the monogrammed pillowcases, and a welcoming note from their hosts in their room.

> **Walk through the latticed archway into a nostalgic world of pinafores and quilts, warmth and hospitality. Whether or not your childhood included visits to Grandma's house, you'll feel as if it did when you visit the Grant Corner Inn.**

Most of the rooms are on the first three floors. Each has its own decor, with brass and four-poster beds, quilts, and tieback curtains. Every room has a private phone, TV, air conditioning, and a ceiling fan. Some have small refrigerators, covered in frills. The rooms aren't large, but the ambience makes up for any lack of space. Adjoining rooms with shared bath are a good choice for families. The rooms range from one twin bed to one king-size and have enough space for a rollaway. Room 11 is perfect for a child, for it has a single brass bed and is filled with stuffed toys.

Five blocks away is Grant Corner Inn Hacienda, an adobe-style condominium with two guest rooms upstairs and a living room, dining room, and kitchen downstairs. Its modern decor includes cathedral ceilings and skylights. The entire unit can accommodate up to eight; each guest room can be rented individually. Both have queen-size beds; one has a beehive fireplace. Rates range from $90 for one room to $250 for eight people renting the entire unit.

Guests in both the main house and the condominium eat a breakfast feast in the inn's dining room or on the front porch, draped with hanging plants. There are two entrées, perhaps pumpkin raisin pancakes or artichoke mushroom crêpes with sour cream sauce, along with homemade jellies and breads, fruit frappes, a selection of fine teas, and fresh coffee. The breakfasts are so special that even fried eggs, bacon, and home fries taste like elegant treats. Brunch is served on Saturdays from 7:30 A.M. to noon and on Sundays from 8 A.M. to 1 P.M.

These meals are so popular that the inn sells its own cook-book, along with jellies and country crafts. If you're in the area and want to eat at the inn, be sure to make reservations.

Guests at Grant Corner Inn can use a sports club ten minutes away, which offers tennis, racquetball, indoor and outdoor pools, a whirlpool, sauna, and massage.

Guadalupe Inn

604 Agua Fria
Santa Fe, NM 87501
505-989-7422

*A friendly,
family-run inn*

Innkeepers: The Quintana family.
Accommodations: 12 rooms, all with private bath. **Rates:** $125–$175 single or double; $15 each additional person. **Included:** Full breakfast. **Added:** 10.25% tax. **Payment:** Major credit cards. **Children:** Over 14 welcome. **Pets:** Not permitted. **Smoking:** Not permitted. **Open:** Year-round.

Along Agua Fria, a street that was once part of the Camino Real, the historical route that led all the way to Mexico, is a new inn with long-standing ties to its locale. The inn was built in 1992 by the Quintanas on land that had been in their family for four generations; their grandfather's store once stood on the property. The Guadalupe inn combines the best of modern conveniences with time-honored traditions.

The 12 guest rooms are in two long buildings, all different in size and shape. Much of their decor has been handcrafted by local artisans or family members. Innkeeper Henrietta Quintana carved many of the headboards, a nephew created the copper light fixtures, and the oil paintings on the walls are by a Santa Fe artist. Some rooms have outdoor sitting areas, four have large Jacuzzi tubs, and seven have fireplaces.

All rooms have private baths, telephones, televisions, and air conditioning.

The Celebration room is especially popular with honeymooners. It has a front living room; in the bedroom the colorful headboard was made by Henrietta with locally gathered willows, and in the bath there's an extra-large claw-foot tub with shiny brass fixtures. The inn also has a two-bedroom suite, and one guest room is accessible to the handicapped.

> **Genuinely warm and hospitable, the Quintanas are among the best reasons to stay at the Guadalupe Inn. Henrietta speaks three languages — English, Spanish, and sign. As a native of Santa Fe, she can share with you her knowledge of the "City Different."**

The full breakfasts are served on long pine tables in the cheerful breakfast room. Breakfast includes pastries, fruit, and an egg dish of your choice, but specialties of the house include Santa Fe omelettes, huevos rancheros, and chile rellenos souffle — using fresh chiles whenever possible.

For pianists, there's a piano in the breakfast room, and nearby is a hot tub for everyone to enjoy.

Hotel Plaza Real

125 Washington Avenue
Santa Fe, NM 87501
505-988-4900
800-279-7325
Fax: 505-988-4900

> *A new hotel near Santa Fe's historic plaza*

General Manager: Rand Levitt. **Accommodations:** 56 rooms. **Rates:** $130–$375; suites $165–$375. **Included:** Continental breakfast. **Added:** 10.25% tax. **Payment:** Major credit cards. **Children:** Under 12 free in room with parents. **Pets:** Not permitted. **Smoking:** Permitted. **Open:** Year-round.

Completed in 1990, the hotel Plaza Real was built in a traditional Territorial style to complement the architecture of the neighborhood. It is small for a downtown hotel, but its unassuming quality is part of its appeal — as is a staff that aims to please.

The lobby is tasteful, with wrought-iron chandeliers, Native American sculptures, sofas, and an unusual painted chest with matching sideboard. La Piazza bar just off the lobby is even more intimate. Most of the guest rooms are in two-story townhouses flanking an open walkway that begins outside the lobby. The

> **A Continental breakfast buffet of home-baked muffins, pastries, granola, and fresh fruit is served in the upstairs common room of the main building. For a $3 service charge, it will be delivered to your room.**

suites, which make up the better part of the hotel, are comfortably appointed with commodious southwestern furniture made from fine woods. Most of the rooms have fireplaces, king-size bed or two double beds, small refrigerators, wet bars, tile baths, ceiling fans, and balconies.

In-room massages can be arranged, and the hotel has an affiliation with a local health club that guests can use for a fee. Also convenient is the hotel's underground parking garage at $5 per day.

Hotel St. Francis

210 Don Gaspar Avenue
Santa Fe, NM 87501
505-983-5700
800-529-5700
Fax: 505-989-7690

> *A graceful
> historic hotel*

Managers: Team managed. **Accommodations:** 83 rooms. **Rates:** $105–$135; suites $175–$350. **Added:** 10.25% tax. **Payment:** Major credit cards. **Children:** Under 12 free in room with parents. **Pets:** Not permitted. **Smoking:** Nonsmoking rooms available. **Open:** Year-round.

In a town that dates from 1610, a hotel built in 1924 is a relative newcomer. Yet the St. Francis, which was renovated in 1987, adds charm and flavor to the cultural capital of the

Southwest. A wide front porch with white wrought-iron furniture, great for people-watching, opens onto Don Gaspar Avenue, only a block and a half from the Plaza. The hotel's high-ceilinged lobby has an elegant look, with classic white columns, Queen Anne furniture, and saltillo tile floors. In keeping with the mood, afternoon high tea is served in the lobby in front of a roaring fire in the winter months, and on the verandah in warm weather. The hotel's restaurant features a changing menu from a variety of cuisines. In the summer you can dine in the pleasant garden courtyard.

> **On Water is the St. Francis' restaurant. Its inventive menu, which changes regularly, is highly regarded in the Santa Fe area.**

There's a hint of romance and history throughout the St. Francis. The halls leading to the guest rooms are wide and grand, with white walls, deep blue carpets, and sitting areas next to the stairwell. There's an old-fashioned switchboard right next to the modern pay phones.

The guest rooms, though relatively small, are delightfully decorated, featuring white iron and brass beds, period furniture, dried flower arrangements, and paisley and burgundy fabrics. The beds have pillow shams and dust ruffles, and each room has its own guardian angel. The bathrooms, also on the small side, are adorned with marble. Other amenities include safes for valuables and small refrigerators.

In order to maintain the hotel's original flavor, it was decided not to add a swimming pool during renovation, as it would have required substantial alteration of the building's structure. With all that Santa Fe has to offer, you probably wouldn't have much time to swim anyway.

Inn of the Anasazi

113 Washington Avenue
Santa Fe, NM 87501
505-988-3030
800-688-8100
Fax: 505-988-3277

*Earthy elegance
permeates this
intimate hotel*

Managing Director: Merry Stephen.
Accommodations: 51 rooms and 8 suites. **Rates:** $220–$260;
suites $360–$420. **Added:** 10.25% tax. **Payment:** Major credit
cards. **Children:** Under 12 free in room with parents; $10 additional for rollaways. **Pets:** Small pets allowed for a $30 additional charge. **Smoking:** Nonsmoking rooms available. **Open:**
Year-round.

The Inn of the Anasazi was developed by Robert Zimmer, a
well-known hotelier who also had a hand in creating the first-
class Bel-Air, Mansion on Turtle Creek, and Hana Maui hotels. With the Inn of the Anasazi, Zimmer wanted to build a
deluxe hotel, but one that
was in keeping with the
values of the American
Indian Anasazi it was
named for.

**For a truly unique dining
experience, the concierge,
who is herself a Navajo,
can arrange special meals
at local pueblos for guests.**

As you walk past the
terra cotta pots filled
with native and flowering
plants at the inn's en-
trance, the smell of cedar
incense greets you in the lobby. The lobby, with a warming
blaze in the fireplace in winter, sets the tone for the rest of
the inn. The flagstone floor, potted cacti, and overstuffed
leather chairs have a down-to-earth feel. You'll find no pre-
tentious or overtly ornate objects here.

The guest rooms are furnished in the same vein. Decorated
in beige and other earthy colors with pine four-poster beds,
soft down comforters, easy chairs, basket lamps, hand-woven
rugs, and folk art made by local artisans, the rooms seem pristine and natural. The unusual "Do Not Disturb" signs —
Anasazi motifs painted on blocks and strung on bolo tie cords
— have confused more than one guest. And although a great
effort has been made to create an age-old flavor throughout the hotel, modern comforts have not been forgotten. All

rooms have coffeemakers, gas fireplaces, safes, televisions, and VCRs. Suites come with a stereo and CD player. There's a video library available through room service, and if the hotel does not have a film you want, they'll send someone out to rent one for you.

A stone water wall runs between the second and third floors. On the ground floor, guests are welcome to use the library (where the bookshelves are filled with artifacts rather than books) and the living room. There's a wine cellar in the basement that can be rented for private parties. The inn's restaurant puts an inventive southwestern and Native American spin on such dishes as chile glazed duck with mango cilantro vinaigrette ($16.75) and grilled lamb loin with tomatilla-serrano vinaigrette and a spring squash tart ($19), and serves all three meals. In-room massages are available, as is aromatherapy. Valet parking is $10 per day.

Inn on the Alameda

303 East Alameda
Santa Fe, NM 87501
505-984-2121
800-289-2122
Fax: 505-986-8325

A small hotel offering personal service

General Manager: Fritz Mercer. **Accommodations:** 42 rooms. **Rates:** $150–$180 single, $180–$210 double; suite $350–$400. **Included:** Continental breakfast. **Added:** 10.25% tax. **Payment:** Major credit cards. **Children:** Free in room with parents. **Pets:** Permitted. **Smoking:** Nonsmoking rooms available. **Open:** Year-round.

Only two blocks from the Plaza, this pueblo-style adobe lodging is a quiet retreat, secluded from the hubbub yet within easy walking distance of many attractions. The inn opened in

1986, and in a short time became one of the most popular in Santa Fe. Some of the inn's buildings are over 80 years old, yet there's a fresh look throughout. When you enter the inn, it's as though you're entering someone's home.

The guest rooms are spacious and airy, reflecting their southwestern locale but with a modern flair. Much of the furniture is handmade, such as the aspen-pole beds, flagstone tables, and mirrors framed in hammered tin. Wood is an important accent, from pine ceilings to latilla chairs. Most of the rooms

> **One of the best things about the Inn on the Alameda is the service. The manager visits with guests at breakfast, and the desk clerks are sincere when they ask how they can help you.**

have a private patio or balcony, and all have air conditioning, cable TV, terrycloth robes, and phones. The rooms have either one king- or two queen-size beds. Six casitas have private entrances, wet bars, and sitting areas in front of cozy fireplaces. The baths are above average for the area, with theatrical bulb lighting and full-length mirrors.

Breakfast is served buffet-style next to the library, or it can be brought to your room from 7:00 to 11:00 A.M. for a service charge. Typical fare is coffeecake, croissants, blueberry muffins, raisin rolls, bagels, fresh fruit and juice, and coffee. At night the breakfast room becomes a gathering spot where drinks are served at the latilla bar. Out in the courtyard, an enclosed blue tile whirlpool is shaded by apricot trees — truly a romantic nook.

La Fonda

100 East San Francisco Street
Santa Fe, NM 87501
505-982-5511
800-523-5002
Fax: 505-988-2952

> *A Santa Fe tradition on the plaza*

General Manager: James Bradbury. **Accommodations:** 153 rooms. **Rates:** $155–$170 single, $170–$185 double; suites $225–$450. **Added:** 10.25% tax. **Payment:** Major credit cards. **Children:** Under 12 free in room with parents. **Pets:** Not permitted. **Smoking:** Nonsmoking rooms available. **Open:** Year-round.

For those who like to be at the center of activity, La Fonda is the place. Its motto, "The world walks through our lobby," has the ring of truth during busy periods. Right on the plaza, it's a nucleus for tourists. Step outside to an ongoing Indian market. Walk a half block to St. Francis Cathedral. Cross the plaza to the Palace of the Governors and the Museum of Fine Arts.

At the hotel you can sign up for sightseeing tours, river rafting, the Cumbres and Toltec Scenic Railway, even trips to the Grand Canyon. You can also start your Santa Fe shopping; there's an art gallery and many fine shops right in the hotel.

> **If you're interested in the history of Santa Fe and the area, be sure to stop by La Fonda's newsstand. It looks like any hotel gift shop, but inside is one of the best selections of regional guides around.**

While the town records show that Santa Fe has had a *fonda*, or inn, since it was founded in 1610, the present La Fonda was built in 1920 on the site of an earlier hotel. This version is a rambling adobe filled with local flavor and a festive spirit.

The guest rooms come in standard, deluxe, mini-suites, and suites. Color spills from the rooms in the form of gaily painted headboards, rich teal or rose carpeting, bright white old-fashioned bedspreads, and hand-decorated Spanish colonial furniture. Sofas and small refrigerators add to your comfort, while carved wood molding adds to each room's individuality.

Standing in the halls, you'll swear that a band of elves had a marvelous time decorating everything in sight. Look in one direction to see a flock of birds in midflight. Turn the other way: the air-conditioning vents are trimmed in bright designs. Even the elevator entrance didn't escape.

La Plazuela, the hotel's main restaurant, is in a festive courtyard, where brightly painted windows screen diners from the busy lobby. You'll feel as though you're in Mexico as you eat New Mexican specialties under a skylit viga roof. La Plazuela serves all three meals. Lunch entrées range from $7 to $13; dinner entrées start at $10.

La Terraza, overlooking St. Francis Cathedral, offers rooftop dining during the summer. Weather permitting, lunch is served from 11:30 A.M. to 5:00 P.M. and cocktails from 5:00 P.M. until closing, occasionally with entertainment. The Bell-tower, with magnificent city and mountain views, serves cocktails seasonally. There's also a French pastry shop and crêperie at La Fonda, and La Fiesta lounge offers nightly entertainment just off the lobby.

An outdoor pool, two indoor hot tubs, and a cold plunge pool are on the first floor. Massages are available by appointment. Garage parking is available for guests at $2 per night.

Spencer House Bed and Breakfast

222 McKenzie Street
Santa Fe, NM 87501
505-988-3024

A bit of English country in the heart of Santa Fe

Innkeepers: Keith Spencer-Gore and Michael McHugh. **Accommodations:** 4 rooms. **Rates:** $85–$115. **Minimum stay:** 2 nights on weekends. **Included:** Full breakfast and afternoon tea. **Added:** 10.25%. **Payment:** Major credit cards. **Children:** Over 12 welcome. **Pets:** Not permitted. **Smoking:** Not permitted. **Open:** Year round.

In the Eastside historic district of Santa Fe, the Spencer House breaks ranks with its neighbors. The 1920s home is an adobe, but its overall appearance, right down to its pitched, red tile roof, is more Mediterranean in flavor than the traditional southwestern-style adobes that surround it. Once inside the inn's front door you'll feel as though you've stepped into an English country cottage, which may seem surprising until you meet innkeeper Keith Spencer-Gore, who was born and raised in England and received his early training in the hospitality business there.

The rooms, with country antiques, Ralph Lauren fabrics, lace curtains, and dried floral wreaths, are cheerful and cozy. Room One has a four-poster queen bed, Three an antique brass bed, and Two is a delight with wicker chairs, folk art, and twin beds covered in black and white checked spreads.

The cottage, with a private entrance, is the most spacious as well as the most southwestern in tone of all of the guest rooms. Decorated in bold red, beige, and black southwestern prints, it has a high queen-size pine bed with steps on either side, a coordinating pine armoire with TV, and a pine wardrobe. There's also an oversized wicker chair with an ottoman for relaxing in front of the kiva fireplace, and a private patio. All rooms have air conditioning, ceiling fans, and private baths.

> **Just four blocks from the Santa Fe plaza, Spencer House is convenient to downtown sights.**

Breakfasts of poached pears, baked apples, waffles served with yogurt, French toast, or cereal, juice, and fruit are served in the dining room in an enclosed sun porch, which the innkeepers themselves added onto the original home. At afternoon tea, which includes a selection of herbal and English teas as well as a homemade treat such as carrot cake, cheesecake, scones, or trifle, Keith's British heritage is once again in evidence. Guests are welcome to enjoy the inn's pleasant living room, whose fireplace is often set with a blazing fire in cooler weather.

Water Street Inn

427 West Water Street
Santa Fe, NM 87501
505-984-1193

> *A quiet, professionally run inn*

Innkeepers: Dolores and Al Deitz. **Accommodations:** 8 rooms. **Rates:** $75–$135 single or double; $15 each additional person. **Included:** Breakfast and afternoon hors d'oeuvres. **Added:** 10.125% tax. **Payment:** Major credit cards. **Children:** $15 per day if eating breakfast. **Pets:** With prior approval only. **Smoking:** Not permitted. **Open:** Year-round.

Tucked away next to a popular Santa Fe restaurant, the Water Street Inn is one of the classiest bed-and-breakfasts in town. Run by a pleasant couple from Louisiana, the inn offers guests a combination of southern hospitality and Santa Fe charm.

Guest rooms are tastefully furnished and immaculate. Sunny Room 1, in light blue and cream, is a favorite, with a four-poster bed, a ceiling fan, Mexican chairs, a brick floor, and a private patio. Room 2 has a fireplace and a nice sitting area.

> It's hard to believe that this attractive, 70-year-old adobe once housed apartments, but the advantages today are private baths and good soundproofing between the rooms.

Room 3 has a cypress four-poster bed from Louisiana, invitingly topped with a pink floral spread and down comforter. Afghan rugs accent the sitting room floor and walls. Room 4 is the largest, and Room 6, with pine twin beds, is the smallest, though it has the use of a balcony across the hall with fine sunset views. Room 7 has a four-poster pine bed, wicker easy chairs, a wood-burning stove, and its own private entrance via a spiral staircase. Room 8 has a king-size bed and fireplace. All of the rooms have cable TV, telephones, and air conditioning.

A breakfast of homemade breads and muffins, fresh fruit, and yogurt, nicely laid out on a tray, arrives at your door in the morning, and there is always a pot of hot coffee ready in the downstairs reception area. In the evenings, hors d'oeuvres are served with wine, sometimes on the upstairs portal to take advantage of the beautiful New Mexico sunsets. Complimentary soft drinks, tea, and coffee are always available in the downstairs common room.

TAOS

Casa Benavides

137 Kit Carson Road
Taos, NM 87571
505-758-1772
505-758-8891
Fax: 505-758-5738

> *A B&B with
> unusual variety*

Innkeepers: Tom and Barbara McCarthy. **Accommodations:** 28 rooms. **Rates:** $80–$195 single or double; additional $15 per day each additional person. **Included:** Full breakfast and afternoon tea. **Added:** 10.31% tax. **Payment:** Major credit cards. **Children:** Welcome. **Pets:** Not permitted. **Smoking:** Not permitted in guest rooms. **Open:** Year-round.

With 28 guest rooms, Casa Benavides is the largest bed-and-breakfast in Taos. Yet each room is individually decorated, and the hosts go to such great lengths to welcome every guest that visitors feel like they're staying in a private home.

> **At Casa Benavides you'll find rooms of all shapes, sizes, and decor.**

The guest rooms are spread among a group of close-knit buildings about a block from the plaza. The main building has five guest suites, including La Victoriana, Dona Tules, and the Flagstone. La Victoriana lives up to its name with Victorian furnishings, lace curtains, and a Tiffany lamp. The masculine Flagstone suite, decorated in gray, black, and white, has Native American art, a leather couch, a fireplace, and a flagstone floor. The Dona Tules is a pretty, feminine room with a chintz day bed and matching pillows, chintz curtains with flouncy valances, a white brass bed, a beautiful dresser with curly maple trim, old photographs, and a Tiffany lamp with beaded fringe.

The Artist's Studio now houses two guest suites. El Mirador upstairs is quite large and is attractively furnished in southwestern style. It has an efficiency kitchen, a view of Taos Mountain, and a kiva fireplace. La Fuente, downstairs, is also southwestern in theme and has a full kitchen. The rest of the guest rooms are in the Benavides house (the childhood home of innkeeper Barbara McCarthy — her maiden name was Benavides) and an old trading post. The staff will patiently describe each room for you when you make your reservation, or they can send you information with brief descriptions of all of the rooms.

Breakfasts, on Mexican china atop pink and purple tablecloths, are served in the pleasant breakfast room in the main building. The meal includes granola, fruit, yogurt, homemade tortillas, muffins, and Mexican eggs, as well as pancakes, waffles, or French toast. Afternoon tea is served with a different homemade treat each day (the brownies made with homemade raspberry jam are especially tasty), and guests are welcome to use the outdoor hot tub at their leisure.

Casa de las Chimeneas

Box 5303
405 Cordoba Road
Taos, NM 87571
505-758-4777
Fax: 505-758-3976

A romantic hideaway minutes from Taos plaza

Innkeeper: Susan Vernon. **Accommodations:** 3 rooms, 1 suite. **Rates:** $115–$125 single, $120–$135 double; suite $145–$155. **Added:** 10.5% tax. **Included:** Breakfast and afternoon hors d'oeuvres. **Children:** Welcome, $15 additional if cot is needed. **Pets:** Not permitted. **Smoking:** Permitted only outside. **Open:** Year-round.

Casa de las Chimeneas, set apart from its humbler surroundings by a light adobe wall that encompasses the property, is a lush oasis. About half a mile from the Taos plaza, the inn is a world unto itself. Birds sing from the canopies of the majestic cottonwoods above. During the warmer months, gardens that border the house and fill the backyard come to life. There are daisies, iris, tulips, daffodils, geraniums, roses, petunias, snapdragons and more — creating a kaleidoscopic bouquet of color everywhere you look. Mexican fountains bubble busily, and the whole effect is both invigorating and pastoral.

Innkeeper Susan Vernon has taken the same care in decorating the guest rooms and common areas of the bed-and-breakfast as she did in creating her magnificent gardens. A ficus tree grows up through the center of the entrance hallway. The living room, where guests are welcome to lounge, is comfortably elegant in southwestern style. Breakfast may include huevos rancheros, cheese crêpes and blueberries, eggs Benedict, green chile strata, or French toast made with orange date-nut bread and topped with bananas and cinnamon maple syrup. Cold drinks are always available in the dining room's wet bar as well as in the tiled bars in each guest room.

> Artfully presented hors d'oeuvres are served in the dining room on a long pine table, perhaps caviar cream pie or baked potatoes with cheese and cracked red pepper. They are often garnished with edible flowers and herbs from the garden.

Although the inn has only four guest rooms, each is tastefully appointed. The Library suite is the largest, with two rooms. One could happily pass any dreary winter day holed up in its library, with its floor-to-ceiling bookshelves filled with magazines and books and its game table with a giant backgammon board and jigsaw puzzles. A large cable TV is hidden in an armoire. Best of all, there's a fireplace to relax in front of on chilly nights. The romantic bedroom has a queen-size brass bed, eyelet lace pillow covers, and a hand-stitched patchwork quilt. The bathroom is sweet, with strawberries hand-painted on the Talavera tile (each bath has its own motif — strawberries, grapes, and so on). The owner calls the walk-in closet in the Library suite the "Imelda Marcos," for it has numerous shelves that could probably hold hundreds of pairs of shoes.

The other three guest rooms, named Blue, Garden, and Willow, are equally appealing, and each has a kiva fireplace. All of the rooms have their own thermostats, top-of-the-line linens, high-quality mattresses, wool mattress pads, natural soaps, and extra towels.

Susan, who had her own wedding at the inn, knows how important the right bed-and-breakfast is on one's honeymoon. She welcomes newlyweds with a bottle of champagne adorned with flowers. Guests celebrating birthdays, anniversaries, or other notable events also receive special treatment. For everyday indulgences, there's a hot tub in the backyard garden that's ideal for unwinding after a long day of sightseeing or skiing.

El Rincón Bed and Breakfast

114 Kit Carson Street
Taos, NM 87571
505-758-4874

A family-run inn with lots of visual appeal

Innkeepers: Nina Meyers and Paul "Paco" Castillo. **Accommodations:** 12 rooms, all with private bath. **Rates:** $45–$105 single, $49–$175 double. **Included:** Continental breakfast. **Added:** 10.25% tax. **Payment:** Major credit cards. **Children:** Welcome. **Pets:** With approval; additional $5 per day. **Smoking:** Permitted. **Open:** Year-round.

Only half a block from the Taos plaza, El Rincón is a charming and unusual B&B. With a compact design, the inn has rooms tucked away on several levels, some opening onto a courtyard.

The owners take great pride in seeing that their guests enjoy a pleasant and visually memorable stay. Each room offers a different mood. The work of local artists abounds, from santos in wall niches to hand-carved doors to intricately crafted furniture. Flowers spill out everywhere.

Most of the building is a hundred years old; the "newer" section has been around for 90 years, although some rooms have been added in the 1990s as the inn has expanded. Next door is the Original Trading Post of Taos, founded years ago by the Indian trader Ralph Meyers, the father of today's innkeeper, Nina.

La Doña Luz room is the most private, standing alone in a separate building in front of the Trading Post. In the 1800s, the building was a popular bar that D.H. Lawrence later frequented. It is now decorated with sheepskin rugs, a handsome batik print, Spanish colonial furniture, and retablos painted by Anne Forbes, a Taos artist. It also has a skylit hot tub, a full kitchen, and a washer and dryer.

The other rooms are equally engaging. The Yellow Bird Deer Room is filled with Indian paintings, pottery, Hopi kachina dolls, Navajo rugs, Taos drums, and Sioux beaded moccasins. Los Angelitos is adorned with angels from all over the world. The Santiago Room is luxuriously furnished in a European-Spanish style. The blanket chest at the end of the black and brass king bed is topped with kilim pillows. There's a fireplace to take off the winter chill, and most of the dark, carved furniture is from Spain. The colorful tile bath is partially lit by a skylight. The room also has air conditioning and mountain views.

> The guest room Doña Luz is named for a well-known Taos hostess who entertained Kit Carson, Governor Charles Bent, and other generals of the day.

Los Flores is popular with honeymooners because of its two-person Jacuzzi surrounded by a tile mural depicting the Garden of Eden. At press time work was underway on two additional rooms. One has two fireplaces and a rooftop hot tub. The other, called the Nina Christine for innkeeper Nina Meyers, who was born here, has eastern European and southwestern furnishings. All rooms have televisions with VCRs (guests can borrow movies from the inn's extensive collection) and refrigerators. Most rooms also have fireplaces.

The dining room is charming, with an old hand-dug well, though breakfast is served on the cheerful patio in good weather. Guests can choose the time that best fits their schedule. The menu usually includes fruit, muffins, yogurt, cereal, and fresh orange juice.

Hacienda del Sol

Box 177
109 Mabel Dodge Lane
Taos, NM 87571
505-758-0287

*Famous artists
and writers once
visited this adobe*

Innkeepers: John and Marcine Landon. **Accommodations:** 9 rooms.
Rates: $55–$110 single, $65–$120 double; suite $115. **Included:** Breakfast. **Added:** 10.313% tax. **Payment:** Cash or check.
Children: Additional $20 per night; $10 per night for a crib.
Pets: Not permitted. **Smoking:** Not permitted. **Open:** Year-round.

Years ago, when art patron Mabel Dodge Luhan was searching for a home for herself and her Indian husband, Tony, one of her choices was the adobe house now known as Hacienda del Sol. D.H. Lawrence, Georgia O'Keeffe, Willa Cather, Thomas Wolfe, and Aldous Huxley all came to call. Today, the 180-year-old house has a feeling of history, enhanced by the efforts of the Landons. They enjoy introducing visitors to Taos, suggesting sights, and talking about the area's history.

Don't despair when they give you directions. Yes, Hacienda del Sol is directly behind Lotta Burger, about a mile north of downtown. When you turn off Highway 64 onto the little dirt road leading to the front door, you may have second thoughts. But once you step inside the courtyard, you never think again about the commercial development nearby. On an acre lot graced with ancient cottonwoods and ponderosa pines, the Hacienda adjoins Indian reservation land of more than 95,000 acres, providing an uninterrupted view all the way to Taos's Magic Mountain. Inside, ancient vigas, kiva fireplaces, oak and brick floors, and handmade furniture please the eye.

Guest rooms include La Sala del Don ("Tony's Room"), a

large room with a kiva fireplace and a queen-size Spanish bed. Windows open onto peaceful gardens with hundred-year-old apple trees. La Sala del Sol, which opens onto the patio, is decorated in peach tones with aspen-pole beds and a bent-willow chair.

The most popular guest room is Los Amantes ("the Lovers' Room"). Not only is it romantically appointed, but it's next to the spa room, with a black marble hot tub on a mahogany platform. There's even a skylight above the tub. The bedroom includes a fireplace and a wooden Mexican bed with metal accents, and French doors open onto the back courtyard.

> **Most of the art in the house is for sale. Many paintings are by Carol Pelton, a former owner, or by local Native American artists.**

If Los Amantes is booked, there are two casitas apart from the main house that also afford lots of privacy. For families or couples traveling together, they can be connected to form a suite. The casitas both have front porches with fabulous mountain views. Nearby, there's a large outdoor hot tub with a redwood sundeck, also with unrivaled mountain views. A sign-up sheet ensures that guests won't be interrupted.

Breakfast always consists of fresh fruit, a hot entrée, fresh juice, and the inn's own blend of coffee; it is served outdoors in the warmer months or in front of the fire in the winter. Afternoon snacks are served in the living room or on the patio when weather permits.

Quail Ridge Inn Resort

P.O. Box 707
Taos, NM 87571
505-776-2211
800-624-4448
Fax: 505-776-2949

> *A resort
> on the road to
> Taos Ski Valley*

General Manager: Peter French. **Accommodations:** 110 units. **Rates:** $85–$125; suites $150–$350 for 4–6. **Added:** 12.3125% tax and service charge. **Payment:** Major credit cards. **Children:** Under 18 free in room with parents. **Pets:** Not permitted. **Smoking:** Permitted. **Open:** Year-round.

Adobe casitas hug the ground at the foot of the Sangre de Cristo Mountains, blending unpretentiously into the landscape. The town of Taos is four miles to the south; Taos Ski Valley is 12 miles north. Quail Ridge Inn offers the essence of Taos, from its southwestern style architecture to its recognition of local art.

> **One of the true delights of this inn is sitting on an adobe patio, gazing at the distant mountains by day or the star-sprinkled sky by night.**

This year-round resort is always brimming with activity. Tennis is one of its biggest attractions — if you can take your eyes off the view long enough to play — with eight Laykold courts, including two under a bubble, a tennis pro, clinic instruction, and tournaments. There is no outdoor court fee for guests; indoor courts cost $15 an hour.

Quail Ridge's landscaped 20-meter pool and deck is one of the most attractive in New Mexico. There's also a large hot tub, a children's pool, and a fitness center.

When snow blankets the nearby mountains, Quail Ridge becomes a ski lodge. At this inn, skiers can easily combine a sports vacation with trips into Taos. Nonskiers can find plenty to do in town.

The simple accommodations, furnished in a southwestern style, include hotel rooms, with a queen-size bed and a queen-size sleeper sofa; studios, with a Murphy bed, sitting area, full kitchen, and patio or balcony; one-bedroom suites (hotel room plus studio); and two-bedroom suites (two hotel rooms plus studio). Every room has a kiva fireplace as well as a TV and telephone. The individually owned units are well decorated. The kitchens are fully equipped, with countertop appliances and cookware as well as a full-size refrigerator and stove, dishwasher, and garbage disposal.

Carl's French Quarter is the inn's restaurant, with such specialties as trout amandine, shrimp Créole, and veal Marsala. Prices range from $12 to $19.

The Taos Bed & Breakfast Association

P.O. Box 2772
Taos, NM 87571
505-758-4747
800-876-7857

*An association of
fine Taos inns*

President: John Landon. **Accommo-dations:** About 83 rooms in 14 inns. **Rates:** $55–$185. **Included:** Breakfast. **Added:** 10.25%–10.313% tax. **Payment, Children, Pets, Smoking:** Policies vary from inn to inn. Check with individual innkeepers before making reservations. **Open:** Most open year-round.

As the Taos area has become a more popular tourist destination, the number of inns has grown, and it has actually become harder in some ways to make a lodging decision. This association of 14 inns can help narrow your choice. While association inns offer potential visitors lots of variety, all members must maintain a standard of cleanliness and hospitality in order to remain part of the association.

Many of these B&Bs have views of the spectacular mountains and scenery surrounding picturesque Taos, and some are filled with original art, often done by the owners themselves. Some inns are in historic homes, others are newly built, but all feature southwestern-style architecture.

Breakfast gets special attention at these inns, and some properties provide afternoon hors d'oeuvres as well.

The Taos Inn

125 Paseo de Pueblo Norte
Taos, NM 87571
505-758-2233
800-TAOS-INN
Fax: 505-758-5776

*This historic
hotel is a
Taos landmark*

Manager/Owner: Carolyn Haddock.
Accommodations: 39 rooms. **Rates:** $80–$195. **Added:** 10.25% tax. **Payment:** Major credit cards. **Children:** Free in room with parents. **Pets:** Not permitted. **Smoking:** Nonsmoking rooms available. **Open:** Year-round.

In keeping with its history, the Taos Inn is a center of activity in this popular tourist town. The plaza is only a block away, and within a few blocks are dozens of galleries, shops, and restaurants. The hotel's lobby, originally a small plaza with the town well in the center, is still a gathering spot for locals, artists, and travelers.

The hotel is unique in that it is composed of several houses that once faced the tiny plaza. In 1936, Helen Martin, the widow of popular Doc Martin, the town's only physician for many years, bought the houses, enclosed the plaza, and converted it all into a hotel. In 1982, the hotel was lovingly restored, resulting in an inn that exudes a sense of history combined with modern comfort. Now on the National and State Registers of Historic Places, it is a Taos landmark.

Fewer than half the guest rooms are in the main building. Only a few steps behind it is the Sandoval House, dating from the 1850s, with six rooms. Because of the age of the building, the rooms here tend to be the smallest — taller patrons need to stoop to get through the doors. An additional 16 rooms are in a one-story complex surrounding a courtyard to one side of the Sandoval House. The courtyard rooms, built in the 1930s, are the inn's most spacious.

Each room is different, but all are steeped in southwestern decor, from bedspreads woven by Zapotec Indians especially for the inn to hand-crafted Taos furniture. Most rooms have kiva fireplaces crafted by local adobe artist Carmen Velarde, and are decorated with Indian designs. All the rooms have comfortable seating, TVs, and phones. When the inn opened in 1936, it was the first building in Taos to have indoor plumbing. Today, the bathrooms, of average size, are colorfully tiled and have tub-showers. Some rooms also have vanities with lavatories. Most rooms have fans; only three have air conditioning.

The small two-story lobby has an informal feeling conducive to relaxing in southwestern surroundings. In its center is a tile fountain, once the town's well. To one side of the lobby is the Adobe Bar, popular with Taos residents and visitors alike. It features New Mexican fare, a great espresso and dessert menu, live entertainment, a variety of international beers, and a host of specialty drinks. In summer, the outdoor patio is inviting.

> **A popular lodging for skiers, the inn offers ski packages, and the shuttle bus to Taos Ski Valley stops at the front door. Also on the grounds is a small swimming pool, open in summer, and a hot tub is open year-round.**

Next to the lobby on the opposite side is Doc Martin's Restaurant, in a building that was once the good doctor's home and office; the birthing room is now a cozy dining area. But history only counts for so much in a dining establishment; the best reason to visit Doc Martin's is the outstanding cuisine. Specializing in international dishes and emphasizing fresh, indigenous foods, the dinner menu changes daily. Diners can expect such innovative entrées as grilled Pacific red snapper with a citrus glaze or buffalo medallions with a roasted garlic cream and corn demiglace. The extensive wine list is one of the best in the state, and selections from the list are available to take home.

Breakfast is no ordinary meal at Doc Martin's either. Piñon nut waffles, specialty omelettes, blue corn and blueberry hotcakes, and stuffed sopapillas ($4.50–$7) are a wonderful way to start the day. Offered at lunch are New Mexican or seafood dishes; some, such as shrimp burritos, combine elements of both ($6–$8).

Twice a year, the inn hosts a Meet the Artist series, from mid-May to mid-June and from mid-October to mid-December. On Tuesdays and Thursdays, Taos artists talk about their work. Studio tours, demonstrations, slide shows, videos, music, and readings are part of the presentation. Contact the inn for upcoming schedules. Participation is free and open to the public, but seating is limited. Reservations are required for some sessions.

TAOS SKI VALLEY

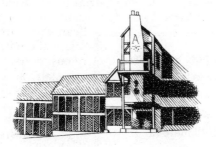

Austing Haus Hotel

Box 8
Taos Ski Valley, NM 87525
505-776-2649
800-748-2932
Fax: 505-776-8751

> *An alpine
> ski lodge*

Innkeeper: Paul Austing. **Accommodations:** 26 rooms. **Rates:** $45–$60 in summer, $88–$145 during ski season. **Included:** Continental breakfast. **Added:** 9.32% tax. **Payment:** Major credit cards; no personal checks. **Children:** Under 5 free in room with parents. **Pets:** Permitted. **Smoking:** Permitted. **Open:** Year-round.

As you drive towards the Taos Ski Basin, you can't miss the Austing Haus Hotel — it has a white and black timber and glass exterior adorned with fanciful flowers. The cheerful building suggests the Bavarian Alps rather than New Mexico, but the two locales may be more similar than their distance would indicate, since their terrain is so similar. The Austing Haus has the flavor of European ski chalet inside as well, especially in the restaurant, which is open only in winter.

The lodge's dining room is light and airy, with large picture windows, plants, stained glass panels, and country quilts on the walls. Queen Anne–style chairs pull up to light wood tables. Entrées such as shrimp scampi, Wiener schnitzel, medallions of beef Bordelaise, and veal Oscar range from $12 to $20. Paul Austing is the chef, serving his specialties of roast duck with black Bing cherry sauce and rack of lamb.

In 1984, Paul Austing and Chuck Jeanette proudly completed the first phase of the hotel, a 14-room post-and-beam lodge with more than 3,000 interlocking joints held together with 1,600 oak pegs. Built of Douglas-fir and ponderosa pine, it is lovingly referred to as "one giant piece of furniture."

Beams are exposed both inside and out. The guest rooms, on two levels, are especially spacious, with queen-size beds and furniture made by Austing. Glass-walled hallways extend the entire length of the building, bringing the wooded terrain closer. In a new 10-room wing, each guest room has a fireplace.

> **The meals here are widely considered to be the best in the ski valley. The menu at the Glass Dining Room proclaims, "If there is something you like that is not on the menu, by just asking it will be prepared for you."**

This is not a place to party late into the night. Since skiers tend to rise early to get the best snow, quiet hours start at 10:30 P.M. and last until 7:00 A.M. Skiers will also appreciate the equipment lockers just off the lobby. The loft hot tub room, a charming nook with views of the snow-covered mountains, is a popular spot for relaxing after a day on the slopes.

Less expensive than most of the accommodations at the ski valley and only a mile from the slopes, the Austing Haus offers excellent service in a pleasant environment. During the off-season, the inn meets the needs of groups, pricing services according to their requirements. For example, groups can cut costs by acting as their own cleanup crew, both in the dining room and in the lodging areas.

St. Bernard Condominiums

P.O. Box 676
Taos Ski Valley, NM 87525
505-776-8506

*Condominiums
offer space
and convenience*

Resident manager: Kathy Humphries. **Accommodations:** 13 2-bedroom condos. **Rates:** $2,100–$2,600 per week for up to 6 people; packages available. **Added:** Tax and gratuity. **Payment:** Major credit cards. **Children:** Welcome. **Pets:** Not permitted. **Smoking:** Not permitted. **Open:** Thanksgiving to mid-April.

The St. Bernard Condominiums, which are about a five-minute walk from the slopes, are convenient to the ski area but are much quieter and less crowded than other accommodations in the village. In a long, three-story building, they overlook the valley.

The two-bedroom, two-bath units, accommodating up to six, are individually owned and decorated. They are roomy, and kitchens come fully equipped with microwaves, garbage disposals, and dishwashers. All of the units have phones, TVs, VCRs, and patios that face the ski slopes: if you want to check out the skiing conditions on the mountain, just step outside. And you won't have to shovel out your car when it snows — there is covered parking next to each unit.

When you make your reservation, ask about ski packages that include a week's lodging, dinners at the hotel, ski lessons, and unlimited use of the ski lifts.

After skiing, guests can use the hot tub and workout room at Hotel St. Bernard, at the base of the slopes. There's also a ski room in the hotel for the exclusive use of condo guests where equipment can be left; you don't have to carry your skis back and forth to the slopes each day. The hotel's restaurant, headed by a French chef, serves dinner.

TERERRO

Los Pinos Guest Ranch

Route 3, Box 8
Tererro, NM 87573
505-757-6213
505-757-6679 in off-season

> *A rustic getaway
> in the
> Pecos wilderness*

Hosts: Bill and Alice McSweeney.
Accommodations: 4 cabins. **Rates:**
$80 daily or $525 weekly per person; children ages 6–13 $60
daily or $390 weekly. **Added:** 7% tax. **Included:** All meals.
Minimum stay: 2 nights. **Payment:** Personal checks; no credit
cards. **Children:** No children under 6 unless with group using
all cabins. **Pets:** Not permitted. **Smoking:** Outdoors only.
Open: June 1 through Labor Day.

If you truly want to get away, Los Pinos may suit your fancy.
From Santa Fe, head east on U.S. 85 to Glorietta. Then take
the road to Pecos and turn north on SR 63 to Tererro — and
you're not even close. The road is dirt from here on. It follows
the Pecos River, here a mountain stream, up the canyon
through forests of aspen, spruce, and fir. At Cowles (a sign
tells you it's a town), go past two ponds and turn left toward
Panchuella Campground. Los Pinos is about a quarter mile up
the narrow dirt trail.

Here in the Pecos Wilderness Area you're in camping country. Los Pinos lets you enjoy the surroundings in comfort,
with hearty meals and hosts who can arrange anything from
fishing to exploring. This is indeed the place for seeing the
country on horseback. Guided trail rides are scheduled according to demand, with up to eight riders in a group
($25–$35 for a half day, $35–$55 for a full day).

Los Pinos is surrounded by a national forest, with mountain lakes and peaks as high as 13,000 feet. On a ride to Grass Mountain, the trail leads through aspen forests, ending at the top of the mountain with a panoramic view of the Pecos Wilderness.

Make no mistake about it, the accommodations are rustic — and therein lies the charm. Four clean and very cozy log cabins, each sleeping up to six, are scattered among the trees. Sit on the front porch or look out the bedroom windows to watch nature's showcase.

Meals are served in the McSweeneys' rambling old lodge. Usually guests show up early to visit on the screened porch, then go inside to feast on Irish pork chops, sauerbraten, turkey, or salmon.

Other favorite pursuits are trout fishing, hiking, and just plain relaxing. The McSweeneys enjoy taking guests to nearby historic areas upon request.

TESUQUE

The Bishop's Lodge

Box 2367
Santa Fe, NM 87504
505-983-6377
800-732-2240
Fax: 505-989-8739

*Santa Fe's
first resort*

Innkeepers: Jim and Lore Thorpe. **Accommodations:** 88 rooms. **Rates:** $125–$280 single, $140–$295 double; suites $170–$350; modified American plan also available. **Added:** 8.75% tax. **Payment:** Major credit cards. **Children:** Welcome. **Pets:** Not permitted. **Smoking:** Permitted. **Open:** Year-round.

Downtown Santa Fe is only five minutes away, but here at the Bishop's Lodge, which occupies 1,000 acres in the foothills of the Sangre de Cristo Mountains, guests find peace and quiet far from the crowds.

The idea of retreating to these juniper-studded foothills at the head of the Tesuque Valley is not without precedent. In fact, at the heart of the lodge's charm, its gentleness and hospitality, is the memory of the man for whom it is named. Archbishop Lamy of Santa Fe, the model for the main character in Willa Cather's *Death Comes for the Archbishop*, came to this spot about a century ago to rest and eventually to retire. Over time he planted an orchard, supplementing the fruit trees planted by the Franciscan fathers during the early 17th century. Remnants of the orchard can still be found on the grounds.

> **In summer, an excellent program for children aged four to twelve includes hiking, swimming, pony rides, and arts and crafts. Teens have their own dining table, and special events such as swim parties are planned, depending upon the number of young guests.**

The archbishop built a private chapel next to his adobe home. It's a simple structure with a vaulted ceiling and painted-glass windows that simulate the stained glass of the cathedrals in his native France. The tiny chapel, now on the National Register of Historic Places, still stands, creating an atmosphere of warmth, peacefulness, and history.

Since 1918, when James R. Thorpe developed the Bishop's Lodge as a ranch resort, three generations of the family have owned and run the lodge. Previously, the property belonged to the newspaper publisher Joseph Pulitzer, who established the Pulitzer Prizes.

In the main lobby, guests can sign up for activities, eat in the central dining room, and enjoy spectacular sunsets from the terrace bar. Life is casual here. While men are asked to wear jackets at dinner and women are requested to "dress accordingly," there's an informal air throughout the resort. Breakfast and lunch are served buffet-style. Cocktails are served in El Charro lounge as well as on the terrace.

The guest rooms are spread out in several lodges. The North and South lodges were fine summer homes prior to World War I; Chamisa Lodge was added in 1994. All reflect their New Mexico heritage. In a wide assortment of sizes and configurations, rooms are especially spacious, well lit, and well furnished. The decor is ranch-style southwestern with kiva fireplaces, simple wooden furniture, and earth-tone fabrics with splashes of color. Some rooms have beamed ceilings, some have private balconies or terraces. The bathrooms are larger than average and designed for convenience. Air conditioning, cable TV, clock radios, in-room safes, twice-daily maid service, plush terry robes, and telephones are standard.

The Bishop's Lodge has an impressive roster of recreational choices. There are facilities for horseback riding, tennis, volleyball, swimming, and skeet shooting as well as lots of extras: a playground complete with a tepee, a children's fishing pond stocked with trout, maps with hiking trails, and lists for birders, who can hope to see over 110 species on the grounds. Golfers are welcome at three private courses in the area.

The lodge also offers an abundance of special activities such as a newcomers' cocktail party held by the Thorpes, exercise classes, fashion shows, storytelling on the front lawn, steak fries, children's cookouts — the list goes on and on. The resort also keeps guests informed of events in the area.

Horseback riding is important here. Most guests ride, whether they are experienced or have never mounted a horse before. With more than 60 horses, the resort offers daily guided rides ($28), plus breakfast and picnic rides.

Rancho Encantado

Route 4, Box 57C
Santa Fe, NM 87501
505-982-3537
800-722-9339
Fax: 505-983-8269

A comfortable resort with old-fashioned hospitality

Owners: The Egan family. **Accommodations:** 22 rooms, 29 condominiums. **Rates:** Main lodge rooms $110–$190, casitas and cottages $125–$260, condominiums $115–$315. **Added:** 8.75% tax. **Payment:** Major credit cards. **Children:** Free in room with parents. **Pets:** Not permitted. **Smoking:** Permitted. **Open:** Year-round.

When you turn into the driveway at Rancho Encantado, you may wonder whether this is really the place that such celebrities as Jimmy Stewart and Robert Redford choose as a vacation retreat. Don't be deterred by the unassuming sign and unpaved road; in Santa Fe, the best addresses are on dirt roads. Rancho Encantado, in operation since 1968, is no exception.

From the gate, a network of dirt roads winds through fragrant piñon and ruddy arroyos on the 168-acre property. Nestled in the high desert beneath the Santa Fe Ski Basin and the Sangre de Cristo Mountains, Rancho Encantado is designed to harmonize with the existing terrain rather than intrude upon it. Although it is only 15 minutes from Santa Fe, 10 minutes from the opera, and five minutes from the artists' community of Tesuque, its location feels remote and private.

> **The handful of guest rooms in the main lodge are decorated in soft pastel colors and blend marble-topped Victorian tables with simpler southwestern pieces. These rooms tend to be more formal than those in the rest of the resort.**

The main lodge seems modest compared with those of similar resorts, but the unpretentiousness of Rancho Encantado is part of its appeal. The lodge's heavy, dark, southwestern-style furniture and comfortable sofas, tile floors, viga ceilings, and small dining room make you feel as though you're visiting someone rather than checking into a hotel. The ranch's "Wall of Fame," featuring photographs of its most famous guests, is in the back sitting room.

Adobe casitas are the primary accommodation here. Each casita has a refrigerator, a kiva fireplace amply stocked with firewood in colder weather, and a cozy sitting area furnished with traditional southwestern pieces in rich earth tones that complement the landscape. All of the casitas have terraces, but numbers 25–32 have the best views of the spectacular sunsets over the distant Jemez Mountains.

Twenty-nine luxury condos with full kitchens have been built across the road, more than doubling the size of the original resort. Some of them may be available for rent. Rates are determined by the number of bedrooms and guests in your party.

Also on the property is the Betty Egan Bed and Breakfast. Mrs. Egan was the matriarch of the Egan family, and the bed-and-breakfast is decorated with her own furnishings — a mixture of antiques and southwestern, Spanish, and Native American pieces. The B&B has four suites, each with a private patio and bath. They share a common living room, dining room, and kitchen. Call for B&B rates.

The superb desert vistas and memorable food make dining at the ranch a rewarding experience. Considered one of the best restaurants in the area, the dining room is popular with Santa Feans and guests alike. The menu consists of New Mexican, fresh seafood (a rarity in the desert), and Continental dishes. A special menu features meals that are low in fat, cholesterol, and sodium, including a delicious Rocky Mountain trout with sun-dried tomatoes, garlic, and basil.

Breakfast has a decidedly New Mexican accent. The dishes are named for local Indian pueblos, such as Santa Clara and Nambe, and include a number of variations of huevos rancheros, some made with chorizo sausage.

Sports play an important role at Rancho Encantado. There is a full-time tennis pro, three tennis courts, including one with a basketball net and backboard for pickup games, an outdoor swimming pool and hot tub that are covered and heated in the winter, and a pool table in the cantina. Perhaps the most popular activity is horseback riding, and trail rides leave from the corral twice daily year-round.

Rancho Encantado's helpful and friendly staff, many of whom have been here for a number of years, add to the relaxed environment.

Texas

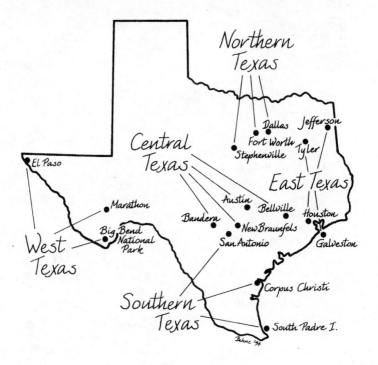

For many, the name Texas conjures up images of oil derricks and acre upon acre of longhorn cattle. But while oil and ranching are two of the state's biggest industries, they represent only a small fraction of the state's identity. There is the sophistication of cities such as Dallas and Houston (now the fourth largest city in the U.S.), the Spanish spirit of San Antonio, and the governmental and educational soul of Austin, the state's capital. To the south you'll find glorious sandy beaches along the Gulf Coast, to the west the captivating high desert and mountainous landscape of Big Bend National Park, to the east a climate and culture akin to that of the Deep South, and in the center is the revered Hill Country where towns still bear the imprint of their European settlers.

Whether you're looking for a beachcombing, river-rafting, cultural, antiquing, hiking, citified, or historic vacation, you're likely to find what you're looking for somewhere in the 262,017 square miles that make up Texas. Wherever you go in the state you're bound to feel welcome because the term "Texas-friendly" is no fabrication. The name Texas comes from the Indian word *tejas*, which means friends, and Texans seem to take their state's name to heart.

The legendary Texas wildflowers are no myth either. Each spring, every open field and hillside seems to be covered in a kaleidoscopic blanket of color. Lovely Texas bluebonnets, the state flower, are among the many flowers that line the state's roadways, making the sometimes vast distances pleasanter to traverse.

Texas also has a lot to offer the visitor in the food department. Naturally the larger cities have their share of fine gourmet and ethnic restaurants, but no trip to Texas would be complete without trying some juicy barbecue, spicy Tex-Mex, or fiery chili, the state dish. Along the Gulf Coast, the seafood is as fresh as it can be, and the shrimp is some of the best anywhere.

The state's history is similarly piquant. Early explorers set up colonies here, famous battles were waged here, presidents were born here, and presidents died here; but through it all Texas has maintained a distinctive and determined personality. As its tourist board proudly proclaims, "it's like a whole other country."

Central Texas

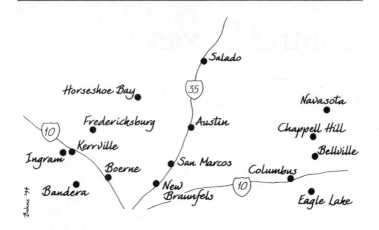

Best Bed-and-Breakfasts

Austin
Southard House
Bellville
High Cotton Inn Bed and Breakfast
Townsquare Inn
Boerne
Ye Kendall Inn
Chappell Hill
Browning Plantation
The Stagecoach Inn
Columbus
Gant Guest House
Fredericksburg
Gastehaus Schmidt
Navasota
The Castle Inn
New Braunfels
Prince Solms Inn
Salado
Inn on the Creek
San Marcos
Crystal River Inn

Best City Stops

Austin
Doubletree Hotel
Four Seasons Hotel Austin
Stouffer Austin Hotel
Wyndham Austin Hotel at Southpark

Best Family Favorites

Kerrville
Inn of the Hills River Resort
Y.O. Ranch Hotel

Best Guest Ranches

Bandera
  Mayan Dude Ranch
Ingram
  Lazy Hills Guest Ranch

Best Historic Hostelries

Austin
  The Driskill Hotel

Best Hunting and Fishing Lodges

Eagle Lake
  The Farris 1912

Best Lakeside

Austin
  Lakeway Inn

Best Resorts

Horseshoe Bay
  Horseshoe Bay Country Club Resort

Best Spas

Austin
  Lake Austin Spa Resort

Aptly located in the center of the vast territory that is Texas is **Austin,** the state capital. Austin is generally considered the most beautiful of the state's major cities, and it is certainly one of the most manageable. From the stately pink granite capitol building (fittingly the country's largest) it is a short walk to the downtown historic district and Sixth Street, Austin's entertainment row. Sixth Street, which used to be called Old Pecan Street, was once the main thoroughfare of the city. Now it's lined with shops, galleries, restaurants, and nightclubs, and is the place to go after dark. The University of Texas is also based in Austin, bringing a youthful energy to the city.

Austin does have a number of museums, such as the Lyndon B. Johnson Library and the Elisabet Ney Museum, devoted to the German-turned-Texan sculptress, but many of the city's attractions are out of doors. There's the Japanese Garden, boating on Town Lake and Lake Austin, the National Wildflower Research Center founded by Lady Bird Johnson, and the waterfall-fed Hamilton Pool on the outskirts of town. Beyond the city limits, it's easy to escape into the surrounding Hill Country.

Talk to most Texans and you're bound to hear raves about Hill Country. While visitors from more mountainous parts of the world may challenge the liberal use of the word hill, the gently rolling hills of the Texas heartland are certainly pastoral and bucolic.

Many Hill Country villages were established in the 1800s by European settlers, and a remarkable number of them have been able to preserve their historical charm. In the tiny town of **Chappell Hill,** where the population is just over 300, some 25 buildings bear historic markers. **Columbus,** ten times the size of Chappell Hill but still a small town, has a wealth of splendid Victorian homes as well.

The influence of early German settlers can still be seen in **Fredericksburg,** one of the most popular Hill Country towns. Fredericksburg's main street, which has its share of country gift shops and antique stores, also has a number of beer gardens serving German food. Rustic "Sunday houses" used by the settlers for shelter on their way to church (churches were few and far between in those days, so a trip to church by rural farmers often entailed an overnight stay) can still be seen in the Fredericksburg area. Also in Fredericksburg are a Pioneer Museum; the Admiral Nimitz Museum of the Pacific War, housed in the highly unusual Steamboat Hotel, built in 1852; and Enchanted Rock State Park, where Indians believed that the 500-foot granite slab was used for human sacrifices. Former president Lyndon B. Johnson's childhood home can be visited in nearby Johnson City.

Boerne, which was established by German settlers in 1851, has some nicely preserved limestone buildings. It also has two caves open to the public: the Cave Without a Name, which was declared too pretty to name, and Cascade Caverns, notable for its underground waterfall. River-rafting fans should head to the rapids in Guadalupe River State Park about 13 miles east of town.

The town of **New Braunfels** celebrates its German heritage with a Wurstfest each November. During the festival, German bands and dance groups perform, and there are historical and art exhibitions — and lots of sausage, of course. The Hummel Museum displays the original works of Sister M. I. Hummel, of porcelain figurine fame. Other area sights include a Classic Car Museum, a Children's Museum, a variety of historic homes, a winery, the Museum of Texas Handmade Furniture, Natural Bridge Caverns, Natural Bridge Wildlife Ranch, and Schlitterbahn, a German-style water amusement park.

Between New Braunfels and Austin is the town of **San Marcos.** LBJ attended school here at Southwest Texas State University. The San Marcos River, considered one of the world's most fertile rivers, originates here. Also in San Marcos, you can take a glass-bottomed boat ride at Aquarena Springs or explore an earthquake-formed cave at Wonder World.

Other notable Hill Country towns are **Bandera,** with its western flavor and dude ranches, and **Kerrville,** home of the Hill Country Museum and Cowboy Artists of America Museum. The **Eagle Lake** area, south and east of Hill Country, is known for duck and goose hunting. At the Attwater Prairie Chicken Refuge, the endangered prairie fowl is preserved.

AUSTIN

Doubletree Hotel

6505 I-35 North
Austin, TX 78752
512-454-3737
800-222-8733
Fax: 512-454-6915

> *A modern hotel
> with a Spanish
> colonial flavor*

General manager: Carl McKee. **Accommodations:** 335 rooms and 15 suites. **Rates:** $120–$180 single, $150–$200 double; suites $350–$550. **Added:** 13% tax. **Payment:** Major credit cards. **Children:** Under 17 free in room with parents. **Pets:** Not permitted. **Smoking:** Nonsmoking rooms available. **Open:** Year-round.

The Doubletree, built in 1984 on the northern edge of Austin, is a charming Spanish colonial–style lodging. The lobby's polished tile floor gleams, and public areas are handsomely decorated with sofas, tapestries, greenery, and flowers. The hotel's focal point is a peaceful inner courtyard with waterfalls, live oak trees, flagstone terraces, bubbling pools, tropical plants, and fountains, one of them from an 18th-century Spanish building. Nearly half of its guest rooms open onto galleries overlooking the courtyard, a sanctuary from the bustling city beyond.

The rooms are spacious and comfortably furnished; some have French doors opening onto small balconies. They are decorated in teal and rose, a color scheme that is carried throughout the hotel, and have writing desks, clock radios, and lounge chairs with ottomans or sofas. All have dressing areas, attractive wallpapered baths, and bath telephones. Two styles of suites are on the Premier Floor, where guests are pampered with Continental breakfast and afternoon hors d'oeuvres. All guests are treated to fresh chocolate chip cookies the night they arrive.

The second-floor fitness room has a sauna and exercise equipment, and there's an outdoor pool and whirlpool spa.

> **The Elisabet Ney room in the Doubletree is a small gallery where local artists exhibit their work.**

The Garden Restaurant is a pleasant dining spot with Mexican pottery and outdoor seating in the courtyard when weather permits. The menu runs from seafood to steak, and dinner entrées range from $8 to $20. The Courtyard Lounge is a cozy bar with overstuffed chairs, a large stone fireplace, and a billiard table.

Just across the street from the hotel are two of Austin's most popular eateries. Guest parking in the hotel's garage is free. Complimentary transportation is offered to the airport and to a number of shops and restaurants within two miles of the hotel. And on top of the hotel is a heliport for quick arrivals and departures.

The Driskill Hotel

604 Brazos
Austin, TX 78701
512-474-5911
800-252-9367
Fax: 512-474-2188

> *A historic hotel blocks from the capitol*

General manager: Tye Hochstrasser. **Accommodations:** 177 rooms and suites. **Rates:** $129 single, $139 double; suites from $175. **Added:** 13% tax. **Payment:** Major credit cards. **Children:** Under 18 free in room with parents. **Pets:** Not permitted. **Smoking:** Nonsmoking rooms available. **Open:** Year-round.

Built in 1886 by a Texas cattle baron, the Driskill is an architectural treasure with an immense arched entrance and ornamented balconies. Its history is intertwined with that of the Lone Star State.

Walk through its doors and you know you're in Texas. Above the registration desk hangs a portrait of Colonel Jesse L. Driskill. Behind it is an expansive painting of the Texas range. Overlooking the lobby is a massive bronze sculpture depicting a dramatic moment in the lives of two cowboys. Portraits of the state's governors line the walls of the handsome lobby bar, and LBJ often made the hotel his campaign headquarters.

> **The Driskill Dining Room, romantically decorated in rose with mirrors, etched glass, and a carved white ceiling, serves steaks and Texas cuisine with a southwestern bent. Down the hall there's a comfortable bar and lounge.**

Throughout the hotel there's a feeling of openness and space, a fitting style for a hostelry that is Texas to the core. The guest rooms occupy two connecting buildings: the 1880s hotel, with high ceilings and several room configurations, and the 1930s tower, with lower ceilings and a more uniform room design.

All the rooms are spacious and tastefully decorated, with touches of grandeur such as crystal drawer pulls on the period furniture. The baths in the tower rooms have adjacent dressing areas.

One of the hotel's banquet rooms is designed around eight mirrors framed in gold leaf, the wedding gift of Mexico's Maximilian to his bride, the Empress Carlotta of Belgium. At the top of each mirror is a gilt medallion likeness of the empress, said to be the most beautiful woman in Europe.

For a small fee, guests may use a health club across the street whose facilities include a workout area with Universal and Nautilus equipment, racquetball courts, a lap pool, a whirlpool, and a sauna. Valet parking at the hotel is $6 per day. Self-parking is also available.

In the heart of downtown Austin, the Driskill opens onto Sixth Street, a lively entertainment area with restaurants, bars, and specialty shops. Sightseeing trolleys stop right in front of the hotel. The Driskill is also just a few blocks from the capitol and the University of Texas.

Four Seasons Hotel Austin

98 San Jacinto Boulevard
Austin, TX 78701
512-478-4500
800-332-3442
Fax: 512-477-0704

> *A top-notch
> lakeside hotel*

General manager: Craig Reid. **Accommodations:** 292 units.
Rates: $155–$185 single, $190–$220 double; suites $225–
$1,200. **Added:** 13% tax. **Payment:** Major credit cards. **Children:** Free in room with parents. **Pets:** Small ones on leash
permitted. **Smoking:** Nonsmoking rooms available. **Open:**
Year-round.

On the shores of Town Lake, ten blocks south of the capitol,
the Four Seasons Austin is a first-class hotel with a southwestern flair. It opened in 1987, setting a new standard for
downtown lodgings.

The lobby, with a stone fireplace and leather chairs, suggests the home of a wealthy Hill Country rancher instead of a
city hotel. Southwestern art, tastefully arranged, adds to the
residential feeling.

Luxury is the tone here; extra touches include terrycloth
robes and hair dryers, pressing within the hour, and twice-daily maid service. More important, the staff is genuinely
friendly and eager to please. The guest rooms are attractive,
decorated in soft earth tones. Although not especially large,
they bespeak comfort with such conveniences as three telephones and digital clocks. "Four Seasons" rooms are more
like suites than standard hotel rooms.

The hotel's serene lakeside setting is used to full advantage; it's like being in a private park. Whether you're eating in
the café, lounging by the pool, or working out in the health

club, the lake is the focal point. Jogging trails line its banks. The health club is far above average, with good exercise equipment, nicely appointed locker rooms, saunas, and a whirlpool.

The Riverside Café, at lake level, serves American cuisine with southwestern and Cajun influences. The kitchen puts its emphasis on freshness, robust sauces, and innovative combinations. Dinner entrées range from $15.50 to $22.50. Lunch buffets are served upstairs in the Lobby Lounge.

Valet parking is available at $8 per day; self-parking is free.

> **By the entrance, lifelike statues of a gardener bending over a flower bed, a pot of fresh flowers in his hand, and a businessman absorbed in the newspaper (and it will be that day's paper) cause many a double take.**

Lake Austin Spa Resort

1705 Quinlan Park Road
Austin, TX 78732
512-266-2444
800-847-5637
Fax: 512-266-1572

> *A friendly staff is a highlight of this lakeside spa*

Executive director: Deborah Evans.
Accommodations: 40 units. **Rates:** 4-day fitness program $500–$640, 1-week program $875–$1,120; 10- and 14-day programs also available. **Included:** All meals. **Minimum stay:** 4 nights. **Added:** 6% tax and a $22 per day service charge. **Payment:** Major credit cards. **Children:** Allowed during family weeks only. **Pets:** Not permitted. **Smoking:** Nonsmoking rooms available. **Open:** Year-round.

In a tranquil setting on the shores of Lake Austin, there's a spa dedicated to fitness education and conditioning. Its atmosphere is unpretentious and friendly; its program is comprehensive, including exercise, nutrition, wellness classes, and beauty services. In a peaceful setting and with personal attention, participants work to achieve their goals, especially weight loss and a more healthful life-style, with the help of a physical fitness staff, a dietitian, and an exercise physiologist.

The spa program is flexible. Guests can choose from 20 daily workouts, including Hill Country walks, low- to high-power aerobics, and an 18-station Swiss Parcourse. Classes on such subjects as relaxation, skin care, and nutrition are integral to the program. For relaxation as well as exercise, there are outdoor and indoor pools, a jogging track, paddle-boats, shuffleboard, and two lighted tennis courts. All the exercise facilities are available around the clock.

Pampering services available at extra charge include skin analysis and facials, massages, manicures, and hair and skin treatments. Spa packages are offered throughout the year.

The main lounge area is appealing, with soothing colors, a stone fireplace, overstuffed chairs, and floral fabrics. The dining room next door is pleasant and casual. Guests are served a thousand-calorie-per-day menu, including dishes like spinach lasagna, chicken fajitas, and vegetable stir-fries. The emphasis is on wholesome food often with a Mexican slant. Many entrées feature fresh vegetables and herbs grown at the resort. For those wishing to continue their healthful eating habits at home, the resort sells its own cookbooks, with delicious low-fat recipes.

The guest rooms in cottages facing the lake have either a king or queen bed, or a full and a twin. They are crisp and clean with a sophisticated country look. Sunny and attractive in blue, white, and yellow, with wicker furniture, beds draped in bunting and topped with floral pillows, the rooms have tile floors, high ceilings, televisions (two movies are shown each night on the house channel), alarm clocks, ceiling fans, and telephones. They are comfortable and welcoming after a hard day's workout.

Lakeway Inn

101 Lakeway Drive
Austin, TX 78734
512-261-6600
800-LAKEWAY
Fax: 512-261-7322

*A lakeside resort
makes the
most of its locale*

General manager: Toby June. **Accommodations:** 137 units. **Rates:** $150 single, $160 double; suites $180. **Included:** Breakfast. **Added:** 6% tax. **Payment:** Major credit cards. **Children:** Free in room with parents. **Pets:** Not permitted. **Smoking:** Permitted. **Open:** Year-round.

On cliffs overlooking Lake Travis about 20 miles west of Austin, Lakeway Inn is at the center of a huge resort and residential community. There are many recreational choices here: two 18-hole championship golf courses, a marina with lots of boats for rent (Jet Skis, fishing, sailing, ski, pontoon, and deck boats), 32 tennis courts at the renowned World of Tennis Club about five minutes from the lodge, horseback riding on 25 miles of trails, several pools, and a spa that offers facials, massages, and manicures and pedicures. There's even a playground for children.

The lake gets top billing. A hillside tram (you'll appreciate it on the way back up) takes guests down to a full-service marina. There is a sailing academy, and fishing trips are available, as are sunset cruises on the lake.

Guest rooms and suites are in low stone buildings near the main lodge. You can rent from one to three segments of a unit. Single bedrooms or bedrooms joined by parlors are spacious and modern, with whitewashed wooden furnishings, southwestern prints, and private balconies that overlook the lake. Many have big stone fireplaces, and executive junior suites have kitchenettes.

The attractive stone lodge houses two dining options, both with lake views. Seafood, southwestern, and Hill Country cuisine dominate the menu ($16–$20) at the Travis Dining Room, while at the Legends pub you'll find burgers and traditional pub fare, as well as shuffleboard and billiards.

Southard House

908 Blanco
Austin, TX 78703
512-474-4731

*A B&B
convenient to
downtown sights*

Innkeepers: Jerry and Regina Southard. **Accommodations:** 16 rooms,
all with private bath. **Rates:** $49–
$79 single, $59–$89 double; suite $129–$159. **Included:** Con-
tinental breakfast on weekdays, full breakfast on weekends;
beverages available. **Minimum stay:** 2 nights on special
Austin weekends. **Added:** 13% tax. **Payment:** Major credit
cards. **Children:** Over 12 welcome. **Pets:** Not permitted.
Smoking: Outside Only. **Open:** Year-round.

On a quiet, tree-lined street just minutes from downtown
Austin, Southard House is an attractive, century-old Greek
Revival and Victorian structure with large, inviting front
porches. Inside, it is warmly furnished with antiques and
original artwork by one of the owners.

Some of the guest rooms have white wrought-iron beds
with brass accents and are covered with elegant lace bedspreads and a profusion of pillows trimmed in lace. Others are
more masculine in tone. Antique washbasins, mirrored
wardrobes, claw-foot tubs, wicker chairs, ceiling fans, sheer
lace curtains, and flowered wallpaper give many of the rooms
a Victorian flavor. The Treaty Oak Room Suite has a sitting
room with a sleeper sofa, a TV, refrigerator, telephone, and
fireplace; the Maisonette room under the eaves has a claw-
foot tub.

On weekends, guests can expect breakfast dishes such as
Belgian waffles with raspberry sauce, eggs Benedict with
chile-hollandaise sauce, and a crustless quiche. During the

week, ample Continental breakfasts consist of cereal, fresh fruit, bagels, and homemade muffins, breads, and cinnamon rolls. Although generally served in the dining room (notice the dragon chandelier), the morning meal moves outdoors to the pleasant gazebo in nice weather.

Because the main house tends to fill up quickly, the Southards have purchased two other homes on the same street and turned them into inns as well. The Peppermint Inn is named for its red and white exterior. It has two suites with kitchenettes.

> **In the evenings, guests enjoy conversing or relaxing with a book on the upstairs porch.**

Rooms at the Lone Star Inn, several doors away, have a western look. Each room has a private entrance, and one has a full kitchen. The swimming pool behind the Lone Star can be used by all guests of Southard House.

Off-street parking is free, and complimentary wine is served upon arrival. Sixth Street, with its collection of restaurants, boutiques, and coffeehouses, is just a few blocks from the inn.

Stouffer Austin Hotel

9721 Arboretum Boulevard
Austin, TX 78759
512-343-2626
800-HOTELS-1
Fax: 512-346-7953

> *Fine accommodations in a suburban setting*

General manager: Gary McGauley.
Accommodations: 478 units. **Rates:** $147 single, $167 double; suites from $195. **Added:** 13% tax. **Payment:** Major credit cards. **Children:** Free in room with parents. **Pets:** Not permitted. **Smoking:** Nonsmoking rooms available. **Open:** Year-round.

In the rolling countryside north of downtown, 15 minutes from the capitol, the Stouffer Austin is a retreat from the city yet near many business addresses, notably the high-tech companies for which Austin is now known. The hotel is part of the Arboretum, a 95-acre development with fancy shops and restaurants as well as sleek office towers. The complex sits on a hillside overlooking the Texas Hill Country, with its cedar forests and limestone cliffs.

At the center of the Stouffer is an atrium, an expansive marble plaza with sculptures, dining kiosks, and sitting areas. Large teak bells hang from above while remarkably lifelike bronze birds appear to soar overhead. Natural plants surround the atrium on every level.

The Pavilion, in the center of the atrium, serves deli sandwiches, salads, fruit, pastries, and beverages around the clock. The Garden Café serves breakfast and lunch, with a pianist to entertain at noontime. On one side is the Trattoria Grande, a northern Italian bistro with excellent food and service with a flair. The arched windows offer unobstructed views of the scenic terrain. The lobby bar has live entertainment in the evenings.

> **Next door to the hotel are the Arboretum shops, from Banana Republic to fancy boutiques, a four-screen movie theater, and the hotel's club, Tangerines.**

The guest rooms, with Queen Anne furniture and Oriental art, are luxurious and large — some of the largest in the city. Many of the rooms have pastoral valley views. Atrium suites have small balconies opening onto the atrium, mini-bars, and separate sitting areas. Conference suites have Murphy beds so that meetings can be held at the suite's own boardroom table. Guests on the private-access Club Floor enjoy concierge services from 6:30 A.M. to 10:00 P.M., complimentary breakfast, evening hors d'oeuvres, and a lounge bar.

The Presidential Suite is truly royal. Chinese palace lions guard the entrance. Inside, giant Oriental vases hold citrus and palm trees, original oils line the walls, and expansive windows provide a fine view. There's a full kitchen and a separate dining room seating ten. In the bath, a small Sony with microcassette recorder lets you watch your favorite program or dictate notes from the double Jacuzzi tub.

All guests are treated to complimentary coffee, a newspaper, and the weather report with their wake-up call. Other amenities include 24-hour room service, free parking, and free transportation to the airport. Valet parking is $7 per day.

For relaxation, there's an especially wide range of choices for a city hotel: an oval outdoor pool in an appealing hillside setting, an indoor pool, a sauna, hot tub, game room, well-equipped exercise room, jogging path, short nature trail, and picnic tables tucked among the trees. A separate elevator takes guests to the pool area; both pools are heated.

Wyndham Austin Hotel at Southpark

4140 Governor's Row
I-35 and Ben White Boulevard
Austin, TX 78744
512-448-2222
800-433-2241
Fax: 512-448-4744

A 14-story hotel with a contemporary look

General manager: John Allsup. **Accommodations:** 313 rooms and suites. **Rates:** $121 single, $141 double; suites $450. **Added:** 13% tax. **Payment:** Major credit cards. **Children:** Under 16 free in room with parents. **Pets:** Not permitted. **Smoking:** 66 nonsmoking rooms. **Open:** Year-round.

Just outside the Wyndham's lobby is a Texas-size, horseshoe-shaped indoor-outdoor pool and a recreation area. A bridge leads across the pool into the fitness center, with its attractive deck area, whirlpool, sauna, and weight and exercise room. Nearby is the hotel's sports court (basketball or volleyball), jogging track, and shuffleboard.

South of downtown, the Wyndham has a relaxing atmosphere, outstanding recreational features, and a hospitable staff.

The rooms have luxurious, modern furnishings, rich fabrics, and colorful artwork. Comfortable seating, TVs with in-house movies, and clock radios add to the pleasure. Some of the ground-floor rooms open onto the pool. Executive suites have a parlor with a conference table, a sitting area with a foldout bed, and one or two connecting bedrooms. Both the Presidential and the Governor's suites have a large parlor and two bedrooms; the former has a whirlpool tub.

Onion Creek Grill, a casual dining room, has all-day service. Pasta and salads are featured, as well as steak and seafood. Sweetwaters Lounge is the hotel's friendly bar.

BANDERA

Mayan Dude Ranch

P.O. Box 577
Bandera, TX 78003
210-796-3312
210-796-3036
Fax: 210-796-8205

*A Texas-friendly,
family-run ranch*

Hosts: The Hicks family. **Accommodations:** 66 units. **Rates:** $95 single, $125 double; suites $190; weekly rates available. **Included:** All meals and horseback riding. **Added:** 10% service charge, 8.1% sales tax. **Payment:** Major credit cards and personal checks. **Children:** Up to 12 years, $40; 13–17 years, $60. **Pets:** Not permitted. **Smoking:** Nonsmoking dining room. **Open:** Year-round.

It doesn't take long to settle into a cowboy frame of mind at the Mayan, a sprawling ranch with plenty of space to ramble and an informal tone conducive to relaxing. The Hicks family has been welcoming guests since the early 1950s, and they have it down pat. Along with hearty cowboy grub, they serve up a big helping of hospitality and fun.

It all starts with orange juice and coffee delivered to your door in the morning, probably by one of the Hicks offspring. Then you choose whether to have breakfast on the trail or in the dining room. We're talking about a real breakfast here: thick bacon, homemade sausage, hash browns, grits, and hot biscuits.

Morning trail rides lead into the hills or down by the cool green Medina River. Guests are entitled to two rides a day, led by well-trained guides. Don't worry if you don't know how to ride; the Mayan Dude Ranch is proud of its instructors. When you aren't riding, there's swimming in the large pool, tubing in the river, fishing, hiking, and playing tennis. During the summer, there's a full roster of group activities, including contests, theme nights, and hayrides. If bad weather drives you indoors, the informal saloon is a good gathering spot over a beer or margarita in the evenings. There's a big-screen TV in the round-up room, and a small game room with video games should keep the children happy.

Accommodations are in stone cottages or in one of three

lodges with six to sixteen rooms each. It's hard to go wrong here, and there's lots of variety. Some of the cottages are designed for large families. The exteriors are rustic, but the interiors are spacious and comfortably western, with ceiling fans, wagon wheel light fixtures, and natural wood everywhere. If views are important to you, be sure to mention it, for some rooms have views of the surrounding hill country. The units are sprinkled through the woods, creating a sense of space.

One of the most attractive features of the ranch is the outdoor deck next to the dining room. It's the perfect place to relax as you watch the sun set beyond the hills, or perhaps you'll catch a glimpse of a deer or the peacock that roams the ranch.

> **Scheduled activities are fewer in the off-season, but they still include riding, cowboy breakfasts, barbecues, and hayrides. Families, groups, seminars, and conventions make up the guest roster. For many, the ranch is the closest thing to the "Wild West" they'll ever experience.**

Reservations, especially for the summer, need to be made well in advance.

BELLVILLE

High Cotton Inn Bed and Breakfast

214 South Live Oak
Bellville, TX 77418
409-865-9796
800-321-9796
Fax: 409-865-5588

*A Victorian B&B
in the country*

Innkeepers: George and Anna Horton. **Accommodations:** 5 rooms with shared baths. **Rates:** $40–$60 single, $50–$70 double. **Included:** Full breakfast. **Added:** 13.75% tax. **Payment:** Major credit cards. **Children:** Infants not encouraged; older children additional $5 per day. **Pets:** Not permitted; boarding available nearby. **Smoking:** Not permitted. **Open:** Year-round.

There is no better place to escape the humdrum than at High Cotton. Anna Horton always wanted to live in the country,

> **High Cotton has a pool out back. There are also two porches to rock on, and a dozen or so antiques shops nearby. The hosts can arrange golf for guests at a local 9-hole course.**

so today she and her husband operate a country B&B in a two-story Victorian with wraparound porches and period furnishings. The mood is informal at High Cotton, making it a great place to relax. Much of its charm is tied to the Hortons, genuinely nice people whose natural enthusiasm and zest for living often spills over to their guests. They revel in serving bounteous breakfasts, with a repertoire too lengthy to list (locally cured bacon, yard eggs, yeast biscuits, grits, rum cake — you get the idea). When the Hortons aren't welcoming guests, they're apt to be out in their cookie kitchen, baking goodies marketed under the name High Cotton Country Cookie and Candy Company. Be sure to try the caramel crisps and the oatmeal raisin spice cookies from their "bottomless cookie jar."

High Cotton's second-floor guest rooms are excellent for small groups as well as couples. No decorating detail has escaped the hosts' notice, and family antiques and memorabilia are the focal point. Uncle Buster's Room has a beautifully carved bed. A beaded gown worn by George's grandmother is displayed in the upstairs parlor. Even the medicine cabinet has a story to tell, with antique gloves and spats on display.

Townsquare Inn

21 South Bell
Bellville, TX 77418
409-865-9021
Fax: 409-865-9021

*A small-town
inn at the center
of activity*

Innkeeper: Deborah Nolen. **Accommodations:** 9 rooms, most with shared baths. **Rates:** $50 single, $55 double; suites $85–$150. **Added:** 12% tax. **Included:** Continental breakfast. **Payment:** Major credit cards. **Children:** Free in room with parents. **Pets:** Not permitted. **Smoking:** Nonsmoking rooms available. **Open:** Year-round.

Part of a group of businesses run by the same owners, the Townsquare Inn is on the second floor of a building that also houses the Tea Rose restaurant, the Tap Room Pub, and

Timeless Interiors design shop. Several antiques shops — one
of Bellville's claims to fame — are within a few blocks. As the
name promises, the inn is indeed on the town square, overlooking the courthouse.

**Continental breakfast is
placed in the kitchenette at
the end of the hall long
before most guests awaken.
But the aroma of country
cooking at the Tea Rose
may entice you to
skip the muffins and head
downstairs.**

Deborah Nolen is an
interior designer, and she
has converted the second-
story space into a lodging
of beauty. Chintz, stained
glass, and greenery play a
large part in the decorating scheme. The keynote
is comfort, from spacious
living quarters to conve-
niences such as clock ra-
dios. Townsquare has two
three-bedroom suites, of
which one, two, or three
bedrooms can be reserved, as well as two adjoining rooms and
a grand suite. Guests in the three-bedroom suites, ideal for
small groups, share a parlor with a TV and game table and a
bathroom with a claw-foot tub and shower.

The Court, with a queen-size bed, and the Chambers, with
twins, adjoin and can be taken separately or together. The
baths are across the hall, one for men and one for women.
The Bell Suite is worth its price tag. It is spacious, with a parlor and private bath, and its decor is decidedly romantic. The
king-size bed is canopied in lace. The elegant bath has a claw-
foot tub, a toilet with a pull chain, and a dressing table.

BOERNE

Ye Kendall Inn

128 West Blanco
Boerne, TX 78006
210-249-2138

*An inn with history
and romance*

Owners: Ed and Vicki Schleyer.
Accommodations: 8 rooms, 3
suites. **Rates:** Rooms $80, suites $125. **Included:** Continental
breakfast. **Added:** 13% tax. **Payment:** Major credit cards. **Chil-**

dren: Additional $10 per child per day. **Pets:** Not permitted. **Smoking:** Not permitted. **Open:** Year-round.

On five acres in the center of the Hill Country town of Boerne, Ye Kendall Inn has a long history of welcoming guests, among them Dwight D. Eisenhower, Jefferson Davis, and Robert E. Lee. The central part of the inn was built in a southern colonial style back in 1859 as the home of Erastus and Sarah Reed. As was common in those days when public accommodations were few and far between, the Reeds occasionally rented out their extra rooms to travelers. In 1878, the inn was turned into a stagecoach inn, and wings were added to both sides of the original structure. In 1909, the inn was renamed for George W. Kendall.

> **A tunnel in the basement, said to have been used to escape unfriendly Indians, once connected the inn to a building a block away. The inn is also rumored to be haunted.**

In 1982, Ed and Vicki Schleyer purchased the property and spent several years restoring the inn, with beautiful results. Today Ye Kendall Inn is a handsome, two-story, honey-colored limestone structure with graceful 200-foot-long porches and gray shutters. Most of the guest rooms are on the second floor; the four that open off the central parlor are part of the original home.

Guest rooms are furnished with American and English antiques, but the Leslie Schoenfeld, Victoria, Edna Davenport, and Sarah Reed rooms are especially romantic. The Leslie Schoenfeld suite is popular with honeymooners. It has a king-size canopy bed with corkscrew posts, high ceilings, a claw-foot tub, and an antique washbasin. The Victoria Suite is a delight. An elegant Victorian sofa with bolster pillows graces the sitting area, windows are draped in lace and fringed chintz, and a two-sided fireplace to warm the sitting area and bedroom at the same time is a focal point. The Edna Davenport has a brass and metal bed; the Sarah Reed has a beautiful carved bed, a pink claw-foot tub, and a rocking chair.

If floral fabrics and lace are not for you, take Time-Life, a masculine room with an animal skin rug, simple metal bed, and old framed Life magazine covers on the walls. The Jane Zoch room, on the first floor, is furnished in dark green and wallpapered with forest scenes. All rooms are air-conditioned.

The inn's surroundings are equally pleasant. In back are a fountain courtyard and a gazebo, and the land stretches down to Cibolo Creek. The front of the inn overlooks the town green. Cascade Caverns are a five-minute drive. Antiquing is also a popular pastime in the area.

Continental breakfast is served in the upstairs parlor. On the first floor are a good Italian restaurant and an attractive boutique.

CHAPPELL HILL

Browning Plantation

Route 1, Box 8
Chappell Hill, TX 77426
409-836-6144

> *Tara in the
> Hill Country*

Innkeepers: Dick and Mildred Ganchan. **Accommodations:** 4 rooms with shared baths in main house, 2 rooms with private bath in separate building. **Rates:** $75–$100 single, $90–$120 double. **Included:** Full breakfast and tax. **Payment:** Personal check. **Children:** Over 12 welcome. **Pets:** Not permitted. **Smoking:** Outside only. **Open:** Year-round.

This grand old mansion set on sprawling grounds is reminiscent of a bygone era. Drive up the gravel road to a world conducive to relaxation: here you can relive the life of southern gentry, sipping cool drinks on the verandah and luxuriating in oversize guest rooms.

Listed on the National Register of Historic Places, the Browning Plantation was built in 1857. Dick and Mildred Ganchan discovered the deteriorated structure in 1980 and decided "somebody had to do something." For the next three years they painstakingly restored it, retaining the historical integrity of the building and transforming it into a magnificent house.

Although furnished with antiques, the Greek Revival home has more comfort than elegance. The guest rooms are enormous. In addition to the expected plantation and tester beds, there are unusual pieces such as a "mammy bench," designed for rocking babies. One doorway still bears marks designating the height of the children who stood against it in 1872.

The third floor is a delight. Throughout the rest of the home the Ganchans remained true to the original design, but in this space, the original attic, they gave their imagination free rein. To supplement the half baths next to each guest room on the second floor, they created two bathrooms with whimsical decor. For ladies, the theme is Victorian bordello — a chandelier, mirrored wall, a soft, fuzzy rug, even a stained glass skylight. The men's bathroom is decidedly masculine — rough cedar walls, a pine dressing table, a zebra-skin rug, and deer antlers doubling as towel racks. From here you can climb to a rooftop observation deck, which offers an excellent view of the surrounding farmland.

So popular is the plantation home that another building has been added. It resembles a 19th-century train depot and is next to a scaled-down model train, the pet project of a "railroad nut" in the Ganchan family.

A swimming pool in the backyard keeps you from losing touch with the 20th century. Also on the grounds is a restored log cabin, now an antiques and crafts shop — a low-key operation, open only on special occasions or when guests ask.

Breakfast is served in the dining room at an antique table. The fare is bountiful, a full country breakfast. Stained glass doors lead to the modern kitchen, built on the site of the original one.

The Stagecoach Inn

Main at Chestnut
P.O. Box 339
Chappell Hill, TX 77426
409-836-9515

> *An old inn
> in a town filled
> with history*

Owners: Elizabeth and Harvin Moore. **Accommodations:** 5 rooms with shared baths, 1 2-bedroom cottage. **Rates:** $90–$100. **Included:** Breakfast. **Added:** 6% tax. **Payment:** Personal check in advance. **Children:** Over age 6 welcome; additional charge for children over 12. **Pets:** Not permitted. **Smoking:** Outside only. **Open:** Year-round.

With fewer than 400 residents, the town of Chappell Hill, Texas, may not be large, but it is filled with history: more than two dozen buildings wear historical markers. The most renowned is the Greek revival–style stone and cedar Stagecoach Inn. Built as an inn in 1850 by Jacob and Mary Haller, the founders of Chappell Hill, it is now listed on the National Register of Historic Places.

> **Guest rooms have been added to the Coach House and the Greek revival–style Weems House, which also stand on the nicely landscaped three-acre property.**

The inn was kept as a residence by the current owners, the Moores, until 1989, when they began welcoming overnight guests. It was beautifully restored and is furnished with fine antiques as well as braided rugs made by Elizabeth Moore.

COLUMBUS

Gant Guest House

936 Bowie Street
P.O. Box 86
Columbus, TX 78934
409-732-5135

> *A cozy hideaway
> in a 19th-century
> German cottage*

Owner: Laura Ann Rau. **Accommodations:** 2 rooms with shared bath.
Rates: $65; both rooms $95. **Included:** Continental breakfast.
Added: 12% tax. **Payment:** Personal checks. **Children:** Over
12 welcome. **Pets:** Not permitted. **Smoking:** Not permitted.
Open: Year-round.

In Columbus, site of one of the oldest settlements in Texas,
you can stay in a tiny restored German cottage dating from
the 1870s. An itinerant
German painter probably
stenciled the walls and
ceilings of this home. His
work, hidden by years of
soot, was uncovered by
Laura Ann Rau when she
set out to restore the gem
of a house. His stenciling
is so charming that the

> **The cottage was moved
> from nearby Alleytown
> to its present location on
> a quiet street in this town
> of 4,500 residents.**

Texas Society of the DAR copied the entire room in the DAR
Museum in Washington, D.C.

Antique furniture, some native to Texas, fills each room.
Two small bedrooms with double beds and a hall sitting room

with a day bed can accommodate up to five people in one party. Don't worry about having to rough it: there's a modern kitchen that guests can use, a small bath with a tub-shower, central air conditioning and heating, and a TV. Breakfast is put·in the refrigerator before your arrival, so you can eat when you choose. A few blocks away are antiques and gift shops for lazy afternoon browsing.

The Rau family also runs a bed-and-breakfast down the street in a lovely Victorian built in 1887. The house, which has been given a state historic marker, has intricate porch trim, three marble mantelpieces, and other fine craftsmanship characteristic of the period. The inn does have modern conveniences, however, such as central heating, air conditioning, and a swimming pool. You might want to inquire about lodging there if the guest house is full.

EAGLE LAKE

The Farris 1912

201 North McCarty Avenue
Eagle Lake, TX 77434
409-234-2546
Fax: 409-234-2598

*A historic
hunting lodge*

Proprietors: William and Helyn Farris. **Accommodations:** 24 rooms, most with shared baths. **Rates:** November–February, rates from $100 per person including all meals; other months, rates from $55 per person including Continental breakfast. **Added:** 10% tax. **Payment:** Major credit cards. **Children:** Restricted. **Pets:** Not permitted inside; kennels available for dogs. **Smoking:** Not permitted.

Open: Guest house open year-round; main lodge closed in summer unless groups rent the entire building.

The Farris 1912 wears two faces. From November through February, the historic hotel, known as "Eagle Lake's birthplace," caters to hunters who come for the excellent duck and goose hunting. During the rest of the year it welcomes sightseers, particularly during March and April, when the fabled Texas wildflowers are at their peak.

Guests are welcome to visit the owners' nearby lakeside property and observe the wildlife. The Attwater Prairie Chicken Refuge, a 3,400-acre sanctuary dedicated to these near-extinct birds, is six miles from the Farris.

> **A sign by the door reads: "Hunters, Unload Guns! No Muddy Boots in Hotel, Please." In a small separate building is a facility for cleaning guns as well as refrigerated storage.**

The area is so popular for bird hunting that the hotel attracts international guests in the winter, for this is no ordinary hunting lodge. Casual elegance is the theme, and the public areas are richly decorated with antique furniture, lace curtains, silver candelabra, mirrors, and floral carpets.

All meals are provided during hunting season. As on a cruise ship, food is omnipresent, with an "eat all you want" philosophy. Continental breakfast is served the rest of the year, except during wildflower season, when lunch is offered daily. For groups and private parties, supplemental food service can be arranged. No gratuities are accepted at any time for lodging or food services.

Accommodations are in the main hotel and in the 1920s guest house next door. The hotel rooms, cheerfully but simply furnished, have double or twin beds, and two have private baths. The VIP Room has an antique spool bed and a twin bed. All the rooms open onto a sprawling mezzanine, a popular gathering spot with couches, easy chairs, and game tables. The suites in the guest house have private entrances, a bath with a shower, a parlor, wet bar, refrigerator, and TV.

FREDERICKSBURG

Gastehaus Schmidt

231 West Main
Fredericksburg, TX 78624
210-997-5612 (10 A.M.–6 P.M.
  weekdays; 1–6 P.M. Saturday)
Fax: 210-997-8282

*A B&B reservation
service for the
Fredericksburg area*

Proprietor: Loretta Schmidt. **Accommodations:** About 50 listings in the Fredericksburg area. **Rates:** From $50 per night. **Included:** Continental or full breakfast in many cases. **Added:** 6–13% tax. **Payment:** Major credit cards. **Children:** Often welcome. **Pets:** Sometimes permitted. **Smoking:** Sometimes permitted. **Open:** Year-round.

Fredericksburg is a popular Hill Country town with many bed-and-breakfasts to choose from, but finding the right one at the right time can be a difficult task. The reservation service Gastehaus Schmidt represents a rich variety of lodgings in the Fredericksburg area, with a number of them reflecting the historic character of the town. You can choose from farms, "Sunday houses" built by pioneer farmers as a place to spend the night when they went to town for church, log cabins, and modern homes. Some homes are occupied by their owners; in others, you have the entire lodging to yourself.

> **Historic homes offered include a log and stone house from the early 1850s and a Victorian charmer only two blocks from the historic district.**

For $4, the service will send you a complete description of their listings. Browsing through the choices gives you a well-rounded view of this community settled by German farmers. Some of the more unusual accommodations offered are guest rooms in a one-room schoolhouse, a limestone barn, and a log cabin on a 26-acre historical site.

HORSESHOE BAY

Horseshoe Bay Country Club Resort

1 Horseshoe Bay Boulevard
P.O. Box 7766
Horseshoe Bay, TX 78654
210-598-2511
800-252-9363 in Texas
800-531-5105 in U.S.
Fax: 210-598-5338

> *A full-service resort on the shores of Lake LBJ*

Executive vice president: Ron Lynn Mitchell. **Accommodations:** 80 hotel rooms, 50 condos. **Rates:** High season $150–$475; low season $120–$386. **Added:** 6% tax. **Payment:** Major credit cards. **Children:** Permitted with restrictions. **Pets:** Not permitted. **Smoking:** Nonsmoking rooms available. **Open:** Year-round.

In the gently rolling Hill Country west of Austin, Horseshoe Bay is a 4,000-acre residential resort community that can boast the best of country life as well as city sophistication. Deer roam freely and the pace of life is slow, but at your fingertips is exceptionally fine dining and a wealth of recreational facilities, including the largest Robert Trent Jones golf complex in the world.

At the heart of the community is Horseshoe Bay Country Club Resort, a private club with extensive facilities for its members and "temporary members," the status accorded guests.

Golfers can choose from three courses on unusually scenic terrain, a combination of cliffside lake views, cedar- and mesquite-studded countryside, and ravines and streams. The Applerock course is considered one of the best resort golf courses in the country. Tee times should be arranged a week in advance.

The tennis complex, covering 18 acres and surrounded by Oriental gardens, has 14 Laykold courts, 4 of them covered. The resort also has several outstanding swimming pools; a two-tier pool fed by waterfalls cascading off bedrock granite outcrops overlooks the golf course. One pool has a spa. Horseback rides follow scenic trails across the countryside. Boat and ski rentals and fishing guides are also available. It's advisable to reserve a boat before you arrive.

> **Enhancing the already beautiful landscape are gardens and fountains, waterfalls and statues. The resort has an idyllic air, restful and pleasing.**

Many of the lodgings, in several low buildings, are directly on the marina. Several styles are available, from one- to three-bedroom units. Refreshingly, the units don't resemble standard condo designs: the space is used innovatively, the interiors are large, the furnishings are modern and well done, and the kitchens and baths have lots of extras.

Dining is a major attraction at Horseshoe Bay. The Captain's Quarters is formal, with a varied menu and an exclusive atmosphere that requires coat and tie for men, evening attire for women. There are also two informal restaurants, romantic in style as well as in their lakeside setting.

INGRAM

Lazy Hills Guest Ranch

P.O. Box G
Henderson Branch Road
Ingram, TX 78025
210-367-5600
800-880-0632
Fax: 210-367-5667

> *A family-run guest ranch for over 30 years*

Hosts: Bob and Carol Steinruck. **Accommodations:** 26 units. **Rates:** $85–$95 single, $130–$140 double; weekly rates available. **Included:** All meals, 6 rides per week. **Minimum stay:** 3 nights in high season; stays of 1 or 2 nights when space is available for an extra $10 per night per room. **Added:** 15% gratuity and 6% lodging tax. **Payment:** Major credit cards. **Children:** Permitted; additional charge based on age. **Pets:** Not permitted. **Smoking:** Permitted. **Open:** Year-round.

Spread over 750 acres in the pastoral Texas Hill Country, the family-run Lazy Hills Guest Ranch offers friendliness and fun. The pace is slow, with time for strolling and relaxing. Horseback riding fits the mood, and guests can choose one of four hour-long rides a day. The price of a week's stay includes six rides; guests staying for a shorter time can pay for guided trail rides at $8 per person per hour. There's also a large swimming pool, a wading pool, a hot tub, a fishing pond, a children's playground with treehouse, an activity hall where line dancing is a popular event, lighted tennis courts, archery, and volleyball, as well as exploring along the creek and hiking in the woods.

> **The family-style dining room is welcoming. The adjacent sitting room has the only TV on the premises. In a nearby building is a game room with pool and Ping-Pong tables, shuffleboard, and electronic games.**

The hosts often cater to groups and are happy to arrange activities suited to the age and interests of their guests. The lodging units are clustered, which makes them ideal for groups. The furnishings are simple, more like those at a real ranch than at many guest ranches. Most of the rooms can sleep up to four. Six units have fireplaces.

Reduced rates are available from September 15 to May 15, except over holidays. No minimum stay is required during the off-season, and B&B rates can be arranged then as well. Groups should inquire about special rates.

KERRVILLE

Inn of the Hills River Resort

1001 Junction Highway
Kerrville, TX 78028
210-895-5000
800-292-5690
Fax: 210-895-1277

*A relaxed,
family-style resort*

General manager: Hans Schlunegger. **Accommodations:** 150
rooms, 68 condos. **Rates:** $55–$65 single, $65–$85 double;
condos $85–$200; additional adults $6. **Added:** 12% tax. **Payment:** Major credit cards. **Children:** Under 12 free in room
with parents. **Pets:** Small ones permitted. **Smoking:** Nonsmoking rooms available. **Open:** Year-round.

In the Texas Hill Country, this resort has a wide range of offerings, both in style of accommodations and in recreation.
Inn of the Hills began welcoming guests in the early 1960s,
and in the mid-1980s it added a condominium complex on the
banks of the Guadalupe River, greatly enhancing its appeal.

**The resort has two
restaurants, Annemarie's
Alpine Lodge, serving
German-American cuisine,
and the River View,
overlooking the river.**

Guests now have a choice
of motel rooms, cabanas,
junior suites, and executive suites in the older
section, or condos with or
without kitchenettes. A
seven-room casa with a
rock-bottomed pool is
ideal for family reunions
or small groups wanting
proximity and privacy.

The motor inn centers around a pleasant swimming pool,
putting green, and playground. While the buildings do reflect
their age, rooms have been recently refurbished and there's a
look of TLC about them. The rooms are pleasantly decorated,
and the grounds are well maintained.

The tower condominium complex provides a river view for
every unit. The condos, ranging from 700 to 1,500 square feet,
are more luxurious than the motor inn lodgings. They have
living rooms, dining rooms, and balconies.

Guests have full use of all the resort's facilities: two outdoor pools, lighted tennis courts, and a 9-hole putting green; a marina with canoes and paddleboats; a fishing pier; rental bikes; and the sports center next door with racquetball, handball, an exercise room, indoor pool, and a bowling alley.

Y.O. Ranch Hotel

2033 Sidney Baker Street
Kerrville, TX 78028
512-257-4440
800-531-2800 in Texas
Fax: 512-896-8189

*Western-style
lodging in the heart
of Hill Country*

General manager: M.E. Rule. **Accommodations:** 200 rooms. **Rates:** $68 single, $88–$98 double; each additional adult $10; suites $150–$230. **Added:** 12% tax. **Payment:** Major credit cards. **Children:** Under 18 free in room with parents. **Pets:** Not permitted. **Smoking:** Nonsmoking rooms available. **Open:** Year-round.

The Y.O. Ranch Hotel is cowboy plush. Stride into the lobby, one of the most distinctive in the Southwest, and you know you're in cattle country. The chandeliers are fashioned from branding irons, and a very lifelike stuffed bear looks as if it's about to strike. Wild game trophies, guns and saddles displayed in glass cases, hand-carved chairs covered in rawhide, and a vaulted wooden ceiling all make you feel as though you're in a wilderness hunting lodge, not in downtown Kerrville.

Although the motel-style lodging is 30 miles from the famed 50,000 acre Y.O. Ranch, the two establishments share a close kinship. A working ranch, the Y.O. has one of the finest herds of Texas longhorns in the country, as well as exotic game. Hotel guests can use a direct phone line to the ranch to sign up for tours. Originally both the hotel and the ranch were owned by the Schreiner family, the descendants of Captain Charles Schreiner. Today the hotel is operated by Holiday Inn.

The guest rooms are comfortable, with country furnishings, saltillo tile floors, larger than average baths, and western prints and antler accents on the walls. Some have balconies overlooking the pool, with its giant Y.O. brand on the bottom. The American Indian suite is decorated with beaded and silver artifacts, arrowheads, and Indian portraits. The Longhorn suite has mementos depicting the history of the breed. Some suites have fireplaces.

Dine at the Sam Houston Room, serving Texas specialties and exotic game, some of which comes from the ranch (entrées range from $13 to $19), and be sure to visit the Elm Waterhole saloon. There's a hot tub next to the pool, a tennis court on the grounds, and a municipal golf course next door.

> **Year-round private game hunts for both native and exotic game are available. Stocked with game animals from all parts of the world, the ranch has herds of axis deer; aoudad, mouflon, and Corsican sheep; American elk; and Indian black buck antelope.**

Ranch tours are offered Tuesday through Sunday for $27, which includes lunch or dinner. Children 7 to 12 pay half price; those under 7 are free.

NAVASOTA

The Castle Inn

1403 East Washington
Navasota, TX 77868
409-825-8051

> *Step into the Victorian era*

Innkeepers: Tim and Helen Urquhart. **Accommodations:** 4 rooms, all with private bath. **Rates:** $84 single, $94 double. **Included:**

Continental breakfast. **Added:** 13% tax. **Payment:** Personal check. **Children:** Over age 13 welcome; additional $20 per day. **Pets:** Not permitted. **Smoking:** Nonsmoking rooms available. **Open:** Year-round.

On eight acres overlooking one of Navasota's main streets, the Castle Inn, built in the 1890s, is indeed a castle, complete with turrets. You enter a world of elegance through a porch enclosed with 110 panes of beveled glass. Built by German craftsmen, the house has nine and a half bays, resulting in octagonal rooms. Curly pine, now extinct, is used throughout the home. So are carved wood trims and ornate brass hardware. Every room is thoughtfully furnished with articles of beauty that have special meaning to the owners. China dolls are dressed in Victorian baby clothes handed down through the family. Two child-size dolls wear costumes that

> **Sliding doors 14 feet tall open into the dining room, the most beautiful room in the house. Its ornate ceiling, hand-painted borders, and tiger oak walls form a work of art.**

Helen Urquhart and her brother once wore for a tap-dance performance. The music room, where socially prominent ladies used to gather for bridge luncheons, is decorated with musical instruments, including a player piano.

The bedrooms are on the second floor. A spool staircase leads past a 20-foot original stained glass window to a parlor and adjoining balcony, where Continental breakfast is served. This is also the gathering spot for wine and cheese in the evenings. The beds are a rosewood Louisiana plantation, a half-tester, or a carved high-back bed. Marble-topped dressers, accent pieces such as fainting couches, and family memorabilia, including heirloom quilts, complete the feeling of Victorian elegance. The Bridal Suite is striking, decorated in fuchsia and pink, with an alcove bed and a claw-foot tub.

NEW BRAUNFELS

Prince Solms Inn

295 East San Antonio Street
New Braunfels, TX 78130
512-625-9169

> *A historic inn
> with lots
> of character*

Owners: Bob and Pat Brent. **Accommodations:** 10 rooms, all with private bath. **Rates:** $60–$110; suites $100–$140. **Added:** 13% tax. **Included:** Continental breakfast. **Minimum stay:** 2 nights on weekends May through September and holidays. **Payment:** Major credit cards. **Children:** Over 12 welcome. **Pets:** Not permitted. **Smoking:** Non-smoking rooms available. **Open:** Year-round.

Built in 1898, the Prince Solms is in a community settled in 1845 by Germans who were led to the new land by Prince Carl of Solms-Braunfels. The family of the hotel's builder were among the original settlers. Today, the trim two-story building, constructed of locally made brick and native timber, is one of New Braunfels's most visible links to its heritage.

The interior, furnished to reflect the inn's history, has a delicate charm. On one side of the central hall is a parlor furnished with antiques, setting the mood for the entire inn. The Princess Sophie Suite across the hall has swags and shutters at the windows, German portraits on the walls, a large sitting room with period furnishings, and a separate bedroom with a king-size bed. The bath is small and modern, and there's also a tiny kitchen. Down the hall is the Prince Carl Suite. Grand and elegant, it is similarly furnished but with a more masculine decor.

The rest of the bedrooms are upstairs, with names suggesting their decor: Peony, Library, Summer House, Magnolia, Rose, and Songbird. It is no surprise that the decorator was able to locate rose, peony, or even magnolia print wallpaper, but where they unearthed such fitting songbird motif wallpaper and upholstery fabric is a mystery and is evidence of the care that went into furninshing each room. The Summer House, appropriately, is furnished with wicker furniture. Book-lovers should request the cozy Library,

> If you're not a guest at the Prince Solms, Wolfgang Keller's restaurant is worth a special trip; for guests, it's a real luxury to have such a fine establishment only a few steps away.

with a stocked bookcase behind its bed. The baths are small but well designed. In addition to central air conditioning, there is a ceiling fan in each room.

A Continental breakfast of fresh pastries, coffee, and tea is laid out on the hall sideboard each morning. Its professional, tastefully elegant style is typical of every aspect of the inn's operation.

In the cellar of the inn is Wolfgang Keller's restaurant, one of the best in the Hill Country, both in cuisine and atmosphere. The restaurant is named in honor of Wolfgang Mozart, and a specially commissioned portrait of the composer hangs on the landing. Soft lighting, exposed brick walls, and classical music add to the romantic ambience. Specialties include Lobster Marquis Lafayette, fried lobster topped with gulf shrimp, avocado, and bernaise sauce; and Jaeger schnitzel, pork seasoned with German mustard, sautéed in red wine with mushrooms, onions, and tomatoes, accompanied by potato pancakes. Reservations are recommended.

Behind the inn there's a shaded courtyard and an 1850s house that, like the inn, is a registered historic building. The Prince Solms is an ideal place to begin exploring New Braunfels — the main plaza is just down the street. The innkeepers are adept at helping visitors plan their stay, and bikes can be borrowed from the inn for local sightseeing.

SALADO

Inn on the Creek

Center Circle
P.O. Box 858
Salado, TX 76571
817-947-5554
Fax: 817-947-9198

*An antique-filled
creekside inn*

Innkeepers: The Epps and the Whistlers. **Accommodations:**
16 rooms. **Rates:** $85–$125. **Included:** Full breakfast. **Added:**
6% tax. **Payment:** Major credit cards. **Children:** Welcome.
Pets: Not permitted. **Smoking:** Not permitted. **Open:** Year-round.

On the banks of shady Salado Creek is a stately Victorian
home with a back porch just made for creek-watching. The
Epps and Whistler families are delightful hosts, making you
welcome with bountiful breakfasts or even elegant dinners. At night, there's chocolate on your pillow.

> **Dinners have become so popular with both guests and the public that the owners bought a 19th-century home to serve as a dining room for up to 50 people.**

The 1880s home was moved to this spot from a nearby town. It took over a year to restore the old house, and its size was doubled in the process. The fine wooden trims of the original home were retained and new trims milled to duplicate them. The result is a picture-perfect home where everything matches, including the exquisite decor.

Guest rooms are all decorated with handsome antiques, and each room has a TV and phone. A favorite is the Tyler Room, a swirl of peach with a white iron bed and wicker furniture. The best room in the house is the McKie Room, on the third floor. It has a brass king-size bed with a canopy, a mirrored armoire, Queen Anne chairs, and an idyllic reading alcove overlooking the creek. Extras befitting its grandeur come with the room: chilled champagne and breakfast in bed.

The creative hosts offer such special events as murder mystery and gourmet weekends. If you wish, they will help you plan your stay in the historic Salado area.

SAN MARCOS

Crystal River Inn

326 West Hopkins
San Marcos, TX 78666
512-396-3739
Fax: 512-353-3248

A well-run, tastefully decorated B&B

Innkeepers: Mike and Cathy Dillon. **Accommodations:** 7 rooms and 4 suites. **Rates:** $50–$70 weekdays, $70–$90 weekends; suites $85–$110. **Included:** Full breakfast. **Added:** 13% tax. **Payment:** Major credit cards. **Children:** Allowed with prior arrangement; $7.50 additional per day if there are three or more people in the room. **Pets:** By prior arrangement only. **Smoking:** In public areas only. **Open:** Year-round.

The Texas Hill Country is made for vacationing. It has everything: scenic beauty, outdoor recreation, and historic sites.

San Marcos, midway between Austin and San Antonio, is a good place to experience this part of Texas.

The picture-perfect Crystal River Inn has a convivial atmosphere, excellent food, and rooms with exquisite decor. While the four Corinthian columns across the front of the house signal grandeur, the mood of the interior is warm and friendly. The gardens, the courtyard, and a second-story verandah are all good places to relax.

> **Special events at the Crystal River Inn range from historical tours to river trips, murder mystery weekends to spa weeks.**

The bedrooms' charming decor seems to spring straight from the pages of a home and garden magazine. Each is named for a Texas river, reflecting the Dillons' affinity for canoeing. Five guest rooms are in the main house. On the ground floor, the Frio Room, with a queen-size bed and wicker furniture, is in cool blue. Connected via a bath is the Pedernales Room, with a canopy bed, fireplace, and fainting couch.

Upstairs the Medina is especially romantic, with a queen-size four-poster bed, rosy colors, and white shutters. The Colorado is a good choice if you aren't partial to ruffles and lace; here symbols of the rugged Southwest predominate. There's an animal-skin rug on the floor and a Mexican leather sofa topped with woven cushions; untwined rope makes an unusual and inventive bed drape. Blanco is a two-bedroom suite. Additional guest rooms are located in the adjacent Young House and in the Rock Cottage, just on the other side of the inn's tranquil gardens.

Breakfast is a main event. The constantly changing menu includes such treats as banana crêpes, stuffed French toast, quiche, and hot breads. Guests may enjoy breakfast in the dining room, in the beautiful gardens, on the patio, or in bed.

East Texas

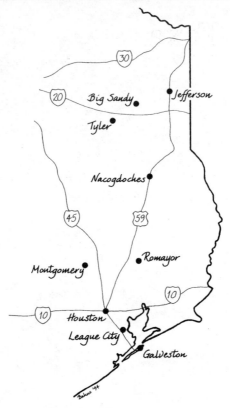

Best Beachside

Galveston
  Hotel Galvez
  The San Luis Resort and Conference Center
  Seascape

Best Bed-and-Breakfasts

Big Sandy
  Annie's Bed and Breakfast
Galveston
  The Gilded Thistle
Houston
  La Colombe d'Or
  Sara's Bed & Breakfast Inn
Jefferson
  McKay House
  Pride House
Nacogdoches
  Llano Grande Plantation Bed and Breakfast
Tyler
  Charnwood Hill
  Rosevine Inn

Best City Stops

Houston
  Four Seasons Hotel Houston
  J. W. Marriott Hotel
  The Lancaster Hotel
  Omni Houston Hotel
  The Ritz-Carlton, Houston
  The Westin Galleria and Westin Oaks
  The Wyndham Warwick

Best Historic Hostelries

Galveston
  The Tremont House

Jefferson
Excelsior House
Wise Manor

Best Lakeside

Montgomery
Del Lago Resort
Romayor
Chain-O-Lakes

Best Resorts

League City
South Shore Harbour Resort and Conference Center

Best Spas

Houston
The Spa at the Houstonian

Because it shares a border with Louisiana, much of East Texas has the feel of the Deep South: antebellum homes, alligators lazing about in the waterways, and bayous shaded by trees draped with Spanish moss. For many years **Nacogdoches,** named for the Nacogdoche Indians, was the gateway to East Texas. The town was visited by the La Salle expedition in 1687, and in 1716 a mission was founded there by the Spanish. Today **Tyler,** home of the East Texas Fair, the nation's largest municipal rose garden (38,000 rose bushes over 22 acres), and a lovely residential area of choice homes called the Azalea District, is one of the region's finest cities. **Jefferson,** to the north, once a busy river port, is now one of East Texas's most historic towns.

To the south, the slower-paced lifestyle gives way to thoroughly modern and multicultural **Houston.** Although Houston was built largely on the Texas oil industry, it has a rich cultural core. By day one can visit the Museum of Fine Arts, the Houston Museum of Natural Science, the Japanese Garden, the Children's Museum, the Houston Zoological Gardens, the Rothko chapel with works by the modern artist, and the Menil Museum, housing John and Dominique de Menil's collection of art ranging from the Byzantine to the surrealist periods. By night you can take in the Houston Ballet or Grand Opera at the handsome Wortham Center, the Houston Symphony Orchestra at Jones Hall, a play at the Alley theater, or a more sporting production at the Astrodome, where tours are given when games are not in progress. Houston has one of the world's largest ports, and NASA's Johnson Space Center, where U.S. spaceflights are monitored, is just 25 miles southeast of downtown. In spring, downtown Houston comes to life with ethnic food, music, and culture during the city's annual International Festival.

In **Galveston,** on the Gulf Coast about an hour's drive from Houston, tenacious residents rebuilt their city after a devastating hurricane in 1900. Galveston has plenty to offer out-of-towners. Many come for the island's beaches, but stately Victorian mansions open to the public, the city's historic Strand district (once called "the Wall Street of the Southwest"), and attractions such as Moody Gardens bring visitors seeking more than a seaside vacation.

BIG SANDY

Annie's Bed and Breakfast

106 West Tyler
P.O. Box 928
Big Sandy, TX 75755
903-636-4355
800-222-6643
Fax: 903-636-4744

> *A house of*
> *seven gables*
> *in the country*

Innkeepers: Sonny and Bonita Allen. **Accommodations:** 13 rooms, some with shared bath. **Rates:** $55–$115. **Included:** Full breakfast. **Added:** 6.25% tax. **Payment:** Major credit cards. **Children:** Additional $12 charge per day for ages 6 and up; children under 5 not permitted. **Pets:** Not permitted. **Smoking:** Not permitted. **Open:** Year-round.

Folks driving through the East Texas countryside do a double take when they get to the little town of Big Sandy and come upon three brightly painted houses clearly kin to Victorian days. It all started with the headquarters for Annie's Attic, a mail-order needlecraft business. Very quickly the operation grew to a group of businesses that now includes Annie's Tea Room (the building bears a Texas historic marker), and Annie's Gift Shop, as well as the bed-and-breakfast.

A turn-of-the-century home with seven gables, the lodging has definite charm. The parlor, with Empire furniture and lace curtains, is the place to meet fellow guests. A wide staircase, excellent for making dramatic entrances, leads to most of the guest rooms. But two of the most desirable rooms are on the first floor. The Queen Victoria is truly romantic — all burgundy and pink, with a brass bed sized for a queen topped with a lace spread, and a private bath. The Prince Albert, which adjoins the Queen Victoria, has its own entrance and a gas-log fireplace and is very attractive with chintz fabrics and a large mirrored armoire.

The upstairs rooms are smaller. The Garden View looks across the street to the tea room's garden. The Sewing Room is furnished with an old sewing machine in its original wooden cabinet. The Hideaway Room, with its brass and metal bed and lavender patchwork quilt, feels like a child's room. The Balcony Room has a private balcony under lacy gingerbread; Garret Room has a sitting area in an alcove, a double bed, a claw-foot tub, and private balcony. Some rooms have lofts, making them excellent for families. Every room has a telephone and a small refrigerator disguised as an old-fashioned safe. Quilts, needlework, and subdued wallpaper add to the cozy feeling. All the bathrooms, even the shared ones, are well decorated and modern.

> **Decorated in deep rose, the bi-level Queen Anne Room is by far the most elegant. Downstairs there's a queen-size bed, sleeper sofa, claw-foot tub, and private balcony. A spiral staircase leads to the loft, with twin beds.**

On weekdays and Sundays, guests eat a bountiful breakfast across the street at Annie's Tea Room, with waitresses in period costume. On Saturdays, a Continental breakfast is served.

GALVESTON

The Gilded Thistle

1805 Broadway
Galveston, TX 77550
409-763-0194
800-654-9380

> *Old-fashioned*
> *Texas hospitality*

Innkeeper: Helen and Pat Hane-
mann. **Accommodations:** 3 rooms, 1 with private bath. **Rates:**
$125–$175. **Included:** Full breakfast and evening refreshments. **Added:** 13% tax. **Payment:** Major credit cards. **Children:** Welcome in 1 guest room, preferably during the week.
Pets: Not permitted. **Smoking:** On verandah only. **Open:**
Year-round.

In all the world, there's only one Helen Hanemann. The best
reason to stay at the Gilded Thistle is to hear her stories and
join in her laughter. Of grandmotherly age, Helen has more
energy than most people half her years, and her wit acts as a
catalyst for her guests' enjoyment. In recent years, her son Pat
has joined her in the operation of the inn, and together they
make hospitality and the comfort of their guests their prime
considerations.

One of the first B&Bs in Galveston, the Gilded Thistle
opened in 1982. The house itself, a Queen Anne, dates from
1893. It has an inherent charm in its curly pine and cypress
trim, oak fireplaces, and wraparound verandahs. This is a
home of warmth as well as character. Teddy bears with
names like Ms. Pernella and Chocolate Drop fill the couches,
spill from the shelves, and sit coyly on the beds. Helen may

try to introduce you to all of them, pointing out the latest additions, presents from her guests. Helen also has a wonderful collection of seashells that figure in her decorating scheme. Many of the furnishings are family heirlooms. Decorative touches came from friends, remembrances of the friendship that Helen engenders.

Considering the numerous collections, the house is remarkably tidy. The guest rooms, all with double beds, are on the second floor. The master bedroom, the only one with its own bath, has a couch and fireplace. The Umbrella Room has an Oriental theme, with Chinese umbrellas. The Treetop Room, once a nursery, looks straight into the uppermost branches of the trees outside. Two rooms have full-length windows that open so one can walk out onto the wraparound porch set with chairs and lots of plants.

> If you want to talk history, Helen is willing and able. A descendant of early West Texas settlers, she can tell you stories of the Texas Rangers. It is said that one of her ancestors, a captain with the Rangers, discovered Carlsbad Caverns while on patrol with his troop.

The Hanemanns still believe in ironing pillowcases and polishing the silver. They also believe in providing their guests with lots of extras. Rooms come equipped with telephones, televisions, VCRs (they have a video library), sodas, candy, ice, books and magazines. For those needing to stay in touch, there's a fax centrally located for guest use. The Gilded Thistle has even installed instruments for the hearing impaired, and Pat is learning sign language.

Inn breakfasts will probably keep you going until midafternoon — or maybe even until afternoon hors d'oeuvres are served. Some guests don't find the need to eat anywhere else in Galveston during their stay. In the morning a tray with juice and coffee arrives at your door, and then at your convenience you head downstairs for a breakfast of homemade preserves, breads, eggs, several breakfast meats, and fresh fruit.

The Gilded Thistle, in the East End Historical District, is seven blocks from the beach and near many of the area's attractions. The Hanemanns have put together a package of tourist information on these local sights for interested guests.

Hotel Galvez

2024 Seawall Boulevard
Galveston, TX 77550
409-765-7721
800-392-4285
Fax: 409-765-7721 ext. 197

> *A beachside hotel
> once called the
> Queen of the Gulf*

General Manager: Brain Kohlweck.
Accommodations: 228 rooms and suites. **Rates:** $70–$120;
suites $175–$350. **Added:** 13% tax. **Payment:** Major credit
cards. **Children:** Under 18 free in room with parents. **Pets:**
Not permitted. **Smoking:** Nonsmoking rooms available.
Open: Year-round.

Galveston has a dual personality, for it is both a beach destination and a historic town. Hotel Galvez, the city's only
beachfront lodging listed in the National Register of Historic
Places, links the two sides of its character.

In 1911, the Spanish-style stucco Hotel Galvez proudly
rose as the "Queen of the Gulf." Eleven years earlier, a de-
structive storm had permanently altered the city's history,
killing 6,000 people and virtually leveling the onetime "Wall
Street of the Southwest." The hotel, built with funds raised
from the community, was the island's first opulent beach attraction and symbolized a city reborn. At that time, Galveston was known as a gambling center and attracted top entertainers to its casinos. The Galvez was their hotel, for not only
was it the finest lodging around, but one of the best casinos in
town was right across the street.

The Spanish architecture of the hotel reflects the island's
heritage. It is named for Bernardo de Galvez, an 18th-century
Spanish governor and general. Galvez never saw Galveston,

but the island was named for him by the chartmaker he commissioned to explore the Texas coast. As governor of Louisiana and Florida, Galvez fought with the colonials against the British in the American Revolution.

The hotel lobby's graceful arches, handsome wood ceiling, and chandeliers create a nostalgic mood. Bernardo's restaurant, just off the lobby, also has a historic ambience (surf and turf entrées run from $12 to $17). Potted palms and ceiling fans line the hall to the light and airy Veranda Bar and the Galvez Lounge, dark and masculine, with live entertainment.

At press time, work was underway to restore the circular drive on the seawall side of the building that was originally the main entrance of the hotel. At the same time an Olympic-size swimming pool with swim-up bar was being built next to the verandah.

> **The Hotel Galvez was restored in 1980, inciting a wave of historic preservation throughout the city. While the guest floors were totally redesigned, the lobby was refurbished to its 1911 charm.**

The guest rooms are ordinary and rather small, with tiny bathrooms. The furnishings are tasteful if not distinctive. The views of the ocean are perhaps less spectacular than they could be, given the parking lot between the hotel and the water; rooms facing the ocean run about $10 more per night than those overlooking the city. The hotel staff is friendly and hospitable. Self-parking is free, and valet parking is $5.

The Galvez is convenient to attractions such as the Strand entertainment area, historic homes and buildings, and the beach, just across Seawall Boulevard. After the 1900 storm, a massive seawall was built along shoreline: as a result, all the structures along the 10.4-mile beach are behind the seawall instead of directly on the beach.

The San Luis Resort and Conference Center

5222 Seawall Boulevard
Galveston, TX 77551
409-744-1500
800-445-0090
Fax: 409-744-8452

A touch of the Caribbean on Galveston Beach

General Manager: Ron Vuy. **Accommodations:** 244 rooms. **Rates:** $84–$139, suites $104–$300. **Added:** 13% tax. **Payment:** Major credit cards. **Children:** Free in room with parents. **Pets:** Not permitted. **Smoking:** Nonsmoking rooms available. **Open:** Year-round.

The San Luis seems to belong in the Caribbean. Perhaps it's the free-form pool with a palapa swim-up bar, tropical gardens, waterfalls, and bridges. Or maybe it's the breezy lobby with its wicker furniture, brass flamingos, and laid-back atmosphere — even the bellmen are casual in their tropical print shirts.

The hotel sits on a hill overlooking the ocean, and the beach is across the street, beyond the seawall that extends along most of Galveston's beachfront.

The San Luis is two lodgings in one. The hotel is a 15-story building with a restaurant and 244 guest rooms overlooking the Gulf. Next door is a sister building with privately owned condominiums, most of which are available for rent. Opened in 1984, the San Luis set a new standard for Galveston beach resorts. It has the Spoonbill restaurant overlooking the pool and gardens, a lounge with live entertainment, two tennis courts, and a beachfront activity center with rental equipment.

The rooms are large and sunny, with tropical print bedspreads, the smell of sea air, and narrow balconies. The bathrooms are small but adequate. The condos range from hotel rooms to large two-bedroom units with kitchens. Access to the condo area is by security key.

Seascape

10811 San Luis Pass Road
Galveston, TX 77554
409-740-1245

Condos right on the beach

Rental manager: Helen Z. Bateman. **Accommodations:** 75 condominiums. **Rates:** 1-bedroom (accommodates 6) $69–$139, 2-bedroom (accommodates 8) $105–$185. **Added:** 13% tax and $1 per night association charge. **Payment:** Major credit cards. **Children:** Free in room with parents. **Pets:** Not permitted. **Smoking:** 2 nonsmoking units available. **Open:** Year-round.

On Galveston Island's West Beach, where the seawall ends, Seascape condominiums are directly on the beach. (Most of Galveston's condos are behind the 10.4-mile-long seawall.) The units are attractive and well furnished, with a pool, kiddie pool, Jacuzzi, and tennis court on the grounds. The management is efficient and accommodating.

The units come in six designs. All have well-equipped kitchens, including a full-size refrigerator (one of the six floor plans has an under-the-counter refrigerator only), dishwasher, two-burner cooktop, mi-

Boardwalks lead over the dunes and onto the beach.

crowave oven, cookware, and tableware. Since these are privately owned condos, all are individually decorated. In addition to the usual sleeping accommodations, the living rooms have sofa beds and the entry halls have two built-in bunk beds. The bathrooms are divided into three compartments, with a total of two toilets, two lavatories, and one tub-shower. One floor plan has two full tub-showers. There is a telephone in each unit.

Parking at Seascape is free. There are coin-operated washers and dryers on two floors of each building, although some units have their own laundry facilities. Housekeeping service is available for an additional charge.

The Tremont House

2300 Ship's Mechanic Row
Galveston, TX 77550
409-763-0300
800-874-2300
Fax: 409-763-1539

*An elegant
historic hotel in
the Strand District*

General Manager: George Van Etten. **Accommodations:** 117 rooms. **Rates:** $135–$180 single, $155–$180 double; suites $250–$450. **Added:** 13% tax. **Payment:** Major credit cards. **Children:** Under 18 free in room with parents. **Pets:** Not permitted. **Smoking:** Nonsmoking rooms available. **Open:** Year-round.

The first Tremont House, built in 1839, was for many years the largest and finest hotel in the Republic of Texas. From its balcony, Sam Houston delivered his last public address. The hotel's guest register included presidents, foreign ministers, and entertainers. Rebuilt in 1872 after a fire seven years earlier, the hotel again welcomed the rich and famous. But after the disastrous 1900 hurricane, the Tremont, like the city itself, never fully recovered, and the hotel was demolished in 1928. Its namesake, in Galveston's Historic Strand District a few blocks from the original hotel site, is in the beautifully restored Leon and H. Blum Building, constructed in 1879.

Designed to recreate the atmosphere of the old Tremont, the hotel is intimate yet grand. At the center of its design is a four-story atrium. About half of the guest rooms overlook the atrium; interior bridges connect the upper halls across it. In the atrium is the Toujouse Bar, featuring a rosewood bar built in 1888, white wicker chairs with flowered cushions, and potted palms. To one side is the Merchant Prince restaurant, named for Leon Blum, Galveston's "Merchant Prince," who had a million-acre empire stretching across Texas. A jewel of a restaurant, the Merchant Prince has a splendid menu featuring nouvelle American cuisine. With entrées such as grilled shrimp over fettuccine in a chili cream sauce, grilled breast of chicken with shiitake mushrooms and pesto, tenderloin of beef with jalepeño béarnaise, and crabmeat with penne and tomato sauce ($10–$17), the restaurant is worth a visit wherever you stay.

> **The Tremont is one of the historic restoration projects of oilman and real estate developer George Mitchell and his wife, Cynthia. The Mitchells have been a prime force behind Galveston's historic preservation movement in recent years.**

The interiors at Tremont House are sophisticated and stylish. Decorated in chic black and white, the high-ceilinged guest rooms have white enamel and brass beds, lace curtains, white eyelet bedspreads, black and white rugs on hardwood floors, and baths with hand-painted Italian tile. Eleven-foot-high windows open onto ironwork balconies. Although the black and white color scheme is used throughout the hotel, no two guest rooms are exactly alike in size, configuration, or furnishings.

Valet parking ($6), a full-time concierge, terrycloth robes, heated towel racks, oversize towels, imported chocolates at turndown, and 24-hour room service are all part of a Tremont House stay. The Tremont's historic downtown location can be a refreshing alternative to the sometimes seedy quality of the strip along Galveston's Seawall Boulevard.

There is no swimming pool at the Tremont, but guests can use the recreational facilities at the Hotel Galvez, a sister property.

HOUSTON

Four Seasons Hotel Houston

1300 Lamar Street
Houston, TX 77010
713-650-1300
800-332-3442
Fax: 713-650-8169

A first-rate hotel across from the convention center

General Manager: Christopher B. Hunsberger. **Accommodations:** 399 rooms and suites. **Rates:** $195 single, $225 double; suites $495. **Added:** 15% tax. **Payment:** Major credit cards. **Children:** Under 12 free in room with parents. **Pets:** Permitted with leash. **Smoking:** Non-smoking rooms available. **Open:** Year-round.

For the traveler who values quality and aesthetics, the 30-story Four Seasons Houston is worth a special trip. Opened in 1982, it is truly elegant — a combination of classic European style and Texas hospitality. The hotel occupies a city block in the downtown business district and is connected by a skywalk to the Park, a three-tier mall with boutiques and restaurants. The George R. Brown Convention Center, a state-of-the-art facility that opened in 1987, is two blocks away.

> **All rooms are luxurious, especially the Four Seasons rooms, which feature a sleeping area in an alcove and a separate sitting area.**

A grand staircase spirals up from the hotel's lobby, joining three floors of public space. On the fourth floor is a nicely landscaped garden with palm trees surrounding the hotel swimming pool, certainly one of the most attractive pools in the city. Men's and women's locker rooms with a whirlpool and sauna are adjacent, as well as a small but fairly well equipped exercise room. Massages and facials are available by appointment. For a $12 daily fee, guests can also use the Houston Center Athletic Club, accessible by indoor walkway, which has racquet sports, jogging, and more extensive exercise equipment.

The guest rooms are decorated in blue and cream with custom furniture. Baths are stylish, with extras such as hair dryers and terry robes. Tower rooms have bay windows that add light. Some rooms overlook the pool deck.

Service is cheerful and professional at the Four Seasons. Bed turndown, 24-hour room service that includes hot entrées at any hour, complimentary shoeshines, 1-hour pressing service, and twice-daily laundry and dry cleaning service are all standard. There's also free limousine service to downtown restaurants, businesses, and entertainment, even on weekends. Valet parking costs $13 per day.

De Ville is an outstanding restaurant, headed by a talented chef bursting with creativity. Featuring gourmet American cuisine with strong Italian influences, the menu changes regularly. There are almost 400 choices on De Ville's wine list. If you're visiting over a weekend, be sure to sample the Italian lunch buffet on Friday or the appetizing brunch on Sunday. The Terrace Café serves lighter fare, and the Lobby Lounge is the place to go for evening cocktails.

J. W. Marriott Hotel

5150 Westheimer Road
Houston, TX 77056
713-961-1500
800-231-6058 in U.S.
800-392-5477 in Texas
Fax: 713-961-5045

Convenient for both shoppers and business travelers

General Manager: Bob Pittenger. **Accommodations:** 494. **Rates:** $139–$149 single, $149–$159 double; suites $500–$600; weekend rates available. **Added:** 15% tax. **Payment:** Major credit cards. **Children:** Free in room with parents. **Pets:**

Small pets accepted with deposit. **Smoking:** Nonsmoking rooms available. **Open:** Year-round.

The J. W. Marriott's lobby gleams with marble, polished paneling, brass, and crystal. A gift shop, hair salon, clothing boutique, and airline reservation desks are off the lobby. The Brasserie, with rare pre-Columbian artifacts, is the hotel's restaurant. Serving steaks, seafood, and pasta, entrées range from $7–$15. The Lobby Lounge is filled with the sound of live piano music.

> **For people on the go, the Brasserie restaurant has breakfast entrées that are ready in five minutes or they're free.**

The guest rooms are decorated with art specially commissioned from local artists. Each room has a sitting area with a couch, easy chair with ottoman, an armoire with a TV, and a convenient desk. The bathrooms have phones, small TVs, terrycloth robes, and built-in hair dryers.

The hotel's health club has good workout equipment and a coed sauna and steam room. The fifth-floor indoor-outdoor pool, although small, is a pleasant gathering spot; there is a food service bar by the indoor portion. The health club has racquetball at $3 per hour.

La Colombe d'Or

3410 Montrose Boulevard
Houston, TX 77006
713-524-7999
Fax: 713-524-8923

> *The charm of a fine country inn in the city*

Owner: Stephen N. Zimmerman.
Accommodations: 6 suites. **Rates:** $195–$600. **Included:** Breakfast selections. **Added:** 15% tax. **Payment:** Major credit cards. **Children:** Free in room with parents. **Pets:** Not permitted. **Smoking:** Permitted. **Open:** Year-round.

La Colombe d'Or combines the style of a country manor with the convenience of a city hotel. Small and intimate, it's also elegant and grand. Once it was the home of a wealthy family;

today it welcomes guests from around the world. Here you are treated as a valued house guest, with an abundance of personal service.

The three-story yellow brick inn, built in 1923, has an attractively landscaped front yard with plants and sculptures, a welcoming front porch, a residential lobby decorated in treasures from Europe, a cozy bar named for the hedonistic wine god Bacchus, and a library where you can sip cognac. While some of the architectural elements have been added, the mahogany staircase and the decorated ceilings are original to the home. The second-floor hallway is lined with paintings, among them a work by Calder and watercolors of Houston landmarks.

> **Always popular with residents, La Colombe d'Or's restaurant gained national attention during the Texas oil crash of the 1980s, when the owner showed solidarity with struggling businessmen by charging for lunch the going rate for a barrel of crude. He's done a brisk business ever since.**

Five guest suites, named after famous artists, are on the second floor. Each one is different — artfully decorated and unusual in its use of space. All have a king-size bed, sitting area, separate dining room, silk flower arrangements, telephone, clock radio, and bathrobes. Some have ceiling fans.

The Renoir Suite, although the smallest, is a favorite. Its dining area is separated from the bedroom by interior columns and draped fabric, yet the theme is Oriental, with Japanese prints, a carved screen for a headboard, and Oriental rugs. Its sunny dining room opens out onto a terrace. The Cézanne was once the master bedroom. Playful paintings hang on the walls, while the floor is covered by a rich Oriental rug. The Degas suite, in rose pastels, looks like an Impressionist painting. Ivy vines grow along the ceiling of its airy dining room. Mauve and burgundy are the dominant colors in the Monet Suite, and there's a Bartlett print in the bath. The Van Gogh Suite, of course, is more flamboyant, in ruddy browns and rusts. The third-floor penthouse is even larger than the suites. It has fine antique furnishings and the luxurious bathroom with an elevated whirlpool tub.

The tempting aromas that waft upstairs are a constant reminder that there is a fine restaurant below. Decorated in soft pink and mauve, the restaurant is sophisticated and grand on a small scale. With an emphasis on regional products and fresh herbs, the cuisine is French Provençal. Entrées such as seafood Monaco, lamb Lyonnaise, and pasta Portofino keep guests from straying too far. The restaurant is open for lunch on weekdays and dinner every day except Sunday.

La Colombe d'Or is about a 5-minute drive from downtown and within easy access of the Galleria, Texas Medical Center, Alley Theater, Wortham Center, and Jones Hall. The University of St. Thomas is a block away. There is 24-hour concierge service; valet parking is free for guests.

The Lancaster Hotel

701 Texas Avenue
Houston, TX 77002
713-228-9500
800-231-0336
Fax: 713-223-4528

> *An intimate
> hotel exudes
> European charm*

Managing director: Charles Graver.
Accommodations: 93 rooms. **Rates:** $185–$205 single, $195–$215 double; suites $325–$800. **Added:** 15% tax. **Payment:** Major credit cards. **Children:** Under 16 free in room with parents. **Pets:** Small pets permitted with a $50 deposit. **Smoking:** Nonsmoking rooms available. **Open:** Year-round.

In the midst of the downtown cultural district, the Lancaster is a small, elegant hotel with European style à la Texas and Service with a capital S. Its look is polished and refined. The lobby, like the rest of the hotel, is intimate, more like a parlor than a standard hotel lobby. Handsome elevators with mirrors and polished wood take guests to their rooms. No more than nine rooms are on each floor, adding to the sense of intimacy.

In truth, the hotel hasn't always been so fine. Built in 1926 as the Auditorium Hotel, it has a colorful history. Gene Autry once rode his horse into the Stage Canteen in the basement. Symphony musicians and circus performers, wrestlers and ice skaters, stayed here. So did the young Clark Gable, and rumor has it that he left his trunk as hostage until he could pay his bill.

In 1982, the building was transformed into a luxury hotel.

The guest rooms have a British theme, with imported English tartan and chintz fabrics and wallpapers, prints of the English countryside, overstuffed chairs with ottomans, and carved two-poster beds. The baths are sleek, in white Italian marble, porcelain, and brass. Live plants and fresh flowers, multiple two-line speaker phones (with fax/pc capabilities), fully stocked refreshment centers, VCRs, twice-daily maid service, terry robes, a newspaper at your door in the morning, and nightly turndown enhance the feeling of luxury.

> **If you enjoy the performing arts, there's hardly a better place to stay in Houston. The Lancaster is next door to the Alley Theater, across the street from Jones Hall, a block from Wortham Center, and within a few blocks of the Music Hall.**

The clubby Bistro Lancaster, whose walls are covered with Gulf Coast scenes, seats fewer than 60 diners. The menu features Gulf Coast cuisine, beef, and venison. The bistro serves all three meals and late night fare and is a popular spot for theatergoers. For recreation and fitness, guests can use the nearby Texas Club ($15 per day). Facilities include a rooftop pool, Nautilus equipment, and squash and racquetball courts.

The hotel has a concierge on duty 24 hours a day, complimentary downtown limousine service, and 24-hour room service. Parking is $12 per day.

Omni Houston Hotel

Four Riverway
Houston, TX 77056
713-871-8181
800-THE-OMNI
Fax: 713-871-8116

> *A tranquil oasis in the bustling city*

General Manager: Hans Strohmer.
Accommodations: 368 rooms. **Rates:** $150–$200, suites $220–$800. **Added:** 15% tax. **Payment:** Major credit cards. **Children:** Under 17 free in room with parents. **Pets:** Under 25 pounds permitted with $25 deposit. **Smoking:** Nonsmoking floors. **Open:** Year-round.

The Omni Houston Hotel is only a few minutes' drive from the Galleria and many business addresses. Its parklike setting, among gleaming office towers, is unexpected. The wooded banks of Buffalo Bayou are on the eastern perimeter, and to the west is a reflection pond, the home of a family of swans, surrounded by weeping willows.

> The hotel's mascots are two beautiful black swans that glide tranquilly across the reflecting pond. Don't get too close, however, or you may find yourself running from a large, irate bird. Apparently the prolific swans are suspicious of intruders, and with good reason, as the cygnets are often given up for adoption.

Just inside, the Palm Court Lounge sets the tone. A lush tropical garden, it has a gentle waterfall, soft piano music, and views of the hotel's pools and fountains. The colors of the garden are repeated throughout, with a profusion of green marble in the lobby accented with Asian screens and modern paintings.

The guest rooms, with luxurious modern furnishings, look out on the grounds or the bayou. All the rooms have overstuffed chairs, remote control TVs, stocked mini-bars, hair dryers, and three telephones (one in the bath) with fax/modem capabilities. Terry robes add to the feeling of luxury. In the baths, large vanities, scales, makeup mirrors, and hair dryers are standard.

A good choice for a weekend retreat or a business stop, the Omni Houston Hotel is geared to recreation. It has two pools, one heated and with underwater music; four tennis courts; and bikes to rent, with trails in nearby Memorial Park. The health club has extensive exercise equipment and a whirlpool.

The dining choices are all good. Café on the Green, open from 6:30 A.M. to midnight, has a sumptuous Sunday brunch. La Réserve serves fine French, American, and regional dishes. Entrées such as smoked chicken and eggplant salad served with a warm goat cheese torta range from $13 to $20. Afternoon tea, evening hors d'oeuvres, and Viennese desserts are all part of the Palm Court Lounge's bill of fare. Downstairs is the Black Swan, a pub named for the hotel's mascots. Offering more than a hundred brands of beer, it serves light evening fare and has live entertainment, board games, darts, and dancing.

The Omni's service is attentive. Self-parking is free, valet service costs $11. Free limousine service is available to the Galleria, and buses to the airport stop at the hotel. Downtown Houston is about 10 miles east of the hotel.

The Ritz-Carlton, Houston

1919 Briar Oaks Lane
Houston, TX 77027
713-840-7600
800-241-3333
Fax: 713-840-0616

> *A classy hotel where service is king*

General Manager: Leigh Keating.
Accommodations: 232 rooms and suites. **Rates:** Rooms from $175, suites from $260; weekend rates available. **Added:** 15% tax. **Payment:** Major credit cards. **Children:** Under 18 free in room with parents. **Pets:** With approval. **Smoking:** Nonsmoking rooms available. **Open:** Year-round.

The Ritz-Carlton is a gleaming palace that combines sophistication with hospitality. Despite its size, it has a residential feeling. No large lobby looms at its front door; instead, guests sign in at an unimposing hall desk. The public spaces are pretty, featuring rotundas with skylights, alcoves with comfortable chairs, and arched corridors with greenery.

Best of all, the hotel treats its guests as honored visitors. Personal preferences are noted and attended to, and staff members call guests by name. Valet parking ($13.50), 24-hour room service, and complimentary transportation to nearby shopping areas are available.

To the strains of harp music, the Lobby Lounge serves high tea as well as light desserts, cordials, chocolate fondues, and champagne in the evenings. Nearby is the handsome bar, resembling an English men's club with an animal hunt theme, with couches, velvet booths, and a fireplace.

The guest rooms are comfortable and pleasing to the eye. The deluxe rooms are especially large, with bay windows and separate sitting areas. The baths are warmly decorated, with marble vanity tops. Suites have canopy beds, expansive wet bars with refrigerators, and large tubs with Jacuzzi jets. Extras include terrycloth robes, a choice of down or synthetic pillows, three phones, and remote control TVs. When you walk into your room you feel expected: the thermostat is set, the lights are on, and soft music is playing. Guests staying on the club floors are treated to five separate food presentations a day in the club lounge.

> **The second-floor pool is a tranquil hideaway. Though the pool is small, the setting is like a garden, far removed from the city streets.**

Dining at the Ritz is a stellar event. Lunch entrées in the Dining Room range from $8 to $14 and include crab and ricotta ravioli with a lightly roasted garlic sauce and grilled jerk chicken breast with orange pasta and papaya vinaigrette. Desserts, made by the hotel's pastry chef, are as beautiful as they are delicious. Meals at the formal Grill incorporate flavors from Asia, Mexico, Italy, the Caribbean, the Middle East, and the Southwest. The fine entrées include Gulf shrimp served with basmati rice and Thai carrot-lime sauce, and lamp chops accompanied by creamed spinach, Navajo sage bread, aioli and pepper essence. Both restaurants use herbs and fresh vegetables from the hotel's rooftop organic garden.

In Post Oak Park off Loop 610 West, the Ritz is a few blocks from the Galleria. It is easy to get to most business addresses, including those downtown. The hotel has its own full-service business center.

Sara's Bed & Breakfast Inn

941 Heights Boulevard
Houston, TX 77008
713-868-1130
800-593-1130
Fax: 713-868-1160

> *A charming B&B in the Heights*

Innkeepers: The Arledges. **Accommodations:** 12 rooms in main house, most with private bath; 1 suite in carriage house. **Rates:** $50–$85, suite $120. **Added:** 15% tax. **Included:** Breakfast. **Payment:** Major credit cards. **Children:** Over 5 permitted; additional $10 per day. **Pets:** Not permitted. **Smoking:** Not permitted. **Open:** Year-round.

Downtown Houston is four miles away — you can see the skyscrapers on the horizon. But here in the Heights, developed in the 1890s as one of Texas's first planned suburbs, you can relive the days of lemonade and cookies, almost forgetting that the gleaming modern city exists. Here Victorian structures dominate; 100 of them are on the National Register of Historic Places. There is a central boulevard set with trees, a park with a lacy gazebo, and a public library that makes you want to curl up for hours.

> **New rooms include the Brady, with a 1940s look, the Western, with a cedar bed and cowboy print wallpaper in the bath, and the Fredericksburg, with vanilla orchid walls and a brass queen bed.**

In the heart of it all is Sara's, a wonderful two-story Victorian gingerbread confection with a wraparound porch, a turret, and a widow's walk. In truth, the entire structure is not as old as its architecture suggests: the core of the house, a one-story cottage, was built in 1898, but the flourishes were added in 1980, and an upstairs addition in 1994.

The Arledges bought the house in 1983 and spent three years renovating it. Now the inn, named for the Arledges' daughter, is fanciful and fun. Sara's is a good place to start a visit to Texas, for many of the rooms in the main house are decorated to evoke one of its towns or cities. You can get a tour of the state while choosing a room. Dallas is sophisticated; Galveston has a nautical theme. Tyler, named for a city famed for its roses, is decorated in a rose motif.

The Austin suite is Sara's most deluxe room. The bedroom is inside a turret; high ceilings and three arched windows bring in lots of light. The iron and brass bed is covered with a fancy white crocheted spread and bed skirt, and a hand-stitched patchwork quilt drapes the foot of the bed for cooler nights. French doors open from the adjoining sitting room onto a large porch overlooking Heights Boulevard. The suite's bath is a genuine delight — it has a separate shower, old-fashioned wooden washstand, and a claw-foot tub invitingly set in an alcove under a front gable.

Breakfast is served in the large, sunny garden room at the back of the house. Guests gather over fresh breads, muffins, or coffee cake. Donna gets up every morning at 5:00 to make them, so you can be sure they're fresh.

Throughout, the inn has a crisp, clean look, and the Arledges are constantly upgrading with their guests' comfort in mind. Guest rooms have telephones, televisions (some with VCRs; the inn has a video library), custom-made mattresses, and a supply of magazines.

The Spa at the Houstonian

111 North Post Oak Lane
Houston, TX 77024
713-680-0626

> *A professionally run, coed spa*

Owner: Kathy Driscoll. **Accommodations:** Spa guests stay at the Houstonian hotel. **Rates:** One-week packages start at $2,350 double. **Included:** All meals, hotel room, and spa program. **Added:** 15% tax on hotel rooms. **Payment:** Major credit cards. **Children:** Not appropriate. **Pets:** Not permitted. **Smoking:** Not permitted. **Open:** Year-round, except for New Year's and Christmas weeks.

The Spa at the Houstonian is a top-rated luxury spa located at the Houstonian, a multifaceted facility comprising a hotel and conference center, health and fitness club, and a center for preventive medicine. Despite its urban location, the Houstonian is a wooded retreat, with winding paths throughout its 18-acre campus. The Spa is headquartered at the Phoenix house, a 1930s mansion that is one of three estates that originally stood on the Houstonian's grounds.

Spa participants check in at the Phoenix House, where they meet with their personal trainer and undergo a complete fitness evaluation in order to design the best program for their individual needs and goals. Participants then work with their personal trainer each day on cardiovascular workouts, weight training, or whatever special program they have set up.

At the Spa, exercise machines are available in endless variety, each machine with a headset for watching television or listening to music. The club has handball courts, tennis courts, swimming pools, an aerobics room with a spring-loaded floor, an indoor gymnasium, an indoor jogging track with banks and hills, a mile-long outdoor track with stretching stations that winds throughout the grounds, locker rooms with whirlpools and saunas, and a complete sports shop in case you forgot any equipment. Classes in traditional aerobics, step aerobics, water aerobics, yoga, and boxercise are available; there's even a golf pro on staff who uses video diagnosis to help golfers improve their game.

For many, beauty is an important part of the spa program at the Houstonian. Treatments that include facials, salt scrubs, seaweed masks, body polishes, and Swedish or sports massages are given in the Phoenix House.

> **Spa guests use the facilities at the Houstonian's fitness club, which are quite simply some of the most extensive in the Southwest.**

Since the facility was once a private home, treatment rooms are more inviting than average, with windows that look out onto the greenery or swimming pool; some even have private baths for freshening up before or after a treatment. A full-service hair salon is also located at the spa.

Spa participants stay in the Houstonian hotel. The guest rooms have a classical look, with such extras as loveseats and comfortable easy chairs, crystal ice buckets and glasses, leather-covered writing desks, and marble accents in the baths.

Spa guests receive meal coupons that can be used at the Center Court in the fitness club, the Houstonian's dining room, or the pleasant Manor House, another one of the original private homes on the property. Since good health is one of the goals of a stay at the spa, the coupons can be applied only toward spa cuisine meals. But although the spa meals are low in calories, they are long in taste. Smoked chicken and apple quesadilla served with sun-dried tomato salsa and pan-seared tuna with white beans, wilted greens, and a basil-tomato fondue are two of the wholesome entrées spa participants are "limited" to.

The Westin Galleria and Westin Oaks

Westin Galleria: 5060 West
  Alabama
Westin Oaks: 5011 Westheimer
Houston, TX 77056
713-960-8100
800-228-3000
Fax: 713-960-6553

> *Twin hotels at
> the popular
> Galleria mall*

Managing director: Raymond Sylvester. **Accommodations:**
Galleria, 485 rooms; Oaks, 406 rooms. **Rates:** $150–$170 single, $165–$190 double; suites $300–$1,200. **Added:** 15% tax.
Payment: Major credit cards. **Children:** Under 18 free in room
with parents. **Pets:** Small ones permitted on leash. **Smoking:**
Nonsmoking rooms available. **Open:** Year-round.

Houston has two Westins, each offering luxury coupled with
vitality. Both are part of a "city under glass," the Galleria
Mall, which was inspired by the Galleria Vittorio Emanuele
in Milan, Italy. Houston's
version has more than
300 shops and restaurants, an Olympic-size
skating rink, and several
cinemas, as well as these
two excellent hotels.

> **You can swim at either
> hotel, play tennis at the
> Galleria, and jog at the
> Oaks. The Galleria also has
> a putting green. Guests can
> also use the University Club
> in the mall, with 10 indoor
> tennis courts, a ball
> machine, whirlpools and
> saunas, and massage.**

The 21-story Westin
Oaks opened with the enclosed mall in 1971. The
24-story Galleria opened
six years later. About a
five-minute walk apart,
the two complement each
other in style and mood.
Guests at either hotel can
charge services to their room at the other.

The guest rooms, furnished in contemporary decor, are
large and well-appointed. Each has a stocked bar and refrigerator, multiple phones, and balconies. Rooms have either one
king- or two queen-size beds. Cable TV is complimentary.

For dining and entertainment, there are six choices. Delmonico's, at the Galleria, offers fine dining. Shucker's Sports
Bar, at the Oaks, serves seafood and casual fare. Both hotels

have informal restaurants. The Roof nightclub, at the Oaks, has live entertainment and happy-hour buffets.

Hotel courtesies include a concierge, 24-hour room service, express check-in and check-out, and valet parking ($13). Self-parking is free.

The Wyndham Warwick

5701 Main Street
Houston, TX 77005
713-526-1991
800-WYNDHAM
Fax: 713-639-4545

Fine art makes this hotel memorable

General Manager: Jeff Wagoner. **Accommodations:** 308 rooms and suites. **Rates:** $149–$169 single, $169–$209 double; $20 each additional person in room; suites start at $175. **Added:** 15% tax. **Payment:** Major credit cards. **Children:** Under 17 free in room with parents. **Pets:** Not permitted. **Smoking:** 3 nonsmoking floors. **Open:** Year-round.

In a fast-paced city where change is the norm, the Warwick is a welcome link to the past. The hotel itself is not particularly old, though. The original structure was built in 1926, but its opulence only dates from 1964, when the hotel was completely renovated by oilman John Mecom, Sr.

The furnishings in the public areas are a virtual museum of European treasures. They include ornate pilasters and exquisite paneling from the Murat palace in France, 18th-century statues from Italy, Baccarat crystal chandeliers with over 5,000 pieces each, a 275-year-old Aubusson tapestry, and a profusion of art — all collected by the Mecoms. John Mecom was a visionary, striking oil where others swore there could be none. He also had an eye for beauty. His business took him around the world, and wherever he went, he added to his collection.

In Houston's museum district — a few blocks from the Museum of Fine Arts, the Cullen Sculpture Garden, the Contemporary Arts Museum, and the Museum of Natural Science — the Warwick is surrounded by beauty. Just outside its doors is one of Houston's favorite landmarks, the Mecom Fountains.

By the 1980s, the hotel had became a little worn around the edges, in contrast with the sparkling luxury hotels that were opening in Houston. So the Trammell Crow Company purchased the hotel, renovated it, and reopened the property as the Wyndham Warwick in 1989, maintaining its status as an elegant hotel whose list of notable guests includes royalty, heads of state, and entertainers.

> **While overseeing the renovation of the hotel, Mecom instructed his wife to use any color she wanted — as long as it was blue. "Green is beautiful, too," he said. "But you look down at the grass to see green. You look up to see blue."**

The guest rooms at the Warwick vary in size and decor. Most are furnished in the style of Louis XV, with marble-topped dressing tables, custom furniture, botanical prints, flowered bedspreads, and a choice of king-size or twin beds. The bathrooms have phones and hair dryers. Lanai rooms, in a separate wing, face the swimming pool. All rooms have two baths and a balcony or patio, with easy access to the men's and women's saunas.

One of the best room choices is a junior suite; some have refrigerators and microwave ovens. Most of the suites are one of a kind, and some have outstanding views of the city to the south. Bob Hope once called this view the prettiest sight in the world.

The Warwick's dining rooms are the Hunt Room and Café Vienna. The Hunt Room, the more formal of the two, is decorated in rich woods and has a fireside setting. The menu is good, with entrées such as capon breasts with artichokes and rack of lamb ranging from $17 to $25. The paneling in Café Vienna came from the Château la Motte au Bots in northern France. There's a pasta bar here at lunch, and dinner entrées range from $7 to $15.

JEFFERSON

Excelsior House

211 West Austin
Jefferson, TX 75657
903-665-2513

A well-restored historic hotel

Owners and Operators: Jesse Allen Wise Garden Club. **Accommodations:** 13 rooms, all with private bath. **Rates:** $45–$70, suites $80–$90. **Added:** Tax. **Payment:** Major credit cards. **Children:** Permitted in one room only. **Pets:** Not permitted. **Smoking:** Not permitted. **Open:** Year-round.

It may surprise the first-time visitor to learn that the now somewhat sleepy town of Jefferson was a bustling port during the 19th century and once had a population of 30,000 people. Steamboats from New Orleans plied Big Cypress Bayou and docked in Jefferson. To accommodate the river traffic, riverboat captain William Perry built the Excelsior House during the 1850s. Today the Excelsior, which was purchased and restored in the 1960s by the Jessie Allen Wise Garden Club, operates much the way it did over a century ago.

Behind the Excelsior is a lovely brick courtyard. Cherubs adorn recesses in the garden wall, birds sing, water spills from a fountain, and wrought-iron chairs invite quiet conversation or private reflection.

The handsome hotel is painted white with black shutters. The guest rooms are decorated with spool beds, marble-topped dressers, and other period furnishings, many of them original to the hotel. One room, the Lady Bird Johnson room, was the former first lady's favorite. Other notable guests at the Excelsior have included Ulysses S. Grant, Oscar Wilde, and Rutherford B. Hayes.

The hotel lobby, as well as the adjoining sitting room and ballroom, all retain their 19th-century flavor. Plush red carpeting, Victorian velvet upholstered sofas, and a glass case displaying old guest registers grace the lobby. Plantation breakfasts are a grand affair in the ballroom, replete with Oriental rugs, pianos, and French crystal chandeliers. Breakfast is the only meal served, and reservations are recommended.

For those who don't have the opportunity to stay at the hotel, historical tours are given by garden club members for a small admission fee.

McKay House

306 East Delta
Jefferson, TX 75657
903-665-7322 Jefferson
214-348-1929 in Dallas

A romantic B&B from a more relaxed era

Innkeepers: Tom and Peggy Taylor.
Accommodations: 7 rooms. **Rates:** $75–$135; suites $115–$135. **Included:** Full breakfast. **Added:** 13% tax. **Payment:** Major credit cards. **Children:** Additional charge if extra bed is needed. **Pets:** Not permitted. **Smoking:** Outside only. **Open:** Year-round.

Flowers spill over a white picket fence in front of this pristine 1850s Greek Revival cottage. McKay House stands proudly in the heart of historic Jefferson, a town little changed since the steamboat era brought it prosperity and notoriety. Across the street is the House of the Seasons, a grand old mansion that is one of the most popular attractions in town. Thirty structures bearing Texas Historic Markers are within a five-block radius. The McKay House itself, built in 1851, is a historic Texas building and is listed on the National Register of Historic Places.

Here on East Delta Street, life moves slowly, so slowly that it doesn't take long to get caught up in the tranquility. The Taylors are adept at creating the illusion of an earlier era. They greet guests with lemonade and tea cakes on the front porch, where you can rock in white wicker chairs or enjoy the porch swing. At

> **Guests are invited to join in the spirit of things by wearing one of the inn's 200 hats to breakfast.**

bedtime, ladies find Victorian nightgowns in the armoire, and men can don long sleep shirts. A Gentleman's Breakfast, consisting of hearty country fare such as French toast, country-cured ham, and zucchini-pineapple muffins is served in period costume in the conservatory overlooking the garden.

On the ground floor of the main house are the three original guest suites, each of which has a 14-foot ceiling, a fireplace, a private bath, and distinctive antique furnishings. The McKay Room, decorated in blue, has a law library and rare papers in honor of Captain Hector McKay, a lawyer and the owner of the house more than a century ago. (McKay gained local fame by serving as the attorney in a well-publicized murder trial.) The Quilt Room has hardwood floors strewn with hooked rugs and hand-sewn quilts on the walls. The Spinning room, originally the formal parlor, is warmly appointed; it adjoins the Jefferson room to form a suite.

Upstairs are two large guest suites. The Grand Gable has peppermint-striped wallpaper and a separate sitting area in a restored Victorian gable. The Garden Suite — in florals, naturally — has a red velvet courting bench and overlooks the garden. The stained glass skylight above its tub can be illuminated at night for a romantic bath. Both have access to a balcony via the upstairs hallway.

Two other guest rooms are in a darling late 1890s Victorian cottage called Sunday House. It reflects a simpler lifestyle than the grand McKay House, but the decor is just as appealing and imaginative. The Keeping Room's furnishings include a mock feather bed, a nightstand made from a butcher block, a coffee mill lamp, a washboard, an old-fashioned icebox, a bench-style rocker that was once a wagon seat, and a Sears & Roebuck catalog from 1909. The bathroom, resembling an old outdoor privy, is an additional touch of whimsy. In the Sunday Room across the hall, a nostalgic air is provided by an antique wedding dress hanging on the wall, a time-worn steamer trunk, and a pull-chain toilet.

Pride House

409 East Broadway
Jefferson, TX 75657
903-665-2675
800-894-3526

*An elegant and
romantic escape*

Innkeeper: Sandy Spalding. **Accommodations:** 10 rooms, all with private bath. **Rates:** $65–$100. **Included:** Full breakfast. **Added:** 13% tax. **Payment:** Major credit cards. **Children:** In the Dependency only. **Pets:** Not permitted. **Smoking:** Outside only. **Open:** Year-round.

Once guests check into the Pride House, they have trouble leaving. Here is the place for a romantic holiday, a true escape from a hurried pace of life. The house, a two-story Victorian trimmed in gingerbread, exudes charm. Of course there's a wraparound porch, set with white wicker rockers and a porch swing for daydreaming on lazy afternoons. Throughout the house there are antique furnishings, swirls of lace, and stained glass windows.

The innkeeper believes in letting guests eat in the privacy of their rooms. Culinary delights appear on the downstairs sideboard at about 8:30 A.M., with coffee available earlier. Favorite dishes include poached pears with crème fraîche served with a praline sauce and "not eggsactly Benedict," Pride

House's version of eggs Benedict. You serve yourself on a tray set with fine china, crystal, and sterling silver.

The six most elegant guest rooms are in the main house. The beautiful Blue Room is especially comfortable, with a king-size bed and several easy chairs. The Bay Room is spectacular, its papered ceiling ablaze with stars. The Golden Era is hard to beat for romance; a half-tester king-size iron bed is set be-

> **In a history-filled East Texas town, Pride House was reportedly the first B&B in Texas, and it sets a high standard.**

neath stained glass bay windows and draped in lace. Most of the bathrooms have showers, but the West Room boasts a claw-foot tub, situated to afford views of the sunset during a luxurious soak.

Four rooms with a country feeling are in a detached building called the Dependency, originally the servants' quarters for the 1888 main house. Here, the Suite is a top choice, with a wood-burning fireplace, a queen-size bed, country furnishings, and a compartmented bath. All rooms have good lighting, soft sun-dried sheets, and super-fluffy towels.

Wise Manor

312 Houston Street
Jefferson, TX 75657
903-665-2386

> *A small B&B run by the local historian*

Owner: Katherine R. Wise. **Accommodations:** 3 rooms, 1 with private bath. **Rates:** $60; suites $75. **Added:** 13% tax. **Payment:** Major credit cards. **Children:** Free in room with parents. **Pets:** Not permitted. **Smoking:** In designated areas only. **Open:** Year-round.

To learn the history of East Texas, especially the charming town of Jefferson, check into Wise Manor and settle down for a talk with the town historian, Katherine Wise. She is proud of the historical marker on her Victorian cottage, and she has been a significant force in the restoration effort that has transformed this tiny town into a top visitor attraction.

Katherine Wise has lived in her historic home since 1929. The entire two-story house is decorated with antiques and family memorabilia, giving it an atmosphere of charm and comfort. Guests can choose from a downstairs bedroom, whose bath has a claw-foot tub, and two upstairs rooms. Double or queen beds are in each room; the larger room upstairs has an additional single bed and a TV.

LEAGUE CITY

South Shore Harbour Resort and Conference Center

2500 South Shore Boulevard
League City, TX 77573
713-334-1000
800-442-5005
Fax: 713-334-1157

A full-service resort between Houston and Galveston

General Manager: Austin Frame. **Accommodations:** 250 rooms and suites. **Rates:** $110–$155 single, $120–$165 double; suites $350–$1,050. **Payment:** Major credit cards. **Children:** Under 14 free in room with parents. **Pets:** Not permitted. **Smoking:** Nonsmoking rooms available. **Open:** Year-round.

South Shore Harbour's location is one of its chief assets. On Clear Lake, an inlet from Galveston Bay, the hotel overlooks a yacht marina and a picturesque lighthouse. About halfway between Houston and Galveston and only minutes from NASA, the resort is ideally situated for sightseeing. Its attractive setting and relaxed atmosphere provide a welcome weekend respite for harried Houstonians.

The nearby fitness center, which guests can use for $5 per day, offers state-of-the-art exercise equipment, jogging tracks, tennis courts (indoor courts are $15 extra), racquetball courts, a lap pool, and a gym. The South Shore Harbour Golf Course is also available for guests. Parasailing or deep-sea fishing excursions can be arranged in the hotel lobby through Clear Lake Charter Boats.

The guest rooms are tastefully and comfortably furnished in rich colors. Jacuzzi suites, with hot tubs placed to take advantage of the view, are a popular choice with couples. And while many hotels have presidential suites that are large for the sake of being large,

> **Humans are not the only ones who appreciate the large pool: the palm tree island in the middle of the pool is the home of a mother duck who returns each year to lay her eggs and raise her ducklings. So treasured are the resident ducklings that the resort's engineering staff have built a special ramp for them.**

the penthouse suites at South Shore Harbour are luxurious but not ostentatious. They have expansive windows that extend the width and height of the two-story suites, bringing the seascape indoors and filling every corner with the rich blues of the ocean and sky.

Dining on seafood in the hotel's Harbour Club while the sun sets over the water is a thoroughly enjoyable experience. Open only to hotel guests and private members, the restaurant feels exclusive. The waiters are attentive and the meals satisfying. Fresh Gulf seafood is the main attraction, but desserts are equally tempting. Deep burgundies, burnished woods, brass railings, and leather sofas complete the setting.

Paradise Reef Restaurant, serving all three meals, is less formal. The nautical Hooker's Nook Bar serves beverages and sandwiches on the pool and marina level. RSVP is the resort's nightclub. Piano music and tropical birds in the hotel's lobby bar create a soothing environment in which to sip cocktails.

South Shore Harbour's 185-foot tropical pool seems end-less. Children will no doubt enjoy swimming under its cas-cading waterfall, and adults find the swim-up bar refreshing.

Room service operates from 6:00 A.M. to midnight, and parking in the hotel's covered garage is free. Hospitality comes naturally to the staff at South Shore Harbour. Service is never forced; the employees just seem to enjoy their work.

MONTGOMERY

Del Lago Resort

600 Del Lago Boulevard
Montgomery, TX 77356
409-582-6100
800-DEL-LAGO
Fax: 409-582-4918

> *A lakeside confer-ence resort ideal for family vacations*

General Manager: Robin Sainty.
Accommodations: 310 tower suites, 52 golf cottages, 16 vil-las. **Rates:** From $100; suites from $250. **Added:** 10% tax. **Pay-ment:** Major credit cards. **Children:** Under 14 free in room with parents. **Pets:** Permitted with prior approval and deposit. **Smoking:** Nonsmoking rooms available. **Open:** Year-round.

Undeniably, Del Lago is a conference center. In fact, check-in is at the conference building instead of the hotel tower. But Del Lago is also a resort, offering couples and families a lake-side vacation complete with a marina, golf course, tennis courts, and health spa.

On the shores of Lake Conroe, northwest of Houston, the resort's 300-slip marina is its focal point. Some guests arrive with their own boats, but others can rent sailboats, ski boats, bass boats, or low pontoons. Ask about reserving a boat when you book your room; weekend rentals should be arranged at least four days ahead.

The 18-hole championship golf course is one of the resort's most popular features. Opened in 1982, the Jay Rivere–Dave Marr course has lush fairways. Tennis is also important at Del Lago. All of the 13 hard-surface courts are lighted, and there's a good pro shop. The spa is outstanding, with a well-equipped exercise room, racquetball courts, sauna, steam, whirlpool, tanning, and massage. All sorts of classes and clinics are geared toward health and fitness, from water exercise to foot massage to nutrition. Guests can use the spa, also a private club, for $5 a day; extra fees are charged for some services.

The 21-story hotel tower, right on the lake, has rooms suited for families. The sleeping and sitting areas are separated, and there's a couch and a small kitchenette fine for snacks. The rooms are all spacious; some have lake views, others have marina views. Golf cottages

> **There's always something special going on at Del Lago: fishing tournaments, family bike rides (rentals are available), or theme buffets. Weekend packages feature golf, tennis, or just getting away.**

have two bedrooms, two baths, a fully equipped kitchen, and a washer and dryer. The lakeside villas are the resort's most deluxe accommodations. They have an open living/dining room, full kitchen, wet bar, two bedrooms, and large oval Jacuzzi tubs in the baths. The villas also have private boat slips.

Café Verde serves all three meals; food service is available by the pool on a seasonal basis. Fiddler's Lounge, overlooking the marina, has pool tables and a big-screen TV. On weekends during the summer, there's live entertainment at Tiffany's.

NACOGDOCHES

Llano Grande Plantation Bed and Breakfast

Route 4, Box 9400
Nacogdoches, TX 75961
409-569-1249

> *A collection of finely restored historic homes*

Hosts: Charles and Ann Phillips. **Accommodations:** In 3 houses. **Rates:** $65–$75 for 1 person, $70–$80 for 2 people; $10 each additional person; reduced rates for stays of more than one night. **Included:** Cook-your-own breakfast. **Added:** 6% tax. **Payment:** No credit cards. **Children:** Accepted only at Gatehouse. **Pets:** Not permitted. **Smoking:** Permitted. **Open:** Year-round.

Hidden away in the pine forests of east Texas, there is an 1840 pioneer-style farmhouse ready to welcome guests, especially those with a bent toward history. The house was once occupied by Taliaferro "Tol" Barret, the man credited with drilling the first producing oil well west of the Mississippi. Today the house is part of Llano Grande Plantation Bed & Breakfast — not a plantation with one large mansion but a group of three homes open to guests.

As it would have been in Barret's day, the front yard of the Tol Barret House is swept clean of grasses, and early Texas flowers such as widow's tear and lantana still bloom. Listed on the National Register of Historic Places, the house has been beautifully restored by Charles and Ann Phillips, both knowledgeable preservationists. They have rebuilt, restenciled, and redecorated the house as well as its period furnishings. Mrs. Barret's "sittin' room," furnished with American Empire pieces, looks much as the lady of the house might have left it. Mr. Barret's general store ledger from 1869 stands open on the writing desk, providing a fascinating look at what people were buying back then. Pictures and portraits of the Barrets can be found in various locations throughout the house, but even pieces not directly related to the Barrets have interesting stories. In the former master bedroom, Charles reconstructed an antique dresser that he rescued as it was about to be burned. Ann made the quilt on the four-poster bed using needlepoint squares her cousin found in a bombed-out home in Germany during WWII.

> After a tour of the historic Tol Barret house, some guests enjoy walking through the woods of the plantation's vast acreage, or trying their luck at angling in the small fishing pond.

The Tol Barret house is treated like a museum; you'll get a tour of the historic home, but B&B guests stay elsewhere. The kitchen and loft, constructed from wood of the same vintage as the house, are connected to the Tol Barret by a covered walkway. This is one of the structures that the Phillipses have turned into B&B accommodations. Downstairs there's a cozy living room with blue gingham curtains, a sofa bed, and a fireplace topped with a clock-jack spit that was used to turn food over the fire, with a pair of longhorns for adornment. In the country kitchen, guests cook their own breakfast. The larder is stocked with such specialties as venison sausage and homemade bread, along with standard fare such as eggs and cereal.

The bedroom upstairs, tucked under the eaves, is straight out of a history book. Rope beds with feather mattresses, patchwork quilts, handmade furniture (Charles made one of the rope beds), braided rugs, and wooden floors make for a snug and comfortable retreat. Ann makes the fresh flower arrangements that accent tables here and there from wildflowers she gathers from the plantation's 600 acres.

About a quarter of a mile down the road is the Phillipses' own home, called the Sparks house after the original owner, with more guest accommodations. Dating to the 1840s, like the Tol Barret, it's also surrounded by trees and seemingly remote from neighbors. At night, with the exception of a few crickets, quiet and calm prevail.

The Sparks house has an elegant parlor on one side of the entrance hall and a cozy den on the other, where the walls are lined with overflowing bookcases (Ann collects mysteries) and old maps of Texas. The parlor ceiling is unusually high for a house of its day; Sparks's wife had him raise the ceiling because she felt it created a greater sense of gentility.

Guests stay on the second floor of the Sparks house, ascending from the back porch via a private stairway to two bedrooms, a central dining area furnished with a wardrobe that belonged to Sparks himself, and a bath. The furnishings are charmingly romantic, reminiscent of pioneer days. Rope beds, patchwork quilts, a doll house, and a loom augment the period flavor, and an embroidered heirloom quilt stitched by Charles's mother adds a personal touch. The original pole rafters of the roof still arch overhead.

Also on the property is the Gate House, a two-bedroom 1930s cottage with a living room and full kitchen. While less historic than the other two houses, the Gate House is a good option for families with children. In addition, the Phillipses are at work restoring another homestead that belonged to Jefferson Simpson, a second cousin of Jefferson Davis, so there may be even more lodging options available during your stay at the plantation.

ROMAYOR

Chain-O-Lakes

P.O. Box 218
Romayor, TX 77368
713-592-2150
Fax: 713-592-8851

A recreation-filled lakeside getaway

Owners: Jim and Beverly Smith.
Accommodations: 30 cabins. **Rates:** $100–$130 double, each additional person $10 per night. **Added:** 6% tax. **Included:** Breakfast and carriage ride. **Payment:** Major credit cards. **Children:** Under 5 free. **Pets:** Not permitted. **Smoking:** Permitted. **Open:** Year-round.

There's a little bit of everything at Chain-O-Lakes. Campsites and a fine restaurant, pedal boats and horse-drawn carriages, a rollicking water slide and quiet nature trails — all are part of the mix.

It's the cozy log cabins, smelling of cedar and scattered among the trees, that make Chain-O-Lakes special. Each one has a wood-burning fireplace, nice furnishings, and perhaps a charming loft bedroom. Central heating and air conditioning enhance the comfort. In the morning, just as the mist is rising from the trees, a horse-drawn carriage arrives at your door to take you to an inn nestled in the woods, where a superb breakfast prepared just for you awaits.

The "chain-o-lakes" is a series of 13 small lakes, most connecting, set in the piney woods of East Texas, 18 miles east of Cleveland and about an hour from Houston. It has been a campground since the 1930s. On weekends and during the summer it is popular with campers and day visitors, who frolic on the beach, go boating and fishing, play volleyball, and ride horses. In the mid-1980s, the Smiths revitalized the campground, adding romantic cabins in the woods and some built on stilts right on the edges of the lakes. From the porches of the lakeside cabins you can see alligators and turtles swimming in the waters below. There are also some older cabins, more rustic and less atmospheric.

> **The huge party barn, with food service sections, entertainment areas, and an upstairs dormitory, is excellent for groups. Conference facilities including a Challenge Course are also available for corporate retreats, seminars, and workshops.**

Chain-O-Lakes's Hilltop Herb Farm Restaurant has a crisp, clean, country feel, and the food is made with only the freshest ingredients, many of which are grown right on the farm. The menu is determined by what is in season and changes on a regular basis; typical dishes include an appetizer of curried chicken cheesecake with mango chutney, an entrée of blackened beef tenderloin with red bell pepper beurre blanc and corn relish, and raspberry Edwardian cream for dessert. Sunday lunch buffets and the five-course Saturday night dinners are so popular that reservations are required. The adjoining gift shop sells the farm's own jams, jellies, sauces, and herbs.

TYLER

Charnwood Hill

223 E. Charnwood
Tyler, TX 75701
903-597-3980
Fax: 903-592-3369

A grand B&B, once the home of Texas oilman H.L. Hunt

Innkeepers: The Walkers. **Accommodations:** 5 rooms, 1 suite, all with private bath. **Rates:** $95–$175; suite $270. **Included:** Full breakfast. **Added:** 13% tax. **Payment:** Major credit cards. **Children:** Not permitted. **Pets:** Not permitted. **Smoking:** Outside only. **Open:** Year-round.

Charnwood Hill, an imposing white brick structure with two-story columns and plentiful porches, was built in the 1850s and has an interesting history. Set amid towering oaks and magnolias, it has been everything from a school and a hospital to an interior design studio. But the home is best known as the 1930s residence of Texas oilman H.L. Hunt. The Walkers bought the home in 1978, decorated it with furnishings befitting an oilman's home, and opened it as a bed-and-breakfast in 1992.

The entrance hallway sets the tone, set off by a beautiful wooden staircase, a library on one side, and an elegant parlor on the other. The high-ceilinged dining room is formal and has chairs trimmed in gold leaf. Nearby, an airy garden room, filled with plants and wicker furniture, is a pleasant spot to curl up with a book or socialize. Guests are also welcome to relax under a wisteria trellis on one side of the house.

The Professor Hand bedroom is the only guest room on the

first floor. A 14-foot ceiling, large wardrobe, marble-topped dresser, and long, shuttered windows add grandeur to the bedroom. Oak fixtures and a gorgeous stained glass window make the bath equally impressive.

The three guest rooms on the second floor open to a large hallway set with rococo-style paintings, and chairs, sofas, and mirrors all trimmed in gold. The JoAnne Miller bedroom is feminine and romantic, with a willow canopy bed, a beaded lace lampshade, and a fainting couch. There's a makeup mirror in the bath and an Oriental stool at the vanity. Rich green and salmon colors, silk flowers in the fireplace, and a dry bird bath holding the book *The Language of Flowers* make the room feel like a garden.

> As befits a house of this stature, Charnwood Hill has an elevator, handy for transporting handicapped guests between the first and second floors.

Masculine tastes are catered to in the Miller Trophy room. It has dark wood paneling, a gun cabinet, bar, and game table. A hunt theme fabric has been used for drapes in the living quarters and as wallcovering in the bath.

The H.L. Hunt room is the most elegant. Tastefully appointed in shades of ivory and powder blue, it has a palatial canopy bed covered with a beautifully embroidered bedspread, leather-topped game table and tile-accented fireplace. The room has a TV/VCR and is popular with honeymooners.

The Margaret and Caroline Hunt suite on the third floor is a surprising contrast to the rest of the home, but it retains much of the art deco flavor it had when it was added on in the 1930s for the Hunt daughters. The 1,500-square-foot suite has a living room, a bath surrounded by glass brick windows, and two bedrooms, each with two built-in twin beds. Interesting alcoves and attractive fabrics add visual appeal.

For a completely different atmosphere and lots of privacy, there's a separate guesthouse. Willow chairs sit on the front porch, and inside, furnishings made from weathered barn wood, southwestern fabrics, and cowboy print cushions give the guesthouse a Texas frontier look. It also has a TV/VCR; all rooms have telephones.

Breakfasts of dishes such as eggs Benedict or French toast topped with hand-picked peaches are served in the sunny breakfast room in the main house.

Rosevine Inn

415 South Vine Avenue
Tyler, TX 75702
903-592-2221

Tyler's first bed-and-breakfast

Innkeepers: Bert and Rebecca Powell. **Accommodations:** 5 rooms, all with private bath. **Rates:** $65–$75 single, $65–$95 double. **Added:** 13% tax. **Included:** Full breakfast. **Payment:** Major credit cards. **Children:** Over 6 welcome; additional $10 per day. **Pets:** Not permitted. **Smoking:** Not permitted. **Open:** Year-round.

The Rosevine Inn combines the best qualities of a B&B, offering hospitality, comfort, convenience, and history. On a hill overlooking the Brick Street District, it has a residential feel, right down to the white picket fence.

On this site once stood the home of Dr. Irwin Pope, the son of one of Tyler's first doctors. Although the original house burned down, the Powells have replicated its 1930s style, placing the present structure over the earlier foundation. Unlike many B&Bs, the Rosevine Inn was designed to accommodate guests. Bert and Becca Powell chose the site for the beautiful, spacious grounds as well as its convenience to the city's attractions.

The well-planned home is comfortable, the living areas homey and intimate and the guest rooms pleasant. Furnishings range from antiques to country collectibles. The Rose room has a rose motif quilt and stained glass panel; the Bluebonnet is attractive in blue and cream and has a white iron and brass bed; the Azalea, with lots of windows, has both a double brass bed and a daybed; and true to its name, the Sunshine room is cheerful.

The most rustic guest room is located upstairs in the red

barn across the lawn from the main house. Its bed is set cozily back in an alcove, and a lace screen separates the bedroom from the bath, with its claw-foot tub. Downstairs is a living room and a game room outfitted with sofas in front of a fireplace, darts, a pool table, and stereo that guests can enjoy. Although you'd swear the barn has been around for years, it was recently built by the Powells. They used old wood and antiques to give it an authentic flavor.

Breakfast is served in the dining room. It's always a grand affair with quiches (often vegetable or sausage), fresh fruit, hot breads (lemon-poppy-seed muffins are a big favorite), and granola. For socializing, guests gather in the main house in the living room or the denlike setting at the top of the stairs, which has couches, a coffeemaker, a vintage wooden radio, and a TV, as well as outside on the patio or in the barn. For total relaxation, the Rosevine has a hot tub, and towels and robes are provided.

> **The Brick Street District, where the Rosevine is located, is an emerging visitor attraction with specialty shops and restored homes. Nearby is the Azalea District, notable for its variety of architectural styles representing many periods in Tyler's history.**

The Powells are a bright, energetic couple, congenial and eager to please. They'll happily direct you to interesting sights, suggest day trips, and recommend local restaurants. At press time they were in the process of acquiring another nearby cottage to expand the inn.

Northern Texas

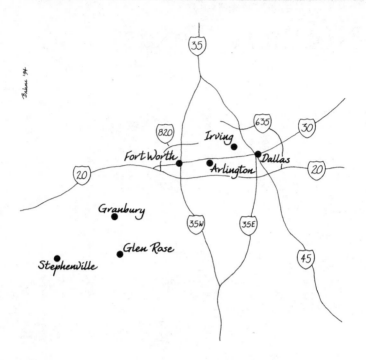

Best Bed-and-Breakfasts

Dallas
  Bed and Breakfast Texas Style
  Hotel St. Germain
Glen Rose
  Inn on the River
Stephenville
  The Oxford House

Best City Stops

Dallas
  The Adolphus
  The Aristocrat
  Fairmont Hotel
  The Grand Kempinski Dallas
  Hotel Crescent Court
  Loews Anatole Hotel
  The Mansion on Turtle Creek
  Melrose Hotel
  The Stoneleigh
  Stouffer Dallas Hotel
Fort Worth
  Radisson Plaza Hotel Fort Worth
  Stockyards Hotel
  The Worthington Hotel
Irving
  Omni Mandalay Hotel at Las Colinas

Best Family Favorites

Arlington
  Radisson Suite Hotel

Best Historic Hostelries

Granbury
  The Nutt House Hotel and Inn

Best Resorts

Irving
Four Seasons Resort and Club

Best Spas

Dallas
The Cooper Aerobics Center

Northern Texas is dominated by the "metroplex," an area that includes **Dallas, Fort Worth,** and the communities lying between the two cities, such as **Arlington** and **Irving.** It takes at least an hour to drive from one end of the metroplex to the other, and within that radius, cultural, sports, amusement, shopping, and dining options abound. Dallas is the commercial hub, Arlington the amusement center, and Fort Worth has a lively arts scene.

Compared with Dallas, Fort Worth can feel like a smallish city, but with a population of almost half a million it is sizable on most other scales. City sights tend to be concentrated in three different areas: the downtown area next to the convention center, the Stockyards, and the museum district. For its prominence in the livestock trade, Fort Worth has often been called "Cowtown." In the Stockyards Historic Area, preserved shops, restaurants, and saloons along Exchange Street serve as reminders of those Old West days. Downtown you'll find a modern water garden and Sundance Square, where lovely Victorian buildings have been gloriously restored.

Fort Worth boasts three fine art museums. The Amon G. Carter Museum houses permanent collections of western artists Frederic Remington and Charles Russell. Home to Kay Kimbell's fine collection of works by European masters, the Kimbell Art Museum regularly features top-notch traveling exhibits. The Modern Art Museum of Fort Worth spotlights the work of contemporary artists. Also worth visiting is the Botanical Garden, the Japanese Garden, the Fort Worth Zoo, and the Fort Worth Museum of Science and History with its Omni Theater and Noble Planetarium.

Although business and Dallas go hand in hand (the city is well known for its huge wholesale apparel market) Dallasites do know how to unwind. Turn-of-the-century buildings in the West End Historic District now house shops, restaurants, and nightclubs, as do the two-story homes in the Deep Ellum Historic District that was the center for African-American businesses in the early 1900s. Both areas come to life at the end of the workday. Old-fashioned trolleys travel along McKinney Avenue, yet another area popular for nighttime entertainment.

Along more educational lines, the Dallas Museum of Art has a permanent collection of pre-Columbian art, and there's a Firefighters Museum, a Center for Holocaust Studies, and a Museum of African-American Life and Culture. Those wanting to delve more deeply into the JFK legacy and that tragic day in November of 1963 should visit the Sixth Floor museum at the former Texas Book Depository. A trip to the top of Reunion Tower offers a splendid view of Dallas's futuristic skyline, particularly colorful at night.

Arlington is the place to go for family entertainment. The Texas Rangers baseball team makes its home in Arlington Stadium, and the Six Flags Over Texas amusement park is here, as is the Wet 'n' Wild waterpark. The International Wildlife Park is a short drive away. In nearby Irving, the Dallas Cowboys play in Texas Stadium, and Las Colinas has a Venetian-style canal system.

When residents of the metroplex want to escape the hustle and bustle of the cities, they go to the green, agricultural counties to the south and west. **Granbury,** on the edge of Lake Granbury, is one of the more popular destinations in the area.

Granbury's picturesque town square, with its opera house, antique shops, and tea rooms, is on the National Register of Historic Places. Travelers also frequent the small town of **Glen Rose** nearby, home of the Fossil Rim Wildlife Center and Dinosaur Valley State Park.

ARLINGTON

Radisson Suite Hotel

700 Avenue H East
Arlington, TX 76011
817-640-0440
800-333-3333
Fax: 817-649-2480

*An all-suite hotel
near the
amusement parks*

General Manager: Audrey Waldrop.
Accommodations: 202 suites. **Rates:** $104 single, $124 double; $10 each additional person. **Included:** Full breakfast and happy hour. **Added:** 13% tax. **Payment:** Major credit cards. **Children:** Under 18 free in room with parents. **Pets:** Not permitted. **Smoking:** Nonsmoking rooms available. **Open:** Year-round.

Six Flags Over Texas, Wet 'n' Wild waterpark, and Arlington Stadium, home of the Texas Rangers, are just a few minutes from this all-suite Radisson, which opened in 1986. Shuttle bus service to these attractions is provided by the hotel. Its exterior arches, lit at night, have a high-energy look. Inside, the lobby is airy and refreshing. Next door is a seven-story atrium — not massive and overpowering but almost intimate.

> **The Radisson is ideal for families because it is close to area attractions and because breakfast is included in the room rate.**

The suites are modern in decor, and all open onto the atrium. Their sitting areas are fairly small but well equipped, with a sofa bed, TV, phone, and wet bar with refrigerator. The bedrooms, decorated in soothing colors, have two double beds or one king-size and a remote-control TV. Downstairs are a heated oval swimming pool, hot tub, steam room, and sauna.

Mandolins Restaurant is elegant, with etched glass at the entrance, soft music in the background, and a menu with such dishes as escallops of veal champignon, coconut-dusted jumbo shrimp, steak au poivre, and grilled lamb. Prices for adults range from $10 to $14; children's are from $4 to $5.

Sunday brunch is a champagne affair, with a buffet featuring everything from fresh fish to eggs Benedict. A special selection is available for children. Mandolins Lounge has live entertainment three nights a week.

DALLAS

The Adolphus

1321 Commerce
Dallas, TX 75202
214-742-8200
800-221-9083
Fax: 214-651-3588

An elegant and historic hotel

Managing Director: Garvin O'Neil. **Accommodations:** 432 rooms and suites. **Rates:** $156–$310 single, $176–$335 double; suites $350–$2,000. **Added:** 13% tax. **Payment:** Major credit cards. **Children:** Free in room with parents. **Pets:** Not permitted. **Smoking:** Nonsmoking rooms available. **Open:** Year-round.

Built in 1912 by the beer baron Adolphus Busch, Dallas's grand and glorious landmark hotel was totally renovated in the early 1980s, combining the grandeur of an earlier era with the comforts of a modern luxury hotel.

The exterior is an extravagance of ornamentation — sculptures, bas-relief figures, gargoyles, heraldic characters, even a corner turret shaped like a beer stein. Classical music appropriately accompanies your entrance into the opulent and tasteful lobby furnished with a wealth of antiques from Europe and Asia as well as the United States. The public areas here are like a museum and include two vast 1660s Flemish tapestries, a six-foot-tall portrait of Napoleon in coronation robes, and carved English Regency oak furniture. There are potted palms in huge Oriental vases, colorful flower arrangements, and multiple sitting areas. The centerpiece of the Adolphus is the French Room, a dining room with a vaulted ceiling, ornate gold leaf moldings, marble floors, columned walls, and rococo murals. On the ceiling, ethereal cherubs holding flower garlands fly beneath a pale blue sky.

Unlike those in new hotels, the guest rooms here come in more than 30 configurations. Retaining their original high ceilings, they are warm yet elegant, decorated in reproduction antique furniture and touches of lace. All the rooms have refrigerators, multiple phones, and TVs in armoires. Down comforters and terrycloth robes add an extra touch of luxury.

> **High tea is served in one part of the lobby, and discreetly tucked away in another corner is an intimate lounge with a billiard table and fireplace.**

The Queen Elizabeth suite has a pair of large private terraces. Skylight suites, on the 19th floor, are expansive, with slanting glass exterior walls, large wet bars, and Asian accents mingled with reproduction period furniture. The Penthouse suite, decorated with art from Tibet, is truly deluxe. There's a four-poster bed in the bedroom, which is big enough to have a sitting area in addition to the suite's large living room. This suite has one and a half baths and a study.

The Adolphus is service-oriented, with a concierge, a multilingual staff, 24-hour room service, and valet parking for $10. Dining choices include the French Room, which serves dinner only (entrées such as New Zealand venison start at $22), and the Bistro, which serves Continental fare in country French decor. The Walt Garrison Rodeo Bar and Grille, with its potted cacti, red-checked napkins, and rodeo paraphernalia, is a fun Texas contrast to the rest of the Adolphus' Old-World style. It serves lunch, dinner, and cocktails.

For light workouts, the Adolphus has a fitness room with treadmills, stair machines, a stationary bicycle, a rowing machine, and free weights. Guests in need of more extensive athletic facilities can use the Texas Club a block away. The Club has an indoor lap pool, racquetball, squash, an indoor track, a gym, Nautilus equipment, and a steam room. The guest use fee at the Club is $10 per day.

The Aristocrat

1933 Main Street
Dallas, TX 75201
214-741-7700
800-231-4235
Fax: 214-939-3639

> *A chic
> downtown hotel*

General Manager: Ghulam M. Khan. **Accommodations:** 172 units. **Rates:** $109–$160 single, $119–$170 double; suites $130–$170. **Added:** 13% tax. **Payment:** Major credit cards. **Children:** Under 12 free in room with parents. **Pets:** Not permitted. **Smoking:** Nonsmoking rooms available. **Open:** Year-round.

The Aristocrat is personable, cozy, smartly decorated, and convenient, designed especially for the corporate traveler.
Built in 1925 by Conrad Hilton, it was the first hotel to bear his name. Since the nearby Adolphus was already the recognized luxury hotel in town, Hilton designed a no-frills property for traveling salesmen. In 1938, Hilton sold the hotel, and over the years it declined. In late 1985, under the guidance of the Texas Historical Commission, it was restored and emerged as the Aristocrat, a jewel worth discovering. Most of the accommodations are luxurious suites formed by combining pairs of the original rooms. Architectural features such as ornate trim and ceiling plaster were preserved, as were the public areas with their wood paneling, etched glass, and period furnishings.

> **Through an extensive skywalk and tunnel system, the Aristocrat is linked to ten or so office buildings. The historic Majestic Theater, home of the Dallas Ballet and Opera, is around the corner, and the Dallas Museum of Art is within walking distance.**

The intimate suites have cherry furniture, sophisticated colors and fabrics, and lots of amenities, creating a feeling of warmth. Each one has a queen-size bed or two doubles, a small refrigerator, remote control TV, three phones (one in the bath), and a separate vanity area.

The Aristocrat Bar and Grill, with large windows, etched

glass partitions, brass railings, and mirrors, is the hotel's pleasant dining spot. Serving full breakfasts, lunch, dinner, and late evening snacks, it features mesquite-grilled dishes and fresh pastas (dinner entrées range from $10–$22). In the mornings, guests can enjoy a cup of coffee in the library. Room service is also available.

The hotel has a small exercise room with a treadmill, Lifecycle and weight machine, or for $10 per day guests can use facilities at the Texas Club several blocks away. Parking in a covered garage across the street is $3 per night.

Bed and Breakfast Texas Style

4224 West Red Bird Lane
Dallas, TX 75237
214-298-5433
214-298-8586 8 A.M.–5:30 P.M.

A reservation service for inns in Dallas and all of Texas

Owner/Director: Ruth Wilson. **Accommodations:** About 180 rooms in about 60 cities, towns, and lake and farm areas. **Rates:** $50–$100; some special listings up to $175. **Included:** Breakfast. **Added:** Tax; varies, but averages 13%. **Payment:** Major credit cards. **Children:** Often welcome. **Pets:** Sometimes permitted. **Smoking:** Sometimes permitted. **Open:** Year-round.

One phone call to Bed and Breakfast Texas Style can help you locate accommodations in an assortment of locales. This reservation service's listings are widespread and offer lots of variety — everything from an executive condo in Dallas to a guest ranch on a lake. Some of the inns were built before the turn of the century, others are sparkling new urban homes. Some have hosts in residence, others are guest houses offering complete privacy.

Accommodations range from budget to luxurious. In addition to listings in Dallas, Houston, and other major metropolitan areas, you can find accommodations in Bryan, Granbury, Midland, Palestine, and Galveston.

The service represents inns of various sizes as well as homes with one or two guest rooms. Ruth Wilson can help guests choose the lodging that is best for their needs. She asks guests to complete evaluation forms so that she can keep close tabs on the lodgings she represents. A current list of accommodations is available for $5.

The Cooper Aerobics Center

12230 Preston Road
Dallas, TX 75230
214-386-0306
800-444-5187
Fax: 214-386-5415

> *The best*
> *exercise facilities*
> *in Dallas*

Founder: Kenneth H. Cooper, M.D.
Accommodations: 62 rooms. **Rates:** $99–$105; group and weekend rates available. **Included:** Continental breakfast and health club use. **Added:** 13% tax. **Payment:** Major credit cards. **Children:** Free in room with parents. **Pets:** Permitted. **Smoking:** Nonsmoking rooms available. **Open:** Year-round.

Billing itself as "the healthiest hotel in town," the Guest Lodge at the Cooper Aerobic Center certainly lives up to its own advertising. The center was founded in 1970 by Dr. Kenneth Cooper, who is widely credited with bringing the importance of aerobic exercise in the prevention of heart disease to the attention of both the medical community and the population at large. As the center's patient register has grown over the years to upwards of 50,000, so too has the complex. On 30 lush acres, landscaped with fragrant catalpa trees, the center includes a research facility in a building that was once a church, a clinic, a fitness center, and the guest lodge.

Out of a necessity to house patients in town for medical check-ups or individuals participating in the Cooper Wellness Program, the guest lodge was opened in 1986. But you needn't be a participant in one of the center's programs to enjoy staying here. The guest lodge is for anyone visiting Dallas who's looking for a health-conscious environment. The fitness center is one of the best in the Southwest. It has extensive exercise machines, a half-court gymnasium with a beautiful arched ceiling — Dr. Cooper wanted to create the feeling of a church — top-of-the-line Cybex weight equipment, two racquetball courts, four outdoor tennis courts, a snack bar, a sports shop, and an outdoor swimming pool heated year-round. Use of the facility is free to all lodge guests. There is an extra fee for massages, done here or in your room.

> **French doors in all of the rooms let in lots of light and open onto private balconies with an inspirational view of the polyurethane jogging track that winds throughout the property.**

At the front of the lodge, the lobby is airy and inviting, with light marble floors, a handsome flower centerpiece, and a sitting area off to one side. A walkway between the two lodge buildings takes you past a pleasant verandah and an outdoor pool to the Colonnade Room, the center's restaurant. In keeping with the Cooper center's focus on a healthy lifestyle, heart-healthy entrées such as spinach lasagna, papaya chicken, and broiled salmon make up about half the menu. Luckily, while the dishes are low in calories (under 300 in most cases), they are long on flavor. If you prefer to dine in the privacy of your room, that can also be arranged.

Guest rooms themselves are quite spacious and tastefully furnished with cherry reproduction furniture, one king or European twin four-poster beds, TVs in armoires, work desks with brass study lamps, and Oriental accents. Suites are extra large, with separate living room, round dining table, wet bar, refrigerator, and stereo. The baths in the suites have separate tubs and showers, but all baths have phones, hair dryers, marble floors and vanities.

The Cooper Aerobics Center is just down the road from the popular Galleria shopping center and 15 minutes from downtown Dallas.

Fairmont Hotel

1717 North Akard Street
Dallas, TX 75201
214-720-2020
800-527-4727
Fax: 214-720-5269

*A sophisticated
downtown hotel*

General Manager: Ray Tackaberry. **Accommodations:** 551 rooms including 51 suites. **Rates:** $125–$215 single, $150–$240 double; suites $325–$1,000. **Added:** 13% tax. **Payment:** Major credit cards. **Children:** Welcome. **Pets:** Seeing eye and hearing dogs only. **Smoking:** Nonsmoking rooms available. **Open:** Year-round.

With sweeping public areas and one of the best-known restaurants in town, the Fairmont, next to the Dallas Arts District, is an excellent base for visiting the city of Dallas.

The lobby lounge is dominated by stunning flower arrangements and an eye-catching contemporary work of art celebrating Cabeza de Vaca, the first European to see the interior of Texas, New Mexico, and Arizona. The Pyramid Lounge has a bright mural depicting events and figures of the 1960s. The Venetian Room is dramatic, with slate-col-

The Texas marble exterior was added in a 1989 multi-million-dollar renovation.

ored walls, red chairs, and Spanish arches. An abundant Sunday brunch is served here in a gondola buffet. Its hallmark dish, pancakes Oscar — buckwheat pancakes sprinkled with brown sugar, covered in meringue, and topped with a strawberry sauce — will satisfy the sweetest tooth.

But it's the Pyramid restaurant, with its intimate settings and award-winning cuisine, that draws the most attention. Entrées, from $19 to $39, include grilled rack of lamb with a pine nut crust and mint horseradish, roast maple leaf duck with a molasses kumquat glaze; and grilled Dover sole with truffle butter sauce. A harpist adds to the ambience, and a Spanish guitarist entertains in the late evenings.

The guest rooms are in two towers. The furnishings are attractive, with such luxuries as down pillows and Irish linens. Amenities include round-the-clock room service, nightly turndown, and twice-daily housekeeping.

The sunny Brasserie restaurant is open 24 hours a day. There is also a sports bar that serves deli lunches on weekdays and is decorated with sports paraphernalia lent by hotel employees. The Olympic-size pool and surrounding patio is big enough to satisfy the needs of such a large hotel, and the views of downtown Dallas from the pool deck are terrific. Guests can also use the facilities at the YMCA next door.

The Grand Kempinski Dallas

15201 Dallas Parkway
Dallas, TX 75248
214-386-6000
800-426-3135
Telex: 795515
Fax: 214-701-0342

A luxury hotel just north of central Dallas

Managing Director: Michael Spamer. **Accommodations:** 527 rooms and suites. Rooms: single $165–$185, double $185–$205; suites $270–$1,200; weekend packages available. **Added:** 13% tax. **Payment:** Major credit cards. **Children:** Free in room with parents. **Pets:** Not permitted. **Smoking:** Non-smoking rooms available. **Open:** Year-round.

In Addison, about 15 minutes from the city, the Grand Kempinski has a spacious feeling that most downtown hotels can't achieve. A glass atrium adds to the lofty quality, while Italian marble throughout provides elegance.

With 37 suites (18 on two levels) and a concierge floor in addition to the standard rooms, there are plenty of choices. The rooms, with French provincial, English country, or Oriental furnishings, have a decidedly masculine air. Special touches include turndown service, fresh flowers, and telephones in the bathrooms.

Not to be missed on a Sunday morning is the champagne brunch in the Malachite Showroom. The vibrant green and black surroundings are striking and sumptuous. The brunch runs about $28 for adults, $14 for children under 12.

Monte Carlo is the hotel's fine restaurant. With silk bougainvillea vines overhead and mosaic floors, it has a Mediterranean bistro flavor. Roast quail and lobster with grilled vegetables are typical dishes. At dinner, entrées range from $20 to $28, while the restaurant's brasserie serves lighter meals at lighter prices.

> **In 1987, Kempinski Hotels, a West German luxury hotel chain, took over this modern property, its first venture in North America.**

Le Café sports a pleasant atmosphere, breakfast and lunch buffets, and traditional favorites. A rose on every table complements the rose and green decor. English teas are served in the Bristol Lounge, and the Atrium Bar has a piano player and complimentary hors d'oeuvres in the evening.

After dinner you can dance the night away in Kempi's, the hotel's nightclub, complete with neon lights and a fog system. If dancing doesn't burn off enough calories, there are four lighted tennis courts, two racquetball courts, two heated pools with adjoining hot tubs — one inside, one outside — and a fitness club.

Concierge, laundry, dry cleaning, telex and fax, and room services are available 24 hours a day. The hotel also offers an executive business center with secretarial support, complimentary limousine service within three miles of the hotel, and free transportation to the nearby Galleria mall. Valet parking is $7; self-parking is $1 in the covered garage and free in the lot.

Hotel Crescent Court

400 Crescent Court
Dallas, TX 75201
214-871-3200
800-654-6541
Fax: 214-871-3272

> *Unparalleled service at a first-rate hotel*

General Manager: Bruno Brunner.
Accommodations: 216. **Rates:** $235–$330 single, $265–$360 double; suites $450–$1,350. **Added:** 13% tax. **Payment:** Major credit cards. **Children:** Free in room with parents. **Pets:** Permitted with damage deposit. **Smoking:** Nonsmoking rooms available. **Open:** Year-round.

Opened in late 1985, the Crescent Court is a Rosewood Hotel, a sister property to the Mansion on Turtle Creek, a mile up the road, and the Bel Air in California. Unlike the other Rosewoods, this hotel is designed for the business traveler. But even if you're in Dallas just for pleasure, it is a hotel well worth discovering.

Although its architect, Philip Johnson, was inspired by the Royal Crescent in Bath, England, the Crescent Court, with its light gray exterior and mansard roof, bears a more remarkable resemblance to a Loire Valley château. And you are treated like the château's lord; the ever-dutiful staff seem to appear magically just when you need them, then discreetly fade and let you have the run of the manor in peace.

Staying here is an immersion in beauty. Your senses will luxuriate in it from the time you enter the lobby, which is adorned with arched windows, Spanish and Italian marble floors, Louis XV furnishings and European art, massive flower arrangements and airy palms. In the background is classical music. The bellman, the desk clerk, and the concierge are more than attentive. Soon you've forgotten the traffic and daily hassle. You can relax. Somebody else will take care of everything.

Make no mistake, however; this is not a retreat. Indeed, there's a vibrancy about the place, a mood that flows from the lobby to the restaurant to the courtyard beyond. The Beau Nash restaurant and bar, named for the arbiter of taste in 18th-century England, is done in dark green marble with floral motifs. It has a lively bis-

> **The hotel is part of a mixed-use project called the Crescent. Off the lobby, a courtyard leads to a three-level marketplace of chic shops and galleries. On the other side of the hotel are three 18-story office towers.**

tro atmosphere and excellent food dominated by salads, pizza, pastas, and grilled dishes. Prices run about $10 per person for breakfast, $15 for lunch, and $20 for dinner.

The Conservatory is the hotel's fine dining room. Entrées include seared salmon with a hard-boiled egg and caper sauce, buttermilk roast pheasant on corn purée, and prime sirloin steak. For special occasions, the hotel's wine cellar can be rented by parties of up to 16 people. A candlelit dinner here, under arched brick ceilings and surrounded by hundreds of vintage wines, is memorable.

The guest rooms are just as beautiful as the public areas. With a residential feeling, they're spacious and aesthetically pleasing in subtle pastels and rich earth tones. French windows open to a view of the courtyard below. The furnishings are comfortably elegant, easy chairs and sofas with down cushions, armoire desks, and original works of art.

It is attention to detail that sets this hotel apart. In your room, expect fresh flowers, three phones, the daily newspaper, hooded terrycloth robes, and brass and marble fixtures in the bathroom. Some suites have wet bars and refrigerators. If you want to be truly pampered, a maid will unpack your luggage. When you need a hem repaired, a seamstress will help. Laundry comes back in a lined wicker basket. Turndown service includes a fresh orchid on your pillow and the weather report for the following day.

The Spa at the Crescent, a luxurious private health and fitness club, is also part of the complex. Rose marble floors surround the whirlpools, and there are plush sofas in the locker room. The wooden lockers are so well equipped — including designer workout clothes — that guests need only bring their athletic shoes. European treatments are combined with America's zest for fitness. Beauty treatments, water therapy and massage, exercise facilities, and nutrition are all included. The Spa also has a food and juice bar.

Hotel guests can use the workout area for $20 per day, and for an additional $30 can work with a private trainer. "Wet area" use is $25. Packages for longer stays are available. The hotel's outdoor pool is free to all guests.

The Crescent Court complex stands on a hilltop on the north side of the city. Between the hotel and Dallas's almost futuristic downtown skyline lies the West End Historical District. The hotel is also near the Arts District and Dallas Market Center. D/FW International Airport is a 20-minute drive, while Love Field is only 10 minutes away.

Hotel St. Germain

2516 Maple Avenue
Dallas, TX 75201
214-871-2516
Fax: 214-871-0740

New Orleans elegance in the heart of Dallas

Proprietor: Claire L. Heymann. **Accommodations:** 7 suites. **Rates:** $225–$600. **Included:** Breakfast. **Added:** 13% tax. **Payment:** Major credit cards. **Children:** Discouraged. **Pets:** Not permitted. **Smoking:** Permitted. **Open:** Year-round except for the first 10 days of August.

The St. Germain is in the McKinney Avenue section of Dallas, a shopping, dining, and entertainment area near downtown. The 1906 Victorian mansion has been beautifully converted into a small luxury hotel by owner Claire Heymann. Named for Heymann's French grandmother and the left bank of Paris (Heymann studied at the Sorbonne), the St. Germain opened in late 1991. It is one of the city's most unusual hotels: with only seven suites, it is small and intimate, yet it offers the same services as larger hotels, such as nightly turndown complete with a chocolate, valet parking, room service, and a round-the-clock concierge.

Outside there's an inviting New Orleans–style walled courtyard with a cherub fountain, flower boxes, and wrought-iron furniture.

The suites are tastefully appointed with fine antiques, elegantly draped canopy beds, and fireplaces. Many of the furnishings came from New Orleans, where the owner lived for a number of years. All suites have cable television, Jacuzzi or deep soaking tubs, terrycloth robes, and French toiletries. Two of the guest suites have private porches accented with fanciful wrought-iron railings. Suite 5 has a brass canopy bed covered in blue and ivory damask and topped by a brass crown. Suite 2 has a crystal chandelier and a wonderful bath. Suite 7 has fabulous arched windows under a gable. Suite 6 is the largest, with 600 square feet of space, and it has a cozy canopied sofa set back in a nook.

In the morning, a silver breadbasket arrives at your door filled with brioches, croissants, sticky buns, fruit danish and other tempting pastries, along with hot café au lait. On Friday and Saturday evenings, meals are served in the hotel's dining room, graced by a magnificent crystal chandelier. While gathering for dinner, guests are served a glass of champagne in either of the two downstairs parlors, one decorated with fluffy sofas and chairs covered in cream damask, the other furnished with red and green velvet sofas. The five-course prix fixe dinner is $65 per person, with entrées ranging from mushroom-crusted swordfish with saffron sauce to mustard-coated, apple bacon–barded breast of pheasant. Dinners are open to the public, and since seating is limited, reservations are necessary.

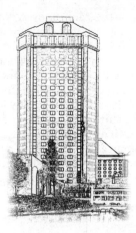

Loews Anatole Hotel

2201 Stemmons Freeway
Dallas, TX 75207
214-748-1200
800-23-LOEWS
Fax: 214-761-7520

*This hotel is a
city unto itself*

Managing Director: Michael French. **Accommodations:** 1,620 units. **Rates:** $170; suites $250–$1,350. **Added:** 13% tax. **Payment:** Major credit cards. **Children:** Under 18 free in room with parents. **Pets:** Not permitted. **Smoking:** Nonsmoking rooms available. **Open:** Year-round.

Although it doesn't look all that imposing from the outside, the Loews Anatole is the kind of hotel in which you need a map and comfortable walking shoes to get around. In a state where everything is big, the Anatole does nothing on a small scale. Spread over 45 acres with seven restaurants, eight lounges, more than a dozen shops, and a huge health spa, it's very nearly a self-contained metropolis. Downtown Dallas is about a five-minute drive away.

This is the largest hotel in the Southwest, and it's worth a stop just to see the Anatole's public areas. Parking is free, so at least pull off Stemmons Freeway and take a look. Two enormous elephants, carved from monkeypod wood by entire villages in Thailand, stand guard inside the tower section. Behind them is an 18th-century white marble Hindustani pavilion from a royal palace in India. Around the corner are exquisite jade screens from the Ching Dynasty. Inside Atrium II hang five fantastic batik banners, created in Ceylon especially for the hotel. The Jade Room, used for receptions, has a magnificent collection of carved jade. Outside the Wedgwood Ballroom, with its collection of pieces dating from the 18th century, is a rare Wedgwood vase nearly five feet tall. And so the collection continues, much of it inspired by Trammell Crow, who developed the hotel as well as the innovative Infomart across the freeway.

> **Naturally, the Anatole can handle large conventions. But groups of all sizes as well as individuals can enjoy its many services.**

Behind the hotel in a southern mansion–style building is the Verandah Club, a health spa with indoor and outdoor jogging tracks; indoor and outdoor pools; tennis, racquetball, and squash courts; a full-size basketball court; exercise rooms; and a sauna, steam room, and whirlpool section. A private club, Verandah, is available to guests for about $12 a day. Extra fees are charged for racquetball. Outdoor swimming is free.

The guest rooms are in two atrium high-rises and a 27-story tower. The traditional furnishings are comfortable if not distinctive. The 70 tower suites have small parlors and elegant baths with marble vanities, phones, and extra amenities. A variety of other suites are also available. Two concierge floors provide Continental breakfast, afternoon wine and cheese, and a full-time concierge.

One can dine at the Anatole at any hour of the day. There are seven restaurants on the premises. The Chanticleer Cafe and atrium deli are open 24 hours, and room service is also available round-the-clock. The Nana Grill on the 27th floor, elegant in burgundy tones, has large windows to take in the city views. Mesquite grilling is the Nana's specialty, and its Sunday brunch is popular. Las Esquina is a Tex-Mex cantina; L'Entre Cote serves Mediterranean cuisine; the Crocodile nightclub is open until 2:00 A.M.; the Rathskeller is a sports bar in the basement; and the Socio Grill offers casual dining at the Verandah club.

The Mansion on Turtle Creek

2821 Turtle Creek Boulevard
Dallas, TX 75219
214-559-2100
800-442-3408
Fax: 214-528-4187

> *A perennial*
> *award-winner*

Managing Director: Jeff Trigger. **Accommodations:** 142 rooms and suites. **Rates:** $235–$330 single, $275–$370 double; suites $495–$1,370. **Added:** 13% tax. **Payment:** Major credit cards. **Children:** $40 extra in room with parents. **Pets:** Permitted with $50 nonrefundable deposit. **Smoking:** Nonsmoking rooms available. **Open:** Year-round.

The only problem with staying at the Mansion is that it spoils you so that you won't want to stay anywhere else. It's a world of quiet opulence, beauty, and attentive service. Beginning at registration, guests' preferences for everything from newspapers to wine are noted and attended to, with records filed for future visits. The staff's hospitality is genuine.

The hotel is indeed a mansion, once the home of the millionaire Sheppard King, set on a terraced hillside in one of Dallas's most prestigious residential areas. Built in 1925, it has a 16th-century Italianate design with imaginative spires and turrets. In 1981, Rosewood Hotels restored the original building, converting it into a fine restaurant and building a complementary hotel tower next door.

At this hotel, the concierge wears a suit, not a uniform. There are no shops off the lobby, no hints of the commercial world. Instead, there's soft music, handsomely arranged fresh flowers, and a bevy of employees (more than two staff members for every guest) to satisfy every whim. The lobby resembles a fine living room, accented with antique mirrors and a Chippendale breakfront.

The guest rooms are exquisite. Decorated in peach, gold, or beige, they have four-poster beds, overstuffed chairs with ottomans, love seats, armoires with TVs, and French doors that open out onto small balconies. Although the rooms are all the same size, those on the upper floors cost more because of the view. The bathrooms are not only luxurious but pleasing to the eye, decorated in marble and brass. Terry robes, bathroom telephones, and turndown service add to the feeling of luxury. In the evening, a treat is delivered, perhaps spiced tea or cookies and milk. Other courtesies include overnight shoeshine and 24-hour pressing and room service.

> **Like its sister hotel, the Crescent Court, the Mansion has a wine cellar that can be used for private dinner parties. The Mansion's wine cellar is stocked with over 28,000 vintage bottles and seats up to 12. Breakfast and lunch are served in the cheerful Promenade.**

Three guest rooms open onto the hotel's attractive pool, which is heated in cooler weather. Guests also have free use of a nearby health club, including transportation.

One of the highlights of staying at the Mansion is dining at its restaurant, an architectural treasure as well as a culinary delight. Much of the grandeur of the original home, such as carved fireplaces and imported marble floors, was retained in its restoration. A dramatic wrought-iron staircase spirals up from the foyer. The ceiling of the main dining room is a composite of 2,400 pieces of enameled and inlaid wood. Stained glass windows depict British barons signing the Magna Carta, and two pairs of early 19th-century Spanish cathedral doors lead to one of the dining areas.

The cuisine does justice to its surroundings. Nouvelle American dishes with a southwestern flair are well prepared and attractively presented. Rack of lamb roasted with rosemary and mustard sauce, Louisiana crabcakes, and lobster tacos are popular favorites. The service is polished but unpretentious. Elaborate weekend brunches are popular with residents as well as hotel guests.

Valet parking costs $10.85; there is no self-parking. About 5 minutes from downtown, the Mansion is near many business, cultural, and shopping areas. D/FW International Airport is a 30-minute drive.

Melrose Hotel

3015 Oak Lawn
Dallas, TX 75219
214-521-5151
800-843-6664
Fax: 214-521-5151

An intimate and centrally located hotel

General Manager: H.L. Yates. **Accommodations:** 184 rooms. **Rates:** $150–$175 single, $160–$185 double; suites $225–$285; weekend rates available. **Added:** 13% tax. **Payment:** Major credit cards. **Children:** Under 17 free in room with parents. **Pets:** Not permitted. **Smoking:** Nonsmoking floors available. **Open:** Year-round.

The Melrose opened in 1924 as an apartment hotel. Restored in 1982, it is now a small luxury hotel with genuine warmth. Its graceful lobby recalls another era, with its marble floors, tall arched windows, and stately white columns. Potted palms, comfortable sofas and easy chairs, and classical music complete the mood.

In the Oak Lawn area, the Melrose is near the West End Marketplace, the Arts District, Dallas Market Center, and the central business district.

Since the guest rooms were once apartments, they are more spacious than usual, and each one is unique in size and decor. All are truly charming, furnished with antique reproductions. Four-poster beds, overstuffed chairs, attractive fabrics, large windows, and wallpapered baths with dressing tables set the tone. The concierge level provides Continental breakfast as well as turndown service with milk and cookies.

The Landmark Café has a splendid art deco setting. Featuring cuisine with strong Cajun and Asian (the hotel is now owned by a Thai company) influences, its enticing menu changes regularly, but you can expect dishes such as roast breast of duck with pecan truffle stuffing, and Cajun-seasoned trout blackened and served with fresh chive butter and New Orleans crawfish cream sauce. Entrées run from $18 to $25. The elegant but cozy Library Bar, doubling as a piano bar, serves lunch and late evening fare.

Hotel parking is free. Complimentary transportation is available to Love Field.

The Stoneleigh

2927 Maple Avenue
Dallas, TX 75201
214-871-7111
800-255-9299 in U.S.
Fax: 214-871-9379

*A charming hotel
in exclusive
Turtle Creek*

General Manager: Greg Harris. **Accommodations:** 150 rooms. **Rates:** $130–$165 single, $145–$180 double; suites $225–$1,000. **Added:** 13% tax. **Payment:** Major credit cards. **Children:** Free in room with parents. **Pets:** Not permitted. **Smoking:** Nonsmoking rooms available. **Open:** Year-round.

This hotel is a gem, hidden in a residential neighborhood on the edge of the prestigious Turtle Creek area. In 1923, the 11-story Stoneleigh opened as a hostelry of distinction. While its doors never closed in the following decades, it definitely declined. Then, in the late 1980s, the Stoneleigh was gloriously reborn, with refurbished interiors, an exterior facelift, and a renewed emphasis on service. Now classical music plays in the background, and antique furniture, marble columns, and fresh flowers grace the lobby.

The beautiful, individually decorated guest rooms, in different shapes and sizes, have armoires, overstuffed chairs, matching drapes and bedspreads, and brass light fixtures. Some suites have kitchens.

Ewald's, serving all three meals, is the Stoneleigh's fine dining restaurant. It's a cheerful and intimate place, where seafood and Continental dishes are dinner highlights, and

Sunday brunch is popular. Prices run from $13 to $22. The cozy Lion's Den Lounge, with pictures of famous visitors on its walls, serves cocktails, lunch, and appetizers.

> In the morning, there's a newspaper at the door. Maid service is twice a day, and turndown includes fancy chocolates. Room service is always available.

Guests at the Stoneleigh have access to some excellent recreational facilities. The owners also have an apartment building next door, also restored, and on its grounds a beautiful shaded pool and tennis courts are hidden in a gardenlike setting. There's also a wonderful rock garden and lily pond, a tranquil spot seemingly far from the city beyond.

Stouffer Dallas Hotel

2222 Stemmons Freeway
Dallas, TX 75207
214-631-2222
Fax: 214-634-9319

> *A 30-story hotel catering to business travelers*

General Manager: Rick Smith. **Accommodations:** 540 rooms. **Rates:** $134–$179 single, $154–$199 double. **Added:** 13% tax. **Payment:** Major credit cards. **Children:** Free in room with parents. **Pets:** Not permitted. **Smoking:** Nonsmoking rooms available. **Open:** Year-round.

The Stouffer Dallas is a sleek, pink Texas granite ellipse, distinctive in its architecture and its service. A wide spiral staircase winds from the center of the lobby to the mezzanine, flanked by a spectacular curved chandelier that is reputedly the longest in the world: 140 feet long, with 7,500 Italian crystals. Asian works of art add aesthetic interest.

But distinctive architecture and art alone do not make a hotel great. It's the people that make Stouffer Dallas special. Throughout the hotel, the staff members are hospitable and attentive, making you feel they're glad you're here. Despite its size, the hotel feels intimate. The public areas are small, almost residential in style. The Bay Tree Grill, serving steaks and seafood, is cozy and elegant. The Charisma Café is casual, serving all three meals.

The guest rooms are refreshingly different, with an Oriental theme. Some rooms have views of downtown. Rooms on the Club floor have TVs in the baths, suites have triangular living rooms, and butlers deliver Continental breakfast, hors d'oeuvres, and beverages to guest rooms on the Butler floor. All guests can request 24-hour room service.

> **Many of the Stouffer's guests are in town to visit the Dallas Market Center, the largest wholesale merchandise market in the world, which is next door. Infomart is also part of the complex. Downtown Dallas is about a 5-minute drive.**

Up on the roof there's a viewing deck, an outdoor pool, and a health club with exercise equipment, a whirlpool, sauna, and steam room. With a wake-up call you get coffee and a morning paper brought to your door. Self-parking is free, an important extra in this metropolitan area. Valet parking is $8.

FORT WORTH

Radisson Plaza Hotel Fort Worth

815 Main Street
Fort Worth, TX 76102
817-870-2100
Fax: 817-870-2100, ext. 1555

> *A historic hotel across from the convention center*

General Manager: Mr. Schafareber.
Accommodations: 517 rooms.
Rates: $128–$140 single, $143–$160 double; suites $225–$1,000; weekend rates available. **Added:** 13% tax. **Payment:** Major credit cards. **Children:** Free in room with parents. **Pets:** Permitted with deposit. **Smoking:** Nonsmoking rooms available. **Open:** Year-round.

The Radisson Plaza Hotel opened in 1921 as the Hotel Texas. At one end of downtown Fort Worth, it reigned for years as the city's social center. Big bands played in its ballroom, and the rich and famous stayed in its guest rooms. The hotel closed in 1979, reopening in 1981. By then it had been named to the National Register of Historic Places.

The 14-story hotel is a rectangle of red brick and terra cotta. While its exterior was virtually unchanged in the renovation, the interior was gutted and is now totally modern. The lobby is soothing, with waterfalls, lush plants, an exotic cockatoo, and reflecting fish ponds.

> **One of the hotel's noteworthy guests was President John F. Kennedy, who spent his last night in the hotel before going to Dallas.**

There are two restaurants. The Café Centennial is casual and relaxed. The Crystal Cactus serves southwestern cuisine. In the evenings, a piano player entertains in the lobby bar beneath a glass atrium.

The guest rooms, traditionally furnished in blue, burgundy, and beige, are masculine and spacious but not particularly distinctive. The plaza level has such extras as Continental breakfast and afternoon hors d'oeuvres. The health club in an adjacent office tower has a heated pool, sauna, and exercise room.

The concierge and staff make every effort to attend to guests' needs. Room service operates from 6:00 A.M. to midnight. Self-parking in an underground garage costs $6 per day; valet parking ($9) is also available. Since the hotel is within a few blocks of I-30, it is easy to reach all the area's sights.

Stockyards Hotel

109 East Exchange
Fort Worth, TX 76164
817-625-6427
800-423-8471
Fax: 817-624-2571

Experience the Old West at this historic hotel

General Manager: Mike Swanson.
Accommodations: 52 rooms. **Rates:** $95 single, $105 double; suites $125–$350. **Added:** 13% tax. **Payment:** Major credit cards. **Children:** Free in room with parents. **Pets:** Not permitted. **Smoking:** Permitted. **Open:** Year-round.

In many ways the Stockyards lives up to the expectations of first-time visitors to Texas, for here they find what they imagine the whole Lone Star State to be. The hotel, in the Stockyards National Historic District of the city affectionately called Cowtown, is a slice of history, reflecting the world of the affluent cattlemen of the early 1900s who dealt at the livestock markets just down the street.

The Bonnie and Clyde Suite, reportedly frequented by the infamous twosome, has appropriate memorabilia, including Bonnie Parker's gun and vintage photographs. The Celebrity Suite, with a celebrity price of $350, has a fireplace and a private deck with a hot tub.

Dating from 1907, the hotel building was transformed in 1983 into a gem of a luxury hotel. Not intended as a historical reproduction, it is inventive and vivacious, capturing the spirit of the era it portrays; outside, western-style shops, restaurants, and saloons line the streets of the former cattle center of the Southwest. Today the area supports thriving tourist businesses and cattle auctions.

The lobby is decorated with leather sofas, carved wooden chairs covered with furry animal hides, bronze sculptures, and western art. One of the most dramatic pieces is a mirror framed in doeskin and topped with antlers.

The guest rooms offer Indian, western, mountain-man, and Victorian decor, all creatively executed. Many decorating touches are unique, such as deerskin headboards and ram's skull chandeliers. The Victorian rooms are soft and feminine, with white wicker furniture, lace curtains, and fringed lamps. There are also king-size beds, baths with chain-pull water closets, and wardrobes that conceal TVs.

In Booger Red's Saloon downstairs, you can order a drink while seated on a saddle mounted on a bar stool. The adjacent restaurant serves southern favorites such as barbecue and chicken-fried steak.

The Worthington Hotel

200 Main Street
Fort Worth, TX 76102
817-870-1000
800-772-5977 in Texas
800-433-5677 in U.S.
Fax: 817-332-5679

*A full-service
downtown hotel*

General Manager: Robert L. Jameson. **Accommodations:** 504 rooms and suites. **Rates:** $129–$169 single, $139–$179 double; suites $300–$400. **Added:** 13% tax. **Payment:** Major credit cards. **Children:** Under 18 free in room with parents. **Pets:** Not permitted. **Smoking:** Nonsmoking rooms available. **Open:** Year-round.

A hospitable staff, a good location, and an excellent fitness club make the Worthington a top-notch hotel. Built in 1981, it occupies three city blocks at one end of downtown Fort Worth. Its ultramodern exterior makes an interesting contrast to Sundance Square, a turn-of-the-century shopping and entertainment area with fancy boutiques and restaurants across the street. For a romantic tour of the city, climb into a horse-drawn carriage right at the hotel's doors. The city's attractions and many business addresses are a short drive away.

The Worthington's fitness club has an indoor pool, outdoor tennis courts, a sun deck, sauna, whirlpool, and exercise room with free weights, Lifecycles, and treadmills. The club is welcoming, from a sociable staff to such extras as a comfortable sitting area with magazines and newspapers, baskets of fruit, and a big-screen TV. The pool and whirlpool are free to hotel guests; the other facilities can be used for a daily fee.

> **The hotel has a distinctive contemporary design. Its marble lobby is softened by gentle waterfalls and lots of greenery.**

Dining gets lots of attention at this hotel. In addition to elegant Reflections and the casual Brasserie LaSalle, it operates the Houston Street Bakery across the street and Firehall Marketplace Deli in Sundance Square. The room service menu is several cuts above average, featuring treats from the bakery as well as the hotel's own kitchen. Afternoon tea and lavish Sunday brunches are Worthington traditions.

Guest rooms in beige, cream, and blue are classy and elegant. They have Oriental accents, rich wood furnishings, servi-bars, and terry robes. Rooms on the Club floor have telephones and hair dryers in the baths and share a lounge and a concierge. Continental breakfast, afternoon hors d'oeuvres, beverages, twice-daily housekeeping service, complimentary shoeshine, nightly turndown, a daily newspaper, and use of the Worthington's fitness center are all included in the Club floor rate.

Throughout the hotel, the staff is Texas-friendly, and a concierge is on duty for special requests. Valet parking costs $9; self-parking is $6.

GLEN ROSE

Inn on the River

209 Barnard Street
P.O. Box 1417
Glen Rose, TX 76043
817-897-2101
Fax: 817-897-7729

> *A delightful inn
> for a country
> getaway*

Innkeeper: Kathi Thompson. **Accommodations:** 22 units, all with private bath. **Rates:** $78–$88 single, $98–$115 double; suites $125–$145. **Included:** Full breakfast. **Added:** 6% tax. **Payment:** Major credit cards. **Children:** Not permitted. **Pets:** Not permitted. **Smoking:** Not permitted. **Open:** Year-round.

The Inn on the River serves up big healthy doses of R&R. Yes, there are sights to see — Dinosaur State Park, Fossil Rim Wildlife Ranch, and the nearby village of Granbury, with its famed opera house — but at the inn, life moves at a comfortably relaxed pace. Just outside the lodging is the tranquil Paluxy River, sheathed in mist in the mornings, and the inn's design takes full advantage of this setting. Its shady grounds slope down to the river, and comfortable lounging areas are sprinkled over the lawn.

> **Breakfasts feature fresh fruit, bacon or sausage, homemade muffins, and a hot entrée such as orange almond pancakes, broccoli and cheddar egg bake, or eggs Florentine.**

Then there's a swimming pool beneath 300-year-old sinewy live oak trees. The majestic trees so impressed one guest in the 1950s that he wrote a song about them called the "The Singing Trees," a song that was later recorded by Elvis Presley.

In 1919 the inn was built as a health resort, taking advantage of the region's mineral waters. In 1984, it was converted into a visually appealing inn. Guest rooms were refurbished with a sense of history coupled with comfort. Overall, the inn has a crisp, clean look, airy and welcoming.

Each room is different, right down to its wallpaper. Many

of the beds have upholstered headboards with spreads to match. Some rooms are decorated in pretty pastels, others are more masculine. Ceiling fans and individual heating and air conditioning units are in every room. But don't look for TVs or phones, for the inn is truly intended as an escape.

On weekends, prix fixe gourmet dinners are served by reservation only in the inn's glassed-in porch overlooking the lawn. Meals may include lobster ravioli with warm dill vinaigrette, smoked duck enchiladas, or pork loin stuffed with apricots, prunes, and sage, and fudge truffle cheesecake or a dark chocolate hazelnut pâté for dessert, but all are beautifully presented and definitely delicious. If your stay at the inn falls on a weekend, be sure to take in a dinner.

GRANBURY

The Nutt House Hotel and Inn

Town Square
Granbury, TX 76048
817-573-5612

A down-home hotel and restaurant on the town square

Owner: Tony Dauphinof. **Accommodations:** 17 units, 9 with shared bath. **Rates:** $45 single, $55 double; suite $85; $5 per day each additional person in room. **Added:** 13% tax. **Payment:** Major credit cards. **Children:** Infants not encouraged. **Pets:** Not permitted. **Smoking:** Not permitted. **Open:** Year-round.

Granbury calls itself "a door to yesterday"; its town square was the first in Texas to be listed on the National Register of

Historic Places. Lining its streets are a bevy of antiques stores, gift shops, tea rooms, and restaurants. The restored Granbury Opera House, one of the region's most popular attractions, overlooks the square. So does the Nutt House Hotel and Inn, a two-story stone building dating from 1893.

> **At the top of the stairs is a gathering spot with a coffee pot; it's a Nutt House tradition that the first guest up in the morning makes the coffee.**

Upstairs is the hotel, straight out of 1919. The rooms, which could use some touching up with a paintbrush, have screened doors, iron beds and simple furnishings, and lavatories. The baths, which could also use some updating, are down the hall; nine rooms share three baths. The suite is suitable for families, with one double and two twin beds, a full kitchen, sitting area, and private bath. Don't expect luxury, phones, or TVs, but the hotel does have central air and heat.

For many, it's the old-fashioned restaurant downstairs that's the best part of staying at the Nutt House. The restaurant serves dinner at midday from Tuesday through Sunday, and supper on weekends. The country food is quite good here; chicken and dumplings, hot water cornbread, and buttermilk pie are specialties. The all-you-can-eat buffet is a real bargain at $6 during the week and $8 on weekends.

About a block away is the Nutt House Bed & Breakfast. There are five rooms, each with a bath and cable TV. A Continental breakfast is included in the room rate.

IRVING

Four Seasons Resort and Club

4150 North MacArthur Boulevard
Irving, TX 75038
214-717-0700
Fax: 214-717-2428

> *A classy resort near Dallas*

General Manager: Jim FitzGibbon.
Accommodations: 365 rooms. **Rates:** $195–$230; suites $365–$1,000. **Added:** 11% tax. **Payment:** Major credit cards. **Children:** Free in room with parents. **Pets:** Small pets only with approval. **Smoking:** Nonsmoking rooms available. **Open:** Year-round.

Hidden between Dallas and D/FW International Airport is a sparkling and innovative community, both an office and a residential development, named Las Colinas. The Four Seasons, which opened in 1986, sits on a hill overlooking a Tournament Players Golf course. It was predated by a sophisticated fitness center, now run by Four Seasons. The combined facilities give vacationers a multifaceted resort. It's also a fine conference center, but that doesn't interfere with a leisure traveler's enjoyment.

The roster of activities offers something for everyone. The 18-hole golf course is the only TPC course in northern Texas and provides elevated areas for watching tournaments, such as the GTE Byron Nelson Classic held each May.

Racquet sports include indoor and outdoor tennis, squash, and racquetball. Several professional tennis events are held on the stadium court during the year. The fitness section has Nautilus equipment, treadmills, bicycles, rowing machines, and a gym. There are also outdoor and indoor pools, jogging tracks, and aerobics classes.

The spa is one of the best equipped in the Southwest.

Workout gear — even sneakers — is provided. Herbal wraps and loofah scrubs, facials, pedicures, saunas, whirlpools, and massages are all included. A trained staff can perform tests geared toward achieving optimal health through exercise and nutrition. Use of the spa facilities is included in the room rate, but services are extra. A round of golf with cart rental can be a little pricey, as are court fees, but packages are offered that combine lodging with sports and spa services.

> **Fifty villa-style rooms added in 1994 overlook the 18th green of the golf course.**

Throughout the resort there is a feeling of spaciousness. Both the public areas and guest rooms overlook lush grounds or a long pool in a shape reminiscent of a golf green. The accommodations get high marks for comfort and luxury. Roomy and tastefully decorated, they have overstuffed chairs with ottomans, three phones, a large tub and separate shower, and balconies. Suites have separate living rooms, two baths, and a writing desk set off in an alcove that's perfect for getting work done.

When it comes to mealtime, it'll be hard to resist the sumptuous buffets at the Café on the Green, a comfortably elegant and attractive dining spot. For those who can put blinders on and pass up the buffet, the restaurant also offers dishes that are low in calories, sodium, and cholesterol. Byron's at the sports club is casual and offers salads and sandwiches at lunch. For evening recreation, the Game Bar has a hunt theme and billiard tables, while the lounge in the lobby area offers a more restful environment in which to enjoy cocktails.

The resort has a professionally run child care center for infants and children up to eight years old. In addition, there are special items on the room service menu just for kids. Hotel parking is complimentary, and valet parking is available.

Omni Mandalay Hotel at Las Colinas

221 East Las Colinas Boulevard
Irving, TX 75039
214-556-0800
1-800-THE-OMNI

A sophisticated hotel in a planned community

General Manager: Bill Thompson.
Accommodations: 420 rooms.
Rates: $140–$160 during the week; $89–$119 on weekends; suites higher. **Added:** 8.25% tax. **Payment:** Major credit cards. **Children:** Under 12, free in room with parents. **Pets:** Under 10 pounds permitted with deposit; pets receive a special amenity. **Smoking:** Nonsmoking rooms available. **Open:** Year-round.

The Mandalay canal at Las Colinas is a touch of Venice in Irving, Texas. The canal winds beneath covered bridges, past cobblestone streets lined with boutiques and eateries, office buildings, and the Mandalay Hotel. Since it's on the canal, guests staying at the hotel can explore the area easily on foot, on bicycles that can be rented from the hotel, or by water taxis, which stop at the hotel's dock.

Because the Mandalay is conveniently located between D/FW airport and downtown Dallas, many weekday guests are business travelers. For them, there's a fully equipped business center. On weekends, the Mandalay's pleasant canalside location draws families. In addition to biking along the canal, families enjoy the hotel's exercise room, outdoor pool, and children's playground. During the summer, there are cook-outs by the pool, and festive theme weekends run periodically throughout the year.

Standard guest rooms are pleasant and attractive. Decorated with marble-topped furnishings and botanical prints, they have sofas, coffeemakers, terry robes, and ironing boards and irons. The baths, while not large, have marble floors and vanities as well as hair dryers and makeup mirrors. Mini-suites, with entrance halls, semicircular living rooms, framed silk embroidery, balconies, and two TVs, are especially attractive.

> **Many visiting business people are Japanese; a Japanese breakfast of miso soup, grilled salmon, rice, and green tea shows up on restaurant and room service menus.**

The hotel's plant-filled lobby houses the appropriately named Les Jardin Bar, which features sandwiches and hors d'oeuvres for lighter appetites. Downstairs, Cafe D'Or serves all three meals including lunch and breakfast buffets. The elegant Enjolie next door is the Mandalay's highly rated fine restaurant, open for dinner only (jackets required). Diners have their choice of ordering à la carte or from a prix fixe menu. Entrées such as pecan-crusted Texas venison chop or stuffed quail with cranberry citrus marmalade are examples of its superior cuisine. On Sunday, a bounteous brunch is served in the Rhapsody room overlooking the canal.

STEPHENVILLE

The Oxford House

563 North Graham
Stephenville, TX 76401
817-965-6885
Fax: 817-965-7555

*A B&B in a
gingerbread-
trimmed Victorian*

Innkeepers: Bill and Paula Oxford.
Accommodations: 4 rooms, all
with private bath. **Rates:** $58 single, $75 double. **Included:**
Country breakfast. **Added:** 13% tax. **Payment:** Major credit
cards. **Children:** Over age 6 welcome; additional $10 charge
per day. **Pets:** Not permitted. **Smoking:** In designated areas
only. **Open:** Year-round.

In 1898, Judge William J. Oxford built a fine Victorian home
in Stephenville. In 1986, his grandson Bill opened it as a B&B,
a gem of a house steeped in local as well as family history.
Bill's wife, Paula, has an obvious love of history, and throughout the house she has woven memorabilia into the design. As
you sip afternoon refreshments, ask her about the home's history and you'll probably get a grand tour. The pump organ is a
family heirloom brought to Texas by wagon. The violins belonged to the good judge himself, as did the law books. The
hats and gloves belonged to his third wife.

The guest room at the top of the stairs has interior columns
and gingerbread trim, plus a stained glass window. There's a
claw-foot tub in the bath and a big basket of towels. Another

room is decorated in peach, featuring a Victorian bed made in Texas. A third room has a sleigh bed and a fainting couch that converts into a single bed.

The Oxfords and their children live elsewhere, but they go out of their way to make you feel welcome. Homemade breads and fruit are served at breakfast with omelettes, quiche, or French toast.

> **With a reservation, you can have high tea in the tea room downstairs or be served a candlelight dinner. Out back are a garden and a gazebo.**

In Stephenville you can visit the Historical House Museum Complex. Other nearby sites include Dinosaur Valley State Park, the Fossil Rim Wildlife Ranch, and the historic village of Granbury.

Southern Texas

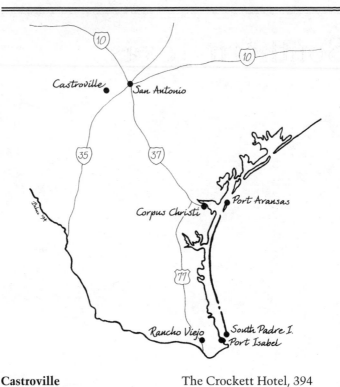

Best Beachside

Corpus Christi
 Best Western Sandy Shores Beach Hotel
Port Aransas
 Port Royal Ocean Resort
South Padre
 Bridgepoint
 Sheraton South Padre Island Beach Resort

Best Bed and Breakfasts

Corpus Christi
 Sand Dollar Hospitality Bed and Breakfast
San Antonio
 Bed and Breakfast Hosts of San Antonio
 Riverwalk Inn

Best City Stops

Corpus Christi
 Corpus Christi Marriott Bayfront
San Antonio
 The Crockett Hotel
 The Emily Morgan Hotel
 The Fairmount Hotel
 La Mansion del Rio
 The Menger Hotel
 Plaza San Antonio
 San Antonio Marriott Rivercenter
 Sheraton Gunter Hotel
 St. Anthony

Best Historic Hostelries

Castroville
 Landmark Inn
Port Aransas
 Tarpon Inn
Port Isabel
 Yacht Club Hotel and Restaurant

Best Resorts

Rancho Viejo
  Rancho Viejo Resort
San Antonio
  Hyatt Regency Hill Country Resort

San Antonio is the gateway to southern Texas and perhaps the most popular tourist destination in all of Texas. The first thing most visitors do when arriving in the city is head straight for the Alamo, appropriately at the city's core. Many remark on the rather diminutive size of the Alamo, forgetting that it was built as a mission and was never meant to be the site of a battle of such mythic proportions.

Until the Texas Revolution, San Antonio was the principal Spanish, and later Mexican, stronghold in the area. Many of the city's first settlers came from the Spanish Canary Islands. In the 19th century, German settlers arrived — their legacy is most evident in the King William district — but the Spanish and Mexican influence still dominates the city. The annual ten-day Fiesta San Antonio in April pays respect to the tenacious Texans such as Davy Crockett and Jim Bowie who held out at the Alamo as long as they could, yet the city's biggest party has an overriding Hispanic flavor. It's this wonderful blending of traditions from several cultures that gives San Antonio its warm and lively spirit.

After the Alamo, most visitors head to the Riverwalk, where happy crowds and riverboat taxis ply the restaurant, shop, and tree-lined Paseo del Rio. Unabashedly touristy, the attractive Riverwalk deserves all the attention it gets, and there are still points along the river where you can find a peaceful niche. Nearby, La Villita, a restored Mexican village that sometimes hosts exhibits such as the Starving Artists Show, offers a quieter option for shopping and dining. Across from La Villita, HemisFair Park was built for the 1968 Texas World's Fair.

Other San Antonio attractions include four missions dating back to the 1700s, the McNay Art Museum with its collection of Post-Impressionist works, Fort Sam Houston, the Hertzberg Circus Museum, El Mercado, the San Antonio Zoo, the San Antonio Museum of Art, the Spanish Governor's Palace, the Botanical Gardens, and the marvelously atmospheric Majestic Theatre. Outside the city, Sea World of Texas and Fiesta Texas are popular with families. The town of **Castro-**

ville, named for its founder Henri Castro, is called the "little Alsace of Texas" because it was settled by Alsatians back in 1844 and retains much of its early character.

Traveling several hours southeast from San Antonio you'll come to **Corpus Christi,** the largest Texas city on the Gulf of Mexico. Windsurfing events are held frequently on the bay, and the Texas State Aquarium is here, as is the U.S.S. Lexington Museum on the Bay, a naval museum housed in an aircraft carrier. At the Bayfront Arts and Science Park you'll find the Art Museum of South Texas, the Harbor Playhouse, the Corpus Christi Museum of Science and History, and Heritage Park, where a collection of Victorian homes has been restored.

One of the best reasons for visiting the Corpus Christi area is the natural beauty of the ocean and its accompanying wildlife. The Padre Island National Seashore offers mile upon mile of pristine, unspoiled beaches, and it is not uncommon to find yourself swimming among turtles and porpoises. **Port Aransas,** on Mustang Island, is popular with fishermen, and the island itself is known for its lovely beaches. The Aransas National Wildlife Refuge in nearby Rockport is home to over 300 species of birds.

South Padre Island, at the southern tip of the state, is Texas's answer to Fort Lauderdale. The beaches here were once as nice as those of North Padre and the National Seashore, but high-rises, surf shops, and fast food restaurants have sprung up along this island's strip. Unless you're between the ages of 18 and 21, it's best to stay away from **South Padre** during spring break. During the rest of the year, South Padre can be a fun destination if you want to combine a beach vacation with shopping trips into Mexico. Brownsville, the largest city in the area, is half an hour from South Padre, and you can easily cross into Matamoros, Mexico from there.

CASTROVILLE

Landmark Inn

402 Florence
Castroville, TX 78009
512-538-2133

*A historic
European-style
inn and park*

Manager: Texas Parks and Wildlife Department. **Accommodations:** 8 rooms, 4 with shared baths. **Rates:** $45–$50 single, $50–$55 double; additional adults $7. **Included:** Continental breakfast. **Added:** 10% tax. **Payment:** Major credit cards. **Children:** Under age 9, free in room with parents; over age 9, $7 per night. **Pets:** Not permitted. **Smoking:** In designated areas only. **Open:** Wednesday through Sunday night only.

Colonists from Alsace settled Castroville in 1844, bringing with them their language, customs, and architecture. Remnants of all three exist in modern Castroville, a town of about 2,000 residents. One of the best-preserved examples of European-influenced architecture is the Landmark Inn, the charming lodging that is the focal point of the Landmark Inn State Historical Park, run by the Texas Parks and Wildlife Department. The Landmark was built in 1849 as a home and general store for Cesar Monod, who became the mayor in 1852. It is open for tours, as is a historic stone grist mill and an exhibit depicting life in early Castroville.

Continental breakfast is served in the inn's 1849 kitchen, and the town has a number of eating establishments, including an Alsatian bakery.

The Landmark is a place for history lovers as well as those who like to get off the beaten track. The inn became the Vance Hotel in the 1850s. According to local legend, a lead-lined water tank on the second floor of the bathhouse was melted down to make Confederate bullets during the Civil War. The Parks Department has made every effort to preserve the historical nature of the structure, so don't expect TVs or telephones, but air conditioning has been added to the six rooms in the main building, and panel heaters are supplied in colder weather.

Your first sight of the inn is of a quaint, two-story, curbside building. In back, the tiny white hotel overlooks beautiful grounds and a graceful garden planted with shrubs and flowers representative of the town's early days. All the rooms in the main building open onto the gardens. The simple guest rooms are furnished with antiques. Don't worry — the historical authenticity doesn't extend to the mattresses.

The old bathhouse has been converted into two small bedrooms, one above the other. Each has a double bed and private bath. While the one on top, number 8, is often booked by honeymooners, people who tend toward claustrophobia or those who are large (whether tall or plump) should avoid it.

CORPUS CHRISTI

Best Western Sandy Shores Beach Hotel

3200 Surfside Boulevard
Corpus Christi Beach
Corpus Christi, TX 78403
512-883-7456
800-528-1234
Fax: 512-883-1437

> *A fun and
> friendly hotel
> on the beach*

Owner: Stern Feinberg. **Accommodations:** 251 rooms. **Rates:** $49–$99 single, $59–$129 double; suites $179–$229. **Added:** 13% tax. **Payment:** Major credit cards. **Children:** Under 12

free in room with parents; over 12 additional $10 per day.
Pets: Not permitted. **Smoking:** Nonsmoking rooms available.
Open: Year-round.

Corpus Christi Beach is a mile-long stretch of sand on Corpus
Christi Bay, about a five-minute drive across Harbor Bridge
from downtown. Best Western Sandy Shores, directly on the
beach, is a good choice for those who want an upbeat environment at a moderate price.

When you enter the lobby, you'll first notice the chairs
shaped like seashells and the bay view beyond. They suggest
the two most prevailing features of the hotel: whimsy and location. There is a spirit of
creativity throughout. Do
you know any other hotel
that has a kite museum?
Sure, it's a small muse-
um, but there's an adjoining kite shop, and the
concept is interesting and
fun. The museum is free,
but you just might be
tempted to purchase a colorful flyer and test it out immediately on the beach.

> **Corpus Christi is a popular
> area for windsurfing, and
> many sailboarding tourna-
> ments are held in front of
> or near the hotel.**

The hotel comprises a motel section built in the 1960s and
a 1980s five-story building. The guest rooms in the newer
building are decorated with beach scenes and wicker chairs.
They tend to be larger than those in the rest of the hotel. The
rooms are comfortable but not luxurious; some have bay
views, and most have balconies. Many rooms in the motel
section open onto the pool deck and have direct access to the
parking lot. Lanai rooms open right onto the beach. Two-
room suites are in the corners of the hotel building, overlooking the bay or downtown Corpus Christi.

In the Espresso coffee shop, every table has a pair of binoculars for watching beach and bay activities. The Pantry will deliver breakfast, pizza, sandwiches, chile relleños, or seafood
platters right to your room, or you can pick up your order and
save the 15% delivery charge. Seafood entrées ($8–$12) dominate the menu at Cal's Calypso Bar and Grille on the hotel's
third floor.

An activities center in the lobby keeps guests informed
about such recreations as golf, fishing, and bike rental. Joggers
will appreciate that the owner, a runner himself, has written

a brochure detailing several routes as well as jogging tips. The pool courtyard is pleasant and family-oriented, with palapas, palms, a kiddie pool, and a Jacuzzi and sauna inside a Japanese pagoda. The beach in front of the hotel is wide, but the sand is fairly coarse. Be advised that jellyfish are numerous in some seasons.

Other attractions in the area include North Padre Island's beautiful beaches, city museums, and a wildlife refuge. The Texas State Aquarium is just down the street, and the hotel is adjacent to the Lexington Aircraft Carrier Museum.

Corpus Christi Marriott Bayfront

900 North Shoreline
Corpus Christi, TX 78401
512-887-1600
800-228-9290
Fax: 512-887-6715

A full-service hotel on Corpus Christi Bay

General Manager: Todd Scartozzi.
Accommodations: 474 rooms. **Rates:** $109–$120 single, $119–$140 double; $12 each additional person; suites $140–$320; lower rates for 7-day prepaid stays. **Added:** 13% tax. **Payment:** Major credit cards. **Children:** Under 17 free in room with parents. **Pets:** Not permitted. **Smoking:** Nonsmoking rooms available. **Open:** Year-round.

There's nothing remarkable about the Marriott from the outside; it's sleek and modern, a white, 19-story rectangle set against the blue bay beyond. But inside, it's a beehive of activity, catering to both business travelers and family groups. There always seems to be something happening here.

The hotel recognizes the bayside setting, and the colors and designs tend to bring the outdoors in. The newly renovated guest rooms are angled for a glimpse of Corpus Christi Bay and are furnished in teal green with traditional furniture, two queen beds or a king, cable TV, and clock radios.

Reflections Restaurant, on the hotel's top floor, has several levels, giving each table an unobstructed view of the bay. Naturally, seafood dishes dominate the menu, and dinner entrées range from $13 to $18. The High Tide is the Marriott's comedy club; there are two shows on Friday and Saturday nights and one on Tuesday, Wednesday, and Thursday nights.

In the second-floor recreational area there's a large whirlpool, Ping-Pong table, weight room, racquetball courts, a sunbathing deck, and indoor and outdoor pools. You can rent bikes, Jet Skis, Sunfish, and fishing equipment at the marina three blocks away.

> **The hotel was originally a Hershey Hotel; the new owners, the Marriott chain, have retained some of their predecessor's traditions; the Chocolate Festival is still held in December, with chocolate buffets, demonstrations, and exhibitions.**

Self-parking in the hotel's covered garage is free; valet parking is $7. Trolleys connect the hotel to shopping centers and area tourist attractions. Downtown Corpus Christi and the exclusive homes along Ocean Drive are just a few minutes away.

Sand Dollar Hospitality Bed and Breakfast

3605 Mendenhall Drive
Corpus Christi, TX 78415
512-853-1222 (8:00 A.M.–9:00 P.M.)
800-264-7782

> *A reservation service for Corpus Christi*

Operator: Pat Hirshbrunner. **Accommodations:** About 24 rooms in host homes in the Corpus Christi area. **Rates:** $50–$90 single, $60–$100 double; suite $200. **Included:** Breakfast in some cases. **Payment:** Personal checks accepted as deposits; major credit cards accepted at some establishments. **Children:** Sometimes permitted with additional charge. **Pets:** Sometimes permitted. **Smoking:** Permitted in some host homes. **Open:** Year-round.

The Sand Dollar Hospitality Bed and Breakfast has a variety of lodgings in this popular coastal region. The reservation service is professionally operated by Pat Hirshbrunner, whose goal is to offer guests a taste of the South with families who exemplify high standards of hospitality.

The service's listings include in-town homes and cottages by the sea. One example is the Harbor View Bed and Breakfast in Port Aransas, which lives up to its name with balconies on each of its three levels that afford excellent views of the harbor. At Sunset Retreat Bed and Breakfast in Ingleside-on-the-Bay, also on the water, you can fish right from the inn's dock.

PORT ARANSAS

Port Royal Ocean Resort

P.O. Box 336
State Highway 361
Mustang Island
Port Aransas, TX 78373
512-749-5011
800-242-1034 in Texas
800-847-5659 in U.S.

> *A beachside condominium resort*

General Manager: Stephen Sheldon. **Accommodations:** 210 condos. **Rates:** 1-bedroom (1–4 persons) $99–$155; 2-bedroom (1–6 persons) $150–$210; 3-bedroom (1–8 persons) $170–$290; special rates for long stays. **Minimum stay:** 2 nights on weekends, 3 nights on holidays. **Added:** 13% tax. **Payment:** Major credit cards. **Children:** Welcome. **Pets:** Not permitted. **Smoking:** Nonsmoking units available. **Open:** Year-round.

On Mustang Island on the Gulf of Mexico, Port Royal is a resort apart from the crowd. Beautiful grounds, attractive condos, and a service-oriented staff make it an excellent destination. Port Aransas, also on the island, is seven miles north. Corpus Christi, on the mainland, is 20 miles away.

The condominiums are in four buildings arranged around one of the best water extravaganzas in Texas. With four pools, waterfalls, a swim-up bar,

> **The three-bedroom units are the most luxurious: they are the only ones that directly face the ocean, and they have extra touches like balcony whirlpools.**

hot tubs, and a water slide, it's the focal point of the resort. Beyond it, a private boardwalk leads over dunes studded with beach grass (and an occasional cactus) onto the wide beach. The resort also has two lighted tennis courts.

Although Port Royal's condos are individually owned, the resort is operated as a hotel, with a full range of services and planned activities during the high seasons. The units are all spacious and nicely appointed; kitchens are fully equipped with dinnerware, a microwave, coffeemaker, and dishwasher. Extra touches include a stereo, whirlpool tub, iron and ironing board, and washer and dryer. Each condo has a private patio or balcony.

The Atrium Restaurant on the top floor of the main building serves all three meals. With rose linen napkins and upholstered booths, the decor is cheerful. Seafood gets top attention, but there are also beef and chicken entrées. Smaller portions at much lower prices are offered for children.

Tarpon Inn

200 East Cotter
P.O. Box 8
Port Aransas, TX 78373
512-749-5555

A long-time landmark in Port Aransas

Manager: Mona Regler. **Accommodations:** 24 rooms. **Rates:** $30–$65; suites $55–$85. **Added:** Tax. **Payment:** Major credit cards; no personal checks. **Children:** Permitted. **Pets:** Not permitted. **Smoking:** Permitted. **Open:** Year-round.

Port Aransas, which is accessible from the mainland via ferry, has long been popular with fishermen because of its prime location in the Gulf of Mexico. In fact the town was once called Tarpon for the trophy fish abundant in its waters. The Tarpon Inn, named for the fish and the town, has been a town landmark in one incarnation or another since 1886.

The original structure was built with lumber taken from a

Civil War barracks by Frank Stephenson, a boat pilot and lighthouse keeper. The inn burned in 1900, and two new structures were built at the same location in 1904. In 1919 the larger building was destroyed by a hurricane but was once again rebuilt, this time to resemble a barracks. That simple structure is what you'll see when you visit the inn today.

The inn is a long, two-story building with porches that run the length of each level. Although plain, the exterior is painted a cheerful blue, and rocking chairs dot the porches, inviting guests to put up their feet and relax.

> **A signed fish scale that is attributed to Timothy Leary (although the innkeeper won't swear by it) reads, "6' 2" 170 pounds — don't know what the fish weighed."**

The inn has a laid-back feel — so casual, in fact, that some quests may not know what to make of the somewhat disheveled lobby. Look past the worn-out sofa to the walls covered in hundreds of fish scales, each signed and dated by the fisherman who caught it, along with the weight and size of the fish. The scales date as far back as 1897, but FDR's (May 8, 1939), and Aimee Semple McPherson's are among the most notable.

Rooms are entered from the long porches. All are different in size and decor. Some are decorated in pastel floral prints, others are rustic, more befitting a seasoned angler. All rooms have private baths, air conditioning, and heat. Televisions and phones have purposely not been added to the rooms, but the innkeeper will take phone messages for guests.

Beulah's, across the grassy lawn behind the inn, is one of the most popular restaurants in the area. Housed in the 1904 structure that did survive the 1919 hurricane, Beulah's serves fresh American variations of French cuisine in a pleasant setting. The menu changes regularly, but diners can expect entrées such as rib-eye steak served with mango salsa, potatoes au gratin, and sautéed vegetables, or crab-stuffed shrimp accompanied by tomato butter and white bean relish.

The Tarpon Inn is about a two-minute drive from both the ferry and the beach.

PORT ISABEL

Yacht Club Hotel and Restaurant

700 Yturria Street
Port Isabel, TX 78578
210-943-1301
Fax: 210-943-1301

> *A 1920s hotel
> and fine seafood
> restaurant*

Owners: Ron and Lynn Speier. **Accommodations:** 24 rooms. **Rates:** $35–$45 single, $42–$52 double; suites $49–$99 for 2; $10 each additional person. **Included:** Continental breakfast. **Added:** 10% tax. **Payment:** Major credit cards; no personal checks. **Children:** Under 12 free in room with parents. **Pets:** Not permitted. **Smoking:** Permitted. **Open:** Year-round.

Across the bridge are the gleaming new condo towers of South Padre Island. But here in the fishing village of Port Isabel, the Yacht Club Hotel puts you in touch with history. The atmosphere is vintage 1920s, the guest rooms are comfortable, and the seafood restaurant is one of the best in the area. The Spanish stucco structure was built in 1926 as an exclusive private club for the most prominent families in the Rio Grande Valley. In 1934, it opened as a fine hotel. But over the years it declined, eventually closing in 1969.

Today the hotel is completely refurbished. New interiors, modern plumbing, and blessed air conditioning have all been added. The overall effect is of a Spanish hacienda. In the back there's a secluded swimming pool bordered by hibiscus. The main dining room, an addition to the original structure, is bright and airy yet in keeping with the Spanish theme.

The guest rooms are small but pleasant, with hardwood floors and white wicker furniture, and are decorated in pastels. The modern baths have white eyelet shower curtains. Telephones, but no TVs, are in each room. Suites are a good choice, with separate bed and sitting rooms. The staff is friendly, setting the tone for guests to socialize.

> **Wherever you stay, there's hardly a better place to enjoy shrimp, trout, and red snapper than the Yacht Club Hotel's restaurant.**

Port Isabel calls itself "the Shrimp Capital of the World," and the hotel maintains a high dining standard. Bread arrives with herbed olive oil, and the fish is so fresh it almost jumps off your plate. If you have room, all the desserts are tempting, but lime pie is the house specialty. The restaurant has a cheerful nautical theme, and entrées range from $13 to $23.

RANCHO VIEJO

Rancho Viejo Resort

P.O. Box 3918
Rancho Viejo, TX 78520
210-350-4000
800-531-7400
Fax: 210-350-9681

> *A golf resort near Mexico and Gulf Coast beaches*

General Manager: Timothy Trapp.
Accommodations: 100 units. **Rates:** $88 single, $113 double; suites $133; villas $206–$309. **Added:** 6% tax. **Payment:** Major credit cards. **Children:** Under 14 free in room with parents. **Pets:** Not permitted. **Smoking:** Permitted. **Open:** Year-round.

About 10 miles north of Brownsville is Rancho Viejo, both an incorporated town and a 1,400-acre resort. The resort consists of two 18-hole championship golf courses, guest villas, private homes, and attractive grounds dotted with palms.

Once the site of a citrus orchard, the resort has retained

some of its history. Casa Grande, the original hacienda, is now a fine supper club (jackets are required) where roving troubadours entertain. Rumor has it that the restaurant is haunted, and some on the resort staff claim to have personally encountered the ghost.

Golf is the headliner at Rancho Viejo. El Diablo and El Angel courses draw visitors all year, especially in the winter, when sun-starved Midwesterners head south. The courses are open only to members, resort guests, and golfers who belong to reciprocating clubs. The greens fee is $35; cart rental is $12 per person. Golf packages are available. Once you check into Rancho Viejo, you can put your wallet aside. Guests simply sign for services, even at the two restaurants, which, like the golf courses, are not open to the public.

> On some evenings, *Delta Dawn,* the resort's riverboat, takes guests for a ride on the waterways that wind through Rancho Viejo.

There's also a great swimming pool with a huge waterfall, swim-up bar, adjacent hot tub, and a snack bar that is open during the summer, as well as two tennis courts.

If resort activities don't keep you busy enough, Mexico is about a 20-minute drive away; the beaches of South Padre are about 30 minutes away. Brownsville has an excellent zoo dedicated to rare and endangered species, and the Confederate Air Force Museum in Harlingen has a collection of American World War II combat aircraft.

The residential-style lodgings are spread across the resort's grounds, with villas facing the waterways or the golf courses. The resort covers a very large area; courtesy vans will also pick you up on request, or you can drive to the dining rooms and recreational facilities. Villas, in two- and three-bedroom styles, some with second-floor bedrooms, have modern furnishings, fully equipped kitchens, and washers and dryers. Executive suites are two-story condo-style units.

SAN ANTONIO

Bed and Breakfast Hosts of San Antonio

123 Auditorium Circle
San Antonio, TX 78205
210-222-8846
800-356-1605
Fax: 210-222-8848

*A well-run B&B
reservation service*

Operator: Lavern Campbell. **Accommodations:** About 60 properties in the San Antonio area. **Rates:** $45–$195. **Included:** Continental breakfast. **Added:** 15% tax within San Antonio city limits. **Payment:** Major credit cards. **Children:** Sometimes permitted. **Pets:** Permitted in one property. **Smoking:** Outside only. **Open:** Year-round.

Lavern Campbell is known for her hospitable and efficient service, and her B&Bs range from families who welcome guests into their homes to inns run by a full-time staff. In a popular tourist city where the hotels are often booked, one phone call to B&B Hosts will help you locate the accommodation that is right for you. B&B Hosts represents a wide variety of inns. Some are near downtown, in the historic King William residential area; others are close to the Riverwalk, Sea World, or the airport.

Listings include the Norton-Brackenridge House, which has won awards for its restoration. It's a Victorian house with four guest rooms.

In the King William area, a new guesthouse includes a downstairs bedroom with a double bed, a loft bedroom with twin beds, and a sofa bed in the living room; bikes are available for exploring the area. Terrell Castle, across from Fort Sam Houston, is one of the most unusual lodgings represented by Lavern's service. Both fanciful and fun, it was built in 1894 to resemble a mix of European castles and French châteaux. It's furnished with antiques and family furnishings. Nine huge guest rooms, including one loft room and another that is hexagonal, are each individually decorated. The lodging is ideal for families traveling with children, who adore the idea of staying in a castle. Freshly baked cookies greet guests upon arrival, and everyone leaves raving about breakfast. Be sure to try the chorizo omelette, a house specialty, served with some of the best homemade salsa you'll ever taste.

The Crockett Hotel

320 Bonham
San Antonio, TX 78205
210-225-6500
800-292-1050
Fax: 210-225-7418

A historic hotel across from the Alamo

General Manager: Kenny Gibson.
Accommodations: 206 rooms and suites. **Rates:** $90–$150 single, $100–$160 double; suites $150–$400. **Added:** 15% tax. **Payment:** Major credit cards. **Children:** Under 18 free in room with parents. **Pets:** Not permitted. **Smoking:** Nonsmoking rooms available. **Open:** Year-round.

Built in 1909, the Crockett Hotel was completely refurbished in 1985, and much care was taken to see that its original character was maintained. You are always aware of the building's age, and the presence of the Alamo just across the street only adds to the ambience.

The hotel is appropriately and simply decorated. The most striking elements in the lobby and adjoining enclosed atrium, once an outdoor courtyard, are the polished slate floors and mellow brick walls, which are exposed in the lobby, softly painted in the atrium.

The guest rooms in the main building, called the Tower, are unpretentious yet comfortable and spacious. Large windows keep them sunny and afford fine city views. The Courtyard rooms are in a separate annex. These rooms are less charming than the older building, but they are popular with families because they have more sleeping space and surround the hotel's tropical garden and swimming pool.

> **Be sure to visit the Tower's rooftop hot tub and sun deck for a bird's-eye view of San Antonio.**

The Crockett has two restaurants, Ernie's Bar & Grill and the Landmark Café. The cafe serves a breakfast buffet. Ernie's is casual, serving burgers and other typical bar fare. Room service is also available.

Valet parking costs $10; self-parking in nearby lots is $5 per day. However, once the car is parked you probably won't have much need for it because the Riverwalk and most city sights are a short walk from the hotel.

The Emily Morgan Hotel

705 East Houston
San Antonio, TX 78205
210-225-8486
800-824-6674
Fax: 210-225-7227

> *This hotel was once the Medical Arts building*

General Manager: Paul Ramsdell.
Accommodations: 177 rooms. **Rates:** $90 single, $100 double; suites $125–$275. **Added:** 15% tax. **Payment:** Major credit cards. **Children:** Under 17 free in room with parents. **Pets:**

Not permitted. **Smoking:** Nonsmoking rooms available. **Open:** Year-round.

The Emily Morgan's neo-Gothic tower with a flag on top catches the eye from almost every street corner in downtown San Antonio. This graceful hotel was built in 1926 as the Medical Arts Building, and you can still see medical symbols above some of the windows. Turned into a hotel in 1985, it is across the street from the Alamo.

> The hotel is named after Emily Morgan, the Yellow Rose of Texas, who is said to have helped Sam Houston bring down Santa Ana.

Inside, the decor is contemporary. Good modern art hangs in the halls and guest rooms. The guest rooms are furnished in gray, teal, and rose tones, and have handsome curly maple dressers and wardrobes. Large windows give the rooms an airy feeling. The bathrooms have scales, though in a city with so many fine restaurants, you may be wise to ignore them. Hair dryers and coffeemakers are also supplied, and many of the rooms have Jacuzzis and mini-refrigerators.

The hotel's Yellow Rose Cafe is open for breakfast and lunch. Guests may also wish to spend some time in the Emily Morgan Bar, the small pool, whirlpool, exercise room, or sauna. Parking in nearby city lots is $6.50 per day.

The Fairmount Hotel

401 South Alamo Street
San Antonio, TX 78205
210-224-8800
800-642-3363
Fax: 210-224-2767

*A luxury hotel
with first-rate
service*

Managing Director: Linda Finger.
Accommodations: 37 rooms and suites. **Rates:** $165–$200 single, $185–$225 double; suites $200–$500. **Added:** 14% tax.
Payment: Major credit cards. **Children:** Free in room with parents. **Pets:** Not permitted. **Smoking:** Nonsmoking rooms available. **Open:** Year-round.

If you like class, pack your bags and head for the Fairmount. To say this wonderful hotel is service-oriented is an understatement. From the moment you drive up until the moment you leave, you are pampered by a warm, friendly staff. The only bad thing about staying here, in fact, is leaving.

Built in 1906 in Italianate Victorian style, the hotel operated until the 1960s, when it was boarded up. In 1985 it made headlines when it was moved six blocks, becoming the largest building ever moved in one piece. The new owners transformed the structure into a luxury hotel and built an addition that complements the original structure.

Each room has a different decor. Common to all are high ceilings, reproduction antiques, bleached wood floors, muted colors, and balconies. The bathrooms have Italian marble and solid brass appointments. Luxury abounds: terry robes, bath telephones, makeup mirrors, oversize towels, remote control TVs with VCRs and a complimentary film library to select from (including a tape of the Fairmount's move), twice-daily maid service, bed turndown, and complimentary shoeshine.

Some rooms are designed for families, with two queen-size beds and milk and cookies for children. The Veranda suites have separate living and sleeping areas, canopy beds, and stereos. The Master Suite is the largest, with all features of Veranda suites plus a whirlpool tub, wet bar, and dressing area.

> **The Fairmount is next to San Antonio's La Villita Historic District, a picturesque assortment of shops and restaurants within a few steps of the famed Riverwalk. Across the street from the hotel are HemisFair Plaza and the city's convention center.**

Polo's, the hotel's restaurant, serves all meals. Dinner entrées such as grilled quail in a raspberry chipolte barbecue sauce, or grilled salmon served with spring rolls and sesame rice, range from $22 to $32. Appetizers include exotic pizzas such as venison sausage and fresh pesto, or brie and almond, and desserts are memorable. Breakfast and lunch are sometimes served on the patio, and Polo's bar has live entertainment in the evening.

Hyatt Regency Hill Country Resort

9800 Hyatt Resort Drive
San Antonio, TX 78251
210-640-1234
800-233-1234
210-681-9681

> *A stylish new resort in Hill Country*

General Manager: Ken Pilgrim. **Accommodations:** 500 rooms, 58 suites. **Rates:** $185–$280; suites $275–$1450; additional persons $25 ($35 in Regency Club rooms); family plans available. **Added:** 15% tax. **Payment:** Major credit cards. **Children:** Under 18, free in room with parents. **Pets:** Not permitted. **Smoking:** Nonsmoking rooms available. **Open:** Year-round.

The Hyatt Regency Hill Country is a grand new resort with an old-fashioned flavor. Although the resort has over 500 rooms, the buildings have been limited to several stories and are constructed from native limestone in a design that resembles a traditional Hill Country home. The result is an appealing structure that truly captures the spirit of yesteryear.

The lobby is homey yet grand, with columns, a vaulted ceiling, and creamy limestone walls. Sitting areas, some in front of fireplaces, are comfortably furnished with with leather sofas or rocking chairs. At the back of the lobby, "Aunt Mary's Porch," set with rocking chairs, overlooks a lush green lawn.

The resort itself is spread over 200 tree-covered acres that were once part of the almost 3,000-acre Rogers-Wiseman ranch. The resort opened in 1993, offering a variety of recreational activities in an attractive setting. There is an 18-hole golf course, tennis courts, and a pro shop catering to enthusiasts of both sports. There's also a health club, a three-quarter-mile jogging track, and a sand volleyball court. Guests can rent bicycles to explore the green grounds.

> **Ideally located for families, the Hyatt is close to Sea World and Fiesta Texas, and not far from downtown San Antonio.**

But the Rambling River waterpark is perhaps the star attraction. The man-made Rambling River meanders and flows just like the natural rivers in the area, and on hot days you can just hop in an inner tube and float the afternoon away. Nearby there are swimming pools, including a kiddie pool and one for adults. There's also a bubbling cauldron of a whirlpool made to look as if it's fed by a natural hot spring.

Dining options abound at the resort as well. Antlers is the fine dining room. With antler chandeliers, an open kitchen, and golf course views, it is pleasant, and dinners ($14–$18) such as chicken and chorizo brochette, or grilled filet steak basted with habañero-achiote butter have a slightly fiery slant. Across the hall, the Cactus Oak Tavern is much more informal and serves deli-style meals. The Spring House Cafe, serving all three meals, has everything from soup, salad, and pizza to steak and pasta; and crayons and coloring book pages are provided for younger diners. Even the resort's General Store has food — make-your-own-pizza, burgers, potato salad, and the like. The store is also stocked with baby food, old-fashioned candy, all kinds of snacks, and beer. For a wider variety of alcoholic drinks, Charlie Long's Bar is the place to go. It has a western theme, a long copper bar, billiards, Ping-Pong, and table-top shuffleboard.

Guest rooms have a country western look — maple furnishings, wrought-iron lamps, and stars for the Lone Star state on the headboards. All rooms have French doors that open onto porches, refrigerators you can fill with goodies from the General Store, TVs hidden in armoires, safes, clock radios, easy chairs with ottomans, and desks. Standard rooms have either a king bed or two doubles. Guests in the Regency Club wing have their own concierge, Continental breakfast, complimentary beverages, afternoon hors d'oeuvres and cocktails, evening desserts, and extra room amenities.

The resort has shuttle service to the airport and both valet and self-parking. Concierge and room service is available, and there are washers and dryers for guest use. For kids, there is Camp Hyatt with special activities every day.

La Mansion del Rio

112 College Street
San Antonio, TX 78205
210-225-2581
800-292-7300 in Texas
800-531-7208 in U.S.
Fax: 210-226-0389

> *A romantic hotel along the Riverwalk*

General Manager: Jan Leenders. **Accommodations:** 337 rooms. **Rates:** $200–$260 with river view, $160–$190 without river view; suites $430–$1,500. **Added:** 15% tax. **Payment:** Major credit cards. **Children:** Permitted. **Pets:** Not permitted. **Smoking:** Nonsmoking rooms available. **Open:** Year-round.

At the heart of this popular tourist town is the Riverwalk, shops and restaurants flanking a gentle, canal-like river. The most charming hotel near the water is La Mansion del Rio, a quiet retreat within a few steps of the Riverwalk's energy. With a Spanish heritage, La Mansion del Rio is the essence of the city, and it envelops you in its charm.

The Spanish colonial building dates from 1852, when it opened as St. Mary's Institute, a Catholic school that became a distinguished law school. A hotel since 1968, it is a composite of classical arches, wrought iron, and red tile. A rambling structure that was added to several times during its years as a school, La Mansion has guest rooms spread over seven floors. Perhaps the most requested rooms are those overlooking the river, which have balconies that are ideal for watching the stream of people on the Riverwalk below. Other rooms open onto two inner courtyards, one with an attractive pool.

> **At the cypress-shaded Riverwalk entrance, a profusion of greenery cascades from stone walls, and an arched bridge spans the waterway.**

Spanish in decor, the rooms all have beamed ceilings, luxurious bedding, and plush carpets. While some of the rooms are rather small, all are attractive and very comfortable. Every room has a dry bar with a refrigerator and a remote TV in an armoire.

Restaurante Capistrano serves southwestern cuisine with an emphasis on authentic Mexican dishes. The romantic Las Canarias restaurant overlooks the river and is known for its fine cuisine. Typical entrées range from $26 to $35. Las Canarias also holds a champagne brunch on Sundays for $20. Other hotel services include a concierge, 24-hour room service, and valet parking ($7).

The Menger Hotel

204 Alamo Plaza
San Antonio, TX 78205
210-223-4361
800-345-9285
Fax: 210-228-0022

> *A historic hotel across the street from the Alamo*

General Manager: J. W. McMillin.
Accommodations: 340 rooms. **Rates:** $98–$108 single, $122–$142 double; $10 each additional person in room; suites $182–$546; weekend packages available. **Added:** 15% tax. **Payment:** Major credit cards. **Children:** Under 18 free in room with parents. **Pets:** Not permitted. **Smoking:** Nonsmoking rooms available. **Open:** Year-round.

The Menger claims to be the oldest continuously operating hotel west of the Mississippi. When William Menger, a German brewer, built it in 1859, he had a practical reason: the patrons of his brewery frequently needed a place to spend the night, and he was tired of converting bar tables into beds. San Antonio was still a frontier town — the Battle of the Alamo had taken place only 23 years earlier — but Menger added a strong dose of refinement, building a fine, beautifully furnished lodging.

> The hotel's pool, surrounded by lush landscaping, is especially beautiful, as is the courtyard, which has a fountain and is used for dining in nice weather.

The Menger has continued to play a part in Texas history. During the Spanish-American War, Teddy Roosevelt recruited Rough Riders in the hotel's bar. The lodging was long popular with visiting cattlemen. Today, with its central location and moderate prices, it attracts families and other vacationers as well as business travelers.

The Menger continues to grow, having sprawled from its original design to include a motor inn. New rooms were also added as the city's Riverwalk expanded. Care was taken to blend the additions as naturally as possible with the old hotel, thus maintaining the Menger's strong sense of history. The spectacular Victorian rotunda, with a stained glass ceiling and two oval, antique-filled mezzanine floors, remains in the original section of the hotel.

To savor the history of the hotel, choose a one-of-a-kind suite such as the Devon Cattle or the King Suite. Each has a large carved bed with a canopy and a parlor with antique furnishings. The Roy Rogers Room was decorated to accommodate Roy and Dale when they visited HemisFair in 1968. All the suites open onto the mezzanines. Other choices include the new guest rooms — top of the line, especially the palatial Presidential Suite; standard rooms, refurbished in the late 1980s; and fairly ordinary motel rooms. The courtyard rooms reflect the garden below, with rich greens, floral fabrics, and botanical prints. The rooms facing the Alamo have beige tones, mirroring the Alamo's honey-colored brick.

The Colonial Room serves southwestern specialties for breakfast, lunch, dinner, and Sunday brunch. The Menger Bar, decorated with photos of Teddy Roosevelt and the hotel's early years, is well worth a visit.

Self-parking in a nearby lot is $5; valet parking is $9.

Plaza San Antonio

555 South Alamo
San Antonio, TX 78205
210-229-1000
800-421-1172
Fax: 210-229-1418

*A downtown
hacienda hideaway*

General Manager: Rod Siler. **Accommodations:** 252 rooms
and suites. **Rates:** $160–$230 single, $180–$250 double; suites
$340–$700. **Added:** 15% tax. **Payment:** Major credit cards.
Children: Free in room with parents. **Pets:** Small pets permitted. **Smoking:** Nonsmoking rooms available. **Open:** Year-
round.

The six-story Plaza San Antonio is only a few blocks from the
Riverwalk, yet secluded and tranquil. From here you can get
to a multitude of attractions within minutes, and retreat to
the hotel's grounds between sightseeing jaunts. A pool surrounded by gardens, two
tennis courts, a croquet
lawn, and a health club
are all on the premises.

**Next door to the main hotel
is the 19th-century school
built for the children of
the German settlers.
Today it's the hotel's conference center.**

The mood is Old Mexi-
co — perfect for enjoying
San Antonio and its mis-
sions, Mexican markets,
and nearby La Villita Historic District. The lobby
entrance is through a lit-
tle Mexican tile courtyard with a fountain. Also on the
grounds are remnants of early Texas. Three historic cottages,
each representing a different style of architecture, add character and also serve practical purposes: the Alsace-Lorraine bungalow and the Victorian cottage are used for private groups,
and the restored Germanic house holds the health club, with
a sauna and exercise facilities, and a front porch swing for
lazy summer evenings.

The guest rooms, in two connecting wings, are spacious
and attractively furnished. Extra pillows make the beds especially inviting. Many rooms have balconies overlooking the
lush gardens. Junior suites have sitting areas with TVs and
another TV in the bedroom. Bathrobes, bottled water, hair
dryers, and cable TV with a movie channel are in every room.

The Anaqua Restaurant, named for the stately trees that generously shade the grounds, has one of the most unusual menus in town. A chef's station, featuring a "hot rock" where food is slow-cooked on granite slabs that come from the German Alps, opens right out into the restaurant. Spanish tapas and an exotic drink such as a kiwi margarita or "banana boat blue" (vanilla bean ice cream with blackberry brandy, fresh bananas, blue curaçao, vodka, and cranberry juice), make fun starters. Go on to a stir-fry of lobster, shrimp, scallops, vegetables, tamarind cashews, and Asian black bean sauce, or an oak-grilled beef filet on smoked chile cream with potato flautas and Zuni corn compote; a tasty dessert completes the meal. For more informal dining and lighter fare, meals are served by the pool or in the Palm Terrace.

Staffed by a concierge, the hotel has 24-hour room service and lots of special touches, from complimentary shoeshines, morning coffee and newspapers, and twice-daily housekeeping service to nightly turndown. Bicycles are available free of charge. There is a poolside bar and a small children's pool. Parking is $5 per day.

Riverwalk Inn

329 Old Guilbeau
San Antonio, TX 78204
210-212-8300
800-254-4440
210-229-9422

A truly unique lodging along the Riverwalk

Innkeeper: Johnny Halpenny. **Accommodations:** 11 rooms, all with private bath. **Rates:** $89–$145; honeymoon suite $160. **Included:** Continental breakfast and evening desserts; champagne in honeymoon suite. **Added:** 15% tax. **Payment:** Major credit cards. **Children:** Welcome; maximum two persons per room. **Pets:** Not permitted. **Smoking:** Outside only. **Open:** Year-round.

The Riverwalk Inn is at once one of San Antonio's newest and oldest lodgings. On the banks of the Riverwalk, about five minutes from the Rivercenter's cluster of shops and restaurants, the inn consists of two log and stone homes that were constructed on the site in 1994 with materials taken from five 1840s Tennessee homesteads. Reconstructed by Jan and Tracy Hammer, who have won awards for earlier restoration projects, the result is an inn that has the look and feel of an authentic 19th-century log cabin.

> **Honeymooners are treated royally at the Riverwalk Inn, with fresh flowers, a bottle of champagne, and a fruit basket upon arrival.**

The setting is idyllic. Long porches set with rocking chairs and queen-size benches overlook a green lawn that stretches down to the river. Only a hint of the 20th-century city can be seen in the distance. In the afternoon there is fresh lemonade and tea, and perhaps a storyteller relating tales of yesteryear or a bluegrass musician strumming an instrument. In the evening, guests sip on glasses of port and feast on "death by chocolate cake" while taking in the river view illuminated by gas lampposts.

In the main reception area, guests serve themselves breakfast from an 1830s dry sink and gather around an antique harvest table. An 1875 post office serves as a room divider, and an old-fashioned hand-pumped vacuum cleaner makes its home in another corner. If you have any questions about the structure's origin, the innkeeper will point out the joist on which are inscribed the words, "Clarence Peterson built this roof in 1842."

Guest rooms are named for historic figures such as Davy Crockett and James Bowie, and they also have an authentic flavor. Pencil-post or four-poster beds, hooked rugs, patchwork quilts, and blanket chests all add to the rustic ambience. Ceilings are washed in blue, in keeping with the German tradition of "sleeping under the sky." Baths have huge walk-in showers with stone floors, and sinks have been built into antique pieces such as grain bins, dry sinks, baker's tables, and ice boxes.

Upstairs rooms have vaulted ceilings, and all but two rooms have gas fireplaces. The Guilbeau room has a private porch, and all rooms have modern conveniences such as refrigerators, ceiling fans, cable TV, and telephones with pc/fax modem capabilities.

Free parking for guests is in a small lot across the street.

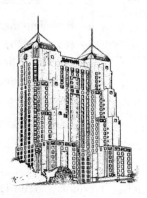

San Antonio Marriott Rivercenter

101 Bowie Street
San Antonio, TX 78205
210-223-1000
800-648-4462
Fax: 210-223-6239

*A modern hotel
at the
Rivercenter*

General Manager: Ed Paradine. **Accommodations:** 1,000 rooms and suites. **Rates:** $119–$170 single, $129–$180 double; suites $250–$850. **Added:** 15% tax. **Payment:** Major credit cards. **Children:** Under 12 free in room with parents. **Pets:** Permitted. **Smoking:** Nonsmoking rooms available. **Open:** Year-round.

The Rivercenter, with its many shops, restaurants, and theaters, has become the hub of activity for San Antonio's celebrated Riverwalk. The 38-story Marriott Rivercenter opened in 1988 to take full advantage of a prime location. Its busy glass-covered atrium lobby mirrors both the hustle and bustle and the glass architecture of the Rivercenter just outside.

The hotel has just about every type of room a traveler could possibly want. In junior-king suites, the bedroom is separated from the sitting area by French doors. Bed–sitting suites are two and a half times larger than a standard room. Two concierge floors serve complimentary breakfast in the morning, hors d'oeuvres in the evening, and late night desserts in the floors' private lounge.

The rooms on the ladies' executive floor have special amenities such as razors, hair dryers, and satin hangers. The marquis floor has somewhat nicer furnishings than the traditional decor in the standard rooms and includes extras such as

> Concert pianists won't have to miss a day's practice if they stay in one of the two presidential suites, which are equipped with baby grand pianos.

shoe polishers and hot taps and instant coffee for making coffee in the room. Some rooms have Riverwalk views. Connecting rooms are available for families.

The Garden Café has a good salad bar and serves breakfast, lunch, and dinner buffets. Occasionally the restaurant holds special events, such as strawberry and seafood festivals, where the food of honor is spotlighted in a variety of dishes. The River Grill, featuring southwestern cuisine, offers elegant dining, with entrées ranging from $17 to $22. After dinner, guests can sample a wide range of liqueurs from the apéritif cart or move over to the Atrium Lounge, where a huge stuffed armadillo is perched at the keys of a player piano.

The hotel has a heated indoor-outdoor pool, the outdoor portion surrounded by an attractive sun deck. If you forgot to pack your bathing suit, you can buy a disposable one at the pool office. A workout room, hot tub, and saunas are all next to the pool area.

The hotel maintains a business center for executives and a laundry room where guests can wash and dry clothes free of charge; a concierge is on duty in the lobby 12 hours a day. Room service is available around the clock. Self-parking is $7 per night, valet parking is $12.

Sheraton Gunter Hotel

205 East Houston Street
San Antonio, TX 78205
210-227-3241
800-222-4276
Fax: 210-227-3299

*This hotel is proud
of its history*

General Manager: David Hansen. **Accommodations:** 322 rooms and suites. **Rates:** $135–$145 single, $145–$165 double; suites $195–$490. **Added:** 15% tax. **Payment:** Major credit cards. **Children:** Under 18 free in room with parents. **Pets:** Not permitted. **Smoking:** Nonsmoking rooms available. **Open:** Year-round.

The Gunter, built in 1909, is a classic, mirroring an earlier, grander era. Its expansive lobby is graced by columns, sparkling crystal chandeliers, and an ornate molded ceiling. Throughout the 12-story hotel, marble floors and walnut paneling date from the time that the Gunter was the largest building in San Antonio. A montage of the hotel's history is displayed near the elevators.

Unlike some historic hotels, the Gunter addresses the modern bent toward recreation and fitness. There is a heated pool on the second floor and an exercise room with Nautilus equipment. For kids, there's a small video arcade in the basement.

Recently redecorated, the spacious yet intimate rooms have Queen Anne furniture. Four different color schemes have been used, so the rooms aren't carbon copies. There's a look of subdued plushness, accented with tradition, from high ceilings to heavy wooden doors.

Just off the lobby and popular with theatergoers is the Houston Street Café, which serves regional favorites in a convivial setting of rich wood and soft lighting. Lively piano music and people-watching on Houston Street entertain guests between courses. The dessert tray is tempting even after a satisfying meal. The pastries are prepared fresh daily by the hotel's well-known bake shop. On Sundays there's a champagne brunch.

Muldoon's, named for Padre Muldoon, an Irish priest who

converted early Texans, is a bar on several levels next to an enclosed glass terrace. Lunch buffets are served upstairs during the week, and happy hours usher in weekday evenings.

Service is important at the Gunter. A friendly staff, valet parking ($9), room service, and a concierge are all part of your stay. Two floors are designated executive levels. In addition to the not-to-be-missed bakery, shops in the hotel include a barber shop and a fancy gift shop. Discount tickets to places such as Sea World and Fiesta Texas are often available at the front desk.

The Gunter is in the heart of downtown, one block from the Riverwalk and five blocks from the Alamo. The Majestic Theater, which attracts top performers, is just across the street. Its ornate Moorish interior is so extraordinary, it's worth the price of a concert ticket just to see it. Machines produce actual clouds that move across its seemingly starlit ceiling, making for a delightful atmosphere and a most memorable evening.

St. Anthony

300 East Travis
San Antonio, TX 78205
210-227-4392
800-338-1338
Fax: 210-227-0915

Both a Texas and a National Historic Landmark

General Manager: Nick Ghawi.
Accommodations: 362 rooms and suites. **Rates:** $120–$156 single, $140–$176 double; suites $235–$475. **Added:** 15% tax.
Payment: Major credit cards, no personal checks. **Children:** Under 18 free in room with parents. **Pets:** Not permitted.
Smoking: Nonsmoking rooms available. **Open:** Year-round.

The St. Anthony grandly reflects the sumptuous grace of an earlier age. Built in 1909 by a prominent cattleman, B. L. Taylor, and a former San Antonio mayor, A. H. Jones, the hotel is European in design and decoration and pure Texan in tradition and hospitality.

Now a Park Lane Hotel, the St. Anthony was for many years owned by railroad builder and rancher R. W. Morrison, who turned it into a showcase for his art collection. Today it's a treasure house of fine furnishings and paintings.

Venetian mosaic tile floors, Oriental rugs, leather sofas, bronze statues, 19th-century Chinese urns, and Empire chandeliers dripping with crystal grace the ornate lobby and public areas. Particularly beautiful is a rosewood and gold leaf grand piano from the czarist embassy in Paris.

A quiet retreat from the flurry is Peacock Alley, which runs parallel to the main lounge and overlooks Travis Park, a spot of green in the midst of downtown. The Alley is a long hall with high ceilings interrupted by tall, arched windows, furnished with large bamboo chairs for intimate conversation; it has been a favorite San Antonio meeting place since the 1930s.

> **Do stop by the Anacacho Ballroom, where Prince Rainier and Princess Grace were once entertained. The Travis Room has a huge painting of cowboys on the range, reflecting the St. Anthony's Texas soul.**

The guest rooms have a sense of refinement with their traditional furniture, matching drapes and bedspreads, and brass accessories. No two rooms are alike, and many have antiques and art objects. Doorbells add a nice touch.

Guests may dine all day at the informal Café, specializing in southwestern and Continental cuisine. For evening and live entertainment, Pete's Pub is the place to go. With its deep green interior and marble tables, it is remarkably elegant for a saloon. Pete's also serves lunch, snacks, and cocktails, and is open until 1:00 A.M.

Unusual for a hotel of its vintage, the St. Anthony has a heated rooftop pool and a large redwood sun deck with a view of downtown, as well as a small fitness room. Other features include room service (6:30 A.M.–11 P.M.) and valet parking ($8). Self-parking in an outdoor lot is also available ($5).

SOUTH PADRE

Bridgepoint

334 Padre Boulevard
South Padre Island, TX 78597
210-761-7969
800-221-1402
Fax: 210-761-2844

> *High-rise luxury on
> South Padre Beach*

Property Manager: Brenda Long. **Accommodations:** About 35 units. **Rates:** 1-bedroom $150–$250; 2-bedroom $175–$300; 3-bedroom $225–$350; 4-bedroom $275–$400; penthouse $275–$425. **Payment:** Major credit cards. **Children:** Welcome. **Pets:** In some units. **Smoking:** Nonsmoking units available. **Open:** Year-round.

For a luxurious vacation high above the crowds, Bridgepoint is the place. About a quarter of the 114 privately owned units in this sleek 28-story beachfront condominium tower are available for rent. While each is individually decorated, they are all super-luxurious.

The units are spacious, airy, and inviting. One-bedroom units have 1,400 square feet; two-bedrooms have 1,800 square feet, three-bedrooms have 2,000 square feet. They have living rooms, dining rooms, and well-equipped kitchens. Each unit has a washer and dryer. Most rooms have ocean views. Penthouses, with three bedrooms and sweeping panoramas, are exquisite.

> **The property itself is top-notch, and the condo manager runs the rental units like a hotel. You're treated like a valued guest.**

There is an attractive outdoor area with a children's pool, a sunken whirlpool tub, an adult pool, and a palapa snack bar. There is also a well-equipped exercise room and two lighted tennis courts. Of course, the beach itself is right outside the front door. Beach umbrellas and chairs are free.

Although South Padre Island is a popular spring break destination, the condos are not rented to students. There is a security gate (a real plus during spring break) and garage parking. A telephone deposit is required of all guests.

Sheraton South Padre Island Beach Resort

310 Padre Boulevard
South Padre Island, TX 78597
210-761-6551
800-672-4747 in Texas
800-325-3535 in U.S.

*A modern
beachside hotel*

General Manager: Jason Dixon. **Accommodations:** 256 rooms. **Rates:** From $129; suites from $172. **Added:** 13% tax. **Payment:** Major credit cards. **Children:** Under 17 free in room with parents. **Pets:** Not permitted. **Smoking:** Nonsmoking rooms available. **Open:** Year-round.

Opened in 1986, the 12-story Sheraton is right on the beach. Every guest room has a balcony and an angled view of the ocean. Decorated in cool colors and with rattan furniture, the accommodations are both attractive and comfortable.

The beachside pool and deck area includes a grill, a palapa bar, a swim-under waterfall, a hot tub, and lots of lounge chairs. Tennis courts are also on the grounds.

The king parlors are worth the extra charge: the sleeping and sitting areas are separated by a floor-to-ceiling armoire housing a swiveling TV. Both king and king parlor rooms are furnished with sleep sofas. The rooms also have air-conditioning units (king parlors have two).

Brandi Renee's Café, facing the ocean, is the hotel's fine dining restaurant, specializing in seafood. Pepper's Lounge has dancing and live entertainment.

West Texas

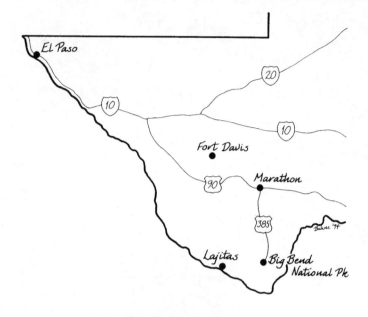

Big Bend National Park
Chisos Mountains Lodge, 417
El Paso
Camino Real Paso del Norte, 419
El Paso Airport Hilton, 421
El Paso Marriott, 422
Fort Davis
Hotel Limpia, 424
Indian Lodge, 426
Prude Ranch, 428
Marathon
Gage Hotel, 429
Terlingua
Lajitas on the Rio Grande, 431

Best City Stops

El Paso
   Camino Real Paso del Norte
   El Paso Airport Hilton
   El Paso Marriott

Best Family Favorites

Fort Davis
   Indian Lodge
Terlingua
   Lajitas on the Rio Grande

Best Guest Ranches

Fort Davis
   Prude Ranch

Best Historic Hostelries

Fort Davis
   Hotel Limpia
Marathon
   Gage Hotel

Best National Park Lodging

Big Bend National Park
   Chisos Mountains Lodge

In West Texas, the state's vastness really begins to sink in. In the central and eastern portions of the state, the population centers are clustered fairly close to one another, but here in West Texas, towns and cities seem few and far between. Sure there are cities, such as Amarillo and Lubbock, but they are not really geared to tourists. Most travelers come to West Texas for the mountains.

The Hill Country often gets top billing in travel literature describing Texas, but West Texas actually has the most spectacular scenery in the state — with large expanses of wide-open space in between. It may surprise some to learn that there are more than 90 peaks in West Texas over a mile high. Most of them are in three areas: the Davis Mountains, **Big Bend National Park,** and Guadalupe Mountains National Park.

At 8,749 feet, Guadalupe Peak in Guadalupe Mountains National Park is the highest point in Texas. The park itself covers 76,293 acres on the Texas–New Mexico border. With 801,163 acres, Big Bend National Park at the Mexico border is more than ten times larger. The terrain of Big Bend ranges from the Chihuahuan Desert to the clear and cool Chisos Mountains, and the wildlife you see varies accordingly, from slithering pink snakes and desert lizards to javelinas and mountain lions. Hiking is popular in both parks, and both are refreshingly less crowded than most national parks, thanks to their remote locations.

Because of its comfortable climate, **Fort Davis** in the Davis Mountains has been a vacation destination for most of this century. Established as an army post in 1854, a museum in re-constructed barracks at the Fort Davis National Historic Site today shows what life was like at the frontier post over a century ago. Visitors to the area also enjoy Davis Mountains State Park, and the McDonald Observatory.

El Paso, a city of over half a million people in the western-most corner of the state, shares a border with Mexico and in many ways seems more Mexican than Texan. With a high percentage of Hispanic residents, and the Mexican city of Juarez just across the Rio Grande it is no wonder there's such a strong Mexican influence on the city. However, its Spanish roots extend back much further than the present-day interaction between the two countries. Cabeza de Vaca visited the area in 1525, then came the Spanish missionaries (some of their missions are still standing and can be toured), but the city really began to develop after Juan Maria Ponce de Leon established a settlement here in 1827.

Situated in a mountain pass (hence its name), El Paso is called the "city in the sun" and attracts those seeking a dry climate. The city also has obvious appeal as a gateway to Mexico. From downtown, you can easily cross into Mexico at several points along the river. Should you venture into Juarez for a little shopping, you won't be alone — there's a steady stream of people from both sides crossing the border at any given time. Other area attractions include the Tigua Indian

Reservation in El Paso, which has both an arts and crafts center and a popular restaurant serving traditional Tigua cuisine. The military base at Fort Bliss has several museums open to the public, and local sporting events include horse-racing at Sunland Park and dog-racing and bull-fighting in Juarez.

BIG BEND NATIONAL PARK

Chisos Mountains Lodge

National Park Concessions
Big Bend National Park, TX 79834
915-477-2291
Fax: 915-477-2352

Friendly and comfortable lodgings

General Manager: Garner B. Hanson.
Accommodations: 72 units. **Rates:** $55–$70. **Added:** 6% tax. **Payment:** Major credit cards. **Children:** Under 12 free in room with parents. **Pets:** Permitted on leash. **Smoking:** Nonsmoking rooms available. **Open:** Year-round.

In Big Bend's "Basin" you'll find Chisos Mountain Lodge, some 5,400 feet above sea level. Surrounded by mountains you can almost touch, the lodge's magnificent setting, friendly service and reasonable prices make it an appealing spot to start your exploration of the park. Since it is the only lodging within the park's boundaries (most visitors camp in the three campgrounds), it is important to make reservations as far ahead as possible. For fall, spring, and major holidays, book at least a year in advance.

Lodging is in motel-style units or stone cottages. The well-maintained motel units have one or two double beds, a bath with tub and shower, and individual air conditioning and heating. The picturesque one-room cottages are tucked away in the trees. They have one to three double beds, baths, and small porches. There are no phones in the rooms, but there always seems to be a pay phone nearby. Nor do the guest rooms have TV, but for news junkies there is one television discreetly placed in a corner of the lobby at the main lodge.

For most people, the lack of televisions and telephones

only adds to the lodge's ambience. In the evening, a quiet calm falls over the park, and visitors retreat to the peace and privacy of their balconies, which have exquisite views of the mountains and wildlife. At dusk, deer and javelinas graze in the area, often coming within a few feet of the buildings.

In each guest room is a newsletter highlighting the week's activities: nature walks, evening lectures, and the like. Hiking, river rafting, and horseback riding are the top attractions in this magically beautiful, rugged, and wild national park.

At mealtime, it is not uncommon to see deer feasting on the shrubbery while you're dining on a freshly prepared dish in the lodge's dining room. The restaurant has splendid views of the Basin and the mountains beyond, and serves meals throughout the day. Its menu is short and simple, with basic American fare such as roast turkey, ham steak, pork chops, steaks, and chef's salads. Whatever you order, it's guaranteed to taste great, and it won't cost you a bundle. Throughout Chisos Mountain Lodge, the mood is convivial, and the setting is hard to beat.

EL PASO

Camino Real Paso del Norte

101 South El Paso Street
El Paso, TX 79901
915-534-3000
800-7-CAMINO
Fax: 915-534-3090

*A historic hotel in
downtown El Paso*

Owner: Hoteles Camino Real, Mexico City. **Accommodations:** 375 rooms. **Rates:** $105–$120; suites $150–$800. **Added:** 14% tax. **Payment:** Major credit cards. **Children:** Under 17 free in room with parents. **Pets:** Small pets only. **Smoking:** Nonsmoking rooms available. **Open:** Year-round.

Staying at the Camino Real Paso del Norte puts you in touch with El Paso's history and at the same time immerses you in beauty and elegance. Built in 1912, the hotel was restored completely and reopened with a new 17-story tower in 1986. The environment is refined, the staff is Texas-friendly, and the combination makes for a top-quality hotel, the finest in the area.

Tradition has it that Pancho Villa wined and dined here between his skirmishes across the border. During the Mexican Revolution, guests were said to have requested rooms on the south side of the hotel so that they could watch the conflict from their windows.

The exquisite Tiffany stained glass dome at the center of the aptly named Dome Bar, off the lobby, takes center stage.

Apricot-colored scagliola columns and walls, crystal chandeliers, and tall, arched windows surrounding the dome combine for a true aesthetic delight. Notice the unusually large light bulbs on the chandeliers. They were selected as a status symbol of sorts; the original owner, Zach T. White, wanted to play up the fact that the Paso del Norte was the first building in El Paso to boast electricity. The massive marble and mahogany bar beneath the famed dome matches it in circumference.

> Local cattlemen had their offices in what is now the hotel's nightclub, Uptown's. Gunfights to settle disputes were not uncommon here, and bullet holes were still visible in the walls until the renovation in 1986.

Next door is the Dome Grill, elegantly decorated in soft yellow, with octagonal columns, high ceilings, and mirrored walls. Dinner entrées feature fresh seafood as well as beef. The imaginative dishes include blue corn crêpes filled with smoked chicken, wild mushrooms, avocado and a creamy mirasol sauce; salmon with shiitake mushrooms in phyllo; and lobster and steak fajitas.

Café Rio, which serves all three meals, has a Southwest theme and regional dishes. It opens onto a courtyard that antedates the original hotel. A plaque commemorates the spot where in 1881 "four men were shot dead in about five seconds," when El Paso was "the wildest 24-hour town in the Old West."

The rooms have Queen Anne–style furniture, with two-poster beds and mirrored armoires that replace closets. The baths have telephones. Suites have hair dryers and coffeemakers. Rooms on the executive floors have fully stocked refrigerators and include breakfast in the morning and hors d'oeuvres and cocktails in the evening. If you need a lot of space, you might choose the Presidential suite, which has two bedrooms, a living room complete with baby grand piano, full kitchen, dining room, and two baths — more than 2,400 square feet in all.

The hotel has a pool, a steam bath, and an exercise complex. Guests requiring a more comprehensive workout can use the facility across the street for $8 per day. Mexico is a mere seven blocks away. The city's civic center is next door. Parking is in the underground garage beneath the hotel.

El Paso Airport Hilton

2027 Airway Boulevard
El Paso, TX 79925
915-778-4241
800-742-7248
Fax: 915-772-6871

*Conveniently located
next to the airport*

General Manager: Rich Cane. **Accommodations:** 272 rooms.
Rates: $92–$102 single, $102–$112 double; suites $99–$129.
Added: 14% tax. **Payment:** Major credit cards. **Children:** Free
in room with parents. **Pets:** With prior approval; deposit may
be required. **Smoking:** Nonsmoking rooms available. **Open:**
Year-round.

Soothing colors and contemporary design greet you at the
El Paso Airport Hilton. Incorporating five buildings, most
of which face the pool, it
is an attractive, low-key
place to stay. The airport
itself is only 200 yards
from the lobby.

**El Paso is dubbed Sun City,
for it boasts sunshine
almost every day of the
year. If you'd like to eat by
the pool, you can simply
pick up a poolside phone
and order lunch.**

The guest rooms are es-
pecially comfortable. The
southwestern prints cre-
ate a friendly atmosphere,
and the beds have conve-
nient attached mirrored
armoires. More than half
of the rooms are suites, with a small parlor with a refrigerator, sofa bed, bedroom, two TVs, and two phones. A few

suites have whirlpool tubs; others have wide-screen TVs and whirlpool baths. Two Jacuzzi suites have enclosed double Jacuzzis surrounded by stained glass windows. Rooms on the executive keyed-access level have extras such as fully stocked bars, hair dryers, and robes. Breakfast and evening hors d'oeuvres are included with the executive level rate.

Magnim's Restaurant, fresh and airy, is delightfully arranged, with lots of intimate dining rooms. Steak, veal, pasta, chicken, and seafood dishes are priced from $13 to $18 on the dinner menu. The bar section of Magnim's has an all-you-can-eat buffet during happy hour for only $5.

The staff is hospitable and helpful. Extra touches include complimentary shuttle service to the airport, a hot tub, a sauna, an exercise room, and handicapped-accessible guest rooms.

El Paso Marriott

1600 Airway Boulevard
El Paso, TX 79925
915-779-3300
800-228-9290
Fax: 915-772-0915

*A friendly
airport hotel*

General Manager: Scott Ringer. **Accommodations:** 296 rooms. **Rates:** Sunday–Thursday $99–$114 single, $114–$129 double; weekend rate $79 single or double including breakfast; suites $225–$425; additional persons $15 per night. **Added:** 14% tax. **Payment:** Major credit cards. **Children:** Free in room with parents. **Pets:** Small ones permitted. **Smoking:** Nonsmoking rooms available. **Open:** Year-round.

At the entrance to the El Paso International Airport, the Marriott exudes Texas friendliness. From the outside, the six-story rectangular building is not distinctive, but its service and hospitality are.

The lobby, with a fountain in the center, is fairly small. Off to one side, La Cascada, which also has a fountain at its entrance, serves meals all day, and specializes in Mexican dishes. Three fresh fish specials each day add depth to the menu. Dinner entrées run from $5 to $9. Chatfield's, behind beveled glass doors, is more intimate. Entrées range from chicken boursin to salmon to prime rib and are priced from $16 to $30. The restaurant, whose philosophy is "bigger is better," also specializes in chocolate soufflés for dessert. The hotel also offers McGinty's Lounge, a popular El Paso night spot.

This Marriott has video check-out and several handicapped-accessible facilities including Braille menus and rooms designed for the hearing impaired.

The guest rooms are fresh and inviting, with matching drapes and bedspreads and plush carpeting. On the concierge level, complimentary Continental breakfast, evening hors d'oeuvres, and dessert are served in a private lounge. There's an office with computer hook-ups and other business equipment for traveling executives. Executive rooms are larger than standard and have a desk, coffeemaker, bottled mineral water, and two phones.

The swim-through indoor-outdoor pool is attractive, and nearby are a Ping-Pong table, exercise room, whirlpool and sauna. A putting green and volleyball court are just beyond the pool.

FORT DAVIS

Hotel Limpia

Box 822
Fort Davis, TX 79734
915-426-3237
800-662-5517

> *A charmingly
> restored
> historic hotel*

Innkeepers: Lanna and Joe Duncan.
Accommodations: 20 rooms and 12
suites. **Rates:** $58–$65; suites $62–$80; cottage $112 for up to
4 people. **Added:** 10% tax. **Payment:** Major credit cards. **Children:** In most rooms, under 12 free in room with parents.
Pets: Permitted. **Smoking:** In public areas only. **Open:** Year-round.

The main structure of the Hotel Limpia was built of native
pink limestone back in 1912 by the Union Trading Company.
Although Fort Davis may seem like a somewhat remote
travel destination for that era, its mile-high elevation insured
a comfortable climate year-round and drew visitors from
throughout Texas, especially those from the southern regions
wanting to escape the intense summer heat. For many years
the hotel flourished and was the center of activity in Fort
Davis for visitors and residents. The town drug store and
town doctor were both located on the property, and on election day, local voting tallies were posted on a chalkboard at
the hotel.

After a fire in 1951 destroyed the building's main corridor,
the hotel was converted into an apartment and office building
that housed the Harvard University Astronomy Offices until
the building was purchased and restored to its original purpose in the late 1970s by J. C. Duncan. In 1990, Duncan's son

Joe and his wife, Lanna, took over operation of the Limpia, and they've created a lodging that is both appealing and comfortable.

The lobby and adjoining living room set the tone. Easy chairs are grouped around a large TV, and a jigsaw puzzle is in progress on the coffee table. Nearby is a glassed-in porch set with plants, rocking chairs, and more games. Ceiling fans gently circulate the air. For those who want formality, there's a small parlor with elegantly upholstered furnishings, a piano, and a fireplace.

The rooms themselves are quite spacious with high ceilings, even upstairs. Some have ornamental pressed tin ceilings, others have rounded walls; both are original to the hotel. All rooms are pleasantly decorated with items such as duvets, abundant pillows, claw-foot tubs, and oak reproduction furniture, with an occasional antique piece. The master suite has two bedrooms and a sunny living room and dining area. Its kitchen was once the darkroom for the Harvard Astronomy offices.

> **Limpia is Spanish for "clean," so some might think the hotel's name means "clean hotel." Actually, the Limpia was named for Limpia Creek in the nearby Davis Mountains.**

Across a courtyard filled with flowers and herbs is the hotel's gift shop and restaurant. The dining room has a country garden flavor with floral carpeting and herbs from the hotel garden drying overhead. Menu items include Texas fare such as catfish and chicken-fried steak (though here it's made with New York strip), as well as some original dishes such as "adobe spaghetti," pasta with a southwestern-style sauce; and "chicken down under," charbroiled chicken breast topped with an onion and mushroom sauce, bacon, mozzarella, and cayenne. Children's portions are available. Upstairs there's a small western bar that occasionally features live music.

As word has spread about the Limpia's resurrection, the owners have found it necessary to add more rooms. The Duncans purchased a 1920s building that was once an annex of the hotel. Since the building had been later turned into apartments, all of the rooms here are one- and two-bedroom suites with separate living rooms, and most have kitchens. Room decor is similar to that of the original hotel.

Across the street from the Limpia, the Duncans have also added rooms in what they call Limpia West. Rooms here resemble more traditional hotel rooms but are comfortable.

For more of a retreat, guests of the Limpia can rent a 1940s cottage at the foot of Sleeping Lion Mountain, about four blocks from the hotel. The cottage has two bedrooms, a full kitchen, and a living and dining room.

The Limpia's staff is Texas-friendly; their warmth adds to the relaxing feel of the place. The Limpia is convenient to Fort Davis National Historic Site, Davis Mountains State Park, and the McDonald Observatory. If you're looking for local sightseeing tips, you need go no further than the hotel lobby, for it also houses the Fort Davis Chamber of Commerce. The town has a number of annual events that tourists seem to enjoy as much as locals, such as the Fourth of July celebration and the fall Moon and Tunes Festival that brings in swing and bluegrass bands.

Indian Lodge

P.O. Box 786
Fort Davis, TX 79734
915-426-3254

A southwestern-style mountain lodging

General Manager: Jerry Cooper. **Accommodations:** 39 rooms. **Rates:** $55–$60; suites $75–$85. **Included:** Full breakfast. **Added:** 10% tax. **Payment:** Major credit cards. **Children:** Under 13 free in room with parents; over 13, additional $10 per day per child. **Pets:** Not permitted. **Smoking:** Not permitted in restaurant or other common areas. **Open:** Year-round except 2 weeks in mid-January.

Indian Lodge is nestled in a valley in the Davis Mountains. The mountains themselves are rugged and distinctive, their rock outcroppings tempered by lush green foliage. The air is fresh with cedar at this tranquil retreat; the elevation is 5,000 feet.

The white adobe Indian Lodge is built on multiple levels. All of its rooms open to the outdoors, some onto verandahs with excellent views of the canyon. Part of Davis Mountain State Park, the lodge is run by the Texas Parks and Wildlife Department. There are no luxuries such as room service, but the rooms all have carpeting, a TV, a phone, and central air conditioning. Rooms have a southwestern look and are decorated in earth tones. Some

> **Old Fort Davis is four miles away; McDonald Observatory, with the 12th-largest telescope in the world, a visitor's center, and tours, is 13 miles from the lodge.**

beds are stenciled in an Indian theme. Junior suites have kiva fireplaces.

The 15 rooms in the original building (with numbers in the 100s) are the most desirable, varying in size and design. Built by the Civilian Conservation Corps in the 1930s, the building's adobe walls are 18 inches thick. Room 121 is the largest, more like a suite than a standard hotel room. The newer rooms, built in 1967, are of average size and have cinder block interior walls.

The lodge's restaurant, the Black Bear, serves three meals a day. Beef, poultry, seafood, and Mexican dinner entrées range from $4 to $12, but buffets are the restaurant's specialty. Holidays such as Thanksgiving, Mardi Gras, and Oktoberfest are celebrated with equal revelry, each with a theme buffet, entertainment, and decor. In December, Santa Claus pays a breakfast visit to the lodge for guests' and area children.

The lodge has a heated pool below the lobby, but the top attractions are in the scenic countryside. Davis Mountain State Park has miles of hiking trails, and campfire programs are presented during the summer.

Prude Ranch

P.O. Box 1431
Fort Davis, TX 79734
915-426-3202
800-458-6232
Fax: 915-426-3502

*A guest ranch in
the heart of the
Davis Mountains*

Owners: The Prude family. **Accommodations:** 35 motel rooms; cottage rooms and bunkhouses. **Rates:** $50–$75 single or double, higher for 3 or 4; group rates available. **Added:** 10% tax. **Payment:** Major credit cards. **Children:** Welcome. **Pets:** Permitted on leash. **Smoking:** Non-smoking rooms available. **Open:** Year-round.

There's nothing fake about Prude Ranch. It's not a Hollywood-style guest ranch with a staff of city folks pretending to be cowhands. It's the real thing: a working ranch long on Texas hospitality and with reasonable rates. The Prude family has welcomed guests since 1911, but the ranch itself dates back to 1898. Three generations of Prudes operate the ranch today, and the fourth generation is in training.

There's often something special going on at Prude Ranch, such as the Davis Mountains Fitness Camp or "Snowbird" week. Summer camps for ages 7–16 are the focal point from mid-June through July.

The ranch raises its own horses and has 60 or more ready to ride. Guided rides cost $10 per hour. In the Davis Mountains at an elevation of 5,500 feet, the ranch has trails crossing miles of scenic terrain. For other recreation, there's a large and attractive heated indoor pool, lighted tennis courts, mountain hikes, and miles of open space.

Meals are served in the large western dining room. The fare is hearty, and the ranch produces much of its own top quality beef, pork, and sausage. A typical dinner, served buffet-style, includes barbecued chicken and beef, potato salad, beans, homemade bread, and cherry cobbler.

The nicest accommodations are those designated as motel, but they bear little resemblance to the image that word usually conjures up. With four units to a building, they are true western in flavor — wooden walls, a solid wood rocker, and cowboy prints on the wall. Happily, there's air conditioning and a ceiling fan, but no TV or phone. The porch is the best part, an excellent setting for putting your feet up and doing some serious mountain-gazing.

Ask about arrangements for groups. Group lodging choices include family rooms that predate the motel units, bunkhouses, campsites, and RV hook-ups.

MARATHON

Gage Hotel

P.O. Box 46
Marathon, TX 79842
915-386-4205
800-884-4243
Fax: 915-386-4510

*A tastefully
restored
historic hotel*

Innkeepers: Bill and Laurie Stevens.
Accommodations: 37 rooms, 29 with private bath. **Rates:** $42 with shared bath; $60–$90 with private bath; suites $135. **Added:** 6% tax. **Payment:** Major credit cards. **Children:** Free

in room with parents. **Pets:** Permitted. **Smoking:** Nonsmoking rooms available. **Open:** Year-round.

Welcome to West Texas. In Marathon, one of the major gateways to Big Bend National Park, the Gage is an oasis, for civilization stops at least 100 miles before you reach its doors.

The hotel was built in 1928 by Alfred Gage, a prosperous banker and rancher from San Antonio. Since there were few places to stay when he visited his 500,000-acre ranch near Marathon, he built the hotel to serve as his headquarters. In 1982, the once-grand hotel was restored, and today it offers an atmosphere quite reminiscent of turn-of-the-century West Texas.

> **Between the main hotel and Los Portales is a wonderful fountain-fed swimming pool. Nearby latilla ramadas provide shade, and terra cotta pots filled with flowers add color.**

The Gage sits right on the edge of U.S. 90. It has a yellow brick exterior, and inside you'll find a treasure trove of unusual furnishings and artifacts, most with a historical tie to West Texas. There are tools crafted by the Tarahumara Indians (now in northern Mexico, they once lived in West Texas), a table designed to hold sheep being sheared, and tiles representing some of the oldest cattle brands in the county. A Spanish colonial trunk came from Peru; the large breakfront was originally in the Gage Inn in England.

Meals are served in a western dining room decorated with Indian artifacts. The innkeeper-chef serves border cuisine. Feast on chargrilled rib-eye topped with avocado and pico de gallo, rellenos and enchiladas, or good ol' chicken-fried steak. Entrées range from $9 to $16.

The guest rooms in the historic hotel have names like Javalina Gap, Ocotillo Flat, and Dagger Mesa. Stillwell's Crossing has an especially handsome brass bed, and Jacal de Luna, with a private bath, is more spacious than the rest. Other rooms are sparely furnished, but all are appealing. Simple iron or wooden beds, woven spreads, saddles, chaps, and hides give them a primitive western atmosphere. Each has a lavatory, an air-conditioner, and a ceiling fan. In keeping with the Old West flavor, there are no modern conveniences, like phones or TVs.

Because of the Stevenses' success in revitalizing the Gage,

they have been able to add 20 new guest rooms in several buildings adjacent to the hotel, called Los Portales. Surrounding a lush garden courtyard, the new rooms are attractively furnished with Spanish Colonial, Mexican primitive, and southwestern pieces. Each room here opens onto a long portal, set with Mexican leather chairs and antique benches offering pleasant seating from which to enjoy the delightful courtyard.

When planning a trip through West Texas, note that the busiest seasons at the Gage are in spring and over holidays; the slow season is mid-July through October.

TERLINGUA

Lajitas on the Rio Grande

Star Route 70
Box 400
Terlingua, TX 79852
915-424-3471
800-527-4078
Fax: 915-424-3277

> *An Old West village on the banks of the Rio Grande*

Managers: The Moores. **Accommodations:** 81 units. **Rates:** $60 single, $65 double. **Added:** 6% tax. **Payment:** Major credit cards. **Children:** Welcome. **Pets:** Small pets permitted. **Smoking:** Permitted. **Open:** Year-round.

There's no doubt about it, Lajitas is a world apart. It's not near anything, unless you count Big Bend National Park, which isn't near anything either. Alpine is 90 miles north, El Paso is 310 miles northwest, San Antonio is 430 miles northeast.

The entire town is a development of the Mischer Corporation designed to bring back an earlier period of Texas history, a time when army troops chased Indians and rustlers holed up in desert hideaways. It started with a real trading post on the banks of the Rio Grande, and now Lajitas is a tourist attraction as well as a small residential community, complete with condos and a few houses. It boasts a 9-hole golf course, swimming pool, tennis courts, livery stable, desert museum, restaurant, saloon, and a handful of shops.

> **The variety of lodgings at Lajitas let you step back in time. It's a perfect place for families or groups to experience the feel of the Old West.**

Each lodging reflects a different aspect of the region's history. The Badlands Hotel is straight out of a cowboy movie. The Cavalry Post Motel was built on the site of the cavalry post where General "Black Jack" Pershing housed his troops in the early 1900s. Guests are housed in style over at the Officers' Quarters, whose exterior is a replica of the officers' quarters in old Fort Davis. A Spanish-style motel, La Cuesta, reflects the area's proximity to Mexico, just across the river.

This is desert country. The river, lined with graceful salt-cedars, marks the southern perimeter, and rugged mountains are in the distance. The landscape is a composite of prickly-pear and ocotillo, yucca and mesquite. Spring and fall are the prime seasons to visit, but the town never closes its doors.

Although air conditioning, phones, and TVs are in all units, each of the four accommodations has its own atmosphere. The upstairs rooms at the Badlands Hotel have an old-fashioned look, with dark wood paneling, wood furniture, and white cotton bedspreads. They open onto a long porch overlooking the town. The Officers' Quarters, in attractive one- and two-story limestone buildings, are more modern. Rooms here are lighter than those at the hotel, with interior colors complementing the creamy stone exterior walls. Some units in the Cavalry Post have fireplaces.

The one- and two-bedroom condos are also a good option. Adobe on the outside, they have stone fireplaces, good kitchens, big bedrooms, and larger than average baths. Clustered in a separate section of the town, they resemble a little village.

For small groups or large families, several houses are also available, each with a dramatic setting overlooking the desert. At the other end of the spectrum are two bunkhouses right across from the Badlands Hotel. Each has two sleeping sections for seven persons each, adjoining baths, and a central sitting area.

The area is rich in recreational opportunities, including excursions into Big Bend, hiking and backcountry trips, and river rafting. Rockhounds, birders, history buffs, and outdoor enthusiasts will luxuriate in the abundance of choices.

What's What

Where's the best place for *you* to stay? Following is a cross reference to accommodation types and special interests.

Archery

New Mexico
   Inn of the Mountain Gods, 159

Badminton

Texas
   Inn of the Hills River Resort, 280

Beach

Texas
   Best Western Sandy Shores Beach Hotel, 383
   Bridgepoint, 411
   Hotel Galvez, 298
   Port Royal Ocean Resort, 387
   The San Luis Resort, 300
   Seascape, 301
   Sheraton South Padre Island Beach Resort, 412

Boating

New Mexico
   The Legends Hotel, 177
Texas
   Del Lago Resort, 326
   Horseshoe Bay Country Club Resort, 277
   Inn of the Hills River Resort, 280
   Lake Austin Spa Resort, 257
   Lakeway Inn, 259
   South Shore Harbour Resort, 324

Canoeing

Cooking Facilities

Croquet

Arizona
New Mexico
Texas

Cross-Country Skiing

New Mexico

Fine Dining

Arizona
New Mexico
Texas

Fishing

Arizona
New Mexico
Texas

Golf

Arizona

Handicapped Access

Hiking

Hunting

Jogging Track

Murder Mystery Weekends

Pets Allowed with Permission

Racquetball

Arizona

Texas

Rafting

Texas

Riding

Sailing

Shuffleboard

Arizona
Arizona Biltmore, 19
Flying E Ranch, 45
Marriott's Camelback Inn, 36
Westward Look Resort, 123
White Stallion Ranch, 124
Wyndham Paradise Valley Resort, 44
Texas
Inn of the Hills River Resort, 280
Lake Austin Spa Resort, 257
Wyndham Austin Hotel at Southpark, 263

Skiing

Arizona
Birch Tree Inn Bed & Breakfast, 58
New Mexico
Austing Haus Hotel, 233
Best Western Swiss Chalet Inn, 167
The Legends Hotel, 177
Quail Ridge Inn Resort, 229
Salsa Del Salto, 187
St. Bernard Condominiums, 235

Smoking Not Allowed

Arizona
Birch Tree Inn Bed & Breakfast, 58
The Bisbee Inn, 92
Canyon Villa, 71
Casa Allegre, 107
Casa Sedona, 72
Casa Tierra, 108
El Presidio Bed & Breakfast Inn, 110
Garland's Oak Creek Lodge, 75
The Inn at Four Ten, 60
Inn at the Citadel, 32
L'Auberge de Sedona, 80
La Posada del Valle, 112
Lynx Creek Farm, 68

Gant Guest House, 273
The Gilded Thistle, 296
High Cotton Inn Bed and Breakfast, 266
Hotel Limpia, 424
Inn of the Hills River Resort, 280
Inn on the Creek, 286
Inn on the River, 368
McKay House, 320
Riverwalk Inn, 404
Rosevine Inn, 334
Sara's Bed & Breakfast Inn, 312
Southard House, 260
The Stagecoach Inn, 272
Ye Kendall Inn, 268

Squash

Arizona
Scottsdale Princess, 41
Texas
Four Seasons Resort and Club, 371
Loews Anatole Hotel, 356

Swimming Hole

Arizona
Garland's Oak Creek Lodge, 75
Junipine Resort Condo Hotel, 79
Texas
Chain-O-Lakes, 330
Del Lago Resort, 326
Hyatt Regency Hill Country Resort, 398
Indian Lodge, 426
Inn on the River, 368
Lakeway Inn, 259

Swimming Pool (indoor)

Arizona
Canyon Ranch Spa, 105
Maine Chance, 21

New Mexico
Barcelona Court All Suite Hotel, 137
Best Western Swiss Chalet Inn, 167
Casita Chamisa, 140
Holiday Inn Pyramid, 142
The Legends Hotel, 177
Ramada Hotel Classic, 146

Texas
Corpus Christi Marriott Bayfront, 385
El Paso Marriott, 422
Four Seasons Resort and Club, 371
The Grand Kempinski Dallas, 350
Hotel Galvez, 298
Inn of the Hills River Resort, 280
J. W. Marriott Hotel, 305
Lake Austin Spa Resort, 257
Loews Anatole Hotel, 356
Prude Ranch, 428
Radisson Plaza Hotel Fort Worth, 363
Radisson Suite Hotel, 342
San Antonio Marriott Rivercenter, 406
Stouffer Austin Hotel, 261
The Worthington Hotel, 366
Wyndham Austin Hotel at Southpark, 263

Swimming Pool (outdoor)

Arizona
Arizona Biltmore, 19
Arizona Inn, 102
The Boulders, 15
Canyon Ranch Spa, 105
Canyon Villa, 71
Casa Allegre, 107
Circle Z Ranch, 97
Copper Queen Hotel, 93
Enchantment Resort, 74
Flying E Ranch, 45
Gold Canyon Ranch, 13
The Graham Bed & Breakfast Inn, 77
Hyatt Regency Scottsdale at Gainey Ranch, 31
John Gardiner's Tennis Ranch on Camelback, 34
Kay El Bar Ranch, 46

Texas

Tennis

Arizona

Trap and Skeet Shooting

New Mexico
Bishop's Lodge, 237
Inn of the Mountain Gods, 159

Volleyball

Arizona
Gold Canyon Ranch, 13
Sheraton Tucson El Conquistador Golf and Tennis Resort, 116
Tubac Golf Resort, 101
Westin La Poloma, 122
Westward Look Resort, 123
New Mexico
Bishop's Lodge, 237
Texas
Chain-O-Lakes, 330
Del Lago Resort, 326
Hyatt Regency Hill Country Resort, 398
Inn of the Hills River Resort, 280
Wyndham Austin Hotel at Southpark, 263

Recommended Guidebooks

These books are excellent sources of information for sight-seeing and restaurant suggestions. This chapter was excerpted from *Going Places: The Guide to Travel Guides* by Greg Hayes and Joan Wright, published by Harvard Common Press.

The Southwest

Ancient Cities of the Southwest: A Practical Guide to the Major Prehistoric Ruins of Arizona, New Mexico, Utah, and Colorado. Buddy Mays, Chronicle Books, $9.95. This beautiful book offers thoughtful descriptions of each ruin in the local and national monuments, tribal parks, primitive areas, and the national parks of four western states. Included are notes on location, access, and, where applicable, a rather dated summary of the hours, facilities, and interpretive services available. An excellent overview.

Fielding's Spanish Trails in the Southwest. Lynn and Lawrence Foster, William Morrow, $12.95. One of three guides from Fielding structured around three famous trails of the western United States. This book should prove of considerable interest to history buffs, as it is laced with descriptions and quotations from those who helped to create these famous trails. Along with the historical pieces is a good deal of information on what to see, where to go, walking tours, hotels, restaurants, and the like.

Great Hot Springs of the West. Bill Kaysing, Capra Press, $14.95. This comprehensive guide to hot springs in Arizona, California, Colorado, Idaho, Montana, Nevada, New Mexico, Oregon, Utah, Washington, and Wyoming offers locations and descriptions, tells whether you need a bathing suit, gives price and phone numbers when possible, and has an appendix with good detail maps. Two hundred hot springs are described; nearly 1,700 appear on the maps. The rest are all free-flowing and yours for the finding!

The Great Towns of the West. David Vokac, West Press, $14.95. This is a guide to out-of-the-way vacation spots, each one a "great town" in its area. Vokac defines a great town as "an independent, unspoiled community rich in human-scale charms and scenic splendor." For each town that meets his criteria he provides a good overview, including detailed notes on history, weather, etc., as well as some possibilities for lodging of every sort, restaurants, camping, shopping, nightlife, sightseeing, special events, and just general enjoyment. A great idea book, it includes towns in Arizona and in New Mexico.

Hiking the Southwest: Arizona, New Mexico and West Texas. Dave Ganci, Sierra Club Books, $12.95. One of a series of pocket-size guides for the hiker and the walker, describing many trails of every length. Contains a good, well-organized planning and preparation section. Each hike is carefully detailed, with references to topographical maps and summaries of important points. Good notes on natural history topics are also included. Occasional trails may have been altered since the guide was written, as it is not updated regularly.

Hot Springs and Hot Pools of the Southwest. Jayson Loam and Gary Sohler, Aqua Thermal, $14.95. A good resource to available hot tubs and spas in motels and inns as well as good descriptions of improved and unimproved hot pools throughout Arizona, California, Nevada, and New Mexico. Good maps and interesting photos supplement this quality guide.

Indian Villages of the Southwest: A Practical Guide to the Pueblo Indian Villages of New Mexico and Arizona. Buddy Mays, Chronicle Books, $9.95. A well-prepared guide to 18 picturesque small Indian pueblos, all but one of which is in New Mexico. A bit of history and thought-provoking discussion is combined with practical information on access, when non-Indians can visit, any admission fees or permission needed to enter, what types of photography are allowed, any interpretive services available, special ceremonies, and an overview of arts and crafts produced by the pueblo. An excellent resource.

Journey to the High Southwest: A Traveler's Guide (4th ed.). Robert Casey, Globe Pequot Press, $19.95. This classic guide to the Four Corners region and the Santa Fe area has gotten even better. Let Casey take you on an exciting tour of the natural wonders, archaeological ruins, Indian reservations, parks, and historic sites of this magnificent region. This edition includes tour information on the Flagstaff and Albuquerque areas and the new Anasazi Heritage Center near Dolores, Colorado, and an expanded shopping guide for southwestern Indian arts and crafts. Guides don't get much better than this.

Landmarks of the West: A Guide to Historic Sites. Kent Ruth, University of Nebraska Press, $19.95. Popular since it appeared in 1963, this guide is now updated. Beautifully designed and well written, with a fascinating collection of new and old photographs and drawings, it is a thoroughly classy, completely intriguing guide to dozens of historic sites throughout the West — all the states west of the Mississippi. For history buffs, this is must reading.

The Sierra Club Guide to the Natural Areas of New Mexico, Arizona, and Nevada. John and Jane Perry, Sierra Club Books, $12. The Natural Areas guides, of which this is a part, include the national parks of the region but go far beyond to address the lesser-known public domain lands (Bureau of Land Management and U.S. forests), wildlife refuges, and other wilderness areas. For each area there is a wealth of detail on its location, physical attributes, the wildlife of the area, the flora, recreational opportunities, and the facilities available. This well-organized, thorough guide presents a multitude of outdoor vacation possibilities, whether you have only a few days or a week to spend. The nationally accepted signs for camping, hiking, hunting, fishing, boating, walking, horseback riding, etc., are used to give you quick visual clues to the appropriateness of a given area to your needs. A wonderful guide for those who love the outdoors.

Traveling Texas Borders: A Guide to the Best of Both Sides. Ann Ruff, Gulf Publishing, $9.95. Interesting things to do along the Texas-Oklahoma and Texas–New Mexico borders.

Two to Twenty-two Days in the American Southwest: The Itinerary Planner. Richard Harris, John Muir Publications, $10.95. Part of a series in which the intent is to let you lead your own tour (it's assumed that you have your own vehicle) by giving you clear, well-planned itineraries for classic three-week vacations. There are also side trips that can expand your trip even further. Or you can jump into the plan at any point if you are rushed. While occasional days offer no more than "R and R," these trips are designed for energetic souls. There is a budget orientation to the guide, with good picks for lodging and restaurants. The whole idea is for you to let the experts lead the way, but not pay someone to actually be there. It's a great idea for those who want some help in planning a vacation.

Arizona

Arizona Hideaways. Thelma Heatwole, Golden West Publishers, $4.50. Choose your destination from this good collection of romantic small Arizona towns in which to spend a tranquil day or two.

Arizona off the Beaten Path! Thelma Heatwole, Golden West Publishers, $5.95. A veteran reporter for the Arizona Republic takes you to her favorite out-of-the-way corners. The descriptions of her adventures will tweak your interest, and simple maps will pin down the location (though you will probably want some additional maps).

Arizona Trails: 100 Hikes in Canyon and Sierra (3rd ed.). David Mazel, Wilderness Press, $14.95. This is one of the many hiking guides from Wilderness Press. It is well done, thorough, and easy to use. The trail descriptions are particularly excellent, and all the specifics of distances, directions, elevation change, etc., are noted. Includes a full-size, separate topographical map. The "topogs" produced by Wilderness Press are particularly good because the routes described in the book are more clearly plotted than the average USGS map, usually in a bright color. An excellent book that we heartily recommend.

Arizona Traveler's Handbook (4th ed.). Bill Weir, Moon Publications, $14.95. This is a very popular title in one of those rare series whose excellence never varies. The orientation is on the young (or young at heart) and adventurous (and usually without a car), but every traveler can glean tremendous value from this superb handbook. Each guide offers an incredible amount of background on the people, arts and crafts, events, and natural history of the area. If you read and study this section before you go, you will be a very well educated traveler. Sightseeing notes are offered in copious detail, and there are always good maps of important areas. Food and lodging recommendations are not neglected, with numerous choices, usually well described, that generally range from budget to moderate. Updated every two years.

Explore Arizona! Rick Harris, Golden West Publishers, $5.95. A good collection of ideas for the explorer — ghost towns, old forts, cliff dwellings, caves, hot springs, ruins, pottery, and lots more. Each idea is accompanied by a useful location map and special notes, which will often remind you to look at, enjoy, and leave the artifacts alone for those who come after you to see as well.

The Hiker's Guide to Arizona. Stewart Aitchison and Bruce Grubbs, Falcon Press, $10.95. One of the Falcon Press series, an excellent collection of hiking guides with a wide array of hikes of varied length. Reproductions of typographical maps are used, and each hike is well discussed, rated, its special attractions summarized, and other USGS maps recommended.

Hiking the Grand Canyon. John Annerino, Sierra Club Books, $15. One of the small-format Sierra Club Hiking Totebook series. See under *Hiking the Southwest,* above.

On Foot in the Grand Canyon: Hiking the Trails of the South Rim (2nd ed.). Sharon Spangler, Pruett Publishing, $12.95. This is an interpretive guide, a hiker sharing her adventures with you. But there are enough practical facts here to help you plan your own hike as well, including appendixes that will give you the word on water available, topographical maps you will need, basic geology, and some day-hike suggestions. Enjoyable and stimulating reading!

One Hundred Best Restaurants in Arizona (14th ed.). John and Joan Bogert, A.D.M. Inc., $4.95. Actually, 172 places are now described in this popular guide. The emphasis is on inexpensive yet excellent dining, and the prices range from downright cheap to moderate. This guide is written the way we like it: anonymous dining done several times over (at least) without any perks. Chances are the authors experienced the same kind of evening you will. Couple this with a bright, informative text, and you have a first-class book. Wonderful — and all the practical data is here too, including access for the disabled. Updated annually.

Outdoors in Arizona: A Guide to Camping. Bob Hirsch, Arizona Highways, $12.95. Here are plenty of camping ideas replete with beautiful color photos, location maps, and charts of important facts. A useful compendium.

Outdoors in Arizona: A Guide to Hiking and Backpacking. John Annerino, Arizona Highways, $12.95. Forty-eight suggested hikes, many with topographical map reproductions, from the author of the Sierra Club's *Hiking the Grand Canyon.* Good ideas and beautiful photos to help you decide where to go.

Roadside Geology of Arizona. Halka Chronic, Mountain Press, $15. A fascinating book on geology "for the rest of us," and right along the highway too! Part of the excellent Roadside Geology Guide series (see *Roadside Geology of New Mexico* under New Mexico, below).

Shifra Stein's Day Trips from Phoenix, Tucson, and Flagstaff: Getaways Less Than 2 Hours Away (2nd ed.). Pam Hait, Globe Pequot, $9.95. This book suggests a great variety of possible trips into the regions immediately next to Phoenix, Tucson, and Flagstaff. The suggested journeys include a clear map, numerous things to do, places to eat, and good ideas for just wandering about, enjoying the sights and sounds of the area.

Travel Arizona: Full Color Tours of the Grand Canyon State. Joseph Stocker, Arizona Highways, $9.95. Sixteen interesting one- to three-day tours are offered for those touring by car. The text is informative, and the beautiful color pictures in this large-format book are typical of those that made *Arizona Highways* magazine famous. There is also a small section of suggested day hikes.

New Mexico

Children's Guide to Santa Fe. Anne Hillerman, Sunstone Press, $4.95. Lots of good ideas for things to do with the kids. In spite of the publication date, most of this information should still be reasonably current, but do check where appropriate.

Escortguide: The People's Connection to New Mexico (3rd ed.). Joan Adams, Escortguide, $7.95. Here is a different sort of book: a directory of all sorts of services, professional guides, bicycling and horseback excursions, unusual sightseeing ideas, lesser-known inns, ranches, and haciendas, and a whole lot more. Some of this information is designed more for New Mexico residents, but a great deal will be useful to the traveler. An excellent resource.

Hikers and Climbers Guide to the Sandias (3rd ed.). Mike Hill, University of New Mexico Press, $12.95. A first-class guide to the beautiful Sandias, east of Albuquerque. There are good sections on weather, plant life, geology, and important notes on hiking and climbing in these rugged mountains. The many trails described vary from very short, easy walk/hikes to strenuous back-breakers. A separate, fold-out topographical map is included.

How to See La Villa Real de Santa Fe: Walking Tour of Historic S.F. Lou Ann Jordan, Sunstone Press, $4.95. An interesting, large-format walking tour booklet done entirely by hand, with illustrations and text about the historic sites.

Insider's Guide to Santa Fe (3rd. ed.). Bill Jamison and Cheryl Jamison, Harvard Common Press, $9.95. This superb, well-researched book covers every need of the traveler to this spectacular city in three parts. Part One describes Santa Fe's heritage — the pueblos, the early Spanish settlers, the coming of the American armies in the early 19th century, and the art colony that has since evolved. Part Two explores the living museum that is Santa Fe — the Plaza, the museums, the fiestas, the mountain trails, and more. Part Three is a great run-down of the best places to stay, eat, and shop. Definitely the best guide to Santa Fe we know.

New Mexico: A New Guide to the Colorful State. Lance Chilton et al., University of New Mexico Press, $22.50. Six excellent authors have created this massive, large-format book as a tribute to the famous 1940 WPA publication of the same name. Here are finely crafted essays on everything from history and politics to arts and literature. The bulk of the book is eighteen well-conceived driving tours to every corner of the state. The maps are clear, and the amount of interesting and useful information is truly remarkable. There is also a helpful section of special events in a month-by-month format. This is one of the great sightseeing guides, destined to be a classic.

New Mexico's Best Ghost Towns: A Practical Guide. Phillip Varney, University of New Mexico Press, $14.95. An excellent large-format guide to the many ghost towns of New Mexico. Varney has put together a great selection of photographs and a fine narrative that is sure to tweak your interest. Included are good directions, some location maps, topographical maps for each area, and comments on how important such maps are to your safe exploration of these ghosts of history.

Roadside Geology of New Mexico. Halka Chronic, Mountain Press, $14.95. This book in the great Roadside Geology series is specifically directed at what you will see from your car window — or what you can see if you pull over at the right time and take a look. It is written for the average person; no need to know all those multisyllabic words. Organized by highway, the book is totally fascinating, and we recommend it highly.

The Santa Fe Guide (7th ed.). Waite Thompson and Richard Gottlieb, Sunstone Press, $6.95. If you put a premium on size, this tiny guidebook will give you a solid overview of history, culture, things to see and do, weather information, and transportation. There is also a list of suggested restaurants, though it notes only the type of food without further comment.

Santa Fe on Foot: Walking, Running and Bicycling Routes in the City Different (rev. ed.). Elaine Pinkerton, Ocean Tree Books, $7.95. A wonderful book on interesting routes to walk, run, or bicycle. The fine text will not only provide you with route information and plenty of background historical material but a pleasurable reading experience as well.

Santa Fe Then and Now. Sheila Morand, Sunstone Press, $14.95. This interesting book shows you how the sights you are seeing now looked 100 years ago. Morand has placed old and new photos side by side and found each place on a street map to let you take a firsthand look.

Six One-Day Walks in the Pecos Wilderness (rev. ed.). Carl Overhage, Sunstone Press, $4.95. This booklet describes in detail six strenuous hikes from 11 to 21 miles for the experienced hiker. Each has a fold-out map and elevation chart. Appropriate topographical maps are recommended, and instructions on how to reach each area are included. Some great ideas, if you are ready to really step on out.

Summer People, Winter People: A Guide to Pueblos in the Santa Fe Area (rev. ed.). Sandra Edelman, Sunstone Press, $4.95. A helpful brochure with overviews of the various pueblos near Santa Fe. Included are the dates of special fiestas, dances, and ceremonies.

Tours for All Seasons: 50 Car Tours of New Mexico. Howard Bryan, Heritage Associates, $4.95. A veteran reporter who writes a weekly column on New Mexico lore for the Albuquerque Tribune, Bryan shares his best automobile tours with you. The dozens of possibilities are grouped by the season in which they most appropriate, and there's a section of trips to do anytime. Simple orientation road maps are included, though you will certainly want to have better ones at hand. There are many good ideas to consider in this compact book.

Texas

The Alamo and Other Texas Missions to Remember. Nancy Foster, Gulf Publishing, $9.95. This large-format book will let you in on a good deal of the history, architecture, and the tours available at various missions in the state. You will also learn about the special events that are held each year. In addition, there are clear locator maps and nicely chosen photographs. A helpful guide to Texas's fascinating history.

Amazing Texas Monuments and Museums: From the Enchanting to the Bizarre. Ann Ruff, Gulf Publishing, $9.95. Where else can you find a guide to monuments erected to the strawberry, pecan, roadrunner, mosquito, and jackrabbit? Where else can you find museums featuring 10,000 birds' eggs or Lee Harvey Oswald's can opener? This is the one, with lots of tombstones too. A lot of sightseeing fun.

Backroads of Texas (2nd ed.). Ed Syers, Gulf Publishing, $12.95. You will find Syers's 62 tours of the backcountry well planned, well written, and just plain fun. It's time to explore the ghost towns, boom towns, farm towns, cow towns, and all those places of interest in between. Comprehensive, compact, and definitely first class.

Beachcomber's Guide to Gulf Coast Marine Life. Nick Fotheringham and S. L. Brunemeister, Gulf Publishing, $12.95. Let this popular naturalist's guide increase your enjoyment of the fascinating Gulf Coast. Instead of puzzling over the shell you just picked up, you will be able to learn something about it, perhaps even identify it precisely.

The Best of Texas Festivals: Your Guide to Rootin' Tootin' Downhome Texas Good Times! Ann Ruff, Gulf Publishing, $9.95. Here is just the ticket — a single resource in a monthly format, giving you all the inside scoop on sixty Texas festivals: a citrus fiesta, a peach jamboree, the fiddlers' festival, and the hushpuppy Olympics. Here is all you need to know plus addresses and phone numbers if you want to know more.

Eyes of Texas Travel Guides. Titles include ***Dallas/East Texas*** (2nd ed.); ***Fort Worth/Brazos Valley; Hill Country/Permian Basin; Panhandle/Plains.*** Ray Miller, Cordovan Press, $10.95–$13.95. This well-known series combines Miller's penchant for history with the facts and figures of modern Texas. Packed with photographs, these regional guides make excellent supplements to more standard travel guides.

Fort Worth and Tarrant County: A Historical Guide. Ruby Schmidt, Texas Christian University Press, $5.95. A very well done assemblage of the history behind a vast array of buildings, homes, churches, cemeteries, schools, etc., in the Fort Worth area. Arranged alphabetically, those in Fort Worth proper are accompanied by several hand-drawn maps. Nonetheless, you will want another map of the surrounding area to help you find other important sites. Most sites have a histori-

cal marker to help you locate them; however, the notes in
this book go well beyond those on the marker itself. An index
allows you to see all the references to one type of historical
site.

Frontier Forts of Texas. Charles Robinson, Gulf Publishing, $9.95. This large-format guide delivers the practical facts
you will need along with fascinating accounts of those adventurous events of yesteryear. The stories cover the more than
two dozen forts that have survived as well as those that were
destroyed. Includes information on visitor facilities and local
events at each of the forts.

Great Hometown Restaurants of Texas. Mary Beverly,
Gulf Publishing, $9.95. This large-format guide is a lot of fun,
with great write-ups on all sorts of intriguing spots where
home-style cooking is the rule. It includes all the practical
data, too, so you won't get lost along the way, but it was published in 1984, so beware of outdated accounts.

A Guide to Bicycling in Texas: Tours, Tips, and More.
George Sevra, Gulf Publishing, $9.95. A great collection of
tours — one-day, intercity, as well as longer routes panning
the entire state — that will prove to you, once and for all, that
Texas is not just "flat and empty." There are also helpful lists
of bicycle shops, sources of maps (though some good-size detail maps are included in this large-format book), and Chambers of Commerce in towns you will pass through and where
you may want to stop and explore a little more.

A Guide to Historic Texas Inns and Hotels (2nd ed.). Ann
Ruff, Gulf Publishing, $9.95. A popular guide from a popular
writer, this large-format book offers excellent descriptions of
the best of the historic lodging spots. The practical facts are
listed separately in the margin for easy access, and each selection is accompanied by a line drawing or photograph. Very
well done.

A Guide to Texas Rivers and Streams. Gene Kirkley, Gulf
Publishing, $12.95. A large-format guide to whitewater ca-
noeing and kayaking, float trips, fishing, and just plain fun
along Texas's many waterways.

Hiking and Backpacking Trails of Texas (3rd ed.). Mickey
Little, Gulf Publishing, $14.95. Here is another fine book that
proves Texas to be something more than flat and empty.
There is some beautiful country out there, and Little has
done a quality job in pointing the way. The state is divided
into four regions in this large-format book. In each region
trails are clearly located, adequate trail notes and distances

included, and maps, sometimes topographical ones, are provided as well. Among your choices are a number of short day hikes.

Historic Homes of Texas: Across the Thresholds of Yesterday. Ann Ruff and Henri Farmer, Gulf Publishing, $18.95. Take a look at the homes built by the cattle and oil barons and the genteel women who came west in times gone by. Each is recognized by the Texas Historical Commission, many are on the National Register of Historic Places, and all are open to the public. Included is all the information you will need to find and enjoy each site. Also included are details for tours of other homes not normally open to the public.

A Marmac Guide to Houston and Galveston. Dale Young, Pelican Publishing, $8.95. One of the Marmac Guides, a series that offers very solid, well-organized views of major cities. You will learn the ropes of each city and some of its history and tradition. There are many hotels and restaurants; each is presented by geographic area, then alphabetically or by type of cuisine. The prices run the gamut, but moderate is the most common. The restaurant section is particularly well done. Other sections cover shopping, sightseeing, museums, sports, nightlife, theater, excursions, walking tours, and transportation. The format will serve you well. Updated every two years.

Ray Miller's Texas Forts: A History and Guide. Ray Miller, Gulf Publishing, $13.95. Miller presents a lively history of the many forts, including the Alamo, that sprung up during the 19th century and were important during the Mexican War, the Indian wars, and the Civil War. Includes many interesting photographs.

Ray Miller's Texas Parks: A History and Guide. Ray Miller, Gulf Publishing, $13.95. You will find good practical information on the numerous parks in the state system, but you'll also get a large measure of the history behind what you see. Some specifics about each park may be dated — call ahead to see — but this is an excellent resource nonetheless.

Shifra Stein's Day Trips from Houston (4th ed.). Carol Barrington, Globe Pequot Press, $9.95. Part of the well-done Shifra Stein's Day Trip Guide series. See *Shifra Stein's Day Trips from Phoenix, Tucson, and Flagstaff* under Arizona, above.

Six Central Texas Auto Tours. Myra McIllvain, Eakin Press, $9.95. These driving tours, filled with historical notes and anecdotes, are all in Central Texas, around Austin. Some of the roads have changed since this book was published, but most of the copious detail should still stand you in good stead.

Texas — Family Style: Parent's Guide to Hassle-free, Fun Travel with the Kids (2nd ed.). Ruth Wolverton, Gulf Publishing, $10.95. This large-format guide has lots of good ideas for what to do with the entire family.

Traveling Texas Borders: A Guide to the Best of Both Sides. Ann Ruff, Gulf Publishing, $9.95. A good description of the many things to do and see along Texas's vast border. Included are activities in Arkansas, Louisiana, Mexico, New Mexico, and Oklahoma. This large-format guide has plenty of interesting suggestions.

Two to Twenty-Two Days in Texas. Richard Harris, John Muir Publications, $10.95. Part of the 22 Days series, this pocket-size guide will help you discover the best of Texas through suggested daily itineraries, rated sightseeing highlights, and dining and lodging recommendations. If you don't have time to take the entire three-week trip, weekend and day trips can easily be extracted from this well-organized book, which covers both metropolitan and rural areas. Maps and driving directions are also included.

Why Stop? A Guide to Texas Historical Roadside Markers (3rd ed.). Claude and Betty Dooley, Gulf Publishing, $16.95. There are more than 2,600 roadside markers in Texas with historical notes on all sorts of subjects. With this guide, you can read the markers without stopping the car. Even if you stop, this will prove a handy resource to keep on the back seat.

Glossary

Adobe: sun-dried brick made of mud and straw.

Adobe-style building: a structure in which the walls are built of adobe bricks and covered with mud plaster; the roof is built by suspending large beams (vigas) from walls, with latillas arranged on top, covered by straw and then soil.

Banco: a curved seating area built into the walls of adobe buildings.

Carne adovada: pork cooked in red-hot chili.

Casita: Spanish for "small house"; used as the equivalent of villa.

Farolitos: votive candles placed in paper bags weighted with sand; used as holiday decorations in New Mexico and Arizona.

Fonda: an inn or restaurant.

Hacienda: an estate, especially one used for ranching; the main house on the estate.

Huevos rancheros: fried eggs covered with spicy red sauce, served on tortillas.

Kiva: a large ceremonial chamber, wholly or partially underground, used by the Pueblo Indians.

Kiva fireplace: a molded fireplace, usually in a corner; also called "adobe fireplace" or "beehive fireplace." The term is commonly used but is considered a misnomer.

Latilla: small wooden poles laid side by side over the main support beams (vigas) to form a ceiling.

Luminarias: small bonfires, usually lit at Christmastime for carolers to gather around and warm themselves.

Metate: a stone with a bowl-shaped depression, used for grinding corn.

Nicho: an arched recess in an adobe wall for displaying figurines, china, religious icons, plants, or other knickknacks.

Posada: a lodge or inn.

Pueblo: a multiple dwelling, typically built of adobe; an Indian village; also, a member of a group of Indian peoples living in pueblo villages. The Native American dwellings, which were first called pueblos by Spanish explorers, are many-roomed structures of two to seven stories, arranged so that the roof of one building is the front yard of the one above. Modern pueblo architecture recalls this historic style.

Relleno: a green chile pepper stuffed with cheese, dipped in batter, then fried.

Retablo: a religious image painted on a wooden panel.

Rincón: Spanish for "corner" or "nook."

Saguaro: a giant cactus that grows in the Sonoran Desert in southern Arizona and the state of Sonora, Mexico; the tree-size cactus is a tall green column with as many as 50 branches, attaining heights of up to 60 feet.

Santos: Spanish for "saints"; refers to carved wooden religious figures.

Sopapilla: puffy fried bread, thought to have originated in what is now New Mexico.

Territorial-style: a style of adobe construction, typically a one-story flat-roofed adobe, symmetrical in design with a central hall and modified Greek Revival trimwork, often painted white; in New Mexico, dating from the mid-19th century.

Viga: large exposed logs that form the support for a ceiling.

Index